CHURCH-STATE ISSUES IN AMERICA TODAY

CHURCH-STATE ISSUES IN AMERICA TODAY

Volume 3: Religious Convictions
and Practices in Public Life

Edited by
Ann W. Duncan and Steven L. Jones

PRAEGER PERSPECTIVES

PRAEGER

Westport, Connecticut
London

Library of Congress Cataloging-in-Publication Data

Church-state issues in America today / edited by Ann W. Duncan and Steven L. Jones.
   p. cm.
   Includes bibliographical references and index.
   ISBN 978-0-275-99367-2 (set : alk. paper) — ISBN 978-0-275-99368-9 (vol. 1 : alk. paper) — ISBN 978-0-275-99369-6 (vol. 2 : alk. paper) — ISBN 978-0-275-99370-2 (vol. 3 : alk. paper)
   1. Church and state—United States.   2. United States—Church history.   I. Duncan, Ann W., 1978–   II. Jones, Steven L., 1971–
BR516.C4925   2008
322'.10973—dc22   2007030692

British Library Cataloguing in Publication Data is available.

Copyright © 2008 by Ann W. Duncan and Steven L. Jones

All rights reserved. No portion of this book may be reproduced, by any process or technique, without the express written consent of the publisher.

Library of Congress Catalog Card Number: 2007030692
ISBN: 978-0-275-99367-2 (set)
       978-0-275-99368-9 (vol. 1)
       978-0-275-99369-6 (vol. 2)
       978-0-275-99370-2 (vol. 3)

First published in 2008

Praeger Publishers, 88 Post Road West, Westport, CT 06881
An imprint of Greenwood Publishing Group, Inc.
www.praeger.com

Printed in the United States of America

The paper used in this book complies with the Permanent Paper Standard issued by the National Information Standards Organization (Z39.48–1984).

10 9 8 7 6 5 4 3 2 1

Contents

	Preface Ann W. Duncan and Steven L. Jones	vii
1	The History and Controversies of the Abortion Debate Francis J. Beckwith	1
2	Religiously Motivated Political Action and Same-Sex Marriage Katherine Stenger	37
3	Conscientious Objection to Military Service in the United States Chad Michael Wayner and James F. Childress	75
4	Religiosity, Public Opinion, and the Stem Cell Debate Eric Matthews and Erin O'Brien	115
5	Tracing Sanctuary and Illegal Immigration as a Church and State Issue Samuel S. Stanton Jr.	141
6	Native American Sacred Sites under Federal Law S. Alan Ray	161
7	Consecrating the Green Movement Nadra Hashim	197
8	Religious Liberty and Authority in Biomedical Ethics Courtney S. Campbell	247
	Appendix: Selected Cases	279
	About the Editors and Contributors	285
	Index	289

Preface

Ann W. Duncan and Steven L. Jones

Congress shall make no law respecting the establishment of religion, or restricting the free exercise thereof.
— The Bill of Rights

Sixteen words. That all it took for the framers of the Constitution to fundamentally alter the social order by separating church and state. No one commenting on their arrangement has managed to be so concise. In the face of two centuries of argument and untold numbers of books and articles exploring every facet of church and state, it is worth remembering that the founders likely thought they were solving a problem, not starting one. To be sure, they knew that Americans would continue to struggle with the relationship between sacred and secular power, but from the Enlightenment on there was a sense that separating these two forces would promote both authentic religion and good government.

The authors of the following chapters cover a number of issues seemingly unrelated to one another. The scarlet thread connecting them all, though, is the fact that even under the formal conditions of separation, religious conviction is a major motivation for political action. In a society that empowers citizens to affect public policy, this fact alone means that issues that on the surface seem unrelated to church and state are often battlegrounds between competing factions, some of which are heavily influenced by religion. When it comes to political action and voting, one person's act of faithfulness is another's instance of religious coercion, and both think they are protected by the Constitution. On the other side, state action in this realm can end up impacting the religious practices of citizens. State action can, knowingly or unknowingly, prevent the free exercise of one religion in the name of the greater good. Zoning laws, for instance, can be experienced by believers as an infringement on their freedom of religion. Conceived of in this fashion, church and state jurisprudence impacts everything from opposing war to the environment, from stem cell research to immigration.

In the first chapter, Francis Beckwith takes up abortion, arguably the most volatile issue in American life. Though the Supreme Court's decision in *Roe v. Wade* does not address the separation of church and state, Beckwith shows how the questions raised by abortion, questions like the origins of life, the nature of human beings, and our obligations to those that cannot protect themselves, are inseparable from religion. The debate over gay marriage, addressed by Katherine Stenger in Chapter 2, is also heavily influenced by religious belief. Aside from a thorough review of current laws, Stenger shows how activists on both sides of this timely issue find guidance, justification, and solace in their religious communities.

In the movie classic *Sergeant York*, Gary Cooper played a World War I hero troubled by the conflicting demands of religious conviction and patriotism. In the real world, this tension has been played out by thousands of conscientious objectors, people whose religious faith requires their refusal to participate in war. In Chapter 3, Chad Wayner and Jim Childress explore this very real conflict and show how difficult it can be for a free society to accommodate religious conviction, particularly in times of national emergency. Eric Matthews and Erin O'Brien, in Chapter 4, take up the cutting edge issue of stem cell research. They show how religious conviction and participation are uniquely powerful in shaping public support or opposition for stem cell research. Given the impassioned opposition to every announcement regarding stem cell research and the almost unlimited hope stem cells inspire among some portions of the medical community, professionals, and patients, religious communities may be the make or break players in this debate.

In Chapter 5 Samuel Stanton takes up an issue that seems be coming to the front burner even as I write this sentence, namely, the practice of sanctuary. Illegal immigration has become a hot topic in America, likely to come up in conversations about health care, race, economics, and even homeland security. Stanton traces the history of sanctuary, both as a theological ideal and legal issue, showing how it poses serious political problems, but also remarkable ministry opportunities, for certain segments of the Christian community in America. Alan Ray, in Chapter 6, focuses on the religious practices of America's only non-immigrant population, Native Americans. Noting the differences in the way Native Americans and Europeans conceptualize religion in the first place, Ray shows how the religious activities of Native Americans have been constrained by social and economic development.

Nadra Hashim takes up the growing evangelical environmental movement in America in Chapter 7. In her wide-ranging essay, Hashim shows how this alliance may break new ground in the relationship between science and religion while at the same time capitalize on and threaten the influence of evangelicalism in American political life. In Chapter 8, Courtney Campbell analyzes some of the most emotionally wrenching issues in church-state jurisprudence as he takes up the rights of families in various religious groups to determine medical care for their sick members. Religious belief can both require extraordinary measures to save lives, even over the advice of medical professionals, and motivate the refusal or suspension of treatment if it violates church doctrine. Given that lives are very often at stake, there are no easy calls in this arena.

1

The History and Controversies of the Abortion Debate

Francis J. Beckwith

Abortion is perhaps the most volatile issue on which the interests and principles embraced by both church and state intersect and sometimes conflict. Consider the following proposed definition of abortion:

Abortion is the procured or spontaneous premature termination of pregnancy that results in the expulsion and/or death of an unborn human being. Unlike spontaneous abortion (or miscarriage), procured abortion is *intended* to terminate a pregnancy.

This definition raises moral and political questions that are addressed explicitly or implicitly by virtually every religious tradition: What is the nature of human beings? Who is and who is not a member of the moral community of persons? What is the extent of my moral obligations to others, and is the fetus (or unborn child) an "other?" Do the special obligations that parents have to their children include a requirement that a pregnant woman carry her unborn child to term?

Governments, in their laws, practices, and traditions, answer identical or similar questions explicitly or implicitly. For example, in the United States of America, the U.S. Supreme Court has held that an unborn human being is not protected under any provision or amendment of the U.S. Constitution. This tells us what the Court understands the Constitution to mean by persons and the extent to which the community may extend its laws to protect the unborn. Thus, the moral and legal permissibility of abortion depends on the nature of the unborn, the mother's bodily rights, and/or how the law ought to address controversial matters of life and death that are also addressed by virtually every religious tradition.

Although some believe that the U.S. Supreme Court has settled the issue of abortion, it is not likely to go away soon. It continues to be the focus of attention whenever the President of the United States appoints someone to the federal bench, as the occupants of the federal bench, especially the Supreme Court, may determine whether abortion will remain a constitutional right. The two major parties are generally divided on the issue, with the Democratic Party being largely supportive of abortion rights and the Republican Party primarily opposed, with notable exceptions in each party. Despite little success in the courts, anti-abortion advocates have managed to pass legislation that either bans, or places restrictions on, abortion. In early 2006, the South Dakota legislature passed a law that would have banned virtually every abortion in that state, though it was eventually overturned by a statewide referendum in the November 2006 election.[1] The U.S. Congress has tried to limit abortion in a variety of ways, including the successful passage in 2003 of a federal ban on so-called "partial-birth abortion." Although the Supreme Court held in *Stenberg v. Carhart* (2000)[2] that Nebraska's prohibition of this procedure is unconstitutional, the federal ban was upheld in *Gonzales v. Carhart* (2007).[3]

Other issues in bioethics, such as embryonic stem cell research and human cloning, raise the same sorts of questions that have been raised about abortion—that is, what is the nature of human beings? Are embryos fully-fledged moral subjects with rights?—and so on. For this reason, resolutions of these issues seem contingent on how American society resolves the issue of abortion. Because the prospect of this is bleak, all of these controversies are here to stay for the foreseeable future.

In order to understand the nature of this controversy in light of broader church-state issues, we will first cover the state's view on abortion. This will be followed by an overview of the different ways in which both secular and religious thinkers have attempted to answer the question of the humanity of the unborn and the obligations and rights of the pregnant woman, questions that have traditionally been answered by religious bodies, including churches. In this chapter's final section, we will examine the case offered by some thinkers who conclude that a pro-life position on abortion, if it were to become law, would violate the separation of church and state because it would place into law a religious view of human nature and obstruct the religious free exercise rights of those who disagree with that view.

ABORTION AND CURRENT LAW

Prior to the mid-1960s in the United States, every state prohibited abortion with differing exceptions including rape, incest, life of the mother, and severe fetal deformity. During the 1960s and early 1970s, some states, including Colorado, New York, and California, began to liberalize their abortion laws, allowing for greater discretion on the part of physicians and patients. These changes were the result of decades of academic and political advocacy calling for differing degrees of decriminalization of abortion. Nevertheless, the abortion rights movement was making its case state by state, with no real prospect of finding a right to abortion in the Constitution that would instantly decriminalize abortion with all the protection that comes along with any fundamental right. For that, the movement needed a principle of law to which they could appeal. But since it was widely believed that local concerns on issues of health and morals were under the legislative power of the states rather than the federal government (including the federal courts), there was no such principle readily available, at least until 1965. It was in that year that the Supreme Court issued its landmark opinion, *Griswold v. Connecticut*.[4]

In that case, the Court ruled as unconstitutional a Connecticut statute that forbade the use of, sale of, and/or the assisting in the use of contraceptive devices. Justice William O. Douglas, who penned the Court's plurality opinion, concluded that the right of privacy grounds this judgment, for the wrongness of this statute lies in its broad scope: it includes the private judgments and activities of couples within the sanctuary of marriage. This right of privacy, according to Douglas, can be gleaned not from a literal reading of the words found in the Bill of Rights but from "penumbras" that stand behind these words, and these penumbras are "formed by emanations from those guarantees that help give them life and substance."[5] What the Court seems concerned about is that Connecticut, through its anti-contraception statute, interfered with the sanctity of marriage and the couple's judgments about intimate matters, including reproduction.[6] In his concurring opinion, Justice Arthur J. Goldberg understood the plurality's rejection of the Connecticut statute as firmly grounded in this notion of marital sanctity.[7]

In the 1972 case *Eisenstadt v. Baird*, the Court ruled that a Massachusetts statute violated the Equal Protection Clause because it provided, in its laws regarding the distribution of contraceptive devices, "dissimilar treatment for married and unmarried persons who are similarly situated."[8] In the words of Justice Brennan, author of the majority opinion:

If under *Griswold* the distribution of contraceptives to married persons cannot be prohibited, a ban on distribution to unmarried persons would be equally impermissible. It is true that in *Griswold* the right of privacy in question inhered in the marital relationship. Yet the marital couple is not an independent entity with a mind and heart of its own, but an association of two individuals each with a separate intellectual and emotional makeup. If the right of privacy means anything, it is the right of the *individual,* married or single, to be free from unwarranted governmental intrusion into matters so fundamentally affecting a person as the decision to bear or beget a child.[9]

It seems that at this point in the historical trajectory of the right of privacy, one could reasonably infer that reproductive liberty was moving in a libertarian direction. Consequently, based on the right of privacy found in *Griswold* and *Eisenstadt* as well as other decisions,[10] in 1973, in the case of *Roe v. Wade*, the Court established a right to abortion.

Roe v. Wade

The case of *Roe v. Wade* (1973) concerned Jane Roe (a.k.a. Norma McCorvey), a resident of Texas, who claimed to have become pregnant as a result of a gang rape (which was found later to be a false charge years after the Court had issued its opinion).[11] According to Texas law at the time (essentially unchanged since 1856), a woman may procure an abortion only if it is necessary to save her life. Because Roe's pregnancy was not life-threatening, she sued the state of Texas. In 1970, the unmarried Roe filed a class action suit in federal district court in Dallas. The federal court ruled that the Texas law was unconstitutionally vague and overbroad and infringed on a woman's right to reproductive freedom. The state of Texas appealed to the U.S. Supreme Court. After the case was argued twice before the Court, it issued *Roe v. Wade* on January 22, 1973, holding that the Texas law was unconstitutional, and that not only must all states including Texas permit abortions in cases of rape but in all other cases as well.

In *Roe*, Justice Harry Blackmun, who authored the Court's opinion, distinguished between different stages of pregnancy. He ruled that aside from procedural guidelines to ensure maternal health, a state has no right to restrict abortion in the first six months of pregnancy. Writes Blackmun:

A state criminal abortion statute of the current Texas type, that excepts from criminality only a *life-saving* procedure on behalf of the mother without regard to pregnancy stage and without recognition of the other interests involved, is violative of the Due Process Clause of the Fourteenth Amendment.

(a) For the stage prior to approximately the end of the first trimester, the abortion decision and its effectuation must be left to the medical judgment of the pregnant woman's attending physician.

(b) For the stage subsequent to approximately the end of the first trimester, the State, in promoting its interest in the health of the mother, may, if it chooses, regulate the abortion procedure in ways that are reasonably related to maternal health.

(c) For the stage subsequent to viability the State, in promoting its interest in the potentiality of human life, may, if it chooses, regulate, and even proscribe, abortion except where necessary, in appropriate medical judgment, for the preservation of the life or health of the mother.[12]

Thus a woman could have an abortion during the first six months of pregnancy for *any* reason she deems fit. Restrictions in the second trimester should be merely regulatory in order to protect the pregnant woman's health. In the last trimester (after fetal viability, the time at which the unborn can live outside the womb) the state has a right, although not an obligation, to restrict abortions to only those cases in which the mother's life or health is jeopardized, because after viability, according to Blackmun, the state's interest in prenatal life becomes compelling. *Roe*, therefore, does not prevent a state from having unrestricted abortion for the entire nine months of pregnancy if it so chooses.

Nevertheless, the Court explains that it would be a mistake to think of the right to abortion as absolute.[13] For the Court maintained that it took into consideration the legitimate state interests of both the health of the pregnant woman and the prenatal life she carries. Thus, reproductive liberty, according to this reading of *Roe*, should be seen as a limited freedom established within the nexus of three parties: the pregnant woman, the unborn, and the state. The woman's liberty trumps both the value of the unborn and the interests of the state except when the unborn reaches viability (and an abortion is unnecessary to preserve the life or health of the pregnant woman) and/or when the state has a compelling state interest in regulating abortion before and after viability in order to make sure that the procedure is performed in accordance with accepted medical standards. Even though this is a fair reading of Roe's reasoning, it seems to me that the premises put in place by Justice Blackmun have not resulted in the sensible balance of interests he claimed his opinion had reached. Rather, it has, in practice, resulted in abortion on demand.

For the Supreme Court so broadly defined health in *Roe*'s companion decision, *Doe v. Bolton* (1973), that for all intents and purposes *Roe* allows for abortion on demand. In *Bolton*, the court ruled that health must be taken in its broadest possible medical context, and must be defined "in light of all factors—physical, emotional, psychological, familial, and the woman's age—relevant to the well being of the patient. All these factors relate to health."[14] Because all pregnancies have consequences for a woman's emotional and family situation, the court's health provision has the practical effect of legalizing abortion up until the time of birth if a woman can convince a physician that she needs the abortion to preserve her emotional health. This is why in 1983 the U.S. Senate Judiciary Committee, after much critical evaluation of the current law in light of the Court's opinions, confirmed this interpretation when it concluded that "no significant legal barriers of any kind whatsoever exist today in the United States for a woman to obtain an abortion for any reason during any stage of her pregnancy."[15]

The Reasoning of *Roe v. Wade*

Because, as we have already noted, the Court had already established a constitutional right to contraceptive use by married couples (*Griswold*) and then by single people (*Eisenstadt*) based on the right of privacy, it would seem that abortion, because it is a means of birth control, would be protectable under this right of privacy. However, in order to make this move, there were at least two legal impediments that the Court had to eliminate:

1. Starting in the nineteenth century, anti-abortion laws had been on the books in virtually every U.S. state and territory for the primary reason of protecting the unborn from unjust killing; and
2. The unborn is constitutionally a person protectable under the Fourteenth Amendment.

Concerning the first obstacle, if, as Justice Douglas asserts in *Griswold*, the "right of privacy [is] older than the Bill of Rights—older than our political parties, older than our school system,"[16] then the Court must account for the proliferation of anti-abortion laws, whose constitutionality were not seriously challenged until the late 1960s, in a legal regime whose legislators and citizens passed these laws with apparently no inclination to believe that they were inconsistent with a right of privacy "older than the Bill of Rights." As for the second impediment, the Court had to show that the unborn is not a person under the Fourteenth Amendment in order to justify abortion. After all, unlike contraception, in which all the adult participants in the sexual act consent to its use, a successful abortion entails the killing of a third party, a living organism, the unborn, who has already come into being.[17] Thus, if the Court had good reasons to reject these two jurisprudential challenges, then it could establish a right to abortion as a species of the right of privacy.

The second impediment was met head on. The Court pointed out that Texas failed to present any textual or case law reasons to believe that the unborn is a person under the Fourteenth Amendment.[18] In addition, Texas' argument that the unborn is in fact a person because its status as a human being is established by the well-know facts of fetal development was rejected by the Court as well. It did so on the grounds that experts, including physicians, philosophers, and theologians, cannot agree on when human life begins.[19]

The first impediment was confronted by appealing to historical evidence. Justice Blackmun agreed with opponents of abortion rights that anti-abortion laws have been on the books in the United States for quite some time. However, according to Blackmun, the purpose of these laws, almost all of which were passed in the nineteenth century, was not to protect prenatal life, but rather, to protect the pregnant woman from a dangerous medical procedure.[20] Blackmun also argues that prior to the passage of these statutes, under the common law, abortion was permissible prior to quickening and was at most a misdemeanor after quickening.[21] (Quickening refers to the "first recognizable movement of the fetus *in utero*, appearing usually from the 16th to the 18th week of pregnancy."[22]) So, because abortion is now a relatively safe procedure, there is no longer a reason for prohibiting it.[23] Consequently, given the right of privacy, and given the abortion liberty that had appeared within common law, there is a constitutional right to abortion.

The history of abortion figures prominently in the Court's opinion in *Roe*.[24] Justice Blackmun, in 23 pages, takes the reader on an historical excursion through ancient attitudes (including the Greeks and Romans), the Hippocratic Oath, the common law, the English statutory law, the American law, and the positions of the American Medical Association (AMA), the American Public Health Association (APHA), and the American Bar Association (ABA). The purpose for this history is clear: if abortion's prohibition is only recent, and primarily for the purpose of protecting the pregnant woman from dangerous surgery, then the Court would not be creating a new right out of whole cloth if it affirms a right to abortion. However, only the history of common law is relevant to assessing the constitutionality of this right, because, as Blackmun himself admits, "it was not until after the War Between the States that legislation began generally to *replace* the common law,"[25] even though, as Joseph W. Dellapenna points out, Justice Blackmun's historical chronology is "simply wrong," for twenty-six of thirty-six states had already banned abortion by the time the Civil War had ended.[26] Nevertheless, when statutes did not address a criminal wrong, common law was the authoritative resource from which juries, judges, and justices found the principles from which, and by which, they issued judgments.

However, since 1973 the overwhelming consensus of scholarship has shown that the Court's history, especially its interpretation of common law, is almost entirely mistaken. Justice Blackmun's history (excluding his discussion of contemporary professional groups) is so flawed that it has inspired the production of scores of scholarly works that are nearly unanimous in concluding that Justice Blackmun's history is not trustworthy.[27]

After *Roe*

From 1973 to 1989 the Supreme Court struck down every state attempt to restrict an adult woman's access to abortion.[28] The U.S. Congress tried, and failed, to pass a Human Life Bill (1981) in order to protect the unborn by means of ordinary legislation, and later it failed to pass a Human Life Amendment (1983) to the U.S. Constitution. Although the Court upheld Congress' ban on federal funding of abortion except to save the life of the mother,[29] it never wavered on *Roe*. Given these political and legal realities, abortion opponents put their hopes in the Supreme Court appointees of two pro-life presidents, Ronald Reagan (1981–1989) and George H. W. Bush (1989–1993), to help overturn *Roe*. Between Reagan and Bush, they would appoint five justices to the Court (Sandra Day O'Connor, Antonin Scalia, Anthony Kennedy, Clarence Thomas, David Souter) who, abortion opponents mistakenly thought, all shared the judicial philosophies of the presidents who appointed them. Ironically, it would be three of those justices—O'Connor, Kennedy, and Souter—who would author the Court's opinion in *Casey v. Planned Parenthood* (1992) and uphold *Roe*. And two of them—O'Connor and Souter—would go even further, joining three of their brethren in *Stenberg v. Carhart* (2000) in holding that Nebraska's partial-birth abortion ban was unconstituitonal.

Nevertheless, three years before *Casey*, the Court seemed to be moving toward a rejection of *Roe*. Many abortion opponents read *Webster v. Reproductive Health Services* (1989)[30] as a sign that the Court was preparing to dismantle the regime of *Roe*. In *Webster* the Court reversed a lower-court decision and upheld several provisions of a Missouri statute that would not have survived constitutional muster in earlier days. First, the Court upheld the statute's preamble, which states that "'[t]he life of each human being begins at conception,' and that '[u]nborn children have protectable interests in life, health, and well-being.'"[31] Furthermore, it requires that under Missouri's laws the unborn should be treated as full persons who possess "all rights, privileges, immunities available to other persons, citizens, and residents of the state,"[32] contingent upon the U.S. Constitution and prior Supreme Court opinions. Because these precedents would include *Roe*, the statute poses no threat to the abortion liberty.

Second, the *Webster* Court upheld the portion of the Missouri statute that forbade the use of government facilities, funds, and employees in performing and counseling for abortions except if the procedure is necessary to save the life of the mother.

Third, the Court upheld the statute's provision that mandates that "[b]efore a physician performs an abortion on a woman he has reason to believe is carrying an unborn child of twenty or more weeks gestational age, the physician shall first determine if the unborn child is viable by using and exercising that degree of care, skill, and proficiency commonly exercised by the ordinarily skillful, careful, and prudent physician engaged in similar practice under the same or similar conditions."[33] In order to properly assess the unborn's viability, the statute requires that the physician employ procedures as are necessary and enter the findings of these procedures in the mother's medical record.[34] In passing this statute, Missouri's legislature took seriously *Roe*'s viability marker—that at the time of viability the state has a compelling interest in protecting unborn life. This is why the Court, in *Webster*, correctly concluded that "[t]he Missouri testing requirement here is reasonably designed to ensure that abortions are not performed where the fetus is viable—an end which all concede is legitimate—and that is sufficient to sustain its constitutionality."[35]

Webster, however, modified *Roe* in at least two significant ways: it rejected both *Roe*'s trimester breakdown as well as its claim that the state's interest in prenatal life becomes compelling only at viability:

[T]he rigid *Roe* framework is hardly consistent with the notion of a Constitution cast in general terms, as ours is, and usually speaking in general principles, as ours does. The key elements of the *Roe* framework—trimesters and viability—are not found in the text of the Constitution or in any place else one would expect to find a constitutional principle.[36]

According to the Court, "we do not see why the State's interest in protecting potential human life should come into existence only at the point of viability, and that there should therefore be a rigid line allowing state regulation after viability but prohibiting it before viability."[37] Although *Webster* chipped away at *Roe*, it did not overturn it.

In *Planned Parenthood v. Casey* (1992), the Court was asked to consider the constitutionality of five provisions of the Pennsylvania Abortion Control Act of 1982, which the state amended in 1988 and 1989.[38] The Court upheld as constitutional four of the five provisions, rejecting the third one (which required spousal notification for an abortion) based on what it calls the *undue burden* standard, which the Court defined in the following way: "A finding of an undue burden is a shorthand for the conclusion that a state regulation has the purpose or effect of placing a substantial obstacle in the path of a woman seeking an abortion of a nonviable fetus."[39] The undue burden standard is, according to most observers, a departure from *Roe* and its progeny, which required that any state restrictions on abortion be subject to strict scrutiny. That is, in order to be valid, any restrictions on access to abortion must be essential to meeting a compelling state interest. For example, laws that forbid yelling "fire" in a crowded theater pass strict scrutiny and thus do not violate the First Amendment right to freedom of expression. The *Casey* Court, nevertheless, claimed to be more consistent with the spirit and letter of *Roe* than the interpretations and applications of *Roe*'s principles in subsequent Court opinions.[40] But the *Casey* Court, by subscribing to the undue burden standard, held that a state may restrict abortion by passing laws that may not withstand strict scrutiny but nevertheless do not result in an undue burden for the pregnant woman. For example, the Court upheld as constitutional two provisions in the Pennsylvania statute—a 24-hour waiting-period requirement and an informed-consent requirement (that is, the woman must be provided the facts of fetal development, risks of abortion and childbirth, and information about abortion alternatives)—that would have most likely not met constitutional muster with the Court's pre-*Webster* composition.[41]

Although the *Casey* Court upheld *Roe* as a precedent, the plurality opinion, authored by three Reagan-Bush appointees—O'Connor, Kennedy, and Souter—rejected two aspects of *Roe*: (1) its requirement that restrictions be subject to strict scrutiny; and (2) its trimester framework (which *Webster* had already discarded). The trimester framework, according to the Court, was too rigid as well as unnecessary to protect a woman's right to abortion.[42] However, the *Casey* Court reaffirmed viability as the time at which the state has a compelling interest in protecting prenatal life.

Casey upheld *Roe* on the basis of *stare decisis* for which the Court provided two reasons: (1) the reliance interest,[43] and (2) the Court's legitimacy and the public's respect for it. Concerning the first, the Court argued that because the nation's citizens had planned and arranged their lives with the abortion right in mind, that is, because they have relied on this right, it would be wrong for the Court to jettison it.[44] And secondly, if the Court were to overturn *Roe*, it would suffer a loss of respect in the public's eye and perhaps chip away at its own legitimacy, even if rejecting *Roe* would in fact correct an error in constitutional jurisprudence.[45] The Court, nevertheless, in its opening comments in *Casey* speaks of abortion as a liberty grounded in the Due Process Clause of the Fourteenth Amendment, an extension of the right of privacy cases mentioned above.[46]

Beginning in 1996, then-President Bill Clinton vetoed several bills passed by the U.S. Congress to prohibit what pro-life activists call "partial-birth abortion."[47] Also known as "D & X" (for dilation and extraction) abortion, this procedure is performed in some late-term abortions. Using ultrasound, the doctor grips the fetus' legs with forceps. The fetus is then pulled out through the birth canal and delivered with the exception of its head. While the head is in the womb the doctor penetrates the live fetus' skull with scissors, opens the scissors to enlarge the hole, and then inserts a catheter. The fetus's brain is vacuumed out, resulting in the skull's collapse. The doctor then completes the womb's evacuation by removing the dead fetus.

Although none of the congressional bills became law, 30 states, including Nebraska, passed similar laws that prohibited D & X abortions. However, in *Stenberg v. Carhart* (2000), the Supreme Court, in a 5–4 decision, struck down Nebraska's ban on partial-birth abortions on two grounds:

1. The law lacked an exception for the preservation of the mother's health, which *Casey* required of any restrictions on abortion.
2. Nebraska's ban imposed an undue burden on a woman's fundamental right to have an abortion.

Although Nebraska's statute had a "life of the mother" exception, the Court pointed out that *Casey* requires an exception for *both* the life and *health* of the mother if a state wants to prohibit post-viability abortions.[48] But Nebraska did not limit its ban to only D & X abortions performed after viability. Its ban applied throughout pregnancy. So, according to the Court, unless Nebraska can show that its ban does not increase a woman's health risk, it is unconstitutional: "The State fails to demonstrate that banning D & X without a health exception may not create significant health risks for women, because the record shows that significant medical authority supports the proposition that in some circumstances D & X would be the safest procedure."[49] But, as Justice Kennedy points out in his dissent, "The most to be said for the D & X is it may present an unquantified lower risk of complication for a particular patient but that other proven safe procedures remain available even for this patient."[50] But the relative risk between procedures, if in fact D & X is in some cases relatively safer,[51] cannot justify overturning the law if the increased risk is statistically negligible and if the State, as the Court asserted in *Casey*[52] and *Webster*,[53] has an interest in prenatal life throughout pregnancy which becomes compelling enough after viability to prohibit abortion except in cases when the life or the health of the mother are in danger.

The Court's second reason for rejecting Nebraska's law is that the ban on D & X imposed an undue burden on a woman's fundamental right to have an abortion. The type of abortion performed in 95 percent of the cases between the 12th and 20th weeks of pregnancy—that is, "D & E" abortion (dilation and evacuation)[54]—is similar to D & X abortion. So, the Court reasoned, if a ban on D & X abortions is legally permissible, then so is a ban on D & E abortions. But that would imperil the right to abortion. Hence Nebraska's ban imposes an undue burden on the pregnant woman and thus violates the standard laid down in *Casey*. But, as both Justice Thomas and Justice Kennedy point out in their separate dissents,[55] by reading Nebraska's law in this way, the Court abandoned its long standing doctrine of statutory construction, that statutes should be read in a way that is consistent with the Constitution if such a reading is plausible. Moreover, Justice Thomas, in a blistering dissent, argues in graphic detail[56] that D & X and D & E procedures are dissimilar enough that it is "highly doubtful that" Nebraska's D & X ban "could be applied to ordinary D & E."[57]

In 2003, President George W. Bush signed into law a federal partial-birth abortion ban[58] that contains both a more circumspect definition of D & X abortion as well as a life of the mother exception.[59] It was immediately challenged in federal court by abortion-choice groups.[60] Nevertheless, on April 18, 2007, in *Gonzales v. Carhart* (2007), the Supreme Court upheld the federal statute.

PHILOSOPHY, RELIGION, AND HUMAN NATURE

Most advocates in the abortion debate, in their more candid moments, will admit that the deep divisions between citizens on this issue are the result of how these citizens answer the most fundamental questions of human existence to which religious traditions have traditionally offered answers. These answers include the nature of human persons and the extent to which human persons have obligations to one another and whether familial obligations—including what, if anything, we owe our children and our parents—ought to be reflected in our laws. This is why philosophers, theologians, and other scholars, in order to support their various views on abortion, have focused on two areas: (1) the nature of human persons, and (2) the extent of a human person's bodily autonomy.

The Nature of Human Persons

Virtually no one disputes that individual human life begins at conception, the *successful* result of the process of fertilization at which the male sperm and the female ovum unite.[61] That is, fertilization is a process, taking between twenty-four to thirty-six hours that culminates in conception. Where there is disagreement is over this question: when during this entity's development does it become immoral to take its life without justification? Or put differently, when does this entity require state protection?

Those who maintain that the unborn—during some, all, or most of its gestation—is not entitled to legal protection by the state argue that it lacks a property that, if present, would make it a *person* (or a subject of moral concern). This is an example of the accidental-essential division employed by some metaphysicians when they discuss, defend, or critique a particular philosophical anthropology. J.P. Moreland illustrates: "If something (say Socrates) has an accidental property (e.g., being white), then that thing can lose the property and still exist. For example, Socrates could turn brown and still exist and be Socrates. Essential properties constitute the nature or essence of a thing; and by referring to essential properties, one answers in the most basic way this question: What kind of thing is *x*?"[62] So, for example, if one states that the unborn is not a moral subject until it is viable, then one is claiming that viability is an essential property of human persons.

Thinkers offer a variety of metaphysical views on the nature of human beings and personhood. Some argue that personhood does not arrive until brain waves are detected (40 to 43 days after conception).[63] Others, such as Mary Anne Warren,[64] define a person as a being who can do certain things, such as have consciousness, solve complex problems, have a self-concept, and engage in sophisticated communication, which would put the arrival of personhood *after birth*. Presenting views similar to Warren's, Michael Tooley[65] and Peter Singer[66] argue that not only is abortion permissible, but so is infanticide, for they maintain that the newborn (for some months after birth) is not a person and thus is not entitled to the protections we accord beings who have such a status. David Boonin takes a more conservative abortion-choice position, maintaining that the unborn does not become a subject of moral rights until the arising of organized cortical brain activity (25 to 32 weeks after conception).[67] Still others, such as L.W. Sumner,[68] take a moderate position and argue that human personhood does not arrive until the fetus is sentient and has the ability to feel and sense as a conscious being. This, according to Sumner, occurs possibly as early as the middle weeks of the second trimester of pregnancy and definitely by the end of that trimester.

There are also theologically-argued variations on these positions. They are, in my judgment, as much based on metaphysical considerations as the secular theories. However, they either rely on or add premises that appeal to Scripture, religious tradition, or theological reasoning. For instance, theologian Beverley Harrison denies the personhood of both the infant as well as the post-viable fetus:

> An infant is a biologically discrete entity, an individual human being—though not a full person. In the first half of pregnancy, a fetus could not be considered this ... There is no analogue between a conceptus and a human being except certain protoplasm—the former is human tissue but not human life ... In regard to infanticide, one has to weigh the moral concerns carefully. It is wise for the community to discourage infanticide and would be unwise to make abortion illegal ... Infanticide is not a great wrong. I do not want to be construed as condemning women who, under certain circumstances, quietly put their infants to death.[69]

Theologian and ethicist Joseph Fletcher, who maintains that his ethical views are within the Christian tradition,[70] presents criteria of personhood that exclude infants.[71] The Religious Coalition for Reproductive Choice (RCRC) affirms that "the common belief is that life begins at birth, when the baby begins to breathe on his/her own and is not dependent on oxygen from the mother. Therefore, Jewish and biblical tradition defined a human being with the word 'nephesh'—the breathing one ... Biblically, a human being is one who breathes."[72] Christian ethicist John Swomley agrees, arguing that "the Bible's clear answer is that human life begins at birth, with the first breath. In *Gen.* 2:7, God 'breathed into his nostrils the breath of life and man became a living being' (in some translations, 'a living soul')."[73]

As one might guess, those who believe that full personhood begins at conception have developed and defended highly sophisticated arguments for their position.[74] These arguments, like those of their adversaries, are put forth to defend a particular metaphysical view of human persons. The following is a brief example of the sort of philosophical anthropology defended by some of these abortion opponents.

According to this view, each kind of living organism or *substance*, including the human being, maintains identity through change and possesses a nature or essence that makes certain activities and functions possible. "A substance's *inner nature*," (emphasis in original) writes Moreland "is its ordered structural unity of ultimate capacities. A substance cannot change in its ultimate capacities; that is, it cannot lose its ultimate nature and continue to exist."[75] Consider the following illustration.

A domestic feline, because it has a particular nature, has the ultimate capacity to develop the ability to purr. It may die as a kitten and never develop that ability. Regardless, it is *still* a feline as long as it exists, because it possesses a particular nature, even if it never acquires certain functions that by nature it has the capacity to develop. In contrast, a frog is not said to lack something if it cannot purr, for it is by nature not the sort of being that can have the ability to purr. A feline that lacks the ability to purr *is still a feline* because of its nature. A human being who lacks the ability to think rationally (either because she is too young or she suffers from a disability) *is still a human person* because of her nature. Consequently, a human being's lack makes sense *if and only if* she is an actual human person.

Second, the feline remains the same particular feline over time from the moment it comes into existence. Suppose you buy this feline as a kitten and name him "Cartman." When you first bring him home, you notice that he is tiny in comparison to his parents and lacks their mental and physical abilities. But over time Cartman develops these abilities, learns a number of things his parents never learned, sheds his hair, has his claws removed, becomes ten times larger than he was as a kitten, and undergoes significant development of his cellular structure, brain and cerebral cortex. Yet, this grown-up Cartman is identical to the kitten Cartman, even though he has gone through significant physical changes. Why? The reason is because living organisms, substances, maintain identity through change.

Another way to put it is to say that organisms, including human beings, are ontologically prior to their parts,[76] which means that the organism as a whole maintains absolute identity through time while it grows, develops, and undergoes numerous changes, largely as a result of the organism's nature that directs and informs these changes and their limits. The organs and parts of the organism, and their role in actualizing the intrinsic, basic capacities of the whole, acquire their purpose and function *because* of their roles in maintaining, sustaining, and perfecting the *being as a whole*. This is in contrast to a thing that is not ontologically prior to its parts, like an automobile, cruise ship, or computer. Just as a sporting event (for example, a basketball game, a tennis match) does not subsist through time as a unified whole, neither will an automobile, ship, or computer.[77] It is, rather, in the words of Moreland, "a sum of each temporal (and spatial) part . . ." Called *mereological essentialism* (from the Greek "meros" for "part"), it "means that the parts of a thing are essential to it as a whole; if the object gains or loses parts, it is a different object."[78] Organisms, however, are different, for they may lose and gain parts, and yet remain the same thing over time.

Thus, if you are an intrinsically valuable human person now, then you were an intrinsically valuable human person at *every moment in your past*, including when you were in your mother's womb, for you are identical to yourself throughout the changes you undergo from the moment you come into existence. But if this were not the case, that it is only one's present ability to exercise certain human functions, such as rationality, awareness of one's interests, and consciousness, that makes one a person, then it is not the organism that is intrinsically valuable, but merely one's states or functions. "It would follow" from this, writes Patrick Lee, "that the basic moral rule would be simply to maximize valuable states or functions." For example, "[i]t would not be morally wrong to kill a child, no matter what age, if doing so enabled one to have two children in the future, and thus to bring it about that there were two vehicles of intrinsic value rather than one. On the contrary, we are aware that persons themselves, which are things enduring through time, are intrinsically valuable."[79]

Among the ways that some thinkers reply to this argument is to advance a case that there is no substantial self that remains the same through all the accidental changes the human being undergoes; that is, there is no absolute identity between any stages in the existence of a human being. Proponents of this view maintain that personal identity consists of a series of experiences that does not require an underlying substance that has these experiences. My "personhood" is merely a string of psychological experiences connected by memory, beliefs, and/or character as well as causal, bodily, and temporal continuity. And because this continuity does not extend to the fetal stages of existence, and perhaps not even to infancy, the unborn and perhaps the newborn are not persons.[80] Some call this the *no-subject* view.[81] Baptist theologian Paul Simmons seems to be embracing this metaphysical perspective as well: "No one can deny that there is a continuum from fertilization to birth, maturity, and adulthood, but not every stage on the continuum has the same value or constitutes the same entity."[82] An implication of this view is that even when a human being becomes a "person" she is literally not the same entity she was ten years ago or even one second ago. That is, she does not maintain absolute identity through change. This view has been subject to trenchant, and I believe convincing, philosophical criticism.[83]

A commitment to materialism provides many thinkers with a motivation for maintaining the no-subject view. The dominant metaphysical view of intellectuals in the West, materialism maintains that all that exists is the physical world and that non-physical things like God, angels, natures, substances, and souls do not actually exist and/or cannot be the object of knowledge. As materialist Paul Churchland writes: "The important point about the standard evolutionary story is that the human species and all of its features are the wholly physical outcome of a purely physical process ... If this is the correct account of our origins, then there seems neither need, nor room, to fit any nonphysical substances or properties into our theoretical account of ourselves. We are creatures of matter. And we should learn to live with that fact."[84]

Another sort of response to the substance view is to agree with the pro-lifer that one's adult self is identical to one's prenatal self, that it is in fact the same substance that remains identical to itself through time, but that intrinsic value is an *accidental*, rather than an *essential*, *property* possessed by human beings as long as they exist.[85] What this means is that you are materially identical to your prenatal self, but that a property you acquire late in your gestation or soon after your birth—for example, sentience, self-consciousness—imparts to you intrinsic vale. So, just as a leaf turns from green to brown in Autumn yet remains the same leaf, you turn from non-person to person, although you remain the same human being. This view is the most dominant one in the literature.

Thus, regardless of what position one may hold on abortion, it depends on a philosophical anthropology that is grounded in some metaphysical perspective. So, for example, if one is a materialist like Churchland, one will likely develop a philosophical anthropology that excludes non-physical properties and substances. Or if one ties the achievement of personhood to the acquisition and development of certain physical properties,[86] one would seem to be accepting the view that the human person is merely a physical system, denying that a human being is a substance ontologically prior to its parts. Or if one argues, like many abortion opponents do, that the human being is a substance that maintains absolute identity through change as long as it exists, then an ordinary adult human being is the same substance that was in her mother's womb from conception, and thus, that unborn entity, who later became the adult, was a person as well. Thus, no position on abortion is without metaphysical presuppositions, regardless of whether those presuppositions are consciously recognized or affirmed by its advocates.

The Extent of a Person's Bodily Rights

Some abortion-choice advocates do not see the status of the unborn as the decisive factor in whether or not abortion is morally or legally justified. They argue that a pregnant woman's removal of the unborn from her body, even though it is foreseeable that it will result in the unborn's death, is no more immoral than an ordinary person's refusal to donate his kidney to another in need of one, even though this refusal will probably result in the death of the prospective recipient. The most important and influential argument of this sort was offered in 1971 by philosopher Judith Jarvis Thomson.[87] Although others, including David Boonin[88] and Eileen McDonagh,[89] have defended revised versions of it, Thomson's case is worth considering for our present purposes. For it is an argument that relies heavily on notions of personal autonomy and individual rights that many religious citizens consider fatal to communitarian understandings of child-bearing and child-rearing that are congenial to their religious traditions. Even though the federal courts and popular pro-choice advocates have not explicitly defended Thomson's argument, much of their rhetoric seems to support an understanding of bodily rights and autonomy consistent with Thomson's position. This will become apparent as we examine the argument.

Thomson's Violinist Argument Thomson writes that it is "of great interest to ask what happens if, for the sake of argument, we allow the premise [that the fetus is a person]. How, precisely, are we supposed to get from there to the conclusion that abortion is morally impermissible?"[90] Thomson's argument, therefore, poses a special difficulty for the pro-life advocate. She grants, for the sake of argument, the pro-lifer's most important premise—the unborn is a subject of moral rights—but nevertheless concludes that abortion is morally permissible. In a sense, her query, at the level of principle, is uncontroversial, for she is simply asking whether it follows from the fact that a living being is intrinsically valuable that it is *never* permissible to kill that being or to act in a way that results in its death. After all, many abortion opponents would answer "no." For many of them argue that one can consistently maintain that all human beings are persons and thus have a *prima facie* right to life, while at the same time holding that there may be some cases in which killing human beings is justified, such as in the cases of just war or self-defense.

Thomson argues that even if the unborn is a person with a right to life, it does not follow that a pregnant woman is morally required to use her bodily organs to sustain the unborn's life. In order to make her case, Thomson offers a story that accentuates what she believes are the relevant principles that support her argument:

You wake up in the morning and find yourself back to back in bed with an unconscious violinist. A famous unconscious violinist. He has been found to have a fatal kidney ailment, and the Society of Music Lovers has canvassed all the available medical records and found that you alone have the right blood type to help. They have therefore kidnapped you, and last night the violinist's circulatory system was plugged into yours, so that your kidneys can be used to extract poisons from his blood as well as your own. The director of the hospital now tells you, "Look we're sorry the Society of Music Lovers did this to you—we would never have permitted it if we had known. But still, they did it, and the violinist now is plugged into you. To unplug you would be to kill him. But never mind, it's only for nine months. By then he will have recovered from his ailment, and can safely be unplugged from you." Is it morally incumbent on you to accede to this situation? No doubt it would be very nice of you if you did, a great kindness. But do you *have* to accede to it? What if it were not nine months, but nine years? Or still longer? What if the director of the hospital says, "Tough luck, I agree, but you've now got to stay in bed, with the violinist plugged into you, for the rest of your life. Because remember this. All persons have a right to life, and violinists are persons. Granted you have a right to decide what happens in and to your body, but a person's right to life outweighs your right to decide what happens in and to your body. So you cannot ever be unplugged from him." I imagine that you would regard this as outrageous . . .[91]

Thomson concludes she is "only arguing that having a right to life does not guarantee having either a right to be given the use of or a right to be allowed continued use of another person's body—even if one needs it for life itself."[92] That is, the unborn does not have a right to life so strong that it outweighs the pregnant woman's right to personal bodily autonomy. Thomson anticipates several objections to her argument, and in the process of responding to them further clarifies her case.

According to Thomson, the pregnant woman consented to sex, but not to the pregnancy that followed if she did not intend to have children. Just as opening my window for the pleasure of fresh air does not entitle a burglar to my belongings even though while opening the window it was foreseeable that a burglar may crawl through the window wanting to steal from me, engaging in sex for pleasure does not entitle the fetus to the pregnant woman's body even though while engaging in sex it was foreseeable that an unborn human being needing the pregnant woman's body for its survival may result.[93]

Responses to Thomson's Argument There is no scarcity of responses to Thomson's argument in the literature.[94] David Boonin presents and critiques sixteen of them, some of which have several variations including counterarguments to rebuttals.[95] However, there is a case against Thomson's argument that combines what are sometimes called the responsibility objection and the parental obligation objection.

Thomson's case seems to depend on the notion that moral obligations must be voluntarily and explicitly accepted in order to have moral, and thus legal, force. But that does not seem correct in some cases. For instance, we do not consider explicit consent to be a necessary condition when we justly ascribe blame and attribute responsibility to a person whose actions resulted in consequences that he did not explicitly intend to bring about. Take, for example, the following tale. Imagine a man and a woman engage in consensual intercourse that results in pregnancy. The couple did not intend this result, for they were careful in their carnal indulgence, employing several of the most efficient and safest forms of birth control. And yet, conception occurred. Rather than exercising her legal right to abort, the woman, who had never fancied herself as a mother, chooses to bring the child to term, for she has not been able to suppress the maternal instincts that welled up inside her from the moment her physician informed her that she was pregnant. The father, however, does not share the mother's excitement. In fact, he loathes the idea of being anyone's father. He wants neither the title nor the responsibility. Soon after the child's birth, the mother seeks from the father financial support for the child that he sired. He rejects her request. She hires an attorney and begins legal action against the father, asking the court to garnish the father's wages until his child is 18 years old. There is no doubt that the father was careful and precautionary in his sexual activity with his child's mother, and he had indicated by both his contraceptive actions and his words that he did not want to become a father. Yet, the child support laws virtually everywhere offer a different moral understanding of this man's responsibility, one that does not put a premium on autonomy, choice, or explicit intention. These laws assert that the father is obligated to provide financial support for his child for no other reason than the one reason he and Thomson would consider not morally relevant: he is the child's father,[96] a status that carries with it a responsibility and obligation because the intercourse in which the father engaged was a consensual act that is naturally ordered toward bringing needy human beings into existence. These laws are grounded in deep moral intuitions that seem *prima facie* correct—intuitions that ground our notion that parents have a natural, pre-political obligation to care for their child even if the child's existence was not the result of a conscious plan to bring the child into being. Our intuitions about parental obligation to children, and society's obligation to its vulnerable immature members, seem to be more well-grounded intuitions than the autonomy to which Thomson appeals.

It would be a mistake, however, to conclude that such parental obligations are based merely on *biology*, for it would follow from this that sperm-donors are morally obligated to care for children sired by their donated seed. Rather, as I have already noted, the father's responsibility for his offspring stems from the fact that he consensually engaged in an act, sexual intercourse, that is naturally ordered to result in reproduction if the sex organs of the participants are functioning properly. This is not an unusual way to frame moral obligations, for we do so even in cases where a particular result is merely foreseeable and not naturally ordered. For example, we hold drunken people whose driving results in manslaughter responsible for their actions, even if they did not *intend* to kill someone prior to becoming intoxicated. Such special obligations, although not *directly* undertaken *voluntarily*, are necessary in any civilized culture in order to preserve the rights of the vulnerable, the weak, and the young. This is why the burglar illustration I borrowed from Thomson fails. As Patrick Lee points out: "[T]he woman's action does not cause the burglar to be in the house but only removes an obstacle; the burglar himself is the primary agent responsible for his being in the house. In the voluntary pregnancy case, however, the baby does not cause his or her presence in the mother's womb; rather, the mother and the father do."[97]

Most people, abortion-choice opponent and supporter alike, agree that in ordinary circumstances, a born child has a natural moral claim upon her parents to care for her, regardless of whether her parents "wanted" her. As Michael Levin points out, "All child-support laws make the parental body an indirect resource for the child. If the father is a construction worker, the state will intervene unless some of his calories he extends lifting equipment go to providing food for his children."[98]

But this means that if Thomson's argument works—that a pregnant woman is not responsible for her unborn fetus in cases of consensual sex—then the moral grounds of our child support laws vanishes. For this would mean that deadbeat dads who may claim to only have consented to sex but not fatherhood would not be morally obligated to pay child support. But since we know that deadbeat dads should pay child support regardless of whether they intended for their partners to become pregnant, then the pregnant woman is obligated to remedy her child's neediness regardless of whether she intended to become pregnant when she consented to sex. Thus, Thomson's case fails.[99]

Boonin offers an argument in reply to the child support objection. He asks us to assume that there is a moral obligation for a deadbeat dad to pay child support (even though Boonin does not believe that there really is such a moral obligation). But even if this is the case, argues Boonin, because a woman has a unique and greater physical burden during pregnancy than a man or woman has to his or her child postnatally, the woman lacks during pregnancy the moral obligation to assist her child that she and the child's father have after birth. Moreover, if we would not require a man to undergo a physical experience similar to pregnancy against his will, then we cannot require a woman to remain pregnant against her will. Boonin employs several analogies, comparing the mother's apparent obligation to her unborn fetus to forced organ donation or temporary use of another's body, which is illegal, and immoral, even if parents are the ones whose bodies are used to help their children.[100]

Some do not find these analogies convincing. For they seem to turn on an account of human beings and procreation for which Boonin does not provide any support—namely, that it is *not rational* to believe that sex is an act whose intelligible point is to bring a needy human being into existence and place it in a congenial environment, the woman's body, whose physical design is ordered toward the caring, sheltering, and nurturing of the fetus. After all, an involuntary organ donor or lender (even if she is the recipient's parent) is typically *not responsible* for the neediness of the organ recipient, and the donor's body is *not* intrinsically ordered toward the donation of organs for a specific person who by nature needs those organs as the woman's body is intrinsically ordered toward the care of her fetus.

Nevertheless, Boonin is correct that there are burdens that attend the condition of pregnancy that cannot be shared with the male parent, for they are unique to the female of the human species. But it is not clear how the difference in parental burdens between the sexes justifies abortion. It seems to me that the correct comparison is between the burdens to be borne by the fetus or its mother (assuming, as Thomson does, that the unborn fetus is a person with a right to life), not between the father and the mother, if the decision to abort the fetus hangs in the balance. For if we were to think of the burden of an ordinary pregnancy as a harm exclusively borne by the woman, as no doubt Boonin does, and compare it to the harm of death borne exclusively by the unborn fetus if it is aborted, "the harm avoided by the woman seeking the abortion," writes Lee, "is not comparable with the death caused to the child aborted. (Recall that burden need only involve nine months of pregnancy; the woman can put the child up for adoption)."[101]

If this response succeeds, then Thomson's violinist illustration does not apply in cases of ordinary consensual sexual intercourse. However, as some have argued, it does apply in cases in which pregnancy results from rape. After all, the above case against the violinist argument relies on moral intuitions about one's responsibility for the foreseeable and/or naturally ordered results of one's *consensual* actions. Rape is not a case of consensual sex. Thus, although Thomson herself does not advance this argument from rape,[102] her argument does seem to apply in cases of rape. Some, however, argue that it does not.[103]

ABORTION, CHURCH, AND STATE

As noted above, because the abortion debate raises many of the same questions that have been answered by virtually every religious tradition, religious groups and their members have been in the forefront of supporting or opposing abortion rights. For example, the Roman Catholic Church as well as most theologically conservative Protestants and Jews (though by no means all) oppose abortion rights. On the other hand, most theologically liberal Protestants and Jews (though by no means all) support a woman's right to choose (with various limitations in the case of some religious bodies). Minority religious groups hold a variety of views, including strong pro-life and strong abortion-rights positions. Thus, it should come as no surprise that some scholars have examined the issue of abortion from the perspective of America's traditions of religious liberty and church-state separation. However, because this approach has been critically applied almost exclusively to religious opponents of abortion-choice, that application will also be our focus. One can only speculate as to why devout pro-choice citizens have not undergone the same scrutiny of their religious motives as have their pro-life counterparts. A reason for this may be that the theological reasons offered by pro-choice citizens—such as appeals to God-given personal liberty and autonomy[104]—nearly always support conclusions that align with the views of secular citizens.

Some thinkers have argued that the framework of *Roe v. Wade* is best justified by the Religion Clauses of the First Amendment and/or what they believe are the philosophical principles that gave rise to our contemporary understanding of these clauses. Among those who hold, or appear to hold, such views are the theologian Paul Simmons[105] and the philosophers Judith Jarvis Thomson[106] and Ronald Dworkin.[107] Although the Supreme Court in its holdings does not explicitly ground the right to abortion in the Religion Clauses, some of its reasoning seems to suggest that the abortion debate is mired in an intractable dispute of conflicting visions of the human person that are religious in quality and that the best way to resolve this debate is to retain the right to abortion. For example, as the plurality in Planned *Parenthood v. Casey* writes,

Our law affords constitutional protection to personal decisions relating to marriage, procreation, contraception, family relationships, child rearing, and education ... These matters, involving the most intimate and personal choices a person may make in a lifetime, choices central to personal dignity and autonomy, are central to the liberty protected by the Fourteenth Amendment. At the heart of liberty is the right to define one's own concept of existence, of meaning, of the universe, and of the mystery of human life. Beliefs about these matters could not define the attributes of personhood were they formed under compulsion by the State.[108]

The First Amendment and Abortion

Simmons suggests that the Supreme Court should "examine abortion as an issue of religious liberty and First Amendment guarantees."[109] For, according to Simmons, the position of abortion opponents—namely, that the fetus is a full-fledged human person from conception—is the result of "speculative metaphysics," indeed, "religious reasoning," and for that reason, ought not to be part of public policy, because if it were it would amount to one religious position being foisted upon those who do not agree with it. This would violate the Establishment Clause, the portion of the U.S. Constitution's First Amendment that asserts that government may not establish a religion.[110] It would also violate the Free Exercise Clause of the First Amendment, for to allow such a public policy would be inconsistent with the Court's obligation "to protect the free exercise of the woman's conscientious (i.e., religious) judgment."[111]

In reply to Simmons,[112] it has been argued that no matter what position the government takes on abortion, it must rely, whether explicitly or implicitly, on some view of the human person that is tied to a metaphysical position that answers precisely the same sort of question that the "religious" positions to which Simmons alludes try to answer. Because these so-called "religious positions," as we saw above, are often defended by arguments that are public (or secular) in their quality and do not rely on appeals to Holy Scripture or religious authority, it is not precisely clear why a public argument that is informed by a citizen's religious belief violates the Constitution while a contrary public argument that is informed by a citizen's secular belief does not.

In terms of constitutional law, the Supreme Court has never suggested or held that with respect to the issue of abortion a citizen's religious motive is relevant to assessing the constitutionality of the citizen's policy proposal. However, Justice John Paul Stevens has argued that the pro-life *position*, rather than the pro-lifer's motive, is religious and thus unconstitutional.[113] But this view seems exclusively held by Justice Stevens. The Court, however, has employed a "religious motive" test to statutes concerning public school prayer[114] and the teaching of creationism in public schools.[115] But in these cases, the activities on which the laws focused seem distinctly religious, unlike the pro-life position on abortion, which is embraced by citizens from a variety of religious traditions and secular philosophies. Examples of the latter include Nat Hentoff (civil libertarian atheist),[116] Doris Gordon (atheist and president of Libertarians for Life),[117] and Joseph W. Dellapenna (law professor and self-described "lapsed Unitarian").[118]

CONCLUSION

Abortion is a political, moral, religious, and legal issue that will not soon go away. Because the issues that percolate beneath it are connected to the deeply held beliefs of the nation's citizens, many of whom are seriously religious, abortion is an issue on which the different answers to the great questions of human existence intersect. This is why virtually every legal or scholarly attempt to resolve the issue has either offered a defense of a particular philosophical or religious view of the human person or bodily rights (as we saw in section II) or attempted to procedurally avoid or exclude some of those views from legal or political consideration (as we saw in sections I and III). Regardless of which tactic is taken, each establishes the fact that the great questions of human existence, the questions to which religious traditions provide answers, loom large in the abortion debate.

It seems then that the abortion debate cannot be politically and legally resolved by merely appealing to apparently neutral principles of political and legal philosophy that are uncontroversial. After all, to say that a woman should have the right to choose to terminate her pregnancy without public justification is tantamount to denying the abortion opponent's position that the unborn are human persons who by nature are worthy of protection by the state. And to affirm that the unborn are human persons that ought to be protected by the state is tantamount to denying the abortion-choice position that a woman has a fundamental right to terminate her pregnancy, because such a termination would result, in most cases, in an unjustified homicide. Abortion is an intractable moral, legal, and social issue that will be with us quite some time.

NOTES

Parts of this chapter are adapted from portions of my book, *Defending Life: A Moral and Legal Case Against Abortion Choice* (New York: Cambridge University Press, 2007).

1. "South Dakota Abortion Ban Rejected," *USA Today*, Nov. 8, 2006, available at http://www.usatoday.com/news/politicselections/vote2006/SD/2006–11-08-abortion-ban_x.htm.
2. *Stenberg v. Carhart*, 120 S. Ct. 2597 (2000).
3. *Gonzales v. Carhart*, 550 U.S. ____ (2007).
4. *Griswold v. Connecticut*, 381 U.S. 479 (1965).
5. Ibid., 486.
6. "We do not sit as a super-legislature to determine the wisdom, need, and propriety of laws that touch on economic problems, business affairs, and social conditions. This law, however, operates directly on an intimate relation of husband and wife and their physician's role in one aspect of that relation." Id. at 482.
7. In his concurrence, Justice Arthur J. Goldberg stated:

The entire fabric of the Constitution and the purposes that clearly underlie its specific guarantees demonstrate that the rights to marital privacy and to marry and raise a family are of similar order and magnitude as the fundamental rights specifically protected . . . The fact that no particular of the Constitution explicitly forbids the State from disrupting the traditional relation of the family—a relation as old and as fundamental as our entire civilization—surely does not show that Government was meant to have the power to do so (Ibid., 494–06 [J. Goldberg, concurring]).

8. *Eisenstadt v. Baird*, 405 U.S. 438, 454 (1972).

9. Ibid., 453.

10. "This right of privacy, whether it be founded in the Fourteenth Amendment's concept of personal liberty and restrictions upon state action, as we feel it is, or, as the District Court determined, in the Ninth Amendment's reservation of rights to the people, is broad enough to encompass a woman's decision whether or not to terminate her pregnancy" (*Roe v. Wade*, 410 U.S 113, 153 [1973]).

11. Abortion-choice advocate and Harvard law professor Laurence Tribe writes: "A decade and a half after the Court handed down its decision in *Roe v. Wade*, McCorvey explained, with embarrassment, that she had not been raped after all; she made up the story to hide the fact she had gotten 'in trouble' in the more usual way" (Laurence Tribe, *Abortion: The Clash of Absolutes* [New York: W. W. Norton, 1990], 10).

12. *Roe*, 410 U.S., 164–165.

13. As the Court writes elsewhere in *Roe*: "The privacy right involved, therefore, cannot be said to be absolute. In fact, it is not clear to us that the claim asserted by some *amici* that one has an unlimited right to do with one's body as one pleases bears a close relationship to the right of privacy previously articulated in the Court's decisions. The Court has refused to recognize an unlimited right of this kind in the past. *Jacobson v. Massachusetts*, 197 U.S. 11 (1905) (vaccination); *Buck v. Bell*, 274 U.S. 200 (1927) (sterilization)." (Ibid., 154)

14. *Doe v. Bolton*, 410 U.S. 179, 192 (1973).

15. Report, Committee on the Judiciary, U.S. Senate, on Senate Resolution 3, 98th Congress, 98–149, June 7, 1983. 6. See also, Report on the Human Life Bill—S. 158; Committee on the Judiciary, United States Senate, December 1981, 5.

16. Ibid.

17. As Justice Blackmun writes in *Roe*: "The pregnant woman cannot be isolated in her privacy. She carries an embryo and, later, a fetus, if one accepts the medical definitions of the developing young in the uterus . . . The situation therefore is inherently different from marital intimacy, or bedroom possession of obscene material, or marriage, or procreation, or education . . . As we have intimated above, it is reasonable and appropriate for a State to decide that at some point in time another interest, that of health of the mother or that of potential human life, become significantly involved. The woman's privacy is no longer sole and any

right of privacy she possesses must be measured accordingly" (*Roe*, 410 U.S., 159) (citations omitted).

18. *Roe*, 410 U.S., 157. Interestingly enough, there was one federal court case, *Steinberg v. Brown*, 321 F. Supp. 741 (ND Ohio 1970), that Texas did not cite that in fact held that the unborn is a Fourteenth Amendment person. The *Roe* Court did cite that case, but in another context. See *Roe*, 410 U.S., 155 (citing *Steinberg*, 321 F. Supp. as well as other cases in which courts have sustained anti-abortion statutes).

19. *Roe*, 410 U.S., 160.

20. Justice Blackmun writes: "[I]t has been argued that a State's real concern in enacting a criminal abortion law was to protect the pregnant woman, that is, to restrain her from submitting to a procedure that places her life in serious jeopardy" (Ibid., 149).

21. Ibid., 132–136. Justice Blackmun writes: "It is thus apparent that at common law, at the time of the adoption of the Constitution, and throughout the major portion of the nineteenth century, abortion was viewed with less disfavor than under most American statutes currently in effect. Phrasing it another way, a woman enjoyed a substantially broader right to terminate a pregnancy than she does in most States today. At least with respect to the early stage of pregnancy, and very possibly without such a limitation, the opportunity to make this choice was present in this country well into the nineteenth century" (Ibid., 140–141).

22. Ibid., 132 (footnote omitted).

23. "Mortality rates for women undergoing early abortions, where the procedure is legal, appear to be as low or as lower than the rates of normal childbirth. Consequently, any interest of the State in protecting the woman from an inherently dangerous procedure, except when it would be equally dangerous for her to forgo it, has largely disappeared" (*Roe*, 410 U.S., 149).

24. *Roe*, 410 U.S., 129–151.

25. Ibid., 139. (emphasis added)

26. Dellapenna, "The History of Abortion," 389.

27. Among these many works are the following: Joseph W. Dellapenna, *Dispelling the Myths of Abortion History* (Durham, NC: Carolina Academic Press, 2006); James S. Witherspoon, "Reexaming *Roe*: Nineteenth-Century Abortion Statutes and the Fourteenth Amendment," *St. Mary's Law Journal* 17 (1985); Krason, *Abortion*, 134–157; Dennis J. Horan and Thomas J. Balch, "*Roe v. Wade*: No Justification in History, Law, or Logic," *The Abortion Controversy 25 Years After* Roe v. Wade: *A Reader*, 2nd ed., ed. Louis P. Pojman and Francis J. Beckwith (Belmont, CA: Wadsworth); Joseph W. Dellapenna, "Abortion and the Law: Blackmun's Distortion of the Historical Record," in *Abortion and the Constitution*; Joseph W. Dellapenna, "The History of Abortion: Technology, Morality and Law," *University of Pittsburgh Law Review* 40 (1979); Martin Arbagi, "*Roe* and the Hypocratic Oath," in *Abortion and the Constitution*; Harold O. J. Brown, "What the Supreme Court Didn't Know: Ancient and Early Christian Views on Abortion," *Human Life Review*

1, no. 2 (Spring 1975); Robert M. Byrn, "An American Tragedy: The Supreme Court on Abortion," *Fordham Law Review* 41 (1973); John R. Connery, S. J., "The Ancients and the Medievels on Abortion: The Consensus the Court Ignored," in *Abortion and the Constitution*; John Gorby, "The 'Right' to an Abortion, the Scope of Fourteenth Amendment 'Personhood' and the Supreme Court's Birth Requirement," *Southern Illinois Law Review* (1979); Janet LaRue, "Abortion: Justice Harry A. Blackmun and the *Roe v. Wade* Decision," *Simon Greenleaf Law Review: A Scholarly Forum of Opinion Interrelating Law, Theology & Human Rights* 2 (1982–83); Marvin Olasky, *Abortion Rites: A Social History of Abortion in America* (Wheaton, IL: Crossway, 1992); and Robert Sauer, "Attitudes to Abortion in America, 1800–1973," *Population Studies* 28 (1974).

28. See, for example, *Planned Parenthood of Missouri v. Danforth*, 428 U.S. 52 (1976) (held as unconstitutional parental and spousal consent requirements as well as a state ban on saline [or salt poisoning] abortions, a procedure that literally burns the skin of the unborn); *Colautti vs. Franklin*, 439 U.S. 379, 387 (1979) (state may not define viability or enjoin physicians to prove the fetus is viable in order to require that they have a duty to preserve the life of the fetus if a pregnancy termination is performed; "viability" is whatever the physician judges it is in a particular pregnancy); *Akron v. Akron Center for Reproductive Health, Inc.* 462 U.S. 416 (1983) (held as unconstitutional: informed consent requirement, 24-hour waiting period, parental consent requirement, compulsory hospitalization for second trimester abortions, and humane and sanitary disposal of fetal remains); *Thornburgh v. American College of Obstetricians and Gynecologists*, 476 U.S. 747 (1986) (struck down as unconstitutional a Pennsylvania statute that (a) required informed consent of abortion's possible risks to the woman, (b) required that the pregnant woman be informed of agencies that would help her if she brought child to term, (c) required that the abortion provider report certain statistics about their patients to the state, and (d) required that a second physician be present at abortion when fetal viability is possible).

29. See *Harris v. McRae*, 448 U.S. 297 (1980).

30. *Webster v. Reproductive Health Services,* 492 U.S. 490 (1989).

31. Ibid., 504, quoting from Mo. Rev. Stat. §§ 1.205.1(1), (2) (1986) (parenthetical insertions are the Court's).

32. Ibid., 504, quoting from Mo. Rev. Stat. §§ 1.205.2 (1986) (footnote ommitted).

33. Ibid., 513, quoting from Mo. Rev. Stat. § 188.029 (1986).

34. Mo. Rev. Stat. § 188.029 (1986), as found in ibid.

35. *Webster*, 492 U.S. 520. "No abortion of a viable unborn child shall be performed unless necessary to preserve the life or health of the woman" (Mo. Rev. Stat. § 188.030 [1986]).

36. *Webster*, 492 U.S. 519

37. Ibid.

38. *Casey*, 505 U.S., 844.

39. Ibid., 877.

40. "Yet it must be remembered that *Roe v. Wade* speaks with clarity in establishing not only the woman's liberty but also the State's 'important and legitimate interest in potential life.' . . . That portion of the decision in *Roe* has been given too little acknowledgment and implementation by the Court in its subsequent cases. Those cases decided that any regulation touching upon the abortion decision must survive strict scrutiny, to be sustained only if drawn in narrow terms to further a compelling state interest . . . Not all of the cases decided under that formulation can be reconciled with the holding in *Roe* itself that the State has legitimate interests in the health of the woman and in protecting the potential life within her. In resolving this tension, we choose to rely upon *Roe*, as against the later cases" (Ibid., 871).

41. The Court in fact explicitly overrules *Akron*, 462 U.S. and *Thornburgh*, 476 U.S.: "To the extent *Akron I* and *Thornburgh* find a constitutional violation when the government requires, as it does here, the giving of truthful, nonmisleading information about the nature of the procedure, the attendant health risks and those of childbirth, and the 'probable gestational age' of the fetus, those cases go too far, are inconsistent with *Roe*'s acknowledgment of an important interest in potential life, and are overruled" (*Casey*, 505 U.S. 882).

42. Ibid., 872.

43. The "reliance interest" is a term of art from contract law that refers to "the interest a nonbreaching party has in recovering costs stemming from that party's reliance on the performance of the contract" (*Black's Law Dictionary*, ed. Bryan A. Garner, 7th ed. [St. Paul, MN: West Group, 1999], 816). The Court took this term from contract of law and applied it to the public's apparent reliance on the right to abortion and the personal and economic benefits that right supposedly entails. Consequently, according to the Court, if it had overturned *Roe*, it would have "breached" its social contract with the public, which would have suffered personal and economic costs as a result.

44. "[F]or two decades of economic and social developments, people have organized intimate relationships and made choices that define their views of themselves and their places in society, in reliance on the availability of abortion in the event that contraception should fail"(*Casey*, 505 U.S. 869).

45. "A decision to overrule *Roe*'s essential holding under the existing circumstances would address error, if there was error, at the cost of both profound and unnecessary damage to the Court's legitimacy, and to the Nation's commitment to the rule of law" (*Casey*, 505 U.S. 869).

46. *Casey*, 505 U.S. 844–853.

47. See "Partial Birth Abortion," Center for Reproductive Rights Home Page, available at http://www.crlp.org/hill_pba.html.

48. Ibid., citing *Casey*, 505 U.S. 879.

49. Ibid., 2610.

50. Ibid., 2628 (J. Kennedy, dissenting).

51. As Justice Kennedy points out in his dissent, there is impressive medical opinion that D & X abortion is not any less risky and may in some cases increase the risk to a woman's health. See Ibid., 2626–2631 (J. Kennedy, dissenting).

52. *Webster*, 492 U.S. 519.

53. *Casey*, 505 U.S. 871. The Court writes: "Even in the earliest stages of pregnancy, the State may enact rules and regulations designed to encourage [a woman] to know that there are philosophic and social arguments of great weight that can be brought to bear in favor of continuing the pregnancy to full term and there are procedures and institutions to allow adoption of unwanted children as well as a certain degree of state assistance if the mother chooses to raise the child herself" (Ibid., 872) (insertion mine).

54. Ibid., 2606.

55. "Were there any doubt remaining the statute could apply to a D & E procedure, that doubt is no ground for invalidating the statute. Rather, we are bound to first consider whether a construction of that statute is fairly possible that would avoid the constitutional question" (Ibid., 2644, citing *Erznoznick v. Jacksonville*, 422 U.S. 205, 216 [1975] and *Frisby v. Schultz*, 487 U.S. 474, 482 [1988]) [J. Thomas, dissenting]). See also, Ibid., 2631 (J. Kennedy, dissenting).

56. Ibid., 2640–2643 (J. Thomas, dissenting).

57. Ibid., 2640.

58. USCS § 1531 (2003).

59. This is what the 2003 federal law asserts: "This subsection does not apply to a partial-birth abortion that is necessary to save the life of a mother whose life is endangered by a physical disorder, physical illness, or physical injury, including a life-endangering physical condition caused by or arising from the pregnancy itself" (18 USCS § 1531 [2003][a]).

60. Robert B. Bluey, "Lawsuits Challenge Partial-Birth Abortion Ban," CNSNews.com (October 31, 2003), available at http://www.cnsnews.com/Culture/archive/200310/CUL20031031c.html.

61. Michael Buratovich, a developmental biologist (Ph.D., University of California, Irvine), points out, in private email correspondence, that because of chromosonal abnormalities, an ovum may undergo complete fertilization but fail conception. Buratovich refers to a work by S. Munne, "Preimplantation Genetic Diagnosis of Numerical and Structural Chromosone Abnormalities," *Reprod Biomed Online* 4, no. 2 (March–April, 2002): 183–196. Hence, that is the reason why conception is defined as the result of a fertlization process that is *successful*.

62. J.P. Moreland, *Body and Soul: Human Nature and the Crisis in Ethics*, ed. J.P. Moreland and Scott B. Rae (Downers Grove, IL: InterVarsity, 2000), 52.

63. See Baruch Brody, *Abortion and the Sanctity of Human Life: A Philosophical View* (Cambridge, MA: MIT Press, 1975).

64. See Mary Anne Warren, "On the Moral and Legal Status of Abortion," in *The Problem of Abortion*, 2nd ed., ed. Joel Feinberg (Belmont, CA: Wadsworth, 1984).

65. See Michael Tooley, "In Defense of Abortion and Infanticide," in *The Abortion Controversy 25 Years After Roe v. Wade*, 2nd ed., ed. Louis Pojman and Francis

J. Beckwith (Belmont, CA: Wadsworth, 1998); and Michael Tooley, *Abortion and Infanticide* (New York: Oxford, 1983).

66. See Peter Singer, "Sanctity of Life or Quality of Life?," *Pediatrics* 73 (July 1973); Helga Kuhse and Peter Singer, *Should the Baby Live?: The Problem of Handicapped Infants* (New York: Oxford, 1985); and Peter Singer, *Rethinking Life and Death: The Collapse of Traditional Ethics* (New York: St. Martin's Press, 1994).

67. David Boonin, *A Defense of Abortion* (New York: Cambridge University Press, 2002), 115–128.

68. See L.W. Sumner, *Abortion and Moral Theory* (Princeton, NJ: Princeton University Press, 1981).

69. Cited in *Policy Review* (32 [Spring 1985]: 14–15) in answer to the question posed to a number of partisans (including Harrison) on the issue of abortion, "Is there a moral difference between feticide and infanticide?"

70. See, for example, Fletcher's comments in Joseph Fletcher and John Warwick Montgomery, *Situation Ethics: Is It Sometimes Right to Do Wrong?* (Minneapolis: Bethany House, 1972).

71. See Joseph Fletcher, "Indicators of Humanhood: A Tentative Profile of Man," *Hastings Center Report* 2 (1972); and Joseph Fletcher, "Four Indicators of Humanhood: The Enquiry Matures," *Hastings Center Report* 4 (1974).

72. "Words of Choice: Countering Anti-Choice Rhetoric," available at www.rcrc.org/pubs/words.html.

73. John Swomley, "When Does Life Begin?," Section 2 of the essay "Abortion: A Christian Ethical Perspective" at www.rcrc.org/religion/es8/section2.html.

74. See, for example, Chapter 6 of this present volume as well as Robert P. George, "Public Reason and Political Conflict: Abortion and Homosexuality," *Yale Law Journal* 106 (1997); Robert E. Joyce, "Personhood and the Conception Event," *New Scholasticism* 52 (1978); Gregory P. Koukl, *Precious Unborn Human Persons* (San Pedro, CA: Stand to Reason, 1999); Lee, *Abortion and Unborn Human Life*; Moreland and Rae, *Body and Soul*; Dianne Nutwell Irving, "Scientific and Philosophical Expertise," *Linacre Quarterly* (Feb. 1993); Patrick Lee and Robert P. George, "The Wrong of Abortion," in *Contemporary Debates in Applied Ethics*, eds. Andrew I. Cohen and Christopher Wellman (New York: Blackwell Publishers, 2005); Patrick Lee, "The Pro-Life Argument from Substantial Identity," *Bioethics* 18, no. 3 (2004); A.A. Howsepian, "Who or What Are We?," *Review of Metaphysics* 45 (March 1992); Schwarz, *The Moral Question of Abortion*.

75. J.P. Moreland, "Humanness, Personhood, and the Right to Die," *Faith and Philosophy* 12, no. 1 (January 1995): 101.

76. J.P. Moreland, *Body & Soul*, 206.

77. Ibid., 178.

78. Ibid.

79. Lee, *Abortion and Unborn Human Life*, 55.

80. See, for example, Peter McInerny, "Does a Fetus Already Have a Future-Like-Ours?," *The Journal of Philosophy* 87 (1990); and Derek Parfit, *Reasons and Persons* (Oxford: Oxford University Press, 1984).

81. This is a name coined by Lee in *Abortion and Unborn Human Life*, 37.

82. Paul D. Simmons, "Religious Liberty and the Abortion Debate," *Journal of Church and State* 32 (Summer 1990): 572.

83. See, for example, Moreland and Rae, *Body and Soul*; and Lee, *Abortion and Unborn Human Life*, Chapters 1 and 2.

84. Paul Churchland, *Matter and Consciousness* (Cambridge, MA: M.I.T. Press, 1984), 12.

85. See, for example, Boonin, *A Defense of Abortion*, Ch. 2, and Dean Stretton, "The Argument from Intrinsic Value: A Critique," *Bioethics* (2000): 228–239.

86. Paul Simmons, for example, writes that prior to viability "the fetus simply is not sufficiently developed to speak meaningfully of it as an independent being deserving and requiring the full protection of the law, i.e. a person. The notion of viability correlates biological maturation with personal identity in a way that can be recognized and accepted by reasonable people." (Paul D. Simmons, "Religious Liberty and Abortion Policy: *Casey* as 'Catch-22'," *Journal of Church and State* [Winter 2000]: 71). He writes in an earlier article, "Viability, by definition, deals with that stage of gestation at which the fetus has a developed neo-cortex and physiological maturation sufficient to survive outside the womb. Biological maturation is correlated with personal identity that can be recognized and accepted by reasonable people" (Simmons, "Religious Liberty and the Abortion Debate," 573).

87. Judith Jarvis Thomson, "A Defense of Abortion," in *The Problem of Abortion*, 2nd ed., ed. Joel Feinberg (Belmont, CA: Wadsworth, 1984), 173–187. This article was originally published in *Philosophy and Public Affairs* 1 (1971), 47–66. References to Thomson's article in this chapter are to the former piece.

88. David Boonin, *A Defense of Abortion* (New York: Cambridge University Press, 2002), 133–281.

89. Eileen McDonagh, *Breaking the Abortion Deadlock: From Choice to Consent* (New York: Oxford University Press, 1996).

90. Thomson, "A Defense of Abortion," 174.

91. Ibid., 174–175.

92. Ibid., 180.

93. Thomson writes: "If the room is stuffy, and I therefore open a window to air it, and a burglar climbs in, it would be absurd to say, 'Ah, now he can stay, she's given him a right to use her house—for she is partially responsible for his presence there, having voluntarily done what enabled him to get in, in full knowledge that there are such things as burglars, and that burglars burgle" (Ibid., 182).

94. See, for example, Keith Pavlischek, "Abortion Logic and Paternal Responsibility: One More Look at Judith Thomson's 'Defense of Abortion,'" *Public Affairs Quarterly* 7, no. 4 (October 1993); Francis J. Beckwith, "Personal Bodily Rights, Abortion, and Unplugging the Violinist," *International Philosophical Quarterly* 32 (1992); Lee, *Abortion and Unborn Human Life*, Chapter 4; and John T. Wilcox, "Nature as Demonic in Thomson's Defense of Abortion," *The New Scholasticism* 63 (Autumn 1989).

95. David Boonin, *A Defense of Abortion* (New York: Cambridge University Press, 2002): 133–281.

96. See "State and Local IV-D Agencies on the Web" (June 15, 2006), Office of Child Support Enforcement, Administration for Children and Families, U.S. Department of Health & Human Services, available at http://www.acf.hhs.gov/programs/cse/extinf.htm.

97. Lee, *Abortion and Unborn Human Life*, 119.

98. Michael Levin, review of *Life in the Balance* by Robert Wennberg, *Constitutional Commentary* 3 (Summer 1986): 511.

99. See Pavlischek, "Abortion Logic and Paternal Responsibility"; and Keith Pavlischek, "Abortion Logic and Paternal Responsibility: One More Look at Judith Thomson's 'Defense of Abortion' and a Critique of David Boonin-Vail's Defense of It," in *The Abortion Controversy*. The latter is a revised version of the former.

100. Boonin, *A Defense of Abortion*, 249–254.

101. Lee, *Abortion and Unborn Human Life*, 118.

102. "Surely the question of whether you have a right to life at all, or how much of it you have, shouldn't turn on the question of whether or not you are the product of rape" (Thomson, "A Defense of Abortion," 175).

103. See Beckwith, *Defending Life*, Chapter 7; and Lee, *Abortion and Unborn Human Life*, 120–124.

104. See, for example, Virginia Ramey Mollenkott, "Reproductive Choice: Basic to Justice for Women," *Christian Scholar's Review* 17 (March 1988); Simmons, "Religious Liberty and the Abortion Debate"; and Simmons, "Religious Liberty and Abortion Policy."

105. See Simmons, "Religious Liberty and Abortion Policy."

106. Judith Jarvis Thomson, "Abortion: Whose Right?," *Boston Review* 20, no. 3 (Summer 1995). Thomson's essay is available at http://bostonreview.mit.edu/BR20.3/thomson.html. All references to Thomson's piece in this chapter are from the online version.

107. Ronald Dworkin, *Life's Dominion: An Argument about Abortion, Euthanasia, and Individual Freedom* (New York: Vintage Books, 1993), 148–178.

108. *Casey*, 505 U.S. at 851 (citations omitted).

109. Simmons, "Religious Liberty and Abortion Policy," 88.

110. Although the original purpose of the Establishment Clause of the First Amendment was to restrain Congress ("*Congress* shall make no law respecting an establishment of religion . . . "), the Supreme Court has incorporated the First Amendment through the Fourteenth Amendment and now applies the former to the states as well. See *Everson v. Board of Education*, 330 U.S. 1 (1947) (Justices unanimously agreed that the Establishment Clause applies to the states through the Fourteenth Amendment).

111. Simmons, "Religious Liberty and Abortion Policy," 88.

112. See Beckwith, *Defending Life*, Chapter 3.

113. Justice John Paul Stevens offers the following analysis of a Missouri statute

that placed restrictions on abortion and included a preamble that asserted that human life begins at conception:

> Indeed, I am persuaded that the absence of any secular purpose for the legislative declarations that life begins at conception and that conception occurs at fertilization makes the relevant portion of the preamble invalid under the Establishment Clause of the First Amendment to the Federal Constitution. This conclusion does not, and could not, rest on the fact that the statement happens to coincide with the tenets of certain religions ... or on the fact that the legislators who voted to enact it may have been motivated by religious considerations.... Rather, it rests on the fact that the preamble, an unequivocal endorsement of a religious tenet of some but by no means all Christian faiths, serves no identifiable secular purpose. That fact alone compels a conclusion that the statute violates the Establishment Clause ... As a secular matter, there is an obvious difference between the state interest in protecting the freshly fertilized egg and the state interest in protecting a 9-month-gestated, fully sentient fetus on the eve of birth. There can be no interest in protecting the newly fertilized egg from physical pain or mental anguish, because the capacity for such suffering does not yet exist; respecting a developed fetus, however, that interest is valid.

(*Webster v. Reproductive Health Services*, 492 U.S. 490, 566–567, 569 (1989)) (J. Stevens, concurring in part and dissenting in part) (citations and footnotes omitted).

114. *Wallace v. Jaffree*, 472 U.S. 38 (1985).

115. *Edwards v. Aguillard*, 482 U.S. 578 (1987). For a critique of the "religious motive" test, see Francis J. Beckwith, "The Court of Disbelief: The Constitution's Article VI Religious Test Prohibition and the Judiciary's Religious Motive Analysis," *Hastings Constitutional Law Quarterly* 33, nos. 2 & 3 (Winter and Spring 2006): 337–60.

116. Nat Hentoff, "Pro-Choice Bigots: A View From the Pro-Life Left," *The New Republic* 207, no. 23 (November 20, 1992): 21, 24–25.

117. Doris Gordon, "A Libertarian Atheist Answers 'Pro-Choice Catholics,'" (January 2003), available at http://www.l4l.org/library/cathchoi.html.

118. Dellapenna, *Dispelling the Myths of Abortion History*. Professor Dellapenna describes himself as a "lapsed Unitarian" on page ix of this book.

FURTHER READING

David Boonin's *A Defense of Abortion* (New York: Cambridge University Press, 2002) is the most comprehensive and rigorously argued philosophical defense of the pro-choice position in print. The esteemed legal philosopher, Ronald Dworkin, is the author of *Life's Dominion: An Argument about Abortion, Euthanasia, and Individual Freedom* (New York: Vintage Books, 1993). Although not a strong work of philosophy, it is a powerful legal brief for the preservation of abortion rights. I have authored an extended defense of the pro-life position on abortion, covering moral, legal, and political arguments: *Defending Life: A Moral and Legal Case Against Abortion Choice* (New York: Cambridge University Press, 2007). Philosopher and Evangelical Christian Robert N. Wennberg defends a moderate pro-choice position on abortion in *Life in the Balance: Exploring the Abortion Controversy* (Grand Rapids: Eerdmans Publishing Company, 1985). In addition to addressing philosophical issues, Wennberg critically engages many of the pro-life biblical arguments. Another theologically rich book is by Nigel M. De S. Cameron and Pamela F. Sims, *Abortion: The Crisis in Morals and Medicine* (Leicester, UK: InterVarsity Press, 1986). Like Wennberg's work, this book addresses both philosophical and theological arguments, though it defends a conservative pro-life perspective. Because the history of abortion was an essential aspect of the reasoning of *Roe v. Wade*, two books, with differing perspectives, are worth consulting: James C. Mohr, *Abortion in America* (New York: Oxford University Press, 1978); and Joseph W. Dellapenna, *Dispelling the Myths of Abortion History* (Durham, NC: Carolina Academic Press, 2006). There are several good anthologies on the issue of abortion, most of which include important legal cases as well as a variety of influential arguments in the history of the contemporary debate. Two of the most recent anthologies are Robert M. Baird and Stuart Rosenbaum, eds., *The Ethics of Abortion: Pro-Life v. Pro-Choice*, 3rd ed. (Amherst, MA: Prometheus Books, 2001) and Louis P. Pojman and Francis J. Beckwith, eds., *The Abortion Controversy 25 Years After* Roe v. Wade: *A Reader*, 2nd ed. (Belmont, CA: Wadsworth, 1998).

2

Religiously Motivated Political Action and Same-Sex Marriage

Katherine Stenger

On November 7, 2006, Arizona voters rejected Proposition 107 by a vote of 52 to 48 percent. That voters would reject a measure on the ballot is nothing extraordinary, but this proposition represented a dramatic departure from an established pattern in the national debate over same-sex marriage. Breaking the trend of votes in 27 other states, Arizona became the first state thus far to defeat a constitutional amendment to define marriage to be between those of the opposite sex. While the active groups were in all respects identical to the groups mobilized in other states, the opponents of Proposition 107 succeeded in shifting the debate away from the dominant frames of morality, family values, and the protection of marriage advanced by groups across the country and toward a frame that benefited their side. The winning argument centered not on the importance of civil rights for gays and lesbians or on equality, but rather on the economic impact the measure would have on *heterosexual* couples living in state-sanctioned domestic partnerships or civil unions.[1] Despite attempts to mobilize opponents of same-sex marriage by the Center for Arizona Policy (a designated "Family Policy Council" affiliated with the conservative Christian organization Focus on the Family), Protect Marriage Arizona (a group funded by a number of groups with religious ties), and the local Catholic bishops, the measure failed to garner the needed support.

The Arizona case illustrates two key factors in the national debate over same-sex marriage highlighted in this chapter: the role of organized groups and the importance of rhetorical framing strategies. Groups reflecting a religious perspective represent a major portion of the active groups in the debate over same-sex marriage and, with the exception of the Arizona case, have dominated the terms of the debate—what scholars call the "framing" of the issue. More generally, religious beliefs and values help drive individual public opinion, compounding the effects of religion on the policymaking process.

The debate over same-sex marriage is complicated by the fact that it is not confined to a single policymaking venue. Instead, local, state, and federal venues have all played host to the policy debate. The national debate over same-sex marriage began in earnest in 1991 when three same-sex couples in Hawaii sued for the right to marry. The years that followed witnessed a flurry of laws and state constitutional amendments denying same-sex marriage benefits and protecting states from recognizing same-sex marriage licenses issued by other states.

One of the most consistent trends in the public debate over same-sex marriage is the media portrayal of the debate as one between a secular left and a largely Christian right. This storyline is driven by a powerful "culture wars" thesis that seemed to be confirmed by the 2004 and 2006 elections when cultural conservatives helped 19 states ratify constitutional amendments to restrict same-sex marriage.[2] A central theme of this chapter, however, is that this narrative oversimplifies the state of religious thinking on the issue. While conservative religious groups are visible and powerful in the policy debate, they are not the only religious groups with a message on the subject of same-sex marriage.

The first section of this chapter provides a brief discussion of the ways in which religious values may impact public policymaking, a summary of the development of debates over homosexuality within religious traditions, and a framework to help conceptualize the ways in which religious groups relate to the debate over same-sex marriage. The second section provides an overview of the policy debate stretching from the legal action in Hawaii in 1991 to the present. The final section focuses more explicitly on the ways in which religious groups participated in the debate as it occurred through the media, using a content analysis of newspaper coverage of the federal debate over same-sex marriage and press releases issued by religious groups.

CONNECTIONS BETWEEN RELIGION, HOMOSEXUALITY, AND POLITICS

Religion and Policymaking

Religious values impact public policy-making at two levels: individual decision-making and group mobilization. While research finds that the American public has become more favorable toward same-sex relationships, much entrenched opposition to these relationships is rooted in religious beliefs.[3] Religious orthodoxy (the extent to which religious faith is an important part of a person's life) and religious tradition, in particular, affect individual-level public opinion.[4] Surveys consistently find a link between religious beliefs and public opinion on homosexuality, gay rights, and same-sex marriage.[5] In general, those with high levels of religious orthodoxy are more likely to oppose homosexuality and same-sex marriage.[6] As Laura Olson, Wendy Cadge, and James Harrison conclude, religion "has a powerful effect on attitudes toward same-sex unions."[7] However, members of certain religious traditions and denominations are more open to homosexuality and same-sex marriage. In particular, non-Christians are more likely to support same-sex marriage, and among Protestants, mainline Protestants are the most open to same-sex marriage.

Scholars find distinct voting patterns among citizens from different religious traditions and with different levels of religious orthodoxy.[8] These patterns do not mean that religious values are the only factors that influence how individual citizens feel about issues or how elected officials vote, but religious values do carry an important weight in political decision-making, especially for members of certain religious traditions and the religiously orthodox. For example, immediately following the 2004 presidential elections, pundits pointed to the impact of ballot initiatives banning same-sex marriage on voter turnout and vote choice. Analyses of election results and polling data suggest that the impact was not as strong as the pundits originally claimed.[9] However, the issue did help mobilize voters in several key swing states such as Ohio and Michigan.[10] Furthermore, many voters saw a clear link between their position on the issue of same-sex marriage and their preferred political candidates.[11]

Religious groups have a long tradition of involvement in the political process.[12] Some organized groups represent single religious denominations, while others are organized around particular issues and represent members from a variety of religious traditions or denominations. These groups are particularly significant because they are involved in every stage of the policy process, from influencing when and where issues are brought to the public agenda (sponsoring statewide ballot initiatives, for example) to mobilizing voter turnout (in support of a candidate or a ballot measure), and from the direct lobbying of elected officials (including campaign donations and independent advertising expenditures) to participation in the legal process (through the sponsoring of legal challenges or filing *amicus curiae* briefs).

At the state and federal level, religious groups have had major influence over a variety of public policies, including those pertaining to gay rights and same-sex marriage.[13] Religious groups fought an attempt by President Bill Clinton to eliminate barriers for gays and lesbians in the military and successfully lobbied for passage of the Defense of Marriage Act.[14] Law professor Didi Herman argues that "antigay measures in the United States are, at their heart, orthodox Christian measures."[15] While this statement may oversimplify the beliefs of orthodox Christians, it reflects the observation that religious groups are influential players in public policymaking. Finally, religious groups also actively seek to influence judicial decisions. The American Center for Law and Justice, American Family Association Law Center, and The Rutherford Institute are among the religiously-motivated organizations that actively pursue legal strategies to complement the legislative strategies of other religious groups.

Many political observers lump these groups together as part of the "Christian Right." While they certainly share policy goals and many connections exist among them, there is also a great deal of decentralization. Religious groups that have led the drive for passage of state defense of marriage acts and constitutional amendments are not monolithic or strategically unified, but they are a part of a semi-structured coalition of conservative religious groups operating at the state level across the country. A handful of national groups such as Focus on the Family (Family Policy Councils), the Christian Coalition, the Catholic Church, and the Church of Jesus Christ of Latter-Day Saints, which have access to politically conservative religious congregations, provide financial and strategic resources as well as fertile ground for recruitment and mobilization. Religious groups that support same-sex marriage do not have such strong organizational networks or the same level of access to religious congregations from which to draw support.

The Contextual Basis of Religious Voices in the Same-Sex Marriage Debate

The impact of religious values in the debate over same-sex marriage is nested within both a theological discussion of homosexuality and a long-standing political struggle by conservative religious traditions to resist secular changes in society. An understanding of these considerations is useful in illuminating the diversity of viewpoints held by those of religious faith and in understanding the motivations of those groups who most actively oppose same-sex marriage rights.

The role of religious groups in the debate over same-sex marriage is tied to a much broader debate over homosexuality within the church.[16] Three issues particularly dominate this discussion: ministry to gays and lesbians, the ordination of gays and lesbians, and the blessing of gay and lesbian relationships. Theological positions concerning homosexuality range from the view that homosexuality is a sin to the belief that sexual orientation is an inherent God-given characteristic. At the most conservative end of the continuum are groups that consider homosexuality to be a sin, such as the Southern Baptist Convention, Orthodox Judaism, the Roman Catholic Church, and many conservative nondenominational churches.[17] Other groups, such as the Reformed Church in America, the Salvation Army, and the Mennonite Brethren Churches emphasize the importance of encouraging gay and lesbian congregants to live in celibacy. Still other groups, such as the Moravian Church, Disciples of Christ, the Evangelical Lutheran Church in America, the Society of Friends (Quaker), the Episcopal Church, and Reform Judaism welcome the participation of gay and lesbian members. A religious community's view of homosexuality has important political repercussions. Political opposition to same-sex marriage is primarily rooted in the belief that homosexuality is a choice and that the choice to pursue a same-sex relationship violates religious teachings.

Views regarding the ordination of gay and lesbian ministers and the blessing of gay and lesbian relationships flow from a religious group's perspective on the nature of homosexuality and factor into a religious group's position on the issue of same-sex marriage. Debates over ordination and same-sex blessings have been particularly heated in mainline Protestant denominations as well as in the Jewish tradition. The United Church of Christ, the Episcopal Church, the Evangelical Lutheran Church in America,[18] the Unitarian Universalist Church, and the Union of American Hebrew Congregations (Reform Judaism) are among the prominent religious groups that ordain gay and lesbian clergy. In December 2006, the highest legal body in Conservative Judaism also announced a decision to allow the ordination of gay rabbis.

The Metropolitan Community Church was the first national religious denomination to offer blessings of same-sex marriages beginning in 1968. Unitarian Universalists approved same-sex union services in 1984 followed by the Reconstructionist Jewish Rabbinical Association in 1996 and the United Church of Christ in 2005. Some Quaker, Episcopal, and Conservative Jewish congregations offer same-sex marriage ceremonies, based on the prerogative of local leaders. In addition to these formal declarations of support for the blessing of same-sex unions, local religious leaders in a host of religious denominations and traditions have endorsed or held ceremonies for same-sex couples.[19]

The role of religious groups in the debate over same-sex marriage is also rooted in a much broader debate over personal morality and the proper role of the government in maintaining a "traditional" model of the family. The latter half of the twentieth century witnessed more women entering the workforce (altering the traditional division of labor within the nuclear family), the liberalization of divorce law (increasing the divorce rate), the emergence of a sexual revolution (including fewer social prohibitions on premarital sex), and the legalization of abortion. Coupled with public debates over the role of religious values in schools and other public places (teaching creationism, school prayer, public displays of crèches, etc.), these changes in society spawned the growth of groups based on the preservation of traditional society.[20] Theologian Jack Rogers points out that most of the opposition to same-sex marriage comes from religious groups—the Catholic and Mormon churches, in particular—that do not ordain women as clergy and that advocate traditional gender roles within the family. Thus, he concludes, the battle over same-sex marriage is simply an extension of the battle to retain male headship and female subjection in the family structure.[21]

The political movement known as "the Christian Right" arose in the late 1970s and centered on the "moral decay" typified by the movement of women into the workforce and the liberalization of sexual mores.[22] It is impossible to fully grasp the motivation of the religious groups opposing same-sex marriage without an acknowledgement of the extent to which these groups perceive same-sex marriage as a direct threat to the traditional family structure. Though religious conservatives are often mocked for advocating a "slippery slope" argument to justify their opposition to same-sex marriage, from their perspective, the dramatic changes in the family structure over the last fifty years are evidence of just that. Same-sex marriage is simply the latest front in a much longer war over the interpretation of the Bible, the proper role of religion in American government, and the structure of the family. As George Chauncey concludes, many opponents of gay marriage view it as "both the ultimate sign of gay equality and the final blow to their traditional ideal of marriage . . ."[23] Thus, argue Clyde Wilcox, Linda Merolla, and David Beer, "many members of the Christian Right regarded the same-sex marriage issue as the defining battle in the culture wars—more important than other gay rights issues and even more immediately critical than abortion."[24]

A Framework for Religious Involvement in the Same-Sex Marriage Debate

With the influence of religious beliefs at both the individual and group level in mind and a fuller understanding of the complex relationship between religious beliefs and sexual orientation, we can categorize the various actors involved in the debate over same-sex marriage who are motivated by religious beliefs. One of the central claims of this chapter is that the Christian Right, while incredibly powerful in this debate, does not encompass all of the viewpoints of the religious community.

This framework, presented in Table 2.1, helps identify the diversity of opinion by highlighting two important dimensions involved in politics: one's position on same-sex marriage and level of involvement in the debate. Some religious groups articulate clear support for government recognition of same-sex marriage while others oppose such action. Some religious groups take an active approach in defense of their position while others refrain from direct political or public action. This framework, then, allows us to identify both the active leaders and the groups that have the potential to be mobilized on either side of the debate.

While the categories represent four levels of belief and activity, the groups mentioned in each category are not necessarily fixed. The groups in quadrants A and B, Active Supporters and Active Opponents, are unlikely to change because of the fundamental belief structures underlying their position on this issue. However, the groups mentioned in quadrants C and D, Passive Supporters and Passive Opponents, have the potential to be mobilized through both political and theological means and pulled or pushed into another category. For example, Active Opponents have successfully used ballot initiatives and constitutional amendments to mobilize the large portion of the population who oppose same-sex marriage but are not active participants in the debate. Theoretically, Passive Opponents could also be turned into Passive Supporters given the right conditions, such as a reframing of the issue or a new and convincing theological interpretation.

To this point, Active Opponents have dominated most of the debate over same-sex marriage. In states across the country, they have successfully mobilized Passive Opponents, and in some cases even Passive Supporters, to support their cause. Active Supporters have maintained a steady presence in the debates at both the national and state levels, but they have neither received the same media attention nor achieved the same level of policy success as have Active Opponents.

Table 2.1 Typology of Religious Group Positions and Activity Levels

	Supports Same-Sex Marriage	Opposes Same-Sex Marriage
Active Involvement	*A—Active Supporters* Leading religious groups in the movement to provide legal recognition to same-sex couples and/or to oppose legislation that would deny benefits or recognition to such couples. *Organized interest groups such as the Religious Coalition for the Freedom to Marry, Dignity USA (Catholic), Soulforce and the Interfaith Alliance.* *Denominations and religious traditions such as the Metropolitan Community Churches, United Church of Christ, Society of Friends (Quaker), Unitarian Universalist.* *Groups within denominations and religious traditions such as Affirmation (United Methodist), More Light Presbyterians (PCUSA), Integrity (Episcopal).*	*B—Active Opponents* Leading religious groups in the movement to deny benefits or legal recognition to same-sex couples. *Organized interest groups such as Focus on the Family, the Christian Coalition, Family Research Council, Concerned Women for America, and the Traditional Values Coalition.* *Denominations and religious traditions such as the Roman Catholic Church, the Church of Jesus Christ of Latter-day Saints (Mormon), the Southern Baptist Convention, and many nondenominational evangelical Protestant congregations.*
Passive Involvement	*C—Passive Supporters* Religious groups that support some degree of legal recognition of same-sex couples or oppose legislation that would deny benefits or recognition to such couples but are not actively involved in the political movement. *Denominations and religious traditions such as The Presbyterian Church (USA), Disciples of Christ, the Episcopal Church, Reform Judaism, and Conservative Judaism*	*D—Passive Opponents* Religious groups that oppose legal recognition of same-sex couples but are not actively involved in the political movement. *Denominations and religious traditions such as the United Methodist Church*

RELIGIOUS GROUPS AND THE DEBATE OVER SAME-SEX MARRIAGE

Several features of American government, such as the division of powers between the states and the national government and the separation of powers between the three branches of government, create a multiplicity of venues for decision-making on the topic of same-sex marriage. There are seven primary venues in which same-sex policymaking occurs in the United States—local governments, state legislatures, state courts, state constitutional amendments, Congress, federal courts, and federal constitutional amendments—and the debate over same-sex marriage has spanned all of these venues. A complete history of the same-sex marriage policy debate would require more space than this chapter allows; this section focuses in on several key moments in the policy debate with a particular emphasis on the role of religiously motivated groups and individuals in the process.

Hawaii

Same-sex marriage as a topic of national political debate began in 1991, when one gay and two lesbian couples in Honolulu, Hawaii, sued the state for the right to marry. Similar legal challenges around the country had upheld the state's prerogative to restrict marriage to opposite sex couples and so it came as a shock to all when, in 1993, the Hawaii Supreme Court ruled that denying these couples a marriage license might violate the equal protection clause of the Hawaii constitution.[25] The ruling in *Baehr v. Lewin* (1993) sent the question back to the trial court to determine whether the state had a compelling reason for the ban on same-sex marriages.[26] In 1996, the trial court found there was no compelling reason and returned the case to the Hawaii Supreme Court. As the first judicial ruling in favor of a same-sex couple on the question of marriage, it sent shock waves through the nation.[27]

While the court did not legalize same-sex marriage, and while the state of Hawaii eventually amended their state constitution to allow the legislature to ban same-sex marriage, the action in Hawaii reminded opponents of same-sex marriage across the country that the legalization of same-sex marriages in one state could directly impact other states through the Full Faith and Credit Clause of the U.S. Constitution. Article IV of the Constitution requires that "full faith and credit" be given to judicial proceedings from other states. In practical terms, it means that states may be obligated to recognize the marriages that occur in other states, even if the couple was ineligible to get married in the new state. Had Hawaii legalized same-sex marriages, couples could have traveled to Hawaii, married, and returned to their home state, which would have been required to recognize their marriage. This possibility mobilized opponents of same-sex marriage across the country. Some groups formed organically in individual states to lobby elected officials, and some were mobilized through loosely coordinated networks organized by national groups. Nearly all of the groups—both local and national—were motivated by religious beliefs.

The Hawaii case is a prime example of the role played by religious groups and individuals motivated by religious beliefs. The initial debate was centered in the courts and, even there, religious groups were involved. Conservative religious groups were particularly active in the judicial proceedings through the submission of *amicus curiae*, or "friend of the court," briefs. National conservative religious groups such as the American Center for Law and Justice, the Rutherford Institute, the Christian Legal Society (on behalf of a range of groups such as the National Association of Evangelicals, the Lutheran Church-Missouri Synod, and the Institute for Religion and Democracy, among others), and the Church of Jesus Christ of Latter-day Saints all submitted briefs to the Hawaii court. A handful of groups with religious ties submitted *amicus* briefs in support of those seeking same-sex marriage rights. The Madison Society of Hawaii, a multi-denominational group advocated in favor of equal treatment of gays and lesbians, and the American Friends Service Committee associated with the Quaker faith also submitted a supporting brief.

Concerned that the Hawaii Supreme Court would soon legalize same-sex marriage in Hawaii, opponents of same-sex marriage encouraged state legislators to place a constitutional amendment on the 1998 ballot that would give the power to define marriage to the Hawaii legislature. A coalition of religiously motivated conservative groups spearheaded the campaign to encourage citizens to vote yes on the amendment (which eventually passed with the support of 70% of the voters). Though some of the groups had local roots, they were also well connected to conservative religious groups from other states. The group with the highest profile was the Alliance for Traditional Marriage (also called "Save Traditional Marriage" or the "Alliance for Traditional Marriage and Values") founded by Mike Gabbard. Gabbard, a strong Catholic elected to the State Senate in 2006, was frequently quoted or referenced in news coverage of the debate over the amendment. Another group with prominent Catholic roots was Pro-Family Hawaii. Led by Daniel McGivern and fellow Catholics from the Star of the Sea parish on the island of Oahu, the group spent nearly $93,000 on the campaign.

These groups built alliances with groups representing the evangelical

Protestant tradition and the Church of Jesus Christ of Latter-day Saints. Other members of the coalition included the Hawaii Family Forum, a Christian advocacy group associated with the national organization Focus on the Family as a part of the organization's Family Policy Council. During the campaign, Focus on the Family provided the coalition with financial and strategic support. The Hawaii Christian Coalition also participated in the debate and the national organization came under fire for undisclosed campaign donations it made during the campaign. One of the largest financial contributions to the campaign came from the Alliance for Traditional Marriage. Nearly half of the $1.2 million spent during the campaign by the group came from the Church of Jesus Christ of Latter-day Saints' central office.

Throughout the campaign, this coalition stressed the message that the purpose of the amendment was to protect "traditional marriage" rather than to deny rights to any group of citizens.[28] In her study of letters to the editor appearing in the two major Hawaii newspapers, Kathleen Hull found that the opponents of same-sex marriage, although religiously motivated, steered away from overtly religious or moral arguments, and instead focused on the importance of protecting the "will of the majority" and criticizing the tactics of opposing groups. Though some writers on both sides of the debate referenced religious beliefs or arguments, these were not the dominant argument frames. In part, this may have reflected a strategic decision to appeal to as many potential supporters as possible by not alienating those who did not share the religious values of the coalition. It also reflects the hesitancy of many Americans to mix religion and politics.[29]

These religiously motivated interest groups drew upon existing connections with churches and national interest groups to craft a defensible message, raise money, and mobilize voters. Throughout both the legal debate and the campaign surrounding the constitutional amendment, conservative religious groups dominated the public coverage of religious views on the issue, even though some religious groups opposed the amendment. A 1997 statement in support of same-sex marriage issued by the Hawaii Council of Churches, "An Interfaith Perspective on Same Gender Marriage," received almost no attention from the media. Recognizing the debates within churches, the Council argued that "while our religious communities are wrestling with the issue of whether same-gender marriages shall be sanctioned within our various traditions, we, the undersigned, believe that an essential distinction must be made between this religious debate and the question of whether couples of the same gender should have access to the legal privileges of marriage as a matter of civil rights."[30] Similarly, the well-established Rainbow of Aloha Metropolitan Community Church, founded in 1973, was not included in media coverage of the debate, and the decision by the American Friends Service Committee to partner with a local gay rights group, *Na Mamo O Hawaii*, also received little attention.

Federal Intervention

Though Hawaiian courts did not ultimately legalize same-sex marriage, the perceived threat was enough to set federal lawmakers on a quest to protect other states from the possibility they would be forced to recognize same-sex marriage certificates from other states. The impetus for a national law that would allow states to ignore the Full Faith and Credit Clause as it applied to same-sex marriage came from a coalition of conservative religious groups, including the Christian Coalition, Colorado for Family Values, the National Legal Foundation, and the American Family Association.[31] The coalition, called the National Campaign to Protect Marriage, first met in a Memphis church basement in January 1996 and issued the "Marriage Protection Resolution," which was later endorsed by all of the Republican presidential candidates at a rally held shortly before the Iowa caucuses.

On May 7, 1996, in response to the Hawaii case and the possible decision in favor of gay marriage, Representative Bob Barr (R-Georgia) introduced legislation that would become the federal Defense of Marriage Act (DOMA). The bill was drafted with the help of Reverend Lou Sheldon of the Traditional Values Coalition, a religiously motivated conservative interest group. In his speech to Congress, Representative Barr, an outspoken critic of gay marriage, argued that "the flames of hedonism, the flames of narcissism, the flames of self-centered morality are licking at the very foundation of our society, the family unit."[32] The Defense of Marriage Act would quench those flames through a two-pronged approach. First, the bill established the right of states to refuse to recognize a same-sex marriage license issued by another state. This provision was designed to protect the laws and amendments passed by state governments from legal challenges. The second prong of the bill formally defined marriage to refer to a legal union between one man and one woman.

When the bill was initially introduced, it drew heavy criticism from gay rights groups such as the Human Rights Committee and Lambda Legal Defense, as well as from civil liberties groups such as the American Civil Liberties Union and People for the American Way. In contrast, conservative religious groups lobbied heavily in favor of the legislation. Christian groups such as Focus on the Family, Concerned Women for America, and the Christian Coalition ran extensive media campaigns to mobilize their members to contact members of Congress in support of the legislation. After a heated debate, the House of Representatives passed the bill in July with 342 (out of 435) voting in favor. The Senate picked up the bill four days later and passed the measure in September with 85 voting in favor. President Bill Clinton, a Democrat, signed the bipartisan bill into law in the middle of the night on September 21, 1996.[33]

Mini-DOMAs

Between 1996 and 2004, thirty-seven state legislatures mirrored the federal government with similar state-level Defense of Marriage Acts (commonly called "mini-DOMAs"). In most cases, legislation establishing state DOMAs was initiated by religious conservatives and national conservative religious groups—in particular, Focus on the Family, the American Family Association, the Christian Coalition, and the Traditional Values Coalition—teamed with local conservative groups to actively mobilize support for the proposals.[34] One comprehensive study found that in the states that considered mini-DOMAs, 81 percent of the legislative sponsors had known links to conservative religious groups, 54 percent of the bills were drafted with the help of conservative religious groups, and conservative religious groups actively lobbied for the bills in all of the states that considered them.[35] As Martin Dupuis noted, "religious views, traditional family values, and the devaluation of marriage were most often cited as reasons for the legislation."[36]

Three separate studies of states' decisions to adopt defense of marriage legislation find that religious groups played a major role in the creation of state laws.[37] Donald Haider-Markel concludes that along with the influence of parties and political elite, the "timing of state adoption of same-sex marriage bans is strongly influenced by religious groups . . ."[38] Sarah Soule adds that state Family Policy Councils, groups loosely affiliated with the national organization Focus on the Family, were instrumental in pushing states to adopt marriage bans. Scott Barclay and Shauna Fisher find that religious groups played a less prominent role in the debate than expected based on other sexual orientation-related measures, though they still find religious groups to be significant players in the policy process.[39] In measuring the influence of religious groups, Barclay and Fisher look to the percentage of the population in each state that identified as Southern Baptist, Catholic, or Mormon (indicators of the strength of opposition to same-sex marriage), as well as the percentage of the population that was Jewish (indicator of the strength of support for same-sex marriage). This method accounts only for the Active Opponents referenced in Table 2.1 and may underestimate the

Table 2.2 States with Mini-Defense of Marriage Acts

Pre-DOMA*	1996	1997–1999	2000–2005
Wyoming	Alabama	Arkansas (1997)	California (2000)
Maryland	Alaska	Florida (1997)	Colorado (2000)
Wisconsin	Arizona	Indiana (1997)	West Virginia (2000)
New Hampshire	Delaware	Maine (1997)	Texas (2003)
Utah	Georgia	Minnesota (1997)	New Hampshire (2004)
	Idaho	Mississippi (1997)	Ohio (2004)
	Illinois	Montana (1997)	
	Kansas	N. Dakota (1997)	
	Louisiana	Virginia (1997)	
	Michigan	Hawaii (1998)	
	Missouri	Iowa (1998)	
	N. Carolina	Kentucky (1998)	
	Oklahoma	Washington (1998)	
	Pennsylvania	Vermont (1999)	
	S. Carolina		
	S. Dakota		
	Tennessee		

*State law predating the federal Defense of Marriage Act defines marriage. New Hampshire also passed a state DOMA in 2004

effect the successful mobilization of Passive Opponents and Passive Supporters had in the passage of these state laws.

Vermont's Civil Unions

In the midst of state legislative debates over mini-DOMAs, three Vermont couples sued the state for the right to marry. As with the Hawaii case, both the Roman Catholic diocese of Burlington and the Burlington stake of the LDS church filed briefs opposing the couples, and the Unitarians, Quakers, Congregationalists, Jews, and Presbyterians filed *amicus* briefs in support of the couples' right to marry.[40] In December 1999, the Vermont Supreme Court sided with the couples and ordered the state legislature to devise a method to provide them with the rights of marriage.[41] According to the court, the state constitution required the government to provide same-sex couples with the same rights provided to opposite-sex couples. The court directed the Vermont legislature to find an appropriate way to accommodate same-sex couples but did not outline a specific method of rectifying the problem.

As debate shifted to the state legislature, religious voices continued to play a prominent role. Seventeen religious leaders from a range of faith traditions issued a statement in January urging the legislature to pass a bill legalizing same-sex marriage. The clergy included representatives of the United Methodist Church, the Episcopal Diocese of Vermont, the Unitarian Universalist church, the United Church of Christ, and a Jewish rabbi. As they argued, "human beings are called to live in right relationship with each other and with God. Therefore, legalizing marriage for same gender couples will build community, support the well-being of children and families and promote the common good."[42] Conservative groups were also represented in the debate. Reverend Lou Sheldon, the director of the Traditional Values Coalition, traveled to Vermont to voice his opposition to legislation.[43] Two-thirds of those who provided testimony to the legislature opposing recognition for same-sex couples cited morality or God's will as justification for their opposition.[44]

Despite opposition from some state lawmakers, in April 2000 the Vermont legislature responded with a civil union bill.[45] Preserving the definition of marriage as referring to a male-female partnership, the Vermont civil union legislation provided same-sex couples with all the legal rights and benefits awarded to heterosexual married couples by the state. The law went into effect on July 1, 2001, and almost 1,500 civil unions were performed in the first six months.[46] The policy left many on both sides of the debate dissatisfied. Some advocates of same-sex marriage argued that the policy created a separate and unequal category for same-sex couples and it did not provide the federal benefits and rights conferred upon those who are legally married.[47] In fact, one-third of the witnesses who testified at the legislative hearing in support of legal recognition for same-sex couples argued that marriage, rather than domestic partnerships or civil unions, was the only acceptable policy outcome.[48] Opponents of same-sex marriage viewed it as another step toward the destruction of the traditional family structure.

Federal Marriage Amendment

By the early months of 2003, advocates of same-sex marriage succeeded in winning a handful of court cases and the enactment of a civil union policy in Vermont, but they lost a string of legislative battles at both the national and state levels. Religious groups successfully mobilized to block the possibility that states would be forced to recognize same-sex marriages if they were eventually legalized through a court decision in another state. Though many observers looked with skepticism at the constitutionality of the DOMA, the fact that no state allowed gay or lesbian couples to marry meant that no citizen had the legal standing to challenge the law as a violation of the Full Faith and Credit Clause of the Constitution.

Seeking to guard against the possibility that the laws would be ruled unconstitutional if challenged, opponents of same-sex marriage submitted a proposal to amend the U.S. Constitution to officially define marriage as between a man and a woman. Mississippi Representative Ronnie Shows first proposed an amendment in the 107th Congress. The amendment was drafted with the help of Alliance for Marriage, a religious group started in 1999 with the goal of protecting against changes to the traditional family structure.[49] H.J. Res. 93, introduced in May 2002, had twenty-two cosponsors and died in the House Judiciary Committee. A year later, on May 21, 2003, Colorado Representative Marilyn Musgrave introduced a similar resolution titled the Federal Marriage Amendment.

The proposed amendment received little public attention until a tangentially related Supreme Court ruling on June 26, 2003, catapulted the issue into the national spotlight. Although the Supreme Court's decision in *Lawrence v. Texas* (2003) did not directly address gay marriage, it was widely interpreted as paving the way for same-sex marriage rights. The Court struck down anti-sodomy laws in thirteen states, providing firmer legal ground to supporters of gay marriage.[50]

Three days after the *Lawrence* ruling, Senate Majority Leader Bill Frist (R-Tennessee) announced his support for a constitutional amendment defining marriage as being between a man and woman. In November, Colorado Senator Wayne Allard introduced a companion resolution in the Senate to amend the Constitution. The Senate resolution drew only six cosponsors, but 131 Representatives in the House—both Republicans and Democrats—joined the marriage amendment resolution as cosponsors. Conservative Christian leader Jerry Falwell announced in August that he would dedicate his "talents, time and energies over the next few years to the passage of an amendment to the U.S. Constitution that will protect the traditional family from its enemies who wish to legalize same-sex marriage and other diverse 'family' forms."[51] Other conservative religious groups mobilized in "defense of marriage," sponsoring rallies, mass mail campaigns, and lobbying days. Despite the support of these religious groups, neither the House nor the Senate voted on the resolution that year.

Massachusetts

The political environment changed dramatically on November 18, 2003 when the Massachusetts Supreme Court struck down Massachusetts' legislative ban on same-sex marriage on the grounds that there was "no constitutionally adequate reason for denying civil benefits to same-sex couples." The decision in the case, *Goodridge v. Massachusetts Department of Public Health* (2003), ordered the legislature to remedy the situation within six months, and in a supplemental ruling the court ruled that a civil union bill would not meet the requirements outlined in the original decision.[52] With the option of a Vermont-style civil union off the table, Massachusetts legislators passed a civil marriage policy to provide legal marriage benefits to same-sex couples and became the first state in the nation to legally recognize same-sex marriages.

Marriage Protection Amendment

With a more direct threat of legalized marriage for same-sex couples, Representative Musgrave and Senator Allard resumed their calls for a federal constitutional amendment to define marriage. Allard introduced a new resolution to the Senate (SJ Res 40) in July 2004 and Musgrave introduced HJ Res 106 in the House in September 2004. This new version was renamed the Marriage Protection Amendment. As it declared, "Marriage in the United States shall consist only of the union of a man and a woman. Neither this Constitution, nor the constitution of any State, shall be construed to require that marriage or the legal incidents thereof be conferred upon any union other than the union of a man and a woman."

President George W. Bush initially refused to take a position on the proposed constitutional amendment and it was not until mid-December 2003 that he announced his support for a constitutional amendment to define marriage. In a nationally televised interview, Bush said he would support a constitutional amendment "if necessary" to codify the legal definition of marriage. Bush mentioned the importance of a traditional definition of marriage in his January State of the Union address and issued an even more explicit endorsement of the proposed amendment in a televised speech to the nation on February 24, 2004. Bush argued that "a few judges and local authorities are presuming to change the most fundamental institution of civilization," and concluded, "if we are to prevent the meaning of marriage from being changed forever, our nation must enact a constitutional amendment to protect marriage in America."[53]

Groups on the religious right were among the most active advocates of the amendment. The American Family Association drafted and circulated a petition in support of the amendment that was sent to members of Congress. Focus on the Family, the Traditional Values Coalition, the Southern Baptist Convention, and the U.S. Conference of Catholic Bishops all voiced support for the amendment.[54] Focus on the Family ran newspaper advertisements in 13 states and used James Dobson's daily radio program to mobilize voters to contact their senators and representatives.[55] Along with organized interest groups, leaders from the Catholic Church, Southern Baptist Convention, Mormon Church, Greek Orthodox Church, Church of God in Christ, and Union of Orthodox Jewish Congregations of America gathered in Washington, D.C. in early 2006 to coordinate the efforts of religious supporters of the Marriage Protection Amendment.[56] The push inspired one commentator to note that "Falwell, Dobson, Sheldon, Robertson and their ilk are employing heated rhetoric and an abundance of resources to whip their supporters into a panic over the future of marriage in America. They are urging their members to pressure congressional lawmakers and the president to fall in line."[57]

While they did not attract the same attention, religious leaders opposed to the marriage amendment also mobilized during this period. Representatives of some liberal religious traditions united in the group Clergy for Fairness. In an open letter addressed to the Senate and signed by twenty-four national religious groups, Clergy for Fairness argued that "the Federal Marriage Amendment reflects a fundamental disregard for individual civil rights and ignores differences among our nation's many religious traditions."[58] The group collected over 2,200 signatures from clergy members and religious leaders on a petition opposing the amendment in 2006. This movement on the Left, led by Active Supporters, worked through this petition to mobilize Passive Supporters and Passive Opponents who may have opposed same-sex marriage but did not approve of making such a drastic change to the U.S. Constitution.

Unlike regular legislation, a constitutional amendment requires a two-thirds vote in both chambers before it can be sent for ratification by three-fourths of the states. The Senate took up the measure first, and senators who were opposed to the amendment quickly launched a filibuster of the resolution. Supporters forced a vote of cloture to allow the chamber to discuss the issue, but the motion failed by a narrow margin (48–50) a week after it was introduced, procedurally killing the resolution. The House held a floor vote on the resolution in mid-September, and with a vote of 227–186, supporters failed to garner the two-thirds needed for passage. This scenario repeated itself two years later in the 109th Congress. Musgrave and Allard again introduced identical resolutions in the House and Senate. The Senate version failed on a cloture vote in June 2006 and the House version failed a month later. During debate over the measures, members of Congress liberally referenced biblical texts and advanced arguments rooted in religious beliefs.[59]

State Constitutional Amendments

The first two states to amend their constitutions to define marriage—Alaska and Nebraska—took action years before the Massachusetts decision or the introduction of a federal marriage amendment. In 1998, the Alaska Superior Court found that the state's policy of denying marriage licenses to same-sex couples was unconstitutional. Opponents responded with a proposed constitutional amendment to define marriage sponsored by an evangelical state Senator.[60] Supporters of the amendment offered a strategically calculated frame focusing on marriage and the need to prevent judicial activism rather than outright hostility to homosexuality. With the support of the Catholic archdiocese and the LDS church, religious conservatives mobilized to ratify the amendment in 2000.[61]

While the central fronts of debate moved between federal and state venues, local governments also found themselves in the midst of controversy. Local officials in a handful of cities and counties across the country used their powers to issue marriage licenses to same-sex couples. On February 12, 2004, San Francisco Mayor Gavin Newsom announced that the city would begin issuing marriage licenses to same-sex couples. That decision was immediately followed in Sandoval County, New Mexico, the city of New Paltz, New York, and Multnomah County, Oregon.[62] In all these locales, judges eventually ordered an end to the distribution of marriage licenses and nullified those that were issued.

These local actions coupled with the Massachusetts decision and the failure of the federal government to pass a constitutional amendment opened the floodgates on state-level constitutional amendments. Thirteen states passed amendments in 2004 to define marriage as being between a man and a woman and to refuse state recognition of same-sex marriages performed in other states. According to Wilcox et al., members of the Christian Right had "long anticipated the emergence of the same-sex marriage issue and had planned for the issue for some time."[63] The Christian Right used the decision in Massachusetts as a means of expanding the religious coalition of opponents of same-sex marriage, reinvigorating local and national religious interest groups, and mobilizing voters in support of state-level constitutional amendments and conservative political candidates. Evangelical Christians joined with conservative Catholics, the LDS church, Muslims, and prominent African American pastors to advocate the passage of constitutional amendments defining marriage. New groups formed in states that would be voting on an amendment, and national organizations—which many political observers viewed as weakened after the 2000 elections—made the issue a central focus of their political and fundraising strategies and helped network state and local groups. Conservative religious groups relied on connections with churches and other houses of worship to reach voters. The Alliance Defense Fund, a Christian group that helps coordinate legal and political strategies for the Christian Right, sent letters to pastors encouraging them to talk about the issue of same-sex marriage with their congregations. Focus on the Family even provided ministers with sample sermons on the topic.[64]

Many of the amendments passed in 2004 were in states that featured conservative legislatures and judiciaries and offered little protection to gays and lesbians. It was not a surprise, then, that most of the amendments passed by overwhelming margins. The closest votes were in Oregon and Michigan, where only 57 percent and 59 percent of the public, respectively, voted in favor of the amendments. Mississippi, on the other hand, passed its amendment with the support of 86 percent of the voters. As with state DOMAs, religious groups played a major role in advancing the amendments.

In Ohio, Citizens for Community Values, associated with Focus on the Family, helped to gather the required 323,000 signatures to place the amendment on the ballot and spent $3.5 million on the campaign.[65] The American Family Association of Michigan played a similar role in the passage of an amendment in Michigan. There, evangelicals united with African American clergy and the Catholic Church in leading the campaign for the amendment.[66] In both of these states, representatives of liberal religious traditions also organized to oppose passage of the amendments.

In 2006, the Christian Right relied on many of the same strategies that proved successful in 2004 but faced more organized resistance from supporters of same-sex marriage combined with less enthusiasm from the grassroots. Amendment supporters in the eight states that voted on constitutional amendments in November 2006 were faced with voters who were more concerned with issues such as the war in Iraq, were less threatened by the prospect of legalized same-sex marriage because of conservative judicial rulings in New York and Washington over the summer, and were exposed to middle ground proposals such as civil union or domestic partnership plans advocated by some gay rights groups.[67] In Arizona, opponents were even able to successfully reframe the issue, leading to the first ever defeat of a marriage amendment at the state level. In Colorado, South Dakota, Virginia, and Wisconsin, the measures passed with the support of under 60 percent of the voters.

Looking into the Future

As of August 2007, only one state—Massachusetts (2004)—allows same-sex couples to marry, and only four states—Vermont (2000), Connecticut

Table 2.3 States with Constitutional Amendments Banning Same-Sex Marriage

1998–2003	2004	2005–2006
Alaska (1998)	Arkansas	Kansas (2005)
Hawaii (1998)*	Georgia	Texas (2005)
Nebraska (2000)	Kentucky	Alabama (2006)
Nevada (2002)	Louisiana	Colorado (2006)
	Michigan	Idaho (2006)
	Mississippi	S. Carolina (2006)
	Missouri	S. Dakota (2006)
	Montana	Tennessee (2006)
	N. Dakota	Virginia (2006)
	Ohio	Wisconsin (2006)
	Oklahoma	
	Oregon	
	Utah	

*The amendment passed in Hawaii does not define marriage directly but it instead gives the state legislature the authority to define marriage through legislation.

(2005), New Jersey (2007), and New Hampshire (effective January 2008)—allow same-sex couples to enter into civil unions. Nearly every other state has a legislative or constitutional ban on same-sex marriages.[68] The policy debate, however, is far from over. In Massachusetts, opponents of same-sex marriage convinced state legislators to vote to place the issue on the ballot as a constitutional amendment to allow voters to decide whether to allow same-sex marriages.[69] According to the Massachusetts constitution, the legislature, meeting as a constitutional convention, must agree to the amendment in two concurrent sessions before it can be placed on the ballot. If the next session also approves the measure, the amendment will go to the voters. Massachusetts issued its first marriage license nearly three years ago, but no state has followed its lead in granting full marriage benefits, though several have created alternate methods for same-sex couples to receive benefits. Recent judicial decisions have either rejected claims made by same-sex couples (in Washington State and New York), or turned the task of creating an acceptable alternative over to the state legislature (New Jersey, which established a civil union policy). The Marriage Protection Amendment will likely make a reappearance in the 110th Congress, but with Democratic majorities in both the House and Senate, it is unlikely to advance.

Table 2.4 State Policies Favorable to Same-Sex Couples

Same-Sex Marriage	Civil Unions	Domestic Partnerships or Similar Benefits	Favorable State Supreme Court Decisions
Massachusetts (2004)	Vermont (2000) Connecticut (2005) New Jersey (2007) New Hampshire (2008)	Hawaii (1997) Washington, D.C. (2002) Maine (2004) California (2006) Washington (2007) Oregon (2008)	Hawaii (1996) Alaska (1998) Massachusetts (2003) New Jersey (2006)

RELIGIOUS GROUPS AND MEDIA FRAMING IN THE SAME-SEX MARRIAGE DEBATE

As the debate over same-sex marriage jumped between local, state, and federal legislatures and courts, a battle over the media's framing of the issue developed, led in part by the national religious organizations and local semi-autonomous religious groups that played such a large role in bringing the issue to the national political agenda. This section examines two dominant patterns within the media's coverage of the debate over same-sex marriage. First, two dueling argument frames dominate the debate: traditional family values versus equality.[70] Second, religious groups opposed to same-sex marriage are more prominent in news coverage of the debate than religious groups that support same-sex marriage.

Dueling Frames

Framing involves the strategic packaging of information to communicate a preferred version of political problems, public policies, or potential solutions.[71] "At the most general level, framing refers to the way in which opinions about an issue can be altered by emphasizing or deemphasizing particular facets of that issue."[72] It is an important political strategy because policy issues are inherently multidimensional and are thus ready targets for interpretation. Numerous studies find that frames can dramatically change the decision-making context, especially in terms of what aspects of the policy are most important, and can thereby alter the outcome of debates.[73] Citizens consume frames through a number of media outlets but are only rarely active in the creation of frames. Instead, politicians, scholars, and policy entrepreneurs such as interest group leaders, are responsible for developing issue frames.[74] Groups actively work to shape public debates over policies by injecting their preferred framing of the issue into the debate. At the same time, journalists play a major role in framing because they act as gatekeepers, deciding which information to include in a story and deciding how that information should be presented.

The issue of same-sex marriage can be framed in a variety of ways. In one study of framing that focused on the public debate in Hawaii, Hull identified twenty-seven separate argument frames emerging in letters to the editor in local newspapers.[75] Twelve of these frames appeared in at least 10 percent of the letters. While these frames represent specific distinct arguments, we can also use broader groupings of arguments to help identify patterns in the emerging debate. The most obvious frame for a debate over same-sex marriage involves constructing the issue as a question of moral values. Morality, however, involves at least two separate dimensions—those addressing questions of traditional family values and those addressing aspects of equal rights. Both are grounded in morality (questions of ultimate right and wrong or good and bad) and both have strong ties to religious beliefs, but each emphasizes a different aspect of morality.[76]

In addition to moral frames, the media's coverage of same-sex marriage might also reference frames emphasizing politics, legality, democracy, and economics. A politics frame would emphasize the political strategies and key players involved in the debate as well as framing the issue as a strategic battle between two or more sides. A legality frame would emphasize legal or constitutional issues raised by the policy. A democracy frame would emphasize the will of the people or public opinion surrounding the topic. Finally, an economic frame would emphasize the economic benefits or costs associated with the policy in question. Each of these frames represents relevant considerations that provide an acceptable alternative or complement to moral frames.

Analysis of the media's coverage of the debate over same-sex marriage and the use and development of these various frames helps explain public opinion and the outcome of many policy decisions regarding same-sex marriage. The *Washington Post* and the *New York Times* provided extensive coverage of the policy debates over same-sex marriage between 1995 and 2003—the period immediately preceding passage of the DOMA and continuing past the decision in Massachusetts.[77] In the coverage of same-sex marriage by these national newspapers, moral frames—particularly those advocating the protection of traditional family values—were the dominant frames in the debate. For example, in covering a congressional debate over a domestic partnership law in the District of Columbia in 1995, the *Washington Post* reported that "lawmakers did approve a repeal of the city's domestic partners law after debating *'family values'* and whether the District government should extend health benefits to the domestic partners of its unmarried employees . . . the Republican majority voted yesterday to strike the law from the city code, calling it a *reprehensible 'redefinition' of the family*" [italics added].[78] This argument frame was a powerful and long-lasting frame throughout the debate.

News coverage in the early period of the debate also emphasized the politics frame. Journalists situated the growing debate as a political battle between liberals and religious conservatives—yet did not acknowledge the role of religious liberals. At the same time, some gay rights groups questioned the wisdom of pursuing gay marriage rights when the campaign would divert attention and resources from more important issues such as preventing the spread of AIDS or eliminating job discrimination. Thus, the political frames that developed encompassed both a general strategic analysis of the unfolding debate as well as a strategic debate within the gay and lesbian community regarding tactics and timing.

The months between the introduction and passage of the DOMA marked the only period in the debate when a frame other than morality was the most common frame. In the heat of the debate over the DOMA, the politics frame was used in nearly 70 percent of the articles written on the topic. The *New York Times* began one article written during this period by emphasizing the political strategy behind the gay marriage debate: "Trying to keep the issue of same-sex marriage alive in the Presidential campaign, Ralph Reed said today that the Christian Coalition would push Congress to send President Clinton legislation by Labor Day to deny federal recognition of such unions."[79] Though the politics frame was the most common frame during this period, the morality frame was a close second. Sixty-seven percent of the articles written during these months included the morality frame. Unlike the previous period, however, the morality frame was not solely focused on traditional family values. While 68 percent of the articles included a family values moral frame, 14 percent included an equal rights moral frame. In some cases, these frames appeared in the same article, creating a direct conflict between the two versions of moral frames being developed in the debate.

These months also marked the introduction of a legal frame, which was used throughout the remainder of the debate. Arguments within the legal frame centered on the constitutionality of laws banning or creating gay marriage as well as the principles of federalism. Supporters of gay marriage argued that states should be free to implement gay marriage laws and that the Full Faith and Credit Clause of the Constitution meant that those marriage licenses should be recognized in other states. Opponents argued that states should not be forced to recognize marriage licenses for same-sex couples issued by other states.

In terms of the dominant frames that appeared in the news, there was little change between the debate over DOMA and the state court ruling in Vermont. The morality frame remained the most common frame used in the debate. Nearly 70 percent of the articles written between January 1997 and April 2002 included the moral frame. Of these, most focused on family values morality, but a growing number of articles (30 percent) also focused on equal rights morality. In particular, argument frames regarding discrimination surfaced during this period. Supporters of gay marriage argued that it was important to protect the equal rights of gays and lesbians and to execute marriage laws fairly. Religious groups, when they were mentioned in news articles in connection with moral frames, were more commonly tied to family values moral arguments. About 30% of the articles during this time included the politics frame and one quarter of the articles included a legal frame.

Between May 2002 and December 2003, the variety of frames used in the debate over gay marriage expanded. Until this point, the debate was framed largely in terms of morality and politics, with some attention also paid to legal frames. In this final period of analysis, however, the terms of debate expanded to include democracy and economic frames as well. The moral frame continued its dominance, with 77 percent of the articles in this time period using a moral frame. Again, the family values version of the morality frame was most common, but a significant number of articles (30 percent) also emphasized the equal rights moral frame. A number of religious interest groups worked hard to push this version of the moral frame, issuing a number of press releases that included an equal opportunity frame, but religious groups were almost never associated with the frame in news coverage of the debate.

In addition to the moral frame, over half of the articles used a politics frame and 27 percent used a legal frame. The arguments associated with each of these major frames were similar to those made throughout the debate, although the judicial activism argument was made more frequently. Opponents of gay marriage, in particular religious conservatives, argued that court rulings in favor of gay marriage represented judicial activism in its most egregious form. Unelected judges, they claimed, were forcing their liberal interpretation of the Constitution on a public that was largely opposed to gay marriage.

Finally, joining these staples of the gay marriage debate were the democracy and economics frames that were rarely used in earlier periods of the debate. Nearly 39 percent of the articles used the democracy frame, emphasizing public opinion on the topic of gay marriage. Supporters of gay marriage argued that the public was gradually becoming more receptive to the idea of gay marriage, while opponents argued that public opinion was strongly opposed to the practice. Nearly 23 percent of the articles included the economic frame. This frame was used particularly to promote gay marriage through the argument that gay and lesbian couples needed access to the economic and legal benefits granted to heterosexual couples.

As the example that began this chapter suggests, the framing of the same-sex marriage debate can have a substantial impact on the policy outcomes. In the debate over an amendment to the Arizona constitution, opponents were able to shift the discourse from the family values moral frame to frames emphasizing economic benefits and equal rights morality. This is a significant departure from the established framing pattern in that a frame emphasizing economic benefits to heterosexuals has the potential to mobilize Passive Supporters and Passive Opponents who are usually swayed by the rhetoric of Active Opponents.

Group Representation in Media Coverage of the Debate

Religious groups opposed to same-sex marriage were significantly more prominent in news coverage of the debate than were religious groups in support of same-sex marriage, and therefore had a larger role in the framing process as it was occurring through the mass media. In many ways, this second pattern is a direct result of the first, in that reporters often have a set of preferred frames in mind and turn to sources that will provide support for those pre-selected frames.[80] The process of framing an issue as a moral issue has important consequences on the groups included in a debate and the types of arguments that are included in the debate. The underrepresentation of religious groups supportive of same-sex marriage, however, is also the result of structural differences in mobilization and media strategies.[81]

Fifty-four interest groups were mentioned in the mediated debate over gay marriage that occurred in the pages of the *Washington Post* and the *New York Times* between 1995 and 2003, but most groups were only mentioned a single time. Approximately half of the groups mentioned were religious groups and half were non-religious groups; however, the non-religious groups received more mentions than the religious groups. Table 2.5 lists the top ten groups receiving the most mentions in the media coverage of the debate over gay marriage.

All five of the religious groups among the top ten groups were strongly opposed to gay marriage. Of the 27 religious groups mentioned in this

Table 2.5 Groups in News Coverage of the Same-Sex Marriage Debate, 1995–2003

Group	Number of Mentions	Religiously Affiliated	Position on Same-Sex Marriage
Human Rights Campaign (HRC)	37	No	Support
Family Research Council (FRC)	23	Yes	Oppose
Lambda Legal Defense (LLD)	18	No	Support
Traditional Values Coalition (TVC)	10	Yes	Oppose
American Civil Liberties Union (ACLU)	9	No	Support
Christian Coalition of America (CC)	9	Yes	Oppose
Concerned Women for America (CWA)	8	Yes	Oppose
Focus on the Family (FF)	7	Yes	Oppose
Pew	7	No	Neutral
Freedom to Marry Coalition (FMC)	6	No	Support

Results are based on a content analysis of news articles from the *Washington Post* and *New York Times* between 1995 and 2003

sample of news coverage, 21 were opposed to gay marriage, three supported gay marriage, and three held a middle ground position on the issue. This pattern in media coverage oversimplifies the diversity of viewpoints held by religious groups. Despite the existence of several religious groups actively supporting gay and lesbian marriage, such as Dignity USA, Equal Partners in Faith, and Soulforce, journalists tended to focus their attention on the larger religious groups opposed to the policy.

This trend of overemphasizing the voices of Active Opponents and underemphasizing the voices of Active Supporters was not simply the result of the time frame studied, nor was it the result of the newspapers chosen for study. In examining all of the "major papers" archived by the Lexis-Nexis database between 1995 and 2006, it is clear that this pattern is systemic. Table 2.6 displays the number of times leading interest groups and denominations were mentioned in association with "same-sex marriage" or "gay marriage" during these years. Religious groups opposing same-sex marriage were simply much more likely to be mentioned in media coverage of the debate.

An examination of the press releases issued by a sample of religious groups active in the same-sex marriage debate finds that most religious interest group press releases used moral language and arguments to justify their positions.[82] Three-quarters of the press releases specifically mentioned family values moral frames, and journalists reinforced this by associating religious groups with family values frames in news stories. However, many

Table 2.6 Religious Groups Mentioned in News Coverage, 1995–2006

Year	Opposing Same-Sex Marriage		Supporting Same-Sex Marriage	
	Interest Groups*	Denominations**	Interest Groups[+]	Denominations[++]
1995	20	1	0	1
1996	279	8	4	3
1997	65	1	1	0
1998	122	5	4	2
1999	41	11	7	1
2000	95	16	15	16
2001	29	8	4	10
2002	35	4	3	1
2003	259	120	23	19
2004	893	116	54	41
2005	434	117	22	5
2006	76	41	0	11
Total	2,348	448	137	110

*Interest groups opposing same-sex marriage include: The Family Research Council, the Traditional Values Coalition, the Christian Coalition of America, Concerned Women for America, and Focus on the Family
**Denominations opposing same-sex marriage include: the Catholic Church, the Southern Baptist church, the Church of Jesus Christ of Latter-day Saints (Mormon)
[+]Interest groups supporting same-sex marriage include: Dignity USA, Equal Partners in Faith, Soulforce, the Interfaith Alliance, and the Religious Coalition for the Freedom to Marry
[++]Denominations supporting same-sex marriage include: The Metropolitan Community Church, Unitarian Universalist, Society of Friends (Quaker), and Conservative Judaism
Results are based on a full text search of "Major Papers" using the Lexis-Nexis database. Search terms included "same-sex marriage" or "gay marriage" and the name of the group for each year shown.

of the religious groups also framed the issue in terms of the equal rights moral frame. Though this version of the morality frame was not nearly as prevalent as the family values version, it was still used consistently by religious groups throughout the debate.

In contrast to the way journalists connected religious groups with the family values frame, however, religious groups were almost never associated with the equal rights frame in news coverage of the debate. The repeated use of the equal rights frame by religious groups communicating through group press releases was essentially ignored by journalists in their coverage of religious groups. Several press releases from religious groups expressed the argument that gay marriage is moral if the couple loves one another, but, again, religious groups were never associated with this frame in news articles.[83]

Furthermore, many of the religious groups supporting same-sex marriage were simply ignored by the media. The Religious Action Center of Reform Judaism and Dignity USA each issued a series of press releases on the topic of gay marriage between 1996 and 2003, but the Religious Action Center was never mentioned in the mediated debate and Dignity was mentioned only once over the entire period. Both of these groups used moral argument frames, but they spoke in the language of equal rights rather than family values morality. Activist Alison Beck notes this reclamation of the morality frame, arguing that "by reframing the debate on 'moral values' and embracing the emerging voices in Progressive Christianity and progressive wings of other religious traditions, we can provide a principled faith-based argument for the dignity and equality of all families."[84]

This is perhaps an extreme example of the power of a dominant frame in affecting the type of voices that are heard in mediated debates. The dominance of a particular frame has the effect of silencing voices that could make an important contribution to the national policy debate. The moral frames developed by these groups, which articulated support for gay marriage, were in direct conflict with the moral frames that dominated the debate. For journalists attempting to piece together a consistent narrative with a theme dominated by a moral frame, these alternate moral frames were difficult to incorporate.

Religious groups articulating moral arguments against gay marriage, however, were included in the debate and were successful in moving argument frames into the deliberation. Focus on the Family is one such group that experienced a high level of framing success. A conservative religious organization devoted to protecting traditional family values, Focus on the Family was especially persistent about using argument frames regarding the protection of the traditional family structure and the impact of gay marriage on children. Although the traditional family values frame was used by journalists several times over the course of the debate, the heaviest use of the frame occurred in 2003. The frame was rarely used between 1997 and 2003, but in 2003, Focus on the Family, along with the Family Research Council (FRC) and the National Conference of Catholic Bishops (NCCB), pushed the frame back on to the table. Focus on the Family issued a series of press releases using the traditional family frame in April, June, and July.

Shortly after the group began emphasizing the frame, the traditional family frame appeared in media coverage of the debate and was often attributed to Focus on the Family. As the year progressed, Focus on the Family continued to use the traditional family frame in group press releases, but use of the frame in news articles expanded to a variety of religious groups, including the NCCB, FRC, Eagle Forum, American Values, and Concerned

Women for America. The impact on children argument was rare through most of the debate until 2003. After Focus on the Family emphasized the impact on children argument in press releases issued in June and July 2003, however, the argument was included in a number of articles, three of which specifically mentioned Focus on the Family in conjunction with the argument.

Overall, religious groups were far more likely to be included in the debate over gay marriage when the issue was framed in terms of family values morality. Religious groups that made moral arguments but did not fall on the "right" side of the debate, however, were less likely to be included in the debate. For groups, access to the debate involves more than simply being interested in the issue or actively pursuing media access. It is more deeply connected to the framing of the issue and, furthermore, the extent to which the group's position fit within the dominant story line associated with the frame.

CONCLUSION

The debate over same-sex marriage is far from settled and religious groups will continue to occupy a prominent role in the debate. As this chapter argues, though, the role of religion in this debate is not confined to the right. Liberal religious groups are every bit as active, though significantly less visible, than conservative religious groups. As liberal religious groups have struggled to gain the media visibility that will allow them to share their message and mobilize supporters, conservative religious groups have dominated the framing battle and successfully mobilized people on the basis of religious beliefs to support state bans on same-sex marriage and state constitutional amendments to define marriage.

Supporters of same-sex marriage too often ignored the powerful role religion plays on both sides of the debate. But, as one activist who is both a lesbian and a Christian writes, "interestingly, it is our church that has helped to give us the strength to endure the politics of hate, and the perspective to take the long view in our road to equality . . . While we must continue to champion the principle that one group's religious beliefs cannot dictate the civil rights of others, we must also remember that in the battle for hearts and minds, religious faith is a central compass of morality for many people."[85] Religious values are certainly at the heart of the debate over same-sex marriage. The lesson of this brief overview of the same-sex marriage debate, however, is that the debate is not simply between religious and secular citizens, but also within religious groups and among people of faith.

NOTES

1. Sonya Geis, "New Tactic in Fighting Marriage Initiatives; Opponents Cite Effects on Straight Couples," *Washington Post*, Monday, November 20, 2006.

2. James Davison Hunter articulated the notion of a "culture war," or a political battle between the conservative Religious Right and the secular Left, in his book, *Culture Wars: The Struggle to Define America* (New York: Basic Books, 1991). Many scholars have built on this characterization. See John C. Green et al., *Religion and the Culture Wars: Dispatches from the Front* (Lanham, MD: Rowman & Littlefield, 1996), George Lakoff, *Moral Politics: How Liberals and Conservatives Think, 2nd Edition* (Chicago: University of Chicago Press, 2002), and John Kenneth White, *The Values Divide: American Politics and Culture in Transition* (New York: Chatham House Publishers, 2003). Other scholars, however, challenge this argument. This position is well articulated by Morris P. Fiorina in *Culture War? The Myth of a Polarized America* (New York: Pearson-Longman, 2006).

3. Paul R. Brewer, "The Shifting Foundations of Public Opinion About Gay Rights," *The Journal of Politics* 65, no. 4 (2003): 1208–1220; Clyde Wilcox and Robin Wolpert, "Gay Rights in the Public Sphere: Public Opinion on Gay and Lesbian Equality," in *The Politics of Gay Rights*, eds. Craig A. Rimmerman, Kenneth D. Wald and Clyde Wilcox (Chicago: University of Chicago, 2000); Fiorina, *Culture War?*

4. Scholars use a variety of terms, such as "religious salience," "religious commitment," and "religiosity," to discuss this concept. See David Leege and Lyman Kellstedt, *Rediscovering the Religious Factor in American Politics* (New York: M.E. Sharpe, 1993). Religious tradition refers to "a group of religious communities that share a set of beliefs that generates a distinctive world view" as defined by Lyman A. Kellstedt et al., "Grasping the Essentials: The Social Embodiment of Religion and Political Behavior," in *Religion and the Culture Wars: Dispatches from the Front*, eds. John C. Green, James L. Guth, Corwin E. Smidt and Lyman A. Kellstedt (Lanham, MD: Rowman & Littlefield, 1996), 176. One particularly thorough look at the relationship between religion and public opinion is Andrew Kohut, et al., *The Diminishing Divide: Religion's Changing Role in American Politics* (Washington, D.C.: Brookings Institution Press, 2000).

5. Christopher Z. Mooney, ed. *The Public Clash of Private Values: The Politics of Morality Policy* (New York: Chatham House Publishers, 2001); Clyde Wilcox, *Onward Christian Soldiers? The Religious Right in American Politics* (Boulder, CO: Westview Press, 1996); Gregory B. Lewis, "Black-White Differences in Attitudes toward Homosexuality and Gay Rights," *Public Opinion Quarterly* 67 (2003): 59–78; Kohut et al., *The Diminishing Divide*; Laura R. Olson, Wendy Cadge, and James T. Harrison, "Religion and Public Opinion about Same-Sex Marriage," *Social Science Quarterly* 87, no. 2 (2006): 340–360.

6. Kohut et al., *The Diminishing Divide*; Olson et al., "Religion and Public Opinion About Same-Sex Marriage."

7. Olson et al., "Religion and Public Opinion about Same-Sex Marriage."

8. A. James Reichley, "Faith in Politics," in *Religion Returns to the Public Square: Faith and Policy in America*, eds. Hugh Heclo and Wilfred M. McClay (Washington, D.C.: Woodrow Wilson Center Press, 2003); Green et al., *Religion and the Culture Wars*.

9. Mark J. Rozell and Debasree Das Gupta, "The 'Values Vote'"? Moral Issues and the 2004 Elections," in *The Values Campaign? The Christian Right and the 2004 Elections*, eds. John C. Green, Mark J. Rozell, and Clyde Wilcox (Washington, D.C.: Georgetown University Press, 2006); Alan Abramowitz, "Terrorism, Gay Marriage, and Incumbency: Explaining the Republican Victory in the 2004 Presidential Election," *The Forum*: 2, no. 4 (2004); Barry C. Burden, "An Alternative Account of the 2004 Presidential Election," *The Forum* 2, no. 4 (2004); D. Sunshine Hillygus and Todd G. Shields, "Moral Issues and Voter Decision Making in the 2004 Presidential Election," *PS: Political Science and Politics* 38, no. 2 (2005): 201–09; Fiorina, *Culture War?*

10. Clyde Wilcox, Linda M. Merolla, and David Beer, "Saving Marriage by Banning Marriage: The Christian Right Finds a New Issue in 2004," in *The Values Campaign? The Christian Right and the 2004 Elections*, ed. John C. Green, Mark J. Rozell, and Clyde Wilcox (Washington, D.C.: Georgetown University Press, 2006); Gregory B. Lewis, "Same-Sex Marriage and the 2004 Presidential Election," *PS: Political Science and Politics* 38, no. 2 (2005): 195–199.

11. Olson et al., "Religion and Public Opinion about Same-Sex Marriage."

12. One of the first scholarly works to address the role of religious groups was Luke Ebersole's *Church Lobbying in the Nation's Capital* (New York: The MacMillan Company, 1951).

13. See Sarah A. Soule, "Going to the Chapel? Same-Sex Marriage Bans in the United States, 1973–2000," *Social Problems* 51, no. 4 (2004): 453–477; Craig A. Rimmerman, Kenneth D. Wald, and Clyde Wilcox, eds., *The Politics of Gay Rights* (Chicago: University of Chicago, 2000); Haider-Markel, "Policy Diffusion as a Geographical Expansion of the Scope of Political Conflict; Same-Sex Marriage Bans in the 1990s"; Sara Diamond, *Not by Politics Alone: The Enduring Influence of the Christian Right* (New York: The Guilford Press, 1998); Clyde Wilcox, *Onward Christian Soldiers?*; or Mark J. Rozell and Clyde Wilcox, eds., *God at the Grass Roots, 1996: The Christian Right in the American Elections* (Lanham, MD: Rowman & Littlefield, 1997).

14. Gregory B. Lewis and Jonathan L. Edelson, "DOMA and ENDA: Congress Votes on Gay Rights," in *The Politics of Gay Rights*, eds. Craig A. Rimmerman, Kenneth D. Wald, and Clyde Wilcox (Chicago: University of Chicago, 2000); John C. Green, "Antigay: Varieties of Opposition to Gay Rights," in *The Politics of Gay Rights*, ed. Craig A. Rimmerman, Kenneth D. Wald, and Clyde Wilcox (Chicago: University of Chicago, 2000).

15. Didi Herman, *The Antigay Agenda: Orthodox Vision and the Christian Right* (Chicago: University of Chicago, 1997), 168.

16. David G. Meyers and Letha Dawson Scanzoni devote chapters to an examination of sexual orientation and scriptural references to homosexuality because it is

particularly difficult to critically explore the topic of same-sex marriage in the Christian tradition without devoting time to these theological questions in *What God Has Joined Together: The Christian Case for Gay Marriage* (New York: Harper SanFrancisco, 2005).

17. Some evangelical churches have recently been forced to confront issues of homosexuality close to home with the revelations of gay sex scandals involving high profile ministers, Associated Press, "Evangelical Pastor Confesses to 'Sexual Immorality,'" *New York Times*, November 5, 2006.

18. Some, like the ELCA, require gay and lesbian ministers to remain celibate.

19. Including, the American Apostolic Catholic Church, American Baptist Church, Buddhist, Evangelical Lutheran, United Methodist, Reformed Catholic Church (USA), Reform Judaism, Methodist, Orthodox Catholic Church and Presbyterian Church (USA), and Southern Baptist. See Chris Glaser, "The Love That Dare Not Pray Its Name: The Gay and Lesbian Movement in America's Churches," in *Homosexuality in the Church: Both Sides of the Debate*, ed. Jeffrey S. Siker (Louisville: Westminster John Knox Press, 1994).

20. Chris Bull and John Gallagher provide a thorough overview of the evolution of the debate over gay rights in *Perfect Enemies: The Religious Right, the Gay Movement, and the Politics of the 1990s* (New York: Crown Publishers, 1996), or see William Martin, *With God on Our Side* (New York: Broadway Books, 2005).

21. Jack Rogers, *Jesus, the Bible, and Homosexuality* (Louisville: Westminster John Knox Press, 2006).

22. John C. Green, "Ohio: The Bible and the Buckeye State," in *The Values Campaign? The Christian Right and the 2004 Elections*, eds. John C. Green, Mark J. Rozell, and Clyde Wilcox (Washington, D.C.: Georgetown University Press, 2006); Ruth Murray Brown, *For a "Christian America": A History of the Religious Right* (Amherst: Prometheus Books, 2002); William N. Eskridge, Jr., *Equality Practice: Civil Unions and the Future of Gay Rights* (New York: Routledge, 2002); Patrick Fagan, "Family and Religion: The Center Beam and Foundation of a Stable Nation," in *Faith and Public Policy*, ed. James R. Wilburn (Lanham, MD: Lexington Books, 2002); George Chauncey, *Why Marriage? The History Shaping Today's Debate over Gay Equality* (New York: Basic Books, 2004).

23. Chauncey, *Why Marriage?*, 145.

24. Wilcox et al., "Saving Marriage by Banning Marriage," 57.

25. Martin Dupuis, *Same-Sex Marriage, Legal Mobilization, and the Politics of Rights* (New York: Peter Lang, 2002). Initial attempts by gays and lesbians to gain the right to marry were made through the court system. In a series of lawsuits beginning with *Baker v. Nelson* in 1971, state courts upheld the right of state legislatures to restrict marriage to heterosexual couples. Other cases include *Jones v. Hallahan* (1973) in Kentucky, *Singer v. Hara* (1974) in Washington, *Adams v. Howerton* (1980) in Colorado, *DeSanto v. Barnsley* (1984) in Pennsylvania, and *Dean v. District of Columbia* (1992) in Washington, D.C.

26. *Baehr v. Lewin*, 852 P.2d 44 (Ha. Sup. Ct. 1993).

27. Unlike some of the decisions favoring same-sex marriage that followed the

Hawaii decision, the Hawaii courts did not identify a fundamental right to marry, did not approach the question as an issue of privacy rights, and concluded that same-sex marriage is not essential to liberty or justice. Instead, the court focused on the right to choose a marriage partner free from restrictions imposed the state based on sex. An Alaska trial court that ruled in favor of same-sex marriage in 1998 and the Vermont Supreme Court in 1999 did identify a "fundamental right" to marry the person of choice.

28. Kathleen E. Hull, "The Political Limits of the Rights Frame: The Case of Same-Sex Marriage in Hawaii," *Sociological Perspectives* 44, no. 2 (2001): 207–232.

29. Scholars debate the appropriateness of using religious language or arguments based in religious beliefs in the secular political world. Richard John Neuhaus argues that the exclusion of religious values from public life is detrimental to the health of American democracy in *The Naked Public Square: Religion and Democracy in America* (Grand Rapids: Eerdmans Publishing Company, 1984). Stephen L. Carter makes a similar argument in *The Culture of Disbelief: How American Law and Politics Trivialize Religious Devotion* (New York: Anchor Books, 1993). For an alternate perspective, see Jane Bennett and Michael J. Shapiro, eds., *The Politics of Moralizing* (New York: Routledge, 2002).

30. Accessed on November 25, 2006, from http://www.religioustolerance.org/haw_coc.htm.

31. Lewis and Edelson, "DOMA and ENDA."

32. Margaret Carlson, "The Marrying Kind," *Time*, September 16, 1996.

33. Eskridge, *Equality Practice*.

34. Soule "Going to the Chapel?"

35. Haider-Markel, "Policy Diffusion as a Geographical Expansion of the Scope of Political Conflict."

36. Dupuis, *Same-Sex Marriage, Legal Mobilization, and the Politics of Rights*, 75.

37. Haider-Markel, "Policy Diffusion as a Geographical Expansion of the Scope of Political Conflict"; Donald P. Haider-Markel, "Lesbian and Gay Politics in the States: Interest Groups, Electoral Politics, and Policy," in *The Politics of Gay Rights*, ed. Craig A. Rimmerman, Kenneth D. Wald, and Clyde Wilcox (Chicago: University of Chicago, 2000), 311; Soule, "Going to the Chapel?"; Scott Barclay and Shauna Fisher, "The States and the Differing Impetus for Divergent Paths on Same-Sex Marriage, 1990–2001," *The Policy Studies Journal* 31, no. 3 (2003): 331–352.

38. Haider-Markel, "Lesbian and Gay Politics in the States," 311.

39. Barclay and Fisher, "The States and the Differing Impetus for Divergent Paths on Same-Sex Marriage, 1990–2001."

40. David Moats, *Civil Wars: A Battle for Gay Marriage* (Orlando, FL: Harcourt, 2004).

41. *Baker v. State of Vermont*, 744 A2d. 864 (1999).

42. Linda Bloom, "Bishop Morrison among Supporters of Vermont Same-Sex Union Law," United Methodist News Service, 2000.

43. Dupuis, *Same-Sex Marriage, Legal Mobilization, and the Politics of Rights.*

44. Kathleen E. Hull, *Same-Sex Marriage: The Cultural Politics of Love and Law* (Cambridge: Cambridge University Press, 2006).

45. Moats, *Civil Wars.*

46. Dupuis, *Same-Sex Marriage, Legal Mobilization, and the Politics of Rights.*

47. Chauncey, *Why Marriage?*

48. Hull, *Same-Sex Marriage.*

49. Jeremy Leaming, "Marriage Proposal: Religious Right, Political Allies Launch Crusade to Alter Constitution," *Church and State* (2003): 196–198.

50. *Lawrence v. Texas,* 539 U.S. 558 (2003)

51. Jerry Falwell, *The Federal Marriage Amendment* [Website], NewsMax.com, 2003, available at http://www.newsmax.com/archives/articles/2003/8/7/143308.shtml 2005.

52. *Goodridge v. Massachusetts Department of Public Health,* 798 N.E.2d 941 (Mass. 2003).

53. The entire text of the president's speech is available at http://www.whitehouse.gov/news/releases/2004/02/20040224-2.html.

54. Leaming, "Marriage Proposal."

55. Matthew Hay Brown, "Senate to Revisit Same-Sex Marriage: Hope for a Ban Unites Many Faiths," *Baltimore Sun,* June 5, 2006.

56. Ibid.

57. Leaming, "Marriage Proposal," 198. The quotation refers to Rev. Jerry Falwell, prominent leader in the Religious Right and founder of Liberty University; Dr. James Dobson, head of Focus on the Family; Rev. Lou Sheldon, president of the Traditional Values Coalition; and Rev. Pat Robertson, founder the Christian Coalition, the American Center for Law and Justice, and Regent University.

58. The text of this letter ("Joint Letter from National Religious Groups") as well as the "Open Letter to Congress from America's Clergy," signed by over 2,200 clergy members, is available on the Clergy for Fairness website at http://www.clergyforfairness.org.

59. Frederick Liu and Stephen Macedo, "The Federal Marriage Amendment and the Strange Evolution of the Conservative Case against Gay Marriage," *PS: Political Science and Politics* 38, no. 2 (2005): 211–15.

60. Coolidge, "Evangelicals and the Same-Sex 'Marriage' Debate."

61. Ibid.

62. Chauncey, *Why Marriage?*; Daniel Pinello, *America's Struggle for Same-Sex Marriage* (Cambridge: Cambridge University Press, 2006).

63. Wilcox et al., "Saving Marriage by Banning Marriage," 57.

64. Ibid.

65. Green, "Ohio: The Bible and the Buckeye State."

66. James M. Penning and Corwin E. Smidt, "Michigan: A War on the Home Front?" in *The Values Campaign? The Christian Right and the 2004 Elections,* ed. John C. Green, Mark J. Rozell, and Clyde Wilcox (Washington, D.C.: Georgetown University Press, 2006).

67. Kirk Johnson, "Gay Marriage Losing Punch as Ballot Issue," *New York Times*, October 14, 2006.

68. New Mexico, New York, Rhode Island, and Washington, D.C. are the only states that do not explicitly prohibit marriage for same-sex couples nor provide marriage benefits through same-sex marriage or civil unions.

69. Pam Belluck, "State Legislators Let Same-Sex Marriage Vote Proceed," *New York Times*, January 3, 2007.

70. Barry L. Tadlock, C. Ann Gordon, and Elizabeth Popp, "Framing the Issue of Same-Sex Marriage: Traditional Values Versus Equal Rights," Paper presented at the American Political Science Association, Chicago 2004; Katherine Stenger, "Defining Right and Wrong: Religious Interest Groups and the Creation and Promotion of Morality-Based Arguments in Policy Debates," Paper presented at the Midwest Political Science Association, Chicago 2005.

71. Robert Entman, "Framing: Toward Clarification of a Fractured Paradigm," *Journal of Communication* 43, no. 4 (1993): 51–58; Thomas E. Nelson, Zoe M. Oxley, and Rosalee A. Clawson, "Toward a Psychology of Framing Effects," *Political Behavior* 19, no. 3 (1997): 221–46.

72. Shanto Iyengar, "Speaking of Values: The Framing of American Politics," *The Forum* 3, no. 3 (2005).

73. For an example of this research see Frank Baumgartner and Bryan D. Jones, *Agendas and Instability in American Politics* (Chicago: University of Chicago Press, 1993) or John W. Kingdon, *Agendas, Alternatives and Public Policies*, 2nd ed. (New York: Harper Collins College Publishers, 1995).

74. Donald R. Kinder and Lynn M. Sanders, *Divided by Color: Racial Politics and Democratic Ideals* (Chicago: University of Chicago Press, 1996).

75. Hull, "The Political Limits of the Rights Frame."

76. See George Lakoff's discussion of the development of these versions of morality in *Moral Politics*.

77. These two newspapers were selected for analysis because they are national in scope and are read by opinion leaders and policy elites. Additionally, back copies of each are easy to access and search through the Lexis-Nexis database. I analyzed 172 articles (74 from the *New York Times* and 98 from the *Washington Post*).

78. Howard Schneider and David A. Vise, "Side Issues Divert House Debate on D.C. Budget," *Washington Post*, November 2, 1995.

79. Adam Nagourney, "Christian Coalition Pushes for Showdown on Same-Sex Marriage," *New York Times*, May 30, 1996.

80. See, for example, Shanto Iyengar, "Speaking of Values"; Karen Callaghan and Frauke Schnell, "Assessing the Democratic Debate: How the News Media Frame Elite Policy Discourse," *Political Communication* 18 (2001): 183–212; or Nayda Terkidsen, Frauke Schnell, and Cristina Ling, "Interest Groups, the Media, and Policy Debate Formation: An Analysis of Message Structure," *Political Communication* 15, no. 1 (1998): 45–62.

81. Deana A. Rohlinger, "Framing the Abortion Debate: Organizational Resources, Media Strategies, and Movement-Countermovement Dynamics," *The Sociological Quarterly* 43, no. 4 (2002): 479–507.

82. I examined press releases issued by a sample of active religious interest groups taken from the list of groups mentioned in the newspaper articles from the *Washington Post* and *New York Times*.

83. Hull also makes the observation that argument frames in the debate in Hawaii lacked "any assertion of the positive moral worth of same-sex marriage" Kathleen E. Hull, "The Political Limits of the Rights Frame," 224. This finding may partially reflect the fact that religious groups advocating this frame were not included in media coverage of the debate.

84. Alison Beck, "Taking the Long View: Reflections on the Road to Marriage Equality," *Berkeley Journal of Gender, Law and Justice* 20 (2005): 50–55, 54.

85. Ibid.

FURTHER READING

The movement for gay and lesbian civil rights existed long before same-sex marriage moved on to the national political agenda. In the book, *Why Marriage? The History Shaping Today's Debate Over Gay Equality,* historian George Chauncey provides a thorough summary of the events leading up to the emergence of same-sex marriage as a primary goal for the gay rights movement. Conservative religious groups have been the most vocal and powerful opponents of gay rights groups. Journalists John Gallagher and Chris Bull narrate the history of these sparring partners in *Perfect Enemies: The Religious Right, the Gay Movement, and the Politics of the 1990s.* This book is particularly unique because it directly compares the two movements while providing a focused look at a selection of local, state, and federal debates involving gay rights.

The debate over same-sex marriage raises numerous empirical questions addressed in two edited volumes: *The Politics of Gay Rights* by Craig A. Rimmerman, Kenneth D. Wald and Clyde Wilcox and *The Values Campaign? The Christian Right and the 2004 Elections* by John C. Green, Mark J. Rozell and Clyde Wilcox. *The Politics of Gay Rights* examines the history of the gay movement, oppositions to the movement, particular policies related to gay rights, and the various political arenas in which decisions regarding gay rights are made. John Green provides a particularly interesting analysis of the religious basis of opposition to gay rights (chapter 6) and Donald Haider-Markel provides a thorough overview of policymaking at the state level, with attention to the religious groups active in state debates (chapter 13). *The Values Campaign* focuses on the impact of the Christian Right on the 2004 elections. In one particularly interesting chapter, Clyde Wilcox, Linda Merolla and David Beer examine how religious groups used the issue of same-sex marriage to mobilize voters and to reinvigorate the religious right movement (chapter 3).

3

Conscientious Objection to Military Service in the United States

Chad Michael Wayner and James F. Childress

To the ears of a community threatened by danger and seeped in fear, conscientious objection to military service may sound like a clarion call of individuality amid that anxious time when a political community seeks to assert its identity with one voice. When the objector appeals to his conscience, expressing fidelity to the norms and values of another community, the majority may too hastily mistake it for cowardice or treason. Yet, to recognize such a dissonant voice and grant the objector a special exemption from communal responsibilities may risk the dissolution of a shared communal life. To ignore that voice subjects the objector to the will of a fearful and threatened collectivity.

Conscientious objection then is a node at which basic suppositions about the individual and his[1] relation to the state converge. In the United States, a country whose Bill of Rights is surprisingly silent concerning the freedom of conscience, individual liberty has found its protection primarily through related rights of peaceable assembly, free exercise of religion, free speech, and due process. After over three centuries of grappling with conscientious objectors, the U.S. military currently designates a conscientious objector as one who "is conscientiously opposed to participation in war in any form; whose opposition is founded on religious training and belief; and whose position is sincere and deeply held."[2]

In this chapter, we will briefly survey the development and eventual recognition of conscientious objection by the United States and its military. We will then examine and analyze the arguments that support the current policy of exempting those objectors who sincerely object to war in any form. These arguments—more fully developed—may also provide support for exempting those who object to particular wars, often labeled selective conscientious objectors. We will conclude with some brief reflections concerning the lessons that conscientious objection may teach us about the relationship between the church and state in the United States.

HISTORY AND DEVELOPMENT

Since the earliest decades of European colonization in America, there have been conscientious objectors to military service.[3] Depending on the colony, the treatment of these early objectors differed vastly. At least as early as 1658, Quakers in Maryland who conscientiously refused to train with the local militia suffered stiff fines and the seizure of personal goods.[4] On the other hand, in 1673, the assembly of the colony of Rhode Island enacted a statute that allowed exemption from military training for conscientious objectors but also required them to serve the military in noncombatant roles if the colony came under attack—conveying weak, aged, or "impotent persons" from danger, administering "works of mercy" to the distressed, and serving as watchmen.[5]

A defining characteristic of these early conscientious objections was the consistent appeal to the words of Jesus recorded in the gospels of the New Testament. In 1661, George Fox and a handful of fellow Quakers submitted a "declaration from the harmless and innocent people of God" to King Charles II, noting,

Christ said to Peter, "Put up thy sword in his place" . . . yet after, when [Christ] had bid him put it up, he said, "He that taketh the sword shall perish with the sword" . . . The spirit of Christ, by which we are guided, is not changeable, so as once to command us from a thing as evil and again to move unto it; and we do certainly know, and so testify to the world, that the spirit of Christ, which leads us into all Truth, will never move us to fight and war against any man with outward weapons, neither for the kingdom of Christ, nor for the kingdoms of this world.[6]

On the basis of this testimony and its later development, Quakers in colonial America expected members of the Society of Friends not only to refuse to bear arms, but also to refuse to pay the fine that various colonies levied on those negligent in their militia duties.[7] Going further, some Quakers refused to pay any monies expressly destined for militia purposes.[8]

The words of Jesus also figured prominently in the Shakers' testimony to the legislature of New Hampshire from 1818, which describes the origins of their conscientious refusal not only to bearing weapons but also to hiring substitutes and paying fines:

> Christ ... taught both by precept and example, to love our enemies, to render good for evil, and to do to others as we would that others should do to us. He also commanded saying, put up again thy sword into his place, for all they that take the sword shall perish with the sword ... Christ has said, 'My Kingdom is not of this world.' And we cannot, as we have already shown, intermeddle with the affairs of both.[9]

Clearly it is the teachings of Jesus that sculpt the contours of the Shaker conscience, but perhaps more remarkable is that the Shaker testimony continues on to make a direct appeal for exemption from military service, on the basis of the "natural, inherent, and constitutional rights of conscience."[10] Allowing the Shakers to hire substitutes or pay fines in place of militia service would not sufficiently protect their liberty, as either "would be a virtual acknowledgement that the liberty of conscience is not our natural right; but may be purchased of government at a stated price."[11] In this Shaker testimony, one already begins to see the first indications of a shifting trajectory in the American conversation about conscientious objection. During the earliest years of objection to militia service in colonial America, the central concern of objectors was often to reveal that their *conscience* was the root of their objection, a conscience watered and fertilized by their religious convictions. Later, especially after the Revolutionary War and the ratification of the U.S. Constitution, conscientious objectors increasingly appealed to legislatures for protection, often invoking the language of rights.

In a way, the course of conscientious objection in the United States was decisively set during the congressional debates of the summer of 1789. Amid discussions about the content of what would become the Bill of Rights, James Madison proposed a host of amendments aimed at vesting political power with the people. Madison—among others—sought to address some of the worries that had beset the state legislatures of North Carolina and Rhode Island and made them hesitant to ratify the Constitution. Among the amendments, Madison proposed that "the right of the people to keep and bear arms shall not be infringed; a well armed and well regulated militia being the best security of a free country: *but no person religiously scrupulous of bearing arms shall be compelled to render military service in person.*"[12]

Ultimately, the first two clauses were accepted and approved by Congress, while the last clause—having received approval from the U.S. House of Representatives—was rejected by the U.S. Senate.[13]

Perhaps one of the reasons why the Senate removed the clause shielding the "religiously scrupulous" from militia service was that by 1789 twelve state constitutions already provided protection for the individual's freedom of conscience.[14] As more states were admitted throughout the early nineteenth century, many made express provision for conscientious objectors in their state constitutions, as long as objectors paid a fee for exemption—for example, Illinois (1818), Alabama (1819), Iowa (1846), Kentucky (1850), Indiana (1851), Kansas (1855), and Texas (1859).[15] Yet, despite the wide range of state protections, the qualification that objectors pay a fine or fund a substitute caused many who refused military service to suffer significant penalties.

One such objector was Alexander Rogers, a Rogerene[16] from Waterford, Connecticut, who refused to send his son to drill in the local "train-band." As penalty, Rogers lost his only cow, which he and his family depended upon for milk. In a letter to his fellow countrymen, Rogers invoked a biblical parable, asking "which of you on whom the Lord hath bestowed ten thousand talents should find his fellow servant that owed him fifty pence and take him by the throat, saying, 'Pay what thou owest me,' and on refusal, command his wife and children to be sold and payment to be made?"[17] For Rogers, the commands of Jesus and the state stood in stark contrast, noting that "because I have refused to obey man rather than God, you have taken away the principal part of the support of my family and commanded it to be sold at the post."[18] Like the majority of Quakers, the Rogerenes saw the payment of a fine or the hiring of a substitute to be an act of acquiescence that violated their Christian testimony. Other Christian objectors, like the Mennonites and the Brethren, conscientiously refused to bear arms, but were willing to pay the required fine; consequently, they encountered fewer difficulties in antebellum America.

Yet, it was not only Christian objectors that endured penalties and punishment during this time, for the early part of the nineteenth century also felt the first winds of conscientious objection that did not draw upon religious convictions. In 1828, the American Peace Society was founded upon the unification of the Massachusetts Peace Society and the New York Peace Society. William Lloyd Garrison was a member of this Society until 1838, when he led a group of more radical peace advocates to break from the Society and form the New England Non-Resistance Society. On one occasion, Garrison found himself in court to pay a fine for failing to partake in the "pomp and circumstance" of the local militia muster; he noted that "I am not professedly a Quaker, but I heartily, entirely and practically embrace the doctrine of non-resistance, and am conscientiously opposed to all military exhibitions... I will never obey any order to bear arms, but rather cheerfully suffer imprisonment and persecution."[19] Henry David Thoreau also advocated for the protection of individual liberty, as well as the practice of conscientious objection. In 1846, Thoreau found himself in jail for a single night after refusing to pay six years of poll taxes, since he was scrupulous to guard his acts of allegiance to the state, a state that was at that time embroiled in a war with Mexico, and permitted slavery. In his essay on civil disobedience—an essay which one historian has called the "most uniquely radical document in American history [after the Constitution]"[20]—Thoreau offered the grounds for his selective tax resistance[21]:

After all, the practical reason why, when the power is once in the hands of the people, a majority are permitted... to rule, is not because they are most likely to be in the right, nor because this seems fairest to the minority, but because they are physically the strongest. But a government in which the majority rule in all cases cannot be based on justice, even as far as men understand it. Can there not be a government in which majorities do not virtually decide right and wrong, but conscience?... Must the citizen ever for a moment, or in the least degree, resign his conscience to the legislator? Why has every man a conscience then? I think that we should be men first, and subjects afterward. It is not desirable to cultivate a respect for the law, so much as for the right.[22]

Thoreau refused to pay the tax because he wanted the individual to be able to dictate the times and places where allegiance would be demanded, creating space to occasionally "stand aloof from [the state] effectually."[23] For Thoreau, the authority of government emerged only from the express sanction and consent of the governed; the "really free and enlightened State" is that which recognizes the individual as a higher and independent power.[24]

For many members of historically pacifist churches, the Civil War raised a poignant conflict, as many strongly supported the abolition of slavery alongside their tradition of nonviolence. Initially, the conscription acts of the North and South offered conscientious objectors no avenues for exemption. According to the Enrollment Act of March 3, 1863, conscripts from the northern states were permitted to pay three hundred dollars to avoid military service. However, on February 24, 1864, legislators revised the conscription act such that "members of religious denominations, who shall by oath or affirmation declare that they are conscientiously opposed to the bearing of arms... shall... be considered non-combatants, and shall be assigned by the Secretary of War to duty in the hospitals, or to the care of freedmen, or shall pay the sum of three hundred dollars . . . to be applied to the benefit of the sick and wounded soldiers."[25] Confederate objectors endured greater difficulties than their Union counterparts. As many objectors openly opposed slavery, Southerners found the loyalty of objectors—especially Quakers, Mennonites, and Dunkers—to be suspect. The first conscription act of the Confederacy was passed in April 1862, and it provided exemption for a wide range of occupations—for example, newspapermen, lawyers, school teachers, druggists, ferrymen, tanners, shoemakers, and so on—but not expressly for those who conscientiously opposed military service.[26] Not until October 1862 did the Confederate states pass a law enabling conscientious objectors to be exempt, though it required them to pay five hundred dollars (or hire a substitute) for this act of legislative grace—this amount was more than a year's wages for those objectors who tilled small farms.[27] During the last weeks of the war, the Confederacy passed legislation that banned exemptions from military service in order to alleviate their serious shortage of soldiers.

During the fifty years separating the American Civil War from the First World War, no military conflicts demanded conscription, and few studies exist that document the activity of conscientious objectors during these intervening years. When, upon its entry into World War I, the United States issued its Selective Draft Act of 1917, it did not permit commutation fees or the hiring of substitutes. Draft boards were permitted to designate members of a "well-recognized religious sect or organization" for noncombatant roles that were then yet to be determined by President Wilson.[28] However, in practice, draft boards broadened this criterion, since the late-nineteenth and early-twentieth centuries had brought waves of new immigrants to the United States and seen the emergence of several new indigenous religious sects. Consequently, objectors included not only the more familiar Quakers and Mennonites, but also Molokans, Dukhobors, Adventists, Jehovah's Witnesses, Russellites, Christadelphians, and various Brethren groups.[29]

Support for the war in some places intoned a shrill pitch, so much so that private citizens voluntarily joined the Department of Justice and local police in ferreting out draft evaders. On one occasion, men arriving by ferry in New York City were forced to display their draft cards.[30] Yet, this passionate patriotism was not universal, and the conscription act cast a spotlight upon the increasing number of conscientious objectors who did not belong to an historically pacifist religious community. In fact, the Adjutant General of the Army issued a directive in December 1917 addressing these "nonreligious" objectors, advocating that "until further instructions on the subject are issued 'personal scruples against war' should be considered as constituting 'conscientious objection' and such persons should be treated in the same manner as other 'conscientious objectors' . . . "[31] In practice, however, the Adjutant General's directive had little influence; the primary responsibility for parsing the acceptable objectors from the unacceptable fell on the shoulders of three men on President Wilson's Board of Inquiry: Major Walter Kellogg, U.S. Circuit Court judge Julian Mack, and Harlan Stone of Columbia Law School.[32] Challenges and appeals to the Board's decisions worked their way through the court system during late 1917 and early 1918, marking an important transition in the handling of conscientious objectors. Prior to the First World War, the policy toward and treatment of conscientious objectors was determined by the executive branch of government and military leaders. Following the conscription for the First World War, the court system was increasingly called upon to adjudicate the perceived unfairness of conscientious objector provisions.

Army records note that nearly 65,000 men sought conscientious objector status between May 1917 and November 1918, only a small fraction of the nearly ten million draftees. Nearly 57,000 of these claims were judged to be sincere and valid. Of these objectors, the army inducted nearly 21,000, with 3,989 men maintaining their objections upon arrival in military camp.[33] Ultimately, about five hundred men refused the alternative noncombatant service offered by President Wilson and were subsequently subjected to court martial. Seventeen of these "absolutists" were sentenced to death, and 142 men were given life imprisonment. Though none of these sentences were carried to fruition, the last conscientious objector from the First World War was not pardoned and released until 1933.[34]

Given the widespread support for the war, one historian has noted that "conscientious objection to World War I received almost no support from major churches and synagogues and considerable antagonism from the great bulk of traditional religious people."[35] Objectors who refused the alternative noncombatant service (or were not deemed eligible) faced substantial hardships. Jehovah's Witnesses were routinely jailed, as their beliefs required them to fight in an apocalyptic war at Armageddon (prophesied in the last book of the Bible), but demanded that they not fight in any other wars. Many conscientious objectors were incarcerated alongside traitors, at Leavenworth and Alcatraz. In military camp and in jail, many objectors suffered cruelty and torture, ranging from physical beatings to being strung up by their fingers with nothing but their extended toes to support their bodyweight.[36] Others undertook a hunger strike to protest their treatment and were forcibly fed. As many as seventeen objectors died from pneumonia and other ailments that resulted from the prison conditions.[37] Lillian Schlissel attributes some of the decline in support for conscientious objectors during this period to the changing public image of the objector. Prior to the First World War, the ready image of the conscientious objector in the public mind might be a Quaker colonial like William Penn. During and after the war, given the influx of immigrants and the more vocal and prominent "political" pacifists (like Socialist Eugene Debs), the public increasingly saw the conscientious objector as a political radical, communist, anarchist, atheist, or "yellowback."[38]

These imprisoned conscientious objectors did not go wholly unnoticed by Congress. In 1919, amid increasingly public concerns about the treatment of conscientious objectors, Congress opened hearings that exposed a wide variety of perspectives on conscientious objection, perhaps most memorably, those unsympathetic. In one speech, a Congressman railed against those objectors who were "German sympathizers" and "craven cowards."[39] Yet the experiences of these conscientious objectors had effects that extended far beyond Washington and into years to come. Roger Baldwin, an objector who was director of the American Union against Militarism, received a one-year sentence to federal prison on October 30, 1918, a mere twelve days before the armistice with Germany. In Baldwin's statement to the court on his sentencing day, he remarked that "now comes the government to take me from that service and to demand of me a service I cannot in conscience undertake. I refuse it simply for my own peace of mind and spirit, for the satisfaction of that inner demand more compelling than any consideration of punishment or the sacrifice of friendships and reputation."[40] After his release, Baldwin, Helen Keller, Crystal Eastman, and others joined together in 1920 to form the American Civil Liberties Union, which in later years provided legal counsel for conscientious objectors. In addition, reports of these abuses of conscientious objectors catalyzed the formation of numerous peace organizations, religious and secular. Joining the already existent Fellowship of Reconciliation[41] (1914) were the American Friends Service Committee (1917) and the War Resisters League (1923). The First World War represented the first time that the members of historic peace churches were the minority among pacifists, and slowly and subtly the conversation over conscientious objection began to incorporate a wider array of voices from non-pacifist religious communities and secular organizations.[42]

An additional shift was also taking place. As the voices of conscientious objection appealed to more common understandings of liberty instead of the words of Jesus in the New Testament, they increasingly sought judicial recognition for their asserted rights. In 1930, the Supreme Court heard the case of *United States v. Macintosh*,[43] in which Douglas Macintosh—Baptist pastor and professor of theology at Yale University—was refused American citizenship because he stated on his application that he would not bear arms in defense of the United States unless he believed that the war was morally justified. The justices sustained the denial of citizenship to Macintosh by a vote of five to four, mainly because they construed nationalization as a privilege subject to restrictions laid down by Congress. Justice Sutherland's majority opinion notes that "the privilege of the native-born conscientious objector to avoid bearing arms comes not from the Constitution, but from the acts of Congress." While concurring with this principle, Chief Justice Hughes, in his dissent, argued that acknowledging Congressional authority does not preclude one from also granting space for the authority of conscience, writing that "there is abundant room for enforcing the requisite authority of law . . . and for maintaining . . . the supremacy of law . . . without demanding that either citizens or applicants for citizenship shall assume by oath an obligation to regard allegiance to God as subordinate to allegiance to civil power." This exchange between Sutherland and Hughes fixed the crucial question for the court cases yet to come—even if the authority to extend the privilege of conscientious objection resides in Congress, ought that authority require one's full and unqualified allegiance?[44]

The year 1940 saw the passage of the first prewar national conscription law. The rapid German conquest of Western Europe gave little time for deliberation, but given the relatively fresh memory of the treatment of conscientious objectors in the First World War and the prevalence of active peace societies, the Selective Training and Service Act of 1940 offered significant concessions for members of peace churches and also other pacifists. Perhaps taking inspiration from the early Rhode Island policy on conscientious objectors, the Act exempted those "who, by reason of religious training and belief, [are] conscientiously opposed to participation in war in any form."[45] Even further, those who objected to any participation in noncombatant service under the military's auspices could be assigned "to work of national importance under civilian direction." Not only had Congress broadened the scope of exemption—going beyond members of well-established pacifist religious sects to include all objectors whose conscience was formed by religious training and belief—but it had offered "absolutists" an alternative, nonmilitary service.

In the Second World War, up to fifty thousand men petitioned for conscientious objector status, with some willing to perform noncombatant service, others alternative civilian service, and the remainder—absolutely opposed to any form of alternate service—left to serve time in prison.[46] Although the number of conscientious objectors was less than one-tenth of one percent of the ten million soldiers drafted for the war, Cynthia Eller notes that this represented an eight or ninefold increase in the number of conscientious objectors from the First World War.[47] Most of those willing to serve in noncombatant military roles entered the medical corps. Objectors who labored in alternative civilian service undertook projects in soil erosion control, forestry, and agriculture, doing so without pay, and under the control of the National Service Board for Religious Objectors.[48] Jehovah's Witnesses made up the majority of the nearly six thousand men subjected to incarceration as conscientious objectors, largely due to their "absolutist" position, which refused to accept any form of alternative civilian service.[49] At the end of 1946, well over a year after Japan's surrender, more than three hundred objectors remained incarcerated.[50]

Throughout the war, many objectors pled their case before the courts, often resulting in vastly different outcomes. In a 1943 case—*United States v. Downer*[51]—the Second Circuit Court of Appeals concluded that a deep-rooted conscientious objection based in "a general humanitarian concept which is essentially religious in character" is sufficient to receive conscientious objector status. It initially appeared that the court had established a sweeping interpretive move, expansively broadening the requirement that a conscientious objector derive his objection from his religious training and belief, perhaps going so far as to render this requirement superfluous. While this court broadened the interpretation of religion, it retained the requirement of pacifist convictions for exemption from military service on grounds of conscience. In the same year, this court ruled in *United States v. Kauten*[52] that conscientious objectors who refused to serve in a particular war would not be granted exemption. Judge Augustus Hand argued that these selective objectors were often political objectors, noting that "there is a distinction between a course of reasoning resulting in a conviction that a particular war is inexpedient or disastrous and a conscientious objection to participation in any war under any circumstances . . . The former is usually a political objection, while the latter, we think, may justly be regarded as a response of the individual to an inward mentor, call it conscience or God, that is for many persons at the present time the equivalent of what has always been thought a religious impulse."[53] In the midst of a war in the Pacific and Europe, the court was willing to interpret the "religious training and belief" clause in the broadest sense, but was stringent in its interpretation of the clause that required opposition to "participation in war in any form." Judge Hand's rationale focused on the contrast between those who pursue exemption for reasons of expediency with those who pursue it for reasons of conscience. For this reason, Hand's distinction was important for directing the court's attention in later decisions to the role of the objector's motive in a valid objection.

In 1946, in *United States v. Berman*, the Ninth Circuit Court took up the matter of religious training and belief again, but in direct opposition to the ruling in *Downer*, this circuit court concluded that "religious training and belief" must be interpreted rigidly. Berman was a humanitarian and a socialist, whose objection, while universal (that is, opposed to participation in any war), did not arise from "religious training and belief," and thus the Court found him ineligible for exemption. To remedy this perceived conundrum between *Downer* and *Berman*, Congress revised its selective service policy in 1948, siding with the Ninth Court's reading, by adding the explicit qualification that one's conscience and belief would not qualify for exemption if either included "essentially political, sociological, or philosophical views or a merely personal moral code."[54] In addition, Congress specified that a conscientious objection grounded in one's religious training and belief must include "an individual's belief in a relation to a Supreme Being."[55]

Within the courts, this issue was readdressed in 1965, with the Supreme Court's decision in *United States v. Seeger*. Though Daniel Seeger had applied for conscientious objector status and did not *disavow* a belief in a relation to a Supreme Being, the draft board did not grant his exemption because he did not expressly affirm his belief in a relation to such a Being. In *Seeger*, the Court ruled that it was not the task of a draft board or the courts to determine whether Seeger's given belief about God was true, but merely whether it was truly held. In Seeger's case, the Court found that he truly believed in some relation to some being. In order to clearly establish the judicial precedent for future decisions, the Court proposed a test for evaluating sincerity, namely "a sincere and meaningful belief [is that] which occupies in the life of its possessor a place parallel to that filled by the God of those admittedly qualifying for the exemption . . . " In so doing, the Court avoided facing the constitutional question as to whether this statute violated the Establishment Clause of the First Amendment, but that question would not go away.

Finally, in 1970, the Supreme Court dealt the final blow to the Supreme Being requirement of the Selective Service Act of 1948. In *Welsh v. United States*, the Court exempted from military service even those objectors who held atheistic beliefs, so long as their conscientious objection rested on ethical and moral beliefs. In *Welsh*, Justice Harlan, in a concurring opinion, contended that while Seeger was "a remarkable feat of judicial surgery" because it removed the theistic requirement of the statute, *Welsh* performed "a lobotomy." The *Welsh* decision salvaged the statute's constitutionality, but in so doing, "completely transformed the statute by reading out of it any distinction between religiously acquired beliefs and those deriving from 'essentially political, sociological, or philosophical views or a merely personal moral code.'" Thus, the courts removed one of the central statutory limits on conscientious objection at the same time that the United States was embroiled in an increasingly unpopular war in Vietnam.

However, the Court did not remove all of the limits. In 1971, the Supreme Court revisited the issue of selective objectors in *Gillette v. United States*. By 1971, the United States had been conscripting soldiers for more than half a decade. Local draft boards were inundated with applications for conscientious objector status. 1972 would see over one hundred and thirty objectors exempted from military service for every one hundred soldiers enlisted.[56] By the time the draft ended in 1973, more conscripts were classified as conscientious objectors than were inducted into the army.[57] In *Gillette*, the Court held that only those conscientious objectors who refused participation in any war in any form were exempt from service. Since it would be difficult to set fair standards for draft broads to use in assessing selective objectors, the Court held that Congress had valid, neutral reasons to exempt only absolute or universal objectors. In 1973, amid fervent public protests and heightened criticism, the United States adopted a fully volunteer armed force, which has continued to the present.

Since 1973, conscientious objection to military service now only arises among members of the armed services whose objection coalesced and emerged after enlistment. Between 1985 and 1990, between 90 and 240 enlisted personnel per year applied for conscientious objector status out of a total enlisted force of over two million.[58] In 1990 and 1991, in preparation for a potential military confrontation in the Persian Gulf, between fifteen hundred and two thousand active-duty members and reservists applied for conscientious objector status.[59] Some cities, including San Francisco, Berkeley, and Oakland, declared themselves to be sanctuaries for those soldiers who conscientiously opposed service in the Persian Gulf.[60] Members of Congress discussed the possibility of reinstituting the draft, but concluded that it was not necessary. The National Interreligious Service Board for Conscientious Objectors (NISBCO) estimated that if the draft had been instituted in the early 1990s, up to 20 percent, or 320,000 conscripts would have petitioned for conscientious objector status.[61]

Currently, the Department of Defense Directive 1300.6 is the operative conscientious objector policy for uniformed military personnel. The Directive defines conscientious objection as "a firm, fixed and sincere objection to participation in war in any form or the bearing of arms, by reason of religious training and belief," and it distinguishes two classes of objectors: those who object to any participation in war, and those who object to combatant participation in war.[62] The procedure for granting objector status and discharge requires that a soldier undergo a twofold assessment, by a chaplain and by a psychiatrist. Some commentators worry that this procedure may build in assumptions about a uniformed objector's mental stability that are likely unwarranted.[63] Further, the procedure may cause the evaluation of a soldier's sincerity to rely too heavily on the "orthodoxy" of the objector's claims, requiring that the soldier's beliefs cohere with an established pacifist tradition. An additional concern is that the current policy could be more explicit about providing enlisted personnel with proper and fair treatment in those instances in which the petition for conscientious objector status is denied.[64]

Over the centuries, conscientious objection in early America and the United States has substantially transformed—many more now object, and they do so for a wider variety of reasons. What was originally the province of a handful of Quaker and Mennonite immigrants has grown to include Christians from a wide variety of traditions and communities, and Muslims, humanists, and secularists as well. Legal protections and exemptions for conscientious objectors, though still conceived by many as an act of legislative grace, are more firmly planted in our legal and military codes than ever before. As others have noted, we face a "new conscientious objection" in the United States alongside the "old" forms, as we now protect not only the conscience formed by a religious community, but also that formed by secular beliefs and practices.[65]

CONSCIENTIOUS OBJECTION—PRESENT AND FUTURE

Much of the recent legal and ethical analysis surrounding conscientious objection emerged during a time when the United States was actively drafting its citizens for an increasingly unpopular war.[66] Since the dissolution of the draft, conscientious objection to military service has not received the attention of seasons past. Yet some important ethical and legal issues remain, issues that—were they are taken up by Congress and the courts—would further reveal the contours of the relationship between church and state in the United States. One of the most important is whether there are justifiable reasons for sharply distinguishing between absolute or universal conscientious objectors (UCOs), that is, pacifists who object to participation in any and all wars, from those objectors who are conscientiously opposed to particular wars (selective conscientious objectors or SCOs). If history is instructive, it is likely that selective conscientious objection will again receive the public scrutiny that it did in the United States during the Vietnam War era. Sound and weighty arguments can be made for treating SCOs on par with UCOs, but there are important counterarguments as well. In what follows, we will present three major arguments against exemption for SCOs: the first maintains that the selective conscientious objections are essentially political and do not warrant special protection; a second argument holds that exemptions for SCOs may lead to selective disobedience to the law; finally, a third argument asserts that exempting SCOs will damage the morale and effectiveness of the armed forces. We will assess the adequacy of each argument, and conclude with some reflections on the use of sincerity as a test for conscientious objector exemption from military service.[67]

The Nature of the Selective Conscientious Objector's Claims

A major argument against exemption for SCOs contends that their objections to a particular war are necessarily political rather than a matter of ethical or religious conscience and thus do not merit exemption from military service. As we have already seen, versions of this argument have appeared now and again, particularly in debates about how to characterize objections to military service during the Vietnam War. For instance, a sharp formulation appears in the 1967 Report of the National Advisory Commission on Selective Service, entitled *In Pursuit of Equity: Who Serves When Not All Serve?*:

> [s]o-called selective pacifism is essentially a political question of support or nonsupport of a war and cannot be judged in terms of special moral imperatives. Political opposition to a particular war should be expressed through recognized democratic processes and should claim no special right of exemption from democratic decisions.[68]

If this argument holds, it will obviously provide an important premise for other arguments that oppose exemption for SCOs. Hence, a critical question is whether it is a sound argument. It is important to note that in seeking to determine whether an act of selective conscientious objection is "essentially political," rather than moral, the distinction of interest is between moral and non-moral reasons, not between moral and immoral reasons. The relevant distinction concerns the classification of reasons in terms of their domains, not whether some reasons are, evaluatively speaking, moral or immoral. It is descriptive rather than normative. A reason could be descriptively classified as moral, but, at the same time, be, evaluatively, immoral. Similarly, it could be non-moral but not immoral. For instance, it could be an economic reason but not, for that reason alone, immoral.

A person drafted into military service in a time of war might offer several kinds of reasons for claiming that his participation in a particular war would violate his conscience and that he should be exempted from the requirement to serve in the military:

1. All wars are wrong.
2. Our aims in this war are unjust.
3. The evil effects of this particular war will probably outweigh its good effects.
4. This particular war is wrong because we are directly killing noncombatants.

We are familiar with the first reason as a pacifist reason, offered by the absolute or universal conscientious objector who disavows participation in any war. That reason has a home in religious and secular pacifist traditions, but it may take a variety of forms.[69]

In contrast to the pacifist approach represented in (1), the other three reasons do appear, at first analysis, to operate on a different plane. Rather than addressing all wars, they focus on a particular war, whether in terms of its aims, its probable balance of bad effects over good effects, or its conduct. These claims are not exhaustive possibilities for the SCO, but they do represent major elements in the broad just-war tradition, which has been the dominant moral framework for deliberation about war in Roman Catholic, mainline Protestant, and many secular organizations.[70] The individual SCO is making a claim about his conscience, parallel to the pacifist objector, and he too may draw on a rich historical tradition, again just as the pacifist, in articulating his own conscience. The question that arises then is whether reasons are essentially political rather than moral.

In this discussion, we will stress that the SCO's qualified judgment about war, the complexity of his reasons, and his appeal to the facts of the situation do not necessarily make his position less "moral" than the UCO's. All four judgments focus on a governmental policy of war. This is their subject matter. Hence, the subject matter alone will not warrant a distinction between a political judgment and a moral judgment. UCOs and SCOs alike render a negative judgment on a governmental policy, at least to the extent of indicating that they cannot, in conscience, participate in the implementation of that policy. They may or may not go on to argue that no one should participate in that implementation. Thus, we cannot appeal to the subject matter in order to distinguish moral reasons from political reasons.

Some who charge that selective conscientious objection is "essentially political" concede that both UCOs and SCOs make a judgment about government policy—and hence are "political" in that limited sense—but they further contend that SCOs take an "essentially political" position because they are offering a judgment about their own government's policy.[71] While the UCO condemns all governments for their policies of war, the SCO by contrast specifically condemns the particular policy of war of his own government. However, it is logically possible for the SCO to hold that both belligerents are waging an unjust war (e.g., when two powers are seeking to expand their territorial influence). Nevertheless, it is accurate to say that in many cases (perhaps most) the SCO will hold that his own government's policies are unjust—his own government's war aims are unjust, his own government's warfare is likely to produce a balance of bad over good outcomes, and his own government's military is conducting the war unjustly. Then the question is whether directing a criticism at one's own government's policy of war necessarily makes that criticism "essentially political" rather than moral.

The distinction between *subject matter*—whether war as a social practice or one's own government's particular war—and the *nature of the judgments* made about that subject matter is a crucial one.[72] An agent may make moral, political, economic, aesthetic or other kinds of judgments about governmental policy. Take a non-military example. Suppose we criticize a member of Congress for opposing a bill to protect the environment. We could criticize him or her for yielding to the demands of a particular constituency, perhaps one that could help his or her reelection, or we could criticize it as unethical because it fails to protect the environment, which has intrinsic ethical value, or because it fails to protect human beings whose long-term health could be threatened by environmental degradation. These judgments share a subject matter—a political act—but they are different and have different grounds. One is clearly more political, while the other, in either of its two forms, is clearly more ethical. Again, this is a matter of classification of kinds of reasons, not an evaluation of their merits.

But skeptics of the possibility of exempting the SCO from military service may still wonder whether this distinction between subject matter and the nature of the moral judgment captures what is crucially important. Even if both the UCO and the SCO make a moral judgment about a governmental policy, the skeptic may stress the differences in kinds of moral judgment. For instance, the skeptic may hold that consideration of the consequences of a war, as in the third position above ("the evil effects of this war will probably outweigh its good effects"), is political. But the distinction between consequentialist reasoning (appealing to the probable consequences of courses of actions) and deontological reasoning (appealing to some standards of right and wrong independent of acts' probable effects) does not map onto the distinction between political reasons and moral reasons. Not only will it not enable us to distinguish political judgments from moral judgments, it will not enable us to distinguish SCOs from UCOs. Instead, these two types of reasoning appear in political as well as in a variety of other activities. Even if the government's reasoning about undertaking and conducting a particular war is largely consequentialist in nature, this does not mean that its reasoning is political rather than moral—again, it is a matter of the kinds of reasons, not their merit.

The mode of moral reasoning then—that is, consequentialist or deontological—does not suffice to distinguish SCOs from UCOs. Although many pacifist positions (for instance, those held by many Mennonite, Brethren, and Quakers) are deontological in nature—that is, they hold that pacifism represents the right course of action, without regard for its consequences—pacifist positions may also be grounded in consequentialist judgments, for instance, that all wars produce a net balance of bad over good effects. Similarly, SCOs may employ deontological or consequentialist reasoning or both. Insofar as SCOs draw on the just-war tradition, they are drawing on a tradition that itself embodies both kinds of reasoning. Consider, for example, the criteria of the just-war tradition identified by the U.S. Catholic Bishops in *The Challenge of Peace: God's Promise and Our Response*. The bishops offer several criteria for determining the rightness or justice of waging war (known as *jus ad bellum* criteria): (a) just cause; (b) competent authority; (c) comparative justice; (d) right intention; (e) last resort; (f) probability of success; (g) proportionality. They then identify two criteria for assessing the justice or rightness of the conduct of war (known as *jus in bello* criteria): discrimination and proportionality. Discrimination focuses on distinguishing non-combatants from combatants and refraining from directly attacking non-combatants, while proportionality focuses on the balance of probable good and bad effects in particular actions in war (in contrast to the war as a whole, which is a concern for *jus ad bellum*).

Some critics of a possible legal exemption from military service for SCOs would concede that SCOs may employ deontological reasoning, either alone or in combination with consequentialist reasoning, as in reasons 2–4 above. Nevertheless, they may further argue, SCOs do not experience that "can't help" that marks sincere UCOs. According to John Rohr, selective conscientious objection is not a "'can't help,' but is based on arguments that are constitutional, political and historical—as well as moral or religious."[73]

However, it is not so clear that SCOs do not or cannot experience a "can't help" situation. An agent who appeals to his conscience as a motive for his conduct claims that if he acted against certain moral convictions, he would experience a severe personal sanction: guilt and shame and a loss of integrity, wholeness, and unity in the self.[74] But this experience of conscience, this "can't help," may be the outcome of processes of moral deliberation. Although a person's appeal to his conscience usually involves an appeal to moral standards, conscience is not itself the standard. It is the mode of consciousness resulting from his application of standards to his conduct. As James Childress has written, the appeal to conscience

> is not limited to intuitionists who hear voices of conscience or to fideists who hear the voice of God. It may result from a complex application of several principles to a set of circumstances. The possibility that the war itself may change, or that the agent's interpretation of the facts may change, in no way alters the moral or conscientious nature of his opposition to the war.[75]

Hence, a person's "can't help" in the face of some societal or governmental demand, such as conscription for military service, may emerge from a variety of ethical sources and forces.

Fairness and Respect for Persons

Much hinges on the previous discussion of the nature of the reasons offered by SCOs and UCOs. If one assumes that the UCO's reasons are morally based and the SCO's reasons are politically based, then the ethical principles of fairness and respect for persons would offer very limited support for the SCO's exemption from military service. However, it does not appear possible to slot the SCO's reasons into a non-moral chamber labeled "political." The SCO's reasons belong to the moral domain, just as the UCO's reasons do. Hence, the principles of fairness and respect for persons may support exemption for SCOs just as they do for UCOs.

First, fairness or formal justice at a minimum requires treating relevantly similar cases in a similar way. One could argue that the UCO and the SCO are relevantly similar. At least their reasons are relevantly similar: both are conscientiously opposed to participation in a war for moral and, often, religious reasons. If Congress exempts the UCO from military service, it appears to be unfair not to exempt the SCO because of the content (such as just-war theory) or the scope (such as viewing killing in some wars as justified) of his moral principles.[76] As we have seen, it is hard to view either the content or the scope of his principles as necessitating a label of "political" rather than "moral." An SCO should be entitled to treatment similar to that of the UCO. A policy that exempts the UCO while forcing the SCO to serve is on its face unfair. It puts the SCO at an unfair disadvantage.

Another version of the fairness principle appeared in the argument offered by some members of the National Advisory Commission on Selective Service who contended that a policy restricting exemption to UCOs discriminates against citizens in the mainstream of Jewish, Christian, and hu-

Conscientious Objection to Military Service in the United States • 93

manist thought and practice in the West. It does so, according to this argument, by offering legal recognition to a "minority" or "sectarian" position (pacifism) while excluding the "consensus" position (just-war theory).[77] This argument was rejected by the majority of the commission.

A second argument focuses on equal respect and contends that denying the SCO exemption from military service while granting exemption to the UCO denies the SCO equal respect. If, for the purposes of argument, the principle of respect for persons requires respect for conscientious objection, exemption from military service cannot be justly granted to UCOs and denied to SCOs simply because SCOs appeal to principles of just war rather than pacifism. Nothing in the difference in content or scope of the two sets of principles and moral reasoning provides a warrant for denying exemption to the SCO. The denial is disrespectful to SCOs.

These arguments based on fairness (or formal justice) and on respect for persons offer strong *prima facie* support for the exemption of SCOs from military service, one parallel to the exemption that UCOs enjoy. However, whether such a policy is ultimately viewed as acceptable will depend in part on the prediction and assessment of its consequences, as compared with the narrow exemption granted to UCOs. Opponents of a broader exemption stress that some of the worst consequences can be expected to flow from the difficulties of fairly administering an exemption for SCOs. Hence, the principle of fairness may have more than one implication in the debate about the legal status of selective conscientious objection—it may have both supportive and critical implications.

Consequentialist Arguments

In *Gillette v. United States*, the Supreme Court held that Congress had valid, neutral, and secular reasons to exempt the UCO but not the SCO from military service. The government had offered lines of argument based on (1) the nature of SCO claims (that is, that selective conscientious objection is basically political) and (2) fairness (that the administration of selective conscientious objection would be erratic, uneven, and even unfair). The Court rejected the first line of argument, at least in its narrow sense, emphasizing that selective conscientious objection may be "rooted in religion and conscience," whatever other judgments are involved. Nevertheless, the Court held that the nature of selective conscientious objection, in conjunction with the fairness argument, could support the statutory restriction to UCO. Bad consequences might arise if SCOs were exempted from military service because such an exemption could not be fairly administered in view of the "uncertain dimensions" and "indeterminate scope" of the claims of SCOs. As the Court wrote:

> But real dangers . . . might arise if an exemption were made available that in its nature could not be administered fairly and uniformly over the run of relevant fact situations. Should it be thought that those who go to war are chosen unfairly or capriciously, then a mood of bitterness and cynicism might corrode the spirit of public service and the values of willing performance of a citizen's duties that are the very heart of free government. . . . In light of these valid concerns, we conclude that it is supportable for Congress to have decided that the objector to all war—to all killing in war—has a claim that is distinct enough and intense enough to justify special status, while the objector to a particular war does not.[78]

The Court undertook this analysis of policies in order to determine whether Congress had a neutral, secular justification for drawing the lines as it did. If it found that such a justification existed, the Court could then hold that Congress's refusal to exempt SCOs from military service did not violate either the Establishment Clause or the Free Exercise Clause of the First Amendment. However, it is important to note, the Court's decision did not imply that Congress "would have acted irrationally or unreasonably had it decided to exempt those who object to particular wars."[79] Furthermore, the Court's concern about fairly administering conscientious objector exemptions may also be applicable, to some extent, to pacifists. The administration of a provision for UCOs might favor the "more articulate, better educated, or better counseled," and might favor claims more closely connected to conventional religiosity.

Those who support exempting SCOs from military service attempt to address the Court's concerns about the probable consequences of such a policy. Most often they seek to show that the consequences of such a policy are either not as probable or not as negative as opponents claim. This is their main argumentative strategy, even though occasionally they also adduce the probable good effects of such a policy—for instance, in fostering significant moral discourse about foreign policy and warfare as well as embodying in policy relevant ethical principles such as respect for conscience—and contend that those probable good effects will outweigh the probable bad effects, if any.

In the absence of relevant societal experience or experiments, the consequentialist arguments against SCO exemption from military service are, to a great extent, inevitably speculative. They point to possibilities (what could happen) rather than to probabilities (what probably would happen) as a result of the exemption of SCOs from military service. Ideally, of course, public policy regarding SCOs, and other matters, would rest on sound predictions and evaluations of probable positive and negative consequences. And yet the language of possibility dominates the consequentialist arguments against SCO exemption from military service. One important example is illustrative. The report of the majority of the National Advisory Commission on Selective Service, *In Pursuit of Equity*, which was used by the Supreme Court in *Gillette v. United States*, argued that "legal recognition of selective pacifism could open the doors to a general theory of selective disobedience to law, which could quickly tear down the fabric of government" and "could be disruptive to the morale and effectiveness of the Armed Forces."[80] An evaluation of any proposed policy of exemption for SCOs from military service needs to analyze and assess concerns about these possible consequences, marked as what "could" happen, in light of the best available evidence.

Selective Disobedience to the Law

A first question is whether the argument that the legal exemption of SCOs could or would lead to selective disobedience to the law is well founded. This argument was made in the context of SCO claims for exemption from military service in the heat of the war in Vietnam. It appears to be a version of the thin-edge-of-the wedge or the slippery-slope argument, here stated as an "open door" argument: if we grant X, then Y will follow. If the government grants SCOs legal exemption from military service, "a general theory of selective disobedience to law" could enter the now opened door.

It is possible to respond to this argument in a couple of ways. On the one hand, SCOs were claiming the same right of exemption as UCOs. If the wedge or slippery slope or open door argument holds for SCOs, it would appear also to hold for UCOs. Whether the request for an exemption from conscription for military service is based on UCO claims or SCO claims has no obvious bearing on "selective disobedience to law." After all, both the UCO and the SCO seek exemption from a particular law. It is not clear why their grounds—pacifism or just-war criteria—should or could make any difference. Nor is it clear why granting the SCO an exemption would create this threat of "selective disobedience to law" when the exemption for UCO apparently does not. After all, to take opposition to the payment of a particular tax—an example used by the National Advisory Commission—many UCOs also oppose the payment of taxes that support the military system, and they, as well as some objectors to the war in Vietnam, refused to pay part of their income taxes and the telephone tax surcharge.

On the other hand, the wedge or slippery slope argument may not hold for either UCO or SCO. The legal exemption of conscientious objectors, whether selective or universal, from military service can be sharply distinguished from "selective disobedience to law." In the one case, the government accepts certain reasons for exemption from legal duties; in the other, individuals or groups disobey established legal requirements. It is unclear why legal recognition of certain reasons for exemption from military service would contribute to selective disobedience of law. In a society torn by disagreements over a particular war, as in the case of Vietnam, a number of individuals who were drafted refused to comply. Some of them were SCOs—that is, they were ethically opposed to participation in the war in Vietnam—while some had other reasons for their opposition to military service. Non-compliance, for instance by going underground or into exile, represented "selective disobedience to law." At a minimum, the legal exemption from military service of those who were SCOs would have reduced the number of criminal acts and hence the number of examples of "selective disobedience to law."

It is possible, of course, that fears about the "selective disobedience of law" that could occur in the wake of the legal recognition of SCOs are misdirected. The felt concerns could be somewhat different. Critics of any proposal to exempt SCOs from military service could believe that if the government grants this exemption, it will be unable consistently to deny other conscientious claims for exemption—for example, exemptions from particular taxes. But as Childress has argued, several distinctions are relevant:

The first is between service and obedience. Individuals selected for duties of service are the law's instruments; they carry out the law. Such service is different from obedience, or at the very least, it is a special form of obedience. And the government need not treat conscientious refusals of service and (other) conscientious disobedience in the same way. The second distinction concerns the nature of the service, i.e., the kinds of action required. The society could hold that killing in war is such a distinctive and special kind of action that conscientious scruples to its performance should be respected whether they are universal or selective.[81]

If these distinctions hold, they can reduce some of the concerns about the impact of legal recognition of SCOs on compliance with laws—selective disobedience does not appear to be a likely outcome of the exemption of SCOs from military service.

Numbers

One widespread fear, often submerged rather than surfaced, is that exemption of SCOs could or would allow a de facto referendum through which large numbers of draft-eligible citizens could thwart a national policy reached through legitimate democratic processes. It might be difficult, so the argument goes, to conduct an unpopular war if SCOs were exempted from military service, especially in view of the difficulty of distinguishing sincere objectors from fraudulent ones. Several points are relevant even if together they are not decisive in one direction or the other.

There is some historical precedent in the United Kingdom for exemption of SCOs in wartime, but that historical precedent may have limited relevance for several reasons. Britain's policy of exempting SCOs in World War II did not encounter serious difficulty. But the absence of serious difficulty may have resulted from the fact that during much of World War II Britain was under siege and fighting for its survival against an enemy widely perceived to be evil.[82] The British example only shows that legal recognition of SCO is sometimes feasible even in wartime. But feasiblity may depend on the overall public view of the war itself.

A government cannot reliably predict the number of SCOs in advance of a particular war, much less as the war evolves. By contrast, the number of UCOs is relatively stable and predictable; as a result, policy makers know how to plan for those objections in the context of military conscription. On the one hand, opponents of a legal exemption from military service for SCOs stress that the government may not be able to fight a war effectively if large numbers of citizens are conscientiously opposed to participating in that war on grounds of its injustice. On the other hand, supporters of the legal recognition of SCOs note that a particular war may need to be reconsidered if the number of SCOs is large because many consider the war to be unjust and the government cannot make a cogent case for its justice (in light of the full set of just-war criteria).

In a true emergency, a situation of necessity, it is plausible to hold that a government may justifiably draft both UCOs and SCOs. Faced with such a situation, perceived to be a genuine emergency, a government is likely to have little problem in securing the military personnel it needs—as we noted, Britain in World War II is a good example. But suppose a government believes it cannot effectively fight a war without overriding the objections of conscientious refusers. On the one hand, it is unlikely that these refusers would be effective contributors to the war effort if drafted. So the problem is unlikely to arise in this form. On the other hand, fairness and equal respect could support a very different policy than preferring the UCO to the SCO or even denying all exemptions for both types of conscientious objectors. In limiting the number of exemptions for conscience because of military needs, this different policy, based on fairness and equal respect, would determine by means of a lottery who would be exempted and who would be forced to serve or face criminal penalties. This procedure would also be a fairer way to reduce the numbers of exemptions than, for instance, by restoring the traditional religious requirement.[83] Of course, it would also be important to set the number needed—or exempted—in a non-arbitrary and non-capricious way. But, again, the practical problems of incorporating genuine conscientious objectors into military service would probably be insurmountable.

Morale and Effectiveness of the Armed Forces

As we noted earlier, the National Advisory Commission also feared another possible negative consequence of the exemption of SCOs from military service: "a legal recognition of selective pacifism could be disruptive to the morale and effectiveness of the Armed Forces." Here the commission is making another judgment about what "could" happen and using it as a reason for opposing the legal recognition of SCOs. Hence, it is important to consider the commission's evidence, analysis, and reasoning.

First, the commission holds that "a determination of the justness or unjustness of any war could only be made within the context of that war itself."[84] This is an overstatement. Certainly, some judgments about how the war is being conducted can only be made within the war itself. But this would apply only to the judgments based on *jus in bello* criteria. And even so, the SCO may focus more on policies regarding *jus in bello* than on particular acts. For instance, the SCO may judge the policies of bombing targets or treatment of prisoners of war as unethical without having to see their actual implementation. And there is even more room for the SCO to make judgments about the *jus ad bellum* without being in the war itself.

Second, the report somehow supposes that a legal recognition of SCO places a burden on each citizen and each soldier of determining whether a particular war is just or unjust. According to this report, legal recognition of SCOs would force "upon the individual the necessity" of making that determination and put "a burden heretofore unknown on the man in uniform and even on the brink of combat." In fact, however, a legal provision for SCO would permit individuals to make this determination, without requiring them to do so. Furthermore, even now, under the laws of war, individual soldiers can be held accountable for "crimes of war," for their actions against the "laws of war" (such as killing innocent people), though not for participation in an "unjust" war. It is not clear then why a provision for SCO would have "disastrous" results for the individual soldier, his unit, and "the entire military tradition."[85]

It is not unreasonable to suppose that the morale of military personnel would suffer if large numbers of persons eligible for a draft or already drafted claimed to be SCOs. A government finds it difficult to fight a war that many citizens consider unjust, and military personnel could reasonably view their risks as unwarranted when many other citizens provide only modest support for or even vigorously oppose a particular war. However, it is unclear what the impact of the legal recognition of SCOs would be in such circumstances. On the one hand, exemption of SCOs from military service could provide a pressure valve and even reduce societal protest about an unpopular war. On the other hand, this exemption would enable more people to avoid military service and would raise questions about the equity of the imposition of risks of military service.

To extend this last point, the most likely source of a negative effect on the morale and effectiveness of the armed forces, as the Supreme Court emphasized, is the draftee's sense of unfairness in the distribution of the burdens of military service. Consider a draftee who is conscientiously opposed to a particular war but who, nonetheless, feels bound by the results of the democratic process that produced the current set of political officials who have undertaken a particular war. His own resolve, however, could weaken if the burdens of military service appear to be distributed in an erratic and unfair way. And, the Court continued, erratic and unfair distribution could be expected in view of the "indeterminate scope" of SCO. Thus, in the Court's view, Congress had good reasons to decide "that the objector to all war—to all killing in war—has a claim that is distinct enough and intense enough to justify special status, while the objector to a particular war does not."[86] Nevertheless, according to the Court, Congress would not have acted "irrationally or unreasonably" if it had exempted SCOs.

Of course, it is difficult to predict with any assurance what consequences, both positive and negative, a policy of exemption of SCOs from military service might bring about, in part because of the likely influence of a variety of other factors. Nevertheless, in view of the important ethical principles involved, it is not implausible to argue that the government ought to seek ways to distribute burdens of military service equitably while respecting SCOs as well as UCOs. If a fair administrative procedure cannot be developed, and if the country reaches a state of emergency, universal conscription could, of course, be justified. In such a state of emergency, perceived to be real, conscription would arguably be unnecessary because of the common spirit of patriotism.

Positive Consequences of Selective Conscientious Objection

Proponents of the legal recognition of SCOs not only seek to weaken and counter the arguments offered against such legal recognition; as we have seen, they appeal to a variety of principles, such as fairness and respect for persons, to support a policy of exemption of SCOs from military service. In addition, as we will now see, some proponents also appeal to the possible or probable positive effects of such a policy. One of their arguments is that this policy would elevate "the level of moral discourse on the uses of force" in the society.[87] Presumably, but in ways that are not totally clear, this policy would foster reflection on the criteria of the justice of and in war and the application of these criteria to particular wars.

A counterargument—or at least a cautionary argument—might concede that elevating the level of moral discourse about war is an important goal, but that (1) such a consequence would have little weight by itself in arguing for a policy of SCO exemption from military service; (2) in any event, the elevation of moral discourse about war is not a very probable result of the exemption of SCOs from military service; and (3) it can be sought and achieved in other ways. Indeed, the argument for the positive effect of a policy of the legal recognition of SCOs may encounter the proverbial chicken-egg problem. Rather than elevating society's moral discourse about war, a policy of recognizing SCOs would probably not be feasible without such an elevation. The elevation of societal moral discourse may be a presupposition rather than a probable effect of the legal recognition of SCOs. Furthermore, without this elevation, some of the consequences feared by opponents of SCO exemption may indeed occur. Elements in this elevated moral discourse would include respect for the conscience of the laws, for democratic decision-making, and for the (rebuttable) presumption in favor of compliance.[88]

Another argument for SCO exemption from military service focuses on moral education. It holds that principles or rules such as "never kill in war" are, in the words of philosopher Carl Cohen,

almost sure to lead to error through oversimplification; while principles of a more limited scope, while also uncertain, have a far better chance of approximating the truth, if there is one. We do well, therefore, to credit the conscientious man with limited principles, rather than to discredit him because his principles are limited.[89]

This, Cohen argues, is a matter not only of justice but also of wisdom. This argument is risky, however, because it introduces the question of truth and falsity into the debate about whether conscientious objectors, whether universal or selective, should be excused from social duties. Should the SCO be exempted (a) because his reasons are more likely to be true (because more limited or qualified), or (b) because the principles of respect for persons and fairness support such a policy? According to the main arguments that have been offered to support an SCO exemption, (b) is more plausible and powerful than (a). We will, however, return to the question of truth and falsity in the next section, where we consider the test of conscientiousness or sincerity of claims of conscience in objection to participation in war.

Before we turn to that section, we summarize the array of arguments for and against the exemption of SCOs from military service:

[W]hile the positive consequences sometimes adduced for excusing SCOs from military service are tenuous, other arguments are more compelling. First, the principle of respect for persons supports recognition of the conscience of the selective objector as well as the universal objector. Second, because the UCO and the SCO are relevantly similar, it is unfair to excuse the UCO without also excusing the SCO. Both of these arguments hinge on the nature of the SCO's judgment and reasons. Like universal objection, selective objection may be based on religious and moral principles and may be genuinely conscientious. Although the SCO's opposition is more complex and is based, in part, on the facts of a particular war, it is not necessarily or solely political. Finally, most of the negative consequences of exemption of SCOs from military service that critics anticipate are not very probable, and the critics' claims often rest on conceptual confusions. When conjoined with an analysis of the nature of the claims of SCOs, the principles of respect for persons and fairness support governmental efforts to develop a mechanism to obviate the difficulties of administering a provision for selective conscientious objection in a fair and equitable way. If such efforts fail and serious problems develop for the armed forces or if the government faces an emergency in war, it may be forced to override the claims of conscientious objectors.

The pragmatic consideration (especially the hopelessness of making an adequate soldier out of the conscientious objector) applies to both the UCO and the SCO. Forced participation probably would be detrimental to the war effort, and many would choose jail or exile rather than military service, as they did during the war in Vietnam. Few opponents of selective conscientious objection ever deal explicitly with this consideration either (a) because they believe that the negative consequences of exempting SCOs, for the war and for the society, would outweigh the negative consequences of not exempting them, or (b) because they believe that SCOs are at best political objectors and at worst slackers and that, consequently, the threat of imprisonment for noncompliance would be sufficient to make them adequate combatants.[90]

Conscientiousness and Sincerity

If we determine that SCOs as a class should be exempted from military service, it is still necessary, in practice, to determine who is a member of that class. Over the past century, a crucial criterion for evaluating the UCO has been his conscientiousness or sincerity. Determination of conscientiousness or sincerity in claiming conscientiousness is easier, of course, if combined with the other two traditional criteria of pacifism and religious training and belief. Indeed, pacifism and a narrow interpretation of religious training and belief could be viewed as more or less objective tests of conscientious objection. By contrast, the determination of conscientiousness hinges on subjective considerations—the task is to determine whether beliefs are truly and deeply held. This task has been very important but also very difficult in implementing the policy of exempting UCOs from military service. It became more difficult with the expansion of the notion of religious belief (the "parallel belief" test set by the *Seeger* decision), and it will become even more difficult if selective conscientious objection is legally recognized.

It is important to distinguish, as we suggested earlier, the task of determining the conscientiousness or sincerity of UCOs or SCOs from the task of determining the truth or falsity of their beliefs about war in general or about a particular war. Nevertheless, selective conscientious objection appears to raise more questions about truth or falsity than universal conscientious objection, particularly when the deontological pacifist insists that he simply cannot participate in military service because of God's command, the "hard sayings" in the New Testament, and so on. In a sense, the government undertaking a war must view both UCOs and SCOs as expressing an "erroneous conscience." Still it can view the UCO's "erroneous conscience" as based on mistaken moral principles, but principles that nonetheless should be respected. Strong critics of pacifists often nevertheless view them as performing a valuable service by reminding the society of higher ideals as long as they accept their exemption from military service and do not try to push the state in the direction of pacifism.[91]

From the U.S. government's standpoint, the SCO who appeals to criteria of the just-war tradition, many of which the government itself recognizes—for instance, debates about the Gulf War or the War in Iraq have been conducted in terms of many of those criteria—has an "erroneous conscience" in another sense. An "erroneous conscience" may be mistaken not only in its moral or religious principles but also in its interpretation of the factual situation to which it applies its principles. In recognizing the rights of the "erroneous conscience," the government may find it difficult to accept the SCO's putative factual errors. The government may more readily recognize the rights of the "erroneous conscience" when the putative error appears in the moral principles or values appealed to—for example, "all war is wrong because it is wrong to kill any human being"—than when the putative error concerns what the government is actually doing. An SCO, for instance, could believe that the U.S. government is systematically killing innocent civilians and could offer this as the primary reason for his refusal to serve in the military when drafted. But this factual belief could be mistaken. Even if we say that the primary consideration in conscientiousness is not the truth or falsity of the moral belief but its sincerity, some factual mistakes could, in principle, disqualify an SCO's claim. Nevertheless, it is generally not easy and often impossible to separate out the factual and ethical components of moral judgments about particular wars.

Whether a proposed conscientious objection policy that emphasizes such subjective considerations can be administered evenly and fairly is, as we have seen, an important consideration in its adoption. Sorting out the genuine and spurious claims of conscientious objection will be a difficult administrative task. In this section, we will not consider various proposals about procedures (for example, local boards, appeals boards, and judicial review), even though they also need careful attention. Instead, we will make a few observations about tests of sincerity of claims of conscientious objection.

Why should the state not just accept the potential conscientious objector at his word? Why should the state not accept without question a person's claim to be a conscientious objector on moral, ethical, or religious grounds? Certainly one major reason is that exemption from military service because of conscientious objection imposes greater burdens on others, some of whom have to serve in the place of conscientious objectors and thus bear greater risks of injury and death. Thus, it is important to have some tests of sincerity because conscientious objectors gain, or are thought to gain, some advantage over others by not having to serve as combatants in military service. Further, the principle of respect for persons and their conscience does not require respect for the insincere conscience.

Earlier we suggested that because of the principles of fairness and respect for persons, the state should bear the burden of proof to show that the class of conscientious objectors, whether universal or selective, should not be exempted from military service. This placement of the burden of proof does not imply that the state bears the burden of showing that any particular claimant is not a member of the class of conscientious objectors. It is fair, and not disrespectful, for the state to require such a claimant to show that he really holds the convictions in question deeply and intensely. He should bear the burden of proof because of his presumed interest in avoiding the risks of injury and death in military service. The claimant to conscientious objector status should answer the threshold question of sincerity, but his burden of proof should not be onerous. The standard should not require establishing sincerity beyond a reasonable doubt but only by the preponderance of the evidence, in part because of the complex possible and actual motivations for individuals' requests for exemption from military service. It is not unreasonable that a person who is conscientiously opposed to participation in all wars or in a war that involves what he deems to be immoral killing may also be interested in avoiding the risk of being killed in that context. But then the question becomes: how can reviewers determine whether any particular person's motive of conscience is necessary and/or sufficient for his claim for an exemption from military service?[92]

In efforts to find better tests of sincerity, some have suggested imprisonment or a severe tax or even confiscation of the conscientious objector's property.[93] Such proposals may help us distinguish those who would only have some "pinpricks" of conscience if they had to serve in the military from those "whose consciences, spurred by deeply held moral, ethical, or religious beliefs, would give them no rest or peace if they allowed themselves to become a part of an instrument of war."[94] But such proposals go too far. It is unfair to impose such hard choices on conscience when they can be avoided. Furthermore, the society loses the service that the conscientious objector can provide in other ways. Alternative service not only (partially) satisfies the principle of fairness but also provides one test of sincerity because it reduces (though it does not eliminate) the advantages that the objector might gain.

While demeanor and credibility are obvious tests of sincerity, one of the most important tests is a person's consistency between word and action and over time. It is easier to apply the test of consistency to the UCO than to the SCO, in part because the pacifist's commitments often—though not always—entail a way of life, a vocation, which reflects his overall outlook. In addition, draft boards have often asked hypothetical questions to determine the UCO's consistency across types of situations. One favorite challenge came in the form of a question: "What would you do if your grandmother [or some other beloved and vulnerable person] were attacked by an assailant?" The courts have indicated that such hypothetical questions are irrelevant as a test of the sincerity of UCO to military service because they presuppose that pacifism (as objection to participation in war in any form) necessarily excludes killing in all settings. A person could be a UCO and still support, for example, killing in self-defense in some circumstances.[95] Nevertheless, some hypothetical questions, for example, questions about different wars, can be useful in determining consistency, but the demand for consistency should not exclude the possibility of dramatic conversions. Finally, the demand for consistency should not require absolute certainty that a claimant for conscientious objector status will never change his views in the future.

Most tests of sincerity seek to determine the authority, power, or strength of the relevant convictions for the person who is seeking recognition as a conscientious objector—this fits with the "parallel belief" test set forth by *Seeger*. Historically, some tests have also focused on the process of conscience formation. As we have seen, a central criterion has involved "religious training and belief." It was usually interpreted to include both training *and* religious belief, not training *or* belief. Nevertheless, the Supreme Court tended to concentrate on belief, not training. After *Welsh*, however, a memorandum from the director of the Selective Service held that to

find that a registrant's moral and ethical beliefs are against participation in war in any form and are held with the strength of traditional religious convictions, the local board should consider the nature and history of the process by which he acquired such beliefs. The registrant must demonstrate that his ethical or moral convictions were gained through training, study, contemplation, or other activity, comparable in rigor and dedication to the processes by which traditional religious convictions are formulated.[96]

Attention to such processes could avoid claims of conscience that reflect a "merely personal moral code." Fairness to claimants of conscientious objector status requires that the expected processes of training in conscience not unduly favor more articulate and educated claimants.[97] Testing the sincerity of UCOs has been difficult enough, but testing the sincerity of SCOs, if they ever qualify for exemption as conscientious objectors, will be much more difficult. In addition, the tendency to favor more articulate and educated applicants is likely to be even stronger because of the more complicated processes of reasoning involved in SCO claims.

CONCLUSION

Having briefly surveyed the history and development of conscientious objection in the United States, it is perhaps most striking to our ears to hear how gracefully a testimony of conscience can oscillate between providing a rich, sincere, tradition-shaped account of one's objection while also appealing to prevailing political norms and concepts to encourage its protection. Most exemplary in this regard is the Shaker testimony from 1818 that we briefly noted above, a testimony not bound by our understandings of church and state and their "proper relation." Speaking "bilingually" in this way comes less easily to objectors today than it did in the past, as current generations have been habituated to speak only one language at a time, depending on which side of the separation between church and state they stand.

For a variety of reasons, conscientious objection to military service has not directly engaged the church and state as often as we might suppose. First, many of the early objectors who suffered fines and punishments for their conscientious refusal came from smaller, less hierarchical ecclesial bodies, bodies perhaps less capable of leveraging their shared stance toward military service to successfully petition for exemption. Second, in the twentieth century, when members of mainline Christian churches became more involved in peace societies like the Fellowship of Reconciliation, the state was becoming increasingly accommodative to conscientious objectors. Whereas exemption from military service for conscientious objectors had been limited to members of pacifist denominations, in time Catholics, Methodists, Lutherans, and Presbyterians, among others, could gain exemption from military service, so long as their objection was universal—against all participation in war in any form—and based on religious training and belief, even though the denomination officially accepted a just-war perspective rather than a pacifist one. Third, the First Amendment protection of the free exercise of religion has provided a protective hedge for those members of ecclesial communities that fully share commitments to peace. At least since World War I, members of historically pacifist churches have not had to stand before the courts and defend their conscientious commitments as derivative from their religious training and belief. Instead, the court adjudicated cases in which an objector's practices and beliefs did not fully cohere with his particular religious community, as we observed in the *Seeger* case, or where a given religious community's approach to war did not align with dominant frameworks and categories, as was the case with Jehovah's Witnesses during the Second World War and Black Muslims during the Vietnam War. If an objector could convincingly appeal to shared conscientious commitments, and his community was sufficiently familiar, the protection of religion's free exercise generated few occasions at which his church might feel compelled to engage his state. In the end, some churches whose members spoke with an impassioned voice were not amplified; the amplified voices, if consistent in their objection to war in any form, were protected; and the amplified voices, if sufficiently familiar, could call upon constitutional protections, rather than their church.

The challenge going forward is whether we can recalibrate how we define and assess sincere objections of conscience, whether religious or secular, universal or selective. Since war and conscription can easily lead patriotic citizens to excessive exuberance and demands for conformity, might law and policy anticipate and hedge against such temptations and tendencies? As Lillian Schlissel has observed, "liberty and freedom of conscience may be rallying cries when the nation is at peace, but let the country be threatened and the call is for a closing of the ranks."[98] If conscience and community are often pitted against each other in wartime, as Schlissel suggests, perhaps the task of developing laws and policies to protect the soldier's conscience is more urgent than we think. The shift to an all-volunteer military force has avoided the kinds of conflicts of conscience that conscription in wartime engenders. However, whether and how long the all-volunteer military force can meet U.S. military needs is unclear. Hence, it is important to devote attention once again to laws and policies for conscientious objection.

NOTES

1. We use masculine pronouns throughout because to date military conscription in the United States has focused on males; given the greatly increased role of women in the military, a reinstituted draft may look very different.

2. Department of Defense Directive 1300.6. Certified Current as of November 21, 2003, available at http://www.dtic.mil/whs/directives/corres/rtf/130006x.rtf (accessed May 5, 2007).

3. During the Second World War and Vietnam War, some Hopi draftees appealed to their peace tradition in order to attain conscientious objector status. Though the origin of this American peace tradition precedes European colonization, given the relative lack of influence that this tradition has had upon the development of law and policy in the United States, it will not be explored here, though see Alice Schlegel's "Contentious But Not Violent: The Hopi of Northern Arizona" in Graham Kemp and Douglas Fry's *Keeping the Peace: Conflict Resolution and Peaceful Societies Around the World* (New York: Routledge, 2004), 19–33, and A.W. Geertz's *The Invention of Prophecy: Continuity and Meaning in Hopi Indian Religions* (Berkeley: University of California Press, 1994).

4. Joseph Besse, *A Collection of the Sufferings of the People called Quakers, for the Testimony of a Good Conscience*, Vol. 2 (London, 1753), 378–380.

5. U.S. Selective Service System, *Backgrounds of Selective Service*, 2 vols. (Washington, D.C.: Government Printing Office, 1947).

6. George Fox, *A Declaration from the Harmless and Innocent People of God called Quakers, against all Sedition, Plotters & Fighters in the World . . . Presented unto the King upon the 21th day of the 11th month, 1660* (London, 1684).

7. Peter Brock, *Liberty and Conscience: A Documentary History of the Experiences of Conscientious Objectors in America through the Civil War* (New York: Oxford University Press, 2002), 4.

8. For example, eight Friends wrote a letter to the Governor of New York in 1672, explaining their refusal to pay for repairs at the fort of New York. The letter is included in Peter Brock's *Liberty and Conscience*, 11.

9. Lillian Schlissel, *Conscience in America: A Documentary History of Conscientious Objection in America, 1757–1967* (New York: E.P. Dutton & Co., 1968), 75.

10. Ibid., 73.

11. Ibid., 77.

12. For the entirety of Madison's speech and the debates that followed, see *Annals of Congress: The Debates and Proceedings in the Congress of the United States, 1789–1824* (Washington, D.C.: Gales and Seaton, 1834), Vol. 1, First Congress, First Session, June 1789. An abbreviated text of the speech is found in Schlissel, *Conscience in America*, 45–48. Our own emphasis added.

13. For a more detailed history of the legislative process and Madison's role in it, see Maj. David Brahms, "They Step to a Different Drummer: A Critical Analysis of the Current Department of Defense Position vis-à-vis In-service Conscientious Objectors" in *Military Law Review* 47 (Jan. 1970), 4–9. Brahms notes that the early sessions of the U.S. Senate were closed, and thus no comprehensive record exists that would indicate the reasons why the last clause was stricken.

14. John Whiteclay Chambers II, "Conscientious Objectors and the American State from Colonial Times to the Present," in *The New Conscientious Objection: From Sacred to Secular Resistance*, ed. Charles Moskos and John Whiteclay Chambers II (New York: Oxford University Press: 1993), 29.

15. Schlissel, *Conscience in America*, 57.

16. The Rogerenes were a small pacifist sect, followers of John Rogers (1648–1721), who resided mainly in Connecticut and insisted upon freedom of worship, the importance of education, and an indifference to material goods and wealth. See Ellen Starr Brinton's "The Rogerenes," *The New England Quarterly*, 16, no. 1 (March 1943): 2–19.

17. Rogers' letter is included in Schissel's volume, *Conscience in America*, 60. It also resides in J.R. Bolles and A.B. Williams' *The Rogerenes* (Boston: Stanhope Press, 1904), 386–87.

18. Schlissel, *Conscience in America*, 61.

19. An excerpt can be found in Brock, *Liberty and Conscience*, 101.

20. Schlissel, *Conscience in America*, 59.

21. Thoreau notes in the essay that he did not have conscientious concerns about paying the highway tax, as he was "desirous of being a good neighbor." Further, he did not feel compelled to "trace the course of [his] dollar" in order to avoid those taxes which supported those causes that affronted his conscience.

22. Henry David Thoreau, "Civil Disobedience." In *Walden and Civil Disobedience*. Ed. by Paul Lauter (Boston: Houghton Mifflin, 2000), 18.

23. Ibid., 32.

24. Ibid., 36.

25. *U.S. Statutes at Large*, 38th Congress, 1st Session. Included in Schlissel, *Conscience in America*, 98. Incidentally, Charles Moskos and John Chambers note that this statute could be construed as the first national policy of conscientious objection in the world (*The New Conscientious Objection*, 198).

26. Schlissel, *Conscience in America*, 90.

27. Brock, *A Brief History of Pacifism*, 38.

28. Selective Draft Act of 1917, excerpt in Lillian Schlissel, *Conscience in America*, 133.

29. Schlissel, *Conscience in America*, 129.

30. Ibid.

31. Ibid., 130.

32. Local draft boards could certify a draftee as a conscientious objector, if he was found to be a member of any well-recognized religious sect or organization that forbid its members to participation in war in any form. Yet, some objectors who did not meet these criteria still petitioned for conscientious objector status, and these cases were adjudicated by this three man Board of Inquiry. See Kellogg's personal account of his work on the Board in *The Conscientious Objector* (New York: Boni and Liveright, 1919).

33. Mulford Sibley and Philip Jacob hold that a good number of the 21,000 inducted objectors likely abandoned their objector status upon arrival for military training, given the "pressures of the time." See their *Conscription of Conscience: The American State and the Conscientious Objector, 1940–1947* (Ithaca, NY: Cornell University Press, 1952), 12.

34. Sibley and Jacob, *Conscription of Conscience*, 12–16.

35. Peter Brock, *Pacifism in the United States From the Colonial Era to the First World War* (Princeton: Princeton University Press, 1968).

36. Sibley and Jacob, *Conscription of Conscience*, 15. Perhaps the most gruesome case concerns the death of an objector who was incarcerated in a damp cell for refusing to wear his military uniform (likely a Mennonite who was prohibited from wearing clothes with buttons). In the cell, he caught pneumonia and died. His corpse was sent home to his family, adorned in the very uniform he refused to wear.

37. John Whiteclay Chambers II, "Conscientious Objectors and the American State from Colonial Times to the Present," in *The New Conscientious Objection: From Sacred to Secular Resistance*, ed. Charles Moskos and John Whiteclay Chambers II (Oxford: Oxford University Press, 1993), 33.

38. Schlissel, *Conscience in America*, 179.

39. 66th Congress, 1st Session, Washington 1919.

40. Schlissel, *Conscience in America*, 146–147. From *The Individual and the State, The Problem as Presented by the Sentencing of Roger N. Baldwin*.

41. See Paul R. Dekar, *Creating the Beloved Community: A Journey with the Fellowship of Reconciliation* (Telford, PA: Cascadia Publishing House, 2005).

42. Chambers, *The New Conscience Objection*, 32. See also C. Roland Marchand's *The American Peace Movement and Social Reform, 1898–1918* (Princeton: Princeton University Press, 1972) and Horace C. Peterson's and Gilbert C. Fite's *Opponents of the War, 1917–1918* (Madison, WI: University of Wisconsin Press, 1957).

43. 283 U.S. 605.

44. In 1946, the U.S. Supreme Court heard *Girouard v. United States*, in which the petitioner was a Canadian Adventist seeking citizenship but unwilling to promise to bear arms. Surprisingly similar in many respects to the *Macintosh* case, the

Court found that prevailing precedents in *Macintosh* and *United States v. Schwimmer* (1929) laid down an incorrect rule.

45. Section 5(g), Selective Training and Service Act of 1940.

46. The Selective Service claims that noncombatants numbered 25,000. Cynthia Eller, in her *Conscientious Objectors and the Second World War: Moral and Religious Arguments in Support of Pacifism* (New York: Praeger, 1991) approximates that the number of conscientious objectors in WWII was near 43,000, with 25,000 serving in noncombatant roles, 12,000 working in alternative service roles for the Civilian Public Service, and 6,000 incarcerated (52). Sibley and Jacob put the total number of conscientious objectors close to 50,000 (*Conscription of Conscience*, 83, 104), and Chambers concurs (*The New Conscientious Objection*, 37). Also see Stephen Kohn's *Jailed for Peace: The History of American Draft Law Violators, 1658–1985* (New York: Praeger, 1986), 47.

47. Eller, *Conscientious Objectors*, 52.

48. Chambers, *The New Conscientious Objection*, 37.

49. Moskos and Chambers, *The New Conscientious Objection*, 204.

50. See Scott Bennett's detailed account in "'Free American Political Prisoners': Pacifist Activism and Civil Liberties, 1945–48," *Journal of Peace Research* 40, no. 4 (July 2003): 413–33.

51. 135 F. 2d 521.

52. 133 F. 2d 703.

53. *United States v. Kauten*, 133 F. 2d 703, 1943.

54. 62 *U.S. Statutes*, 612 (1948), Public Law 1759, ch. 625, 80th Congress, 2d sess. (1948).

55. Ibid., Gov't docs. 1948.

56. Kohn, *Jailed for Peace*, 93.

57. Chambers, *The New Conscientious Objection*, 42.

58. Ibid., 43.

59. Moskos and Chambers, *The New Conscientious Objection*, 4.

60. Laurie Goodstein, "Churches Give Resisters Shelter from War's Storm," *Washington Post*, Feb. 27, 1991, A3.

61. Chambers, *The New Conscientious Objection*, 44.

62. Department of Defense Directive 1300.6.

63. Michael Noone, "Legal Aspects of Conscientious Objection: A Comparative Analysis," in *The New Conscientious Objection: From Sacred to Secular Resistance*, ed. Charles Moskos and John Whiteclay Chambers II (Oxford: Oxford University Press, 1993), 190.

64. *U.S. v. Austin* 27 M.J. 227 (1988).

65. We borrow this phrase from Moskos and Chambers, who highlight the global movement from sacred to secular resistance among conscientious objectors in their *The New Conscientious Objection*.

66. For example, see James Finn's edited volume *A Conflict of Loyalties: The Case for Selective Conscientious Objection* (New York: Pegasus, 1968) and John Rohr's

Prophets Without Honor: Public Policy and the Selective Conscientious Objector (Nashville: Abingdon Press, 1971).

67. The section that follows draws heavily for its structure, ideas, and some formulations from James F. Childress, *Moral Responsibility in Conflicts: Essays on Nonviolence, War, and Conscience* (Baton Rouge, LA: Louisiana State University Press, 1982), Chapter 6: "Policies Toward Conscientious Objectors to Military Service."

68. Report of the National Advisory Commission on Selective Service, *In Pursuit of Equity: Who Serves When Not All Serve?* (Washington, D.C.: Government Printing Office, 1967), 50, hereinafter cited as *In Pursuit of Equity*. See also John A. Rohr, *Prophets Without Honor: Public Policy and the Selective Conscientious Objector* (Nashville: Abingdon Press, 1971).

69. See, for example, John Howard Yoder, *Nevertheless: Varieties of Religious Pacifism* (Scottsdale, PA: Herald Press, 1976), and James F. Childress, "Contemporary Pacifism: Its Major Types and Possible Contributions to Discourse about War," in *The American Search for Peace: Moral Reasoning, Religious Hope, and National Security*, eds. George Weigel and John P. Langan, S.J. (Washington D.C.: Georgetown University Press, 1991), 109–131.

70. See National Conference of Catholic Bishops, *The Challenge of Peace: God's Promise and Our Response* (Washington, D.C.: U.S. Conference of Catholic Bishops, Inc., May 3, 1983); James F. Childress, "Just-War Criteria," in *Moral Responsibility in Conflicts*, 63–94.

71. Rohr, *Prophets Without Honor*, 143, 148.

72. Alan Gewirth, "Reasons and Conscience: The Claims of the Selective Conscientious Objector," in *Philosophy, Morality, and International Affairs*, eds. Virginia Held, Sidney Morgenbesser, and Thomas Nagel (New York: Oxford University Press, 1974), 99.

73. Rohr, *Prophets Without Honor*, 22. See also *In Pursuit of Equity*, 50.

74. Childress, *Moral Responsibility in Conflicts*, Chapter 5, "The Nature of Conscientious Objection," reprinted with modifications from *Ethics* 89 (July 1979).

75. Childress, *Moral Responsibility in Conflicts*, 204–205.

76. See Cohen, "Conscientious Objection," 271, 277.

77. *In Pursuit of Equity*, 48–49.

78. *Gillette v. United States*, 401 U.S. 459 (1971).

79. Ibid.

80. *In Pursuit of Equity*, 50 (emphasis added). See the criticisms by Quentin L. Quade, "Selective Conscientious Objection and Political Obligation," in *A Conflict of Loyalties*, ed. James Finn (New York: Pegasus), 195–218.

81. Childress, *Moral Responsibility in Conflicts*, 208–209.

82. For generalizations from the British experience, see Gewirth, "Reasons and Conscience," 98, and David Malament, "Selective Conscientious Objection and the *Gillette* Decision," *Philosophy and Public Affairs*, I (Summer, 1972), 383–385. Contrast with Quade, "Selective Conscientious Objection and Political Obliga-

tion," 205. For a discussion of the British experience, see Denis Hayes, *Challenge of Conscience: The Story of the Conscientious Objectors of 1939–1949* (London: George Allen & Unwin, 1949).

83. Ralph Potter contends that we should restore the religious criterion in order to accommodate SCOs because he believes that we cannot eliminate the religious requirement and the pacifist requirement at the same time. See Potter, "Conscientious Objection to Particular Wars," in Donald A. Giannella ed., *Religion and the Public Order, No. 4* (Ithaca, NY: Cornell University Press, 1968): 44–99. See also Paul Ramsey, "Selective Conscientious Objection," 31–77. For a defense of a lottery, see John Mansfield, "Conscientious Objection—1964 Term," in Donald A. Giannella, ed., *Religion and the Public Order 1965* (Chicago: University of Chicago Press, 1966): 46 n, 73.

84. *In Pursuit of Equity*, 50, my italics.

85. Ibid.

86. *Gillette v. United States*, 401 U.S. 437 (1971).

87. *In Pursuit of Equity*, 49 (a minority position). See also Ralph Potter, "Conscientious Objection to Particular Wars."

88. Paul Ramsey, "Selective Conscientious Objection," 35, and John Courtney Murray, S.J., "War and Conscience," in Finn, ed., *A Conflict of Loyalties*, 19–30.

89. Cohen, "Conscientious Objection," 277.

90. Childress, *Moral Responsibility in Conflicts*, 213–214.

91. Reinhold Niebuhr, "Why the Christian Church is Not Pacifist."

92. C.D. Broad, "Conscience and Conscientious Action," in Joel Feinberg, ed., *Moral Concepts* (New York: Oxford University Press, 1970): 74–79.

93. An internal Selective Service report, prepared by Donald Gurvitz, but not accepted by Selective Service. See George C. Wilson, "Conscientious Objector Problem Seen," *Washington Post*, March 27, 1980.

94. *Welsh v. United States*, 398 U.S. 340 (1970).

95. See *Goldstein v. Middendorf*, 535 F. 2d 1339 (1976).

96. The same point and much of the same language appears in the 1980 proposed revisions in the Selective Service Regulations. See *Federal Register*, XLIV, No. 234 (December 3, 1980): 80138.

97. In this discussion, we have concentrated on whether and which COs should be exempted from military service. We have not included conscientious refusals to register for a draft. For an examination of some ethical issues in the government's response to draft evasion, desertion, civil disobedience, and war crimes after they have occurred, see James F. Childress, "The Amnesty Argument," *Cross Currents*, XXIII (Fall, 1973): 310–28.

98. Schlissel, *Conscience in America*, 24.

FURTHER READING

Among the numerous exemplary works on the history of conscientious objection in the United States, a few are especially notable. Peter Brock's *Liberty and Con-

science: A Documentary History of the Experiences of Conscientious Objectors in America through the Civil War (New York: Oxford University Press, 2002) is an anthology that documents some of the earliest objector testimonies from the seventeenth century up through the American Civil War. A second anthology by Lillian Schlissel—*Conscience in America: A Documentary History of Conscientious Objection in America, 1757–1967* (New York: E.P. Dutton, 1968)—collects those documents that survey the development of conscientious objection from the first years following American independence up through the late 1960s. Many scholars still consider Edward Wright's *Conscientious Objectors in the Civil War* (Philadelphia: University of Pennsylvania Press, 1931) to be the standard study of objectors during the Civil War. Mulford Sibley and Philip Jacob survey the treatment of conscientious objectors in the Second World War in their *Conscription of Conscience: The American State and the Conscientious Objector, 1940–1947* (Ithaca: Cornell University Press, 1952). Finally, Charles Moskos and John Whiteclay Chambers' edited volume—*The New Conscientious Objection: From Sacred to Secular Resistance* (New York: Oxford University Press, 1993)—observes and assesses some of the recent changes in the treatment of conscientious objectors in the United States and throughout the world.

4

Religiosity, Public Opinion, and the Stem Cell Debate

Eric Matthews and Erin O'Brien

If you spent the summer of 1993 in the United States there was no escaping it. Flip the radio dial—a promo for it. Turn on the television—a trailer advertising it. Hit the local mall—t-shirts plugging it. Stop in at the grocery store—cereal boxes featuring it. What is "it"? *Jurassic Park*—a scientific thriller dealing with the creation of dinosaurs. This movie offered most Americans their first exposure to research involving cellular manipulation. It was not pretty. The movie played loose (at best) with the science of stem cell research and molecular biology. Combined with the magic of Hollywood theatrics, moviegoers' first taste of research entailing stem cells suggested chaos. After all, who really wants a dinosaur chasing after them?

Flash forward some 15 years and stem cell research is no longer the province of fantasy and filmmaking for most Americans. It is a scientific and political reality. This shift has moved the topic away from the entertainment of the cinema toward the controversy of the ballot box and the moralism of Sunday pulpits and Saturday synagogues. Stem cell research is now an undeniably salient and contentious political topic. The major party candidates for presidential office usually offer contrasting positions on stem cell research.[1] A candidate's position on the issue can have dramatic effects for campaign coffers.[2] Celebrities and public icons such as Michael J. Fox, former first lady Nancy Reagan, former President Bill Clinton, and the late

Christopher Reeve hold stem cell research up as a promising resource in tackling various diseases. For many prominent religious leaders, however, the term "embryonic stem cell" cues forth a human being "that is worthy of the same protection as all of us, all the more so because it is so tiny and vulnerable."[3] For them, stem cell research represents yet another infringement upon the sanctity of human life.

But how do everyday Americans make sense of these divergent views and organize them to form their own opinions? Opinion polls consistently tell us that Americans disagree when it comes to stem cell research. But, these polls rarely tell us *why* there is such disagreement or *why* the issue is felt so deeply for many Americans. This chapter takes up these "why" questions. It does so by looking at the potentially multifaceted roles for religion. As we will see, the evidence suggests that religion matters when it comes to views on stem cell research. This is not particularly surprising. Our analysis looks at *how* religiosity influences opinion. We examine what aspects of a religious experience typically impact views on stem cell research. To facilitate this more in-depth understanding, we apply Pui-Yan Lam's dimensions of religiosity to more thoroughly investigate the sources of stem cell opinion amongst everyday Americans.[4] Doing so allows for determining what specific aspects of religion influence views on stem cell research. Is it simply identifying with a particular religious group? Is it being deeply embedded in one of these communities? Is it regular church attendance? Is it the personal devotional practices (saying prayers, reading holy books)? Something else? Is it a combination of influences and factors?

The chapter proceeds in four sections. First, we introduce the contours and trends in American public opinion on stem cell research. This section demonstrates how supporters and non-supporters of stem cell research tend to rely on different sources of information when formulating their views. Opponents are considerably more likely to rely on their religious beliefs. In light of this finding, the second section examines the state of public discourse on stem cell research as it relates to religion and the procedures involved in stem cell research. Two defining discourses (or polarities) on stem cell research are unearthed. We will see that Catholic and evangelical churches have taken the most defining stances on stem cell research. Combined with section one, this indicates that the division along religious lines in stem cell opinion is driven, in part, by the fact that particular religious groups offer distinct logics for opposing stem cell research. The third section examines how, exactly, these contrasting views affect public opinion. What aspects of one's religious experience subsequently impact views on stem cell research? Different messages are being sent, but how is it that they are translated to individuals and subsequently felt during opinion formulation? Lam's dimensions of religiosity index allows for teasing these answers out. The fourth and final section summarizes the findings and their implications for politics and public policy.

Uncovering the connections between religious traditions, dimensions of religiosity, and stem cell opinion matters, as religion has always played an important, if contested, role in United States. Today this plays out most saliently with Christian evangelicals. Our research contributes to scholarship that investigates the multifaceted ways in which this group, as well as other religious traditions, impact political processes and outcomes.[5] There are also applications to religious communities more generally. Stem cell research provides yet another policy issue where church leaders and parishioners struggle to answer personal questions related to morals, technology, and the common good. Ronald Cole-Turner gives voice to these struggles, noting that issues like stem cell research may be "mediated in the political arena" and the medical community but are also deeply rooted in religious institutions and values—specifically, "competing views of the dignity of the human embryo."[6] Some religious communities focus on whether it is morally wrong to use cells from embryos for medical research. Others ask whether it is morally wrong to allow human beings to suffer from diseases and illnesses when research might provide assistance. Our research helps determine how these views are differentially internalized and given a voice in the policy arena amongst adherents of the various religious traditions. Examinations of this sort avoid homogenized assumptions about the diversity of religious experiences in the United States while simultaneously recognizing how and why particular traditions are most apt to affect public discourse and public policy today.

The analysis that follows also sheds light on how public opinion takes hold on emerging, potentially morally-laden issues. Over the past decades, medical and technological advances have presented most of us with policy issues nearly unimaginable. In medical research, for instance, "embryology has revealed to us greater detail of the stunning complexity of genetic and cellular processes."[7] As these modern day revelations and technological advancements continue, they present new questions with serious political, social, and religious ramifications. This research contributes to understanding how mass publics formulate their answers to these questions and does so in a manner that specifies how (not just if) religion matters.

It is important to note where stem cell policy research stands. To this point, the federal government has pursued a policy whereby it does not explicitly prohibit embryo stem cell research but also does not officially condone it, encourage it, or support it with public funds (though state governments have often taken more active roles in both directions). According to the National Conference of State Legislatures, "approaches to stem cell research policy range from statues in California, Connecticut, Maryland, Massachusetts and New Jersey and an executive order in Illinois, which encourages embryonic stem cell research, to South Dakota's law, which strictly forbids research on embryos regardless of their source."[8] Other states, including Ohio, California, New Jersey, New York, and Wisconsin are presently funding some level of stem cell research.[9] President Bush has indicated his lack of support for stem cell research. Speaking from his ranch in Crawford, Texas, President Bush stated:

I strongly oppose human cloning, as do most Americans. We recoil at the idea of growing human beings for spare body parts, or creating life for our convenience. And while we must devote enormous energy to conquering disease, it is equally important that we pay attention to the moral concerns raised by the new frontier of human embryo stem cell research. Even the most noble ends do not justify any means. My position on these issues is shaped by deeply held beliefs. I also believe human life is a sacred gift from our Creator. I worry about a culture that devalues life, and believe as your President I have an important obligation to foster and encourage respect for life in America and throughout the world. And while we're all hopeful about the potential of this research, no one can be certain that the science will live up to the hope it has generated.[10]

Many religious traditions and religious organizations support President Bush's decision to not fund stem cell research, citing their religious convictions and beliefs as a deciding factor. The Southern Baptist Convention, the Christian Coalition, the Catholic Bishops Association and Focus on the Family oppose stem cell research, noting that this type of research violates Biblical values and is never ethically justified. Other organizations, such as the Episcopal Church and the Union of American Hebrew Congregations, overwhelmingly support stem cell research, noting the importance of saving human lives and enhancing the lives on earth. See Appendix 4.1 for an overview of how various groups feel about stem cell research. While there is no federal law prohibiting stem cell research, Americans have polarizing views about the use of embryonic stem cells for research purposes.

CONTOURS OF PUBLIC OPINION ON STEM CELL RESEARCH

So just what do Americans think about stem cell research and how much do they think about it? Figure 4.1 begins providing answers. The dotted line represents those who reported hearing "a lot" or "a little" (as opposed to "nothing") about stem cell research.[11] We see that since 2002, over 80

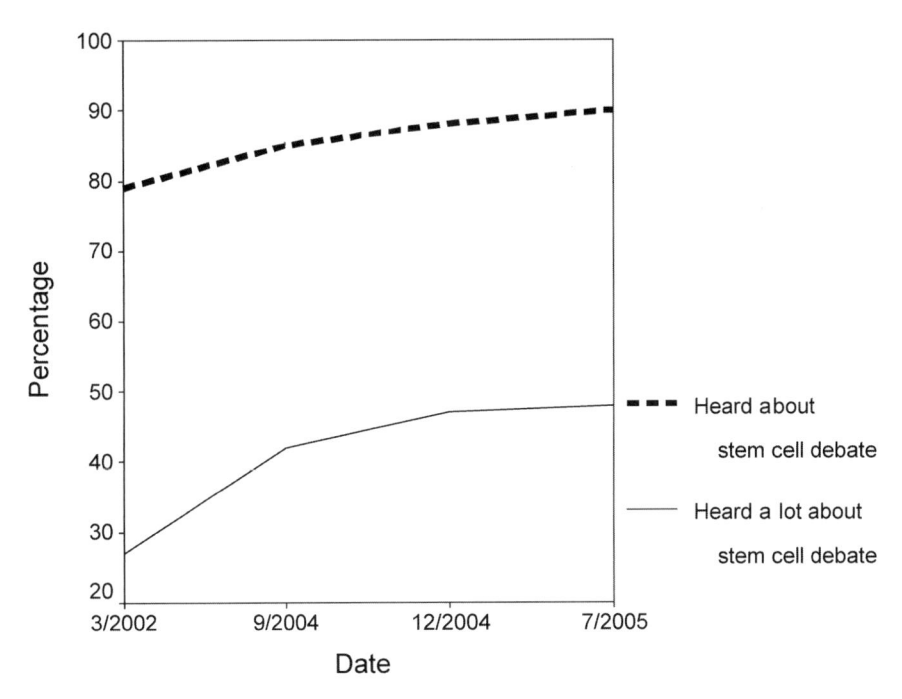

Religiosity, Public Opinion, and the Stem Cell Debate • 119

Figure 4.1 Salience of Stem Cell Research Among Mass Publics Overtime
Source: Pew Forum on Religion and Public Life. Findings released August 2005. Complete report can be downloaded at http://pewforum.org/bioethics/.

percent of Americans reported having heard at least something about stem cell research. This is rather amazing as the specific technologies and procedures of medical research rarely register on the public consciousness.[12] The lack of public opinion data on stem cell research prior to 2002 drives this point home. Simply put, before the turn of the century, stem cell research was of such low salience that those firms who make their living by polling the American public on the major issues of the day did *not* include questions about stem cell research. From Figure 4.1, we see that this changed by the year 2002. It is fair to say there has been a steady uptick in the overall salience of stem cell research since 2002 and that today most Americans have at least heard something about the issue.

A closer read of Figure 4.1 indicates that stem cell research is more than vaguely on the public consciousness. The solid line in the figure isolates the percentage of Americans who report having heard "a lot" about stem cell research. Here we see most dramatically how the issue has jumped onto the political stage and registered amongst mass publics. In March 2002, 27 percent of respondents reporting hearing a lot about stem cell research. By

August 2004, this was up to 42 percent and since then has hovered at just slightly under 50 percent. Thus, almost half of Americans have not only heard of stem cell research—rather, they report hearing a lot about it. There is a nearly infinite range of issues that may resonate for politics, and Figure 4.1 makes clear that stem cell research has emerged on the top.

So Americans are cognizant of stem cell research. But what do they think about it? Figure 4.2 provides the empirical evidence for the opinion divide discussed at the onset. It also indicates that this divide is often understood in moral terms.

The dotted line in Figure 4.2 represents the percentage of respondents who thought it most important to conduct stem cell research. The solid line represents those who thought it most important to not destroy embryos and thus not conduct stem cell research. In March 2002, some 43 percent of respondents favored conducting research while 38 percent favored protecting human embryos over conducting stem cell research (19 percent did not know). Overtime, breakdowns do shift toward favoring the research (52 percent by August 2004), but since December 2004, patterns have held

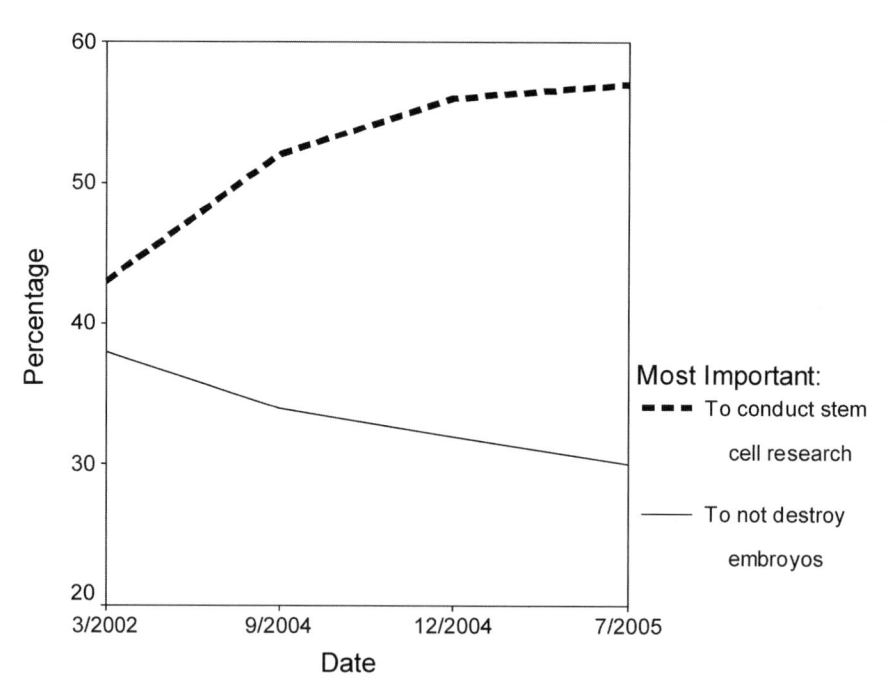

Figure 4.2 Public Opinion on Stem Cell Research Overtime

Source: Pew Forum on Religion and Public Life. Findings released August 2005. Complete report can be downloaded at http://pewforum.org/bioethics/.

relatively stable, with about 55 percent favoring stem cell research and some 30 percent coming out against it, at least in part because they do not wish to destroy human embryos. The divide on stem cell research is very real. It is not quite as stark as in 2002, but polling suggests that it persists and is often understood as a debate between conducting potentially lifesaving research for the common good *and* protecting the sanctity of life.

What explains the difference between those who find that not destroying human embryos resonates most with them and those who find that conducting potentially lifesaving research is more important to them? After all, both lines of reasoning are highly charged and moralistic. Table 4.1 suggests, not surprisingly, that religion plays a key role. The data in Table 4.1 are drawn from a question that asked supporters and non-supporters of stem cell research what was the biggest influence on their views and beliefs pertaining to stem cell research. Religious beliefs are far and away the biggest factor differentiating the two groups. Amongst opponents of stem cell research, over half (52 percent) say their religious beliefs are the biggest influence on their thinking. Just 7 percent of those who favor conducting stem cell research said their religious beliefs were the biggest influence. Supporters were much more likely than non-supporters to report that the media (31 percent versus 13 percent) or their education (28 percent versus 12 percent) drove their views.

Religious beliefs also dominate all other potential sources influencing stem cell opinion. They are the modal category. Religious beliefs do more than differentiate supporters and non-supporters, then. They dominate the

Table 4.1   Influences and Positions on Stem Cell Research

	Conduct research (%)	Not destroy embryos (%)
Biggest influence on views and beliefs pertaining to stem cell research . . .		
Religious beliefs	7	52
Media	31	13
Education	28	12
Personal experience	16	9
Something else	11	8
Friends and family	5	5
Don't know	2	1
	100%	100%

Source: Pew Forum on Religion and Public Life. Findings released August 2005. http://pewforum.org/bioethics/

thought processes of non-supporters and are the single biggest factor influencing opinion across the board.

The contours of public opinion on stem cell research are clear. Stem cell research registers high in the public consciousness; there is a substantial divide between supporters and non-supporters; this divide is couched in moral language; and religious beliefs are absolutely central to understanding the sources of opinion difference. But why? Why is it that those who rely on religious beliefs are more apt to be against stem cell research? This finding at least suggests that those who rely so heavily on their religious beliefs when making up their mind on stem cell research are getting fundamentally different messages than those who rely on the media or their education to formulate opinion. We now take up this issue by summarizing the procedures involved in stem cell research and the corresponding discourses that surround these procedures as they relate to religion. This discussion makes clear that Catholic and evangelical religious traditions have taken the most prominent stance against stem cell research and typically understand the issue as one of protecting the sanctity of human life. Those immersed in these traditions are the most apt to be exposed to the debate on stem cell research as it relates to the moral status of the embryo.

STEM CELL RESEARCH: DOMINANT DISCOURSES, RELIGION, AND THE SCIENCE INVOLVED

The two dominant discourses operating in American politics regarding stem cell research have divergent views on using human embryos for deriving genetic material.[13] Given the importance of religious beliefs when individuals do not support stem cell research, it is not surprising that only one of these polarities is overtly religious. Indeed, only one utilizes direct references to God, scripture, and particular religious conceptions of human life. We focus on the two extremes in order to demonstrate how only one is consciously grounded in religious rhetoric, as this helps illuminate why those relying on their religious beliefs tend to oppose stem cell research.

Dominant Discourses: Polarities Emerge

At one end of the discourse on stem cell research is the view that all life is sacred and that one should never destroy a human being for the benefit of the other. This position assumes a deontological approach by advocating a moral stance noting that "the human individual called into existence by God and made in the divine image and likeness . . . must always be treated as an end in himself or herself, not merely as a means to other ends . . . "[14]

To kill the innocent deliberately is to violate the God-given privilege of re-creation.[15] Creating an embryo outside the human body is also problematic in this view, because it removes the role of parents in the marital relationship, a covenant sanctified by God.[16]

This polarity is closely associated with conservative Christian and evangelical traditions. The Christian Coalition notes that "if the federal government were to allow embryonic stem cell research it would be the first time that our government has declared that a non-consenting human being may be exploited and killed for experimental research purposes." Focus on the Family, which identifies itself as having strong claims to the evangelical community, states that embryonic stem cell research not only kills "the tiniest of human beings," but it violates the medical ethics of "do no harm." (Appendix 4.1 lists just some of the high profile groups associated with either tradition that have come out strongly against stem cell research.)

It is easy to see that the opposition to stem cell research arises from views regarding the sanctity of life and is closely tied to the politics surrounding abortion.[17] Allowing women to donate stem cells from aborted fetuses is thought to encourage abortion and create an "open market" that promotes abortions.[18] While there is a "desire to respect pluralism in a democratic society," this respect for pluralism "is not a morally valid basis for failing to protect the right of each member of the community" under this view.[19]

In sharp contrast to deontological viewpoints on the status of the human embryo, there are other individuals who articulate a developmental view of the embryo. This is the other extreme of the debate. Those in this arena typically view the zygote as not being individualized prior to day fourteen (a pre-embryo) and therefore "too rudimentary in structure [and] development to have moral status or interests in their own right."[20] To those upholding this view, a cost-benefit analysis clearly demonstrates that the potential health benefits of stem cell research far outweigh protecting unformed embryonic cells. Other religious groups, such as the Episcopal Church, note that it is the responsibility of religious individuals to "heal the afflicted."

These two polarities thus turn on the moral status of the embryo. On the one hand, prominent religious traditions equate the embryo with viable human life and oppose stem cell research. On the other hand, proponents typically focus on the many potential medical benefits emerging from stem cell research and do not equate the genetic materials used in the research with viable human life. Again, see Appendix 4.1 for variation within the religious views.

Linking these views to the science of embryonic stem cell research requires some nuts and bolts on the procedures involved. First the key terms:

- *Genes:* a functional unit of heredity located on a specific site on a chromosome. Genes make up specific sections of DNA, which serves as a building block for proteins.
- *Blastocyst:* usually a spherical structure produced by cleavage of a fertilized egg cell; consists of a single layer of cells surrounding a fluid-filled cavity called the blastocel.
- *DNA:* deoxyribonucleic acid, the building block of life, often referred to as the genetic code.
- *Stem Cell:* cells that have the ability to divide for indefinite periods of time in culture and which can give rise to specialized cells.
- *Pluripotent:* cells capable of giving rise to most tissues of an organism.
- *Totipotent:* cells that have unlimited capability. Cells that are referred to as being totipotent have the ability to specialize into a myriad of tissues, membranes, and organs.[21]

Stem cells have the ability to divide for indefinite periods of time into specialized cells. When a single cell is created through fertilization, either through natural means or artificially, this single cell is *totipotent*, meaning that its potential is total. For the first several days after fertilization, the cell continues to divide into identical totipotent cells. During this time period, this mass of totipotent cells could be separated manually or separated naturally and identical twins or identical triplets could be derived from the initial, single totipotent cell. After several cycles of cell divisions, which usually take 3–4 days, totipotent cells begin to specialize, forming a hollow sphere of cells called a *blastocyst*. The blastocyst, which derives from a *blastocel*, has a cluster of cells inside the outer ring referred to as the inner cell mass and an outer layer of cells separated from the inner cell mass by the hollow sphere.

The outer layer cells form the placenta and other tissues necessary for development. The inner cell mass forms most if not all of the tissues of the human body. It is important to note in light of the polarities regarding stem cell research that the inner cell mass on its own cannot create a complete organism because the necessary supporting tissue, derived from the outer cell layers, is not present. Thus, the inner cell mass is referred to as being pluripotent—they may give rise to many types of cells but not all the cells necessary for development. Because their potential is not total (they cannot form complete human structures), they are not referred to a totipotent, nor can they be referred to as being embryos. These pluripotent cells can, however, form specialized cells that have very specific functions. An example of a pluripotent stem cell would be a myocardial stem cell. This pluripotent cell generates the heart's cardiac cells.[22]

Presently, researchers have identified two successful methods of obtaining pluripotent stem cells for research purposes. The first method involves directly removing the inner cell mass of human embryos at the blastocyst stage. Developed by Dr. James Thomson, this procedure utilized pluripotent stem cells from consenting donor couples who had discarded the *in vitro fertilized* (IVF) embryos following successful infertility treatments. Dr. Thomson isolated the inner cell mass, extracted the pluripotent cells and cultured a new pluripotent stem cell line in Petri dishes. For the religious pole on stem cell research, this procedure is problematic because of the fact that the pluripotent stem cells are derived from discarded embryos. Proponents, however, note that the cells harvested do not have the potential to become human.

In contrast to the IVF embryo procedure, Dr. John Gearhart obtained pluripotent stem cells from fetal tissue he obtained in terminated pregnancies (not IVF embryos). Dr. Gearhart isolated inner cell mass material from consenting adult(s) prior to termination of a pregnancy and extracted the blastocysts, generating a new strain of pluripotent stem cells. Removing inner cell mass for the creation of pluripotent new stem cell lines does prevent the embryo from being viable, but as others note, these cells are collected amongst consenting women receiving abortions.[23]

In keeping with the two discourses outlined, there is also considerable discussion of what promise pluripotent stem cell therapy may hold. Pharmaceutical companies and medical researchers argue they can experiment and conduct trials on new medicines in a quicker, more effective manner with pluripotent stem cells.[24] Research at crucial times of pluripotent stem cell division may also allow researchers to identify the factors involved in the cellular decision-making process that results in cell specialization. By knowing when, where, and how to "turn genes on and off," researchers may combat such medical conditions as cancer, leukemia, and birth defects.[25] Finally, pluripotent stem cells may be used in creating therapies which generate new cells and tissues. Pluripoent stem cells have the potential to develop into specialized cells replacing damaged cells and tissues. This discovery has far reaching implications for individuals needing donor organs, for patients suffering from diseases such as Alzheimer's and Parkinson's, as well as for stroke patients, burn victims, arthritis suffers, and those with Lou Gehrig's disease.[26]

The science of stem cell research thus provides fodder for both polarities of the dominant discourses on stem cell research. It is true that as individuals learn more about stem cell research they become more apt to favor it. Indeed, roughly two-thirds of those who had heard a lot about the issue (68 percent) believe it is more important to conduct stem cell research than not to destroy the potential life of embryos. That compares with 49 percent of those who had heard a little about the issue and just a third of those who were unfamiliar with the debate over stem cell research.[27] However, this pattern does not hold so well for those who rely on their religious beliefs for formulating their views on stem cell research.

The puzzle in need of solving is thus complete: stem cell research is a highly visible and a contested political issue. The biggest division between everyday Americans who do and do not support it is whether or not their religious beliefs are the primary source from which they formulate their opinions. Investigation into the two polarities on stem cell research indicates that only one of them makes overt, direct references to religion as it related to the moral status of the procedures involved. The science of stem cell research offers these opponents evidence to support their views but also provides evidence to support the discourse that favors stem cell research and does not make direct religious appeals. Religion thus matters for stem cell opinion in everyday politics and in the cultural discourses surrounding stem cell research. Religion seems to be the fault line along which the stem cell debate divides. In the next section, we put this proposition to a more advanced empirical test by determining how, exactly, religion influences individuals' opinions on stem cell research. Our analysis recognizes there are many aspects of religious experiences and isolates those that are influential when it comes to opinions on stem cell research. We isolate those aspects of religious experiences that specifically activate and reinforce the fault line separating supporters and non-supporters of stem cell research.

USING THE DIMENSIONS OF RELIGIOSITY TO UNDERSTAND VIEWS ON STEM CELL RESEARCH

Religious values "are comprised of a highly complex nexus of human associations steeped in tradition and normative structures. These associations may be voluntary or non-voluntary, relatively large or small, formal or informal, highly institutionalized or loosely knit together."[28] For instance, religiosity may involve formal or informal affiliation with church groups or religious political organizations. It may also involve private and/or public activities such as church attendance, frequency of prayer, Bible/Koran/Torah reading, protest activity, etc. Piu-Yan Lam recognized these gradations (or dimensions of religiosity) and offered a formal operationalization of religiosity's four key components: the affiliative dimension, the participatory dimension, the theological dimension, and the devotional dimension. His subsequent work indicates *these four dimensions differentially influence the processes by which the private aspects of religion merge with the public activities of the religious individual.*[29]

In keeping with our effort to understand how (not just if) religiosity influences opinion on stem cell research, we test for the potential effect each of Lam's measures of religiosity has on stem cell opinion. Doing so determines what, precisely, it is about particular religious experiences that impacts opinion on stem cell research. Lam's dimensions of religiosity help us determine how it is that the macro-level religious perspectives translate and filter through to influence individual-level opinion.

Data, Methodology, and Findings

Our analysis utilizes Pew's "Religion and Public Life" 2002 survey. These data are advantageous as they include questions that operationalize each of Lam's four dimensions of religiosity (described below) and allow for results generalizable to the American population. Individuals were selected for inclusion in the survey via random generation of the last two digits of telephone numbers selected on the basis of area code, telephone exchange (first three digits of a seven-digit telephone number), and bank number (fourth and fifth digits). This ensured all listed and unlisted residential households were in the sampling frame and randomly selected for inclusion. This produced a sample of some 2002 respondents.

We present a series of cross-tabulations that examines the effect of the dimensions of religiosity that in turn may reasonably influence views on stem cell research. The main variable in each model is derived from a question that asked respondents if they supported stem cell research over not destroying human embryos. For researchers this is coded as a dichotomous variable where "yes" answers signify that the individual supports stem cell research (yes = 1, no = 0).

The explanatory variables in each table are those that operationalize Lam's four dimensions of religiosity. The first dimension of religiosity he delineates is the *affiliative dimension*—or simple identification with a particular religious tradition. This aspect of religiosity is what Tocqueville noted when he praised the value of religious groups in promoting civic engagement in the United States.[30] Evidence from the modern day tempers this excitement somewhat, as not all religious bodies promote civic engagement.[31] In light of these differences, Lam identifies five affiliative possibilities: Protestants, Catholics, Mormons, Jews, and others. We also add Evangelicals to the mix (operationalized by "yes" responses to the question of whether or not one has been "born again"). Given the religious links apparent in the anti-stem cell research discourse, we expect Catholics and Evangelicals to be more likely to oppose stem cell research.

Table 4.2 clearly demonstrates the role one's religious affiliation has as it

Table 4.2 Support for Stem Cell Research Based on the Religious Affiliation

Religious Affiliation	% Who Support	% Who Oppose
Protestants	58.1	41.9
Catholics	30.7	69.3
Jews	72.8	27.2
Mormons	28.6	71.4
Others	56.3	43.7
Born Again	33.3	66.7

Source: Pew Forum on Religion and Public Life.

pertains to views pertaining about stem cell research. Protestants, Jews, and those that identify as belonging to a religious faith in the "Other" category support stem cell research at a much higher rate than the other religious traditions/faiths. Jews overwhelmingly support the idea of stem cell research at a 3:1 rate while Protestants and Others support it at much closer margins. Not surprisingly, individuals who identify as being "born-again" do not support stem cell research at a 2:1 rate. Born-again Christians are traditionally thought of as belonging to the conservative spectrum of the Protestant movement, and as such these statistics further show a separation or chasm between the modern/liberal wing of the Protestant church and the conservative wing of the Protestant church in matters of social policy.

Catholics and Mormons do not support stem cell research—Catholics at a 2:1 opposition rate while Mormons are at a much higher opposition rate (72 percent opposed; 28 percent support). It is important to note that both Catholics and Mormons have strong hierarchical leadership structures and that this may affect their overall belief patterns.

These findings are not particularly surprising given the degree to which we have seen that the anti-stem cell research position is associated with the Catholic Church in dominant discourse, as well as the strongly anti-stem cell stance taken by many Catholic Church leaders and groups (Appendix 4.1). Their stance is consistent with the Magisterium of the Catholic Church, which in the encyclical *Evangelium Vitae* states "that from the first moment of its existence, the embryo must be guaranteed unconditional respect which is morally due to the human being in his or her totality and unity in body and spirit."[32] As predicted, those who identify as "evangelical" or "born again" are also less likely to support stem cell research when compared to those who do not identify as such. Here again we see that those churches associated with a strong stance against stem cell research tend to have parishioners who are more apt to take this position.

The second dimension of religiosity outlined by Lam recognizes that identifying as a member of a specific religious tradition does not necessarily indicate the degree to which an individual prioritizes this tradition, and the social/political views it espouses, in their life. This is the *theological dimension* of religiosity. We examine the role this influence has on stem cell opinion by including a cross-tab analysis that assesses *one's belief that religion is important in their life*.[33] Inclusion of the theological dimension, however, begins the process of understanding how (not just whether) religion matters for the stem cell debate.

The findings from Table 4.3 show that as one's religion becomes more important in their life, their support for stem cell research diminishes. It is not just belonging to a particular religious tradition that influences opinion then. The degree of immersion matters tremendously, as there is a difference of 43.6 percentage points between those whose religion is important in their life and those who say religion is not important in their life as it pertains to their support for stem cell research.

Inclusion of Lam's *participatory dimension* of religiosity continues in this regard. Churches, synagogues, mosques, and other places of worship provide "networks for social relations"[34] where participation in sponsored activities can provide civic skills transferable to other arenas, like community volunteering.[35] Alternatively, participation in the activities of religious institutions may undermine participation in secular organizations."[36] The participatory dimension is measured using two bonding activities: frequency of attendance at religious services and volunteering within one's house of worship.

Within the participatory dimension of religiosity, results indicate that as attendance at religious services increases, support for embryonic stem cell research decreases (77.2 percent to 26.4 percent). Levels of involvement in religious activities also have an effect on support levels for embryonic stem cell research. This pattern suggests that it is the formal exposure to religious tenets (through religious services) coupled with the social networks that usually develop from volunteering in one's house of worship that impact

Table 4.3 Support for Stem Cell Research Based on Whether Religion Is Important in Your Life

Religion is	% Who Support	% Who Oppose
Very Important	39.7	60.3
Fairly Important	70.1	29.9
Not Very important	83.3	16.7

Source: Pew Forum on Religion and Public Life

Table 4.4 Support for Stem Cell Research Based on Attendance at Church Services

Attendance at Church...	% Who Support	% Who Oppose
More than once a week	22.8	77.2
Once a week	43.6	56.4
Once/twice a month	57.6	42.4
Few times a year	66.2	33.8
Seldom	73.0	27.0
Never	73.6	26.4

Source: Pew Forum on Religion and Public Life

policy views for stem cell research—those who indicated that they were very involved in their church opposed stem cell research by a 2:1 margin (66.0 percent to 33.1 percent).

Lam's fourth dimension of religiosity, *devotional,* highlights those religious activities undertaken in private and how these may affect views on public policy. Activities like reading the Bible, Koran, Torah or other holy book can certainly be done within the confines of a religious institution. When done in private though, these devotional activities are important "symbolic reinforcements" of individual religiosity that may exacerbate one's internalization of their religious institution's policy views.[37] By the same token, praying on a regular basis may "not necessarily reinforce one's religious values and motivate involvement in community activities and political participation."[38] To differentiate between these potential effects for views on stem cell research, we include a cross-tabs measure of how frequently an individual prays in the model that follows.

This final dimension had a measurable effect on support for embryonic stem cell research. As the frequency of praying increased, the overall support for stem cell research decreased. This has enormous implications on public policy and public opinion. It demonstrates that although praying is an ac-

Table 4.5 Support for Stem Cell Research Based on Church Involvement

Involvement in Church	% Who Support	% Who Oppose
Very involved	33.1	66.9
Somewhat involved	41.6	58.4
Not too involved	55.1	44.9
Not at all involved	65.3	34.7

Source: Pew Forum on Religion and Public Life

Table 4.6 Support for Stem Cell Research Based on Prayer Frequency

Prayer Frequency...	% Who Support	% Who Oppose
Several times a day	35.4	64.6
Once a day	54.0	46.0
Few times a week	55.6	44.4
Once a week or less	71.4	28.6
Never	87.1	12.9

Source: Pew Forum on Religion and Public Life

tivity performed by many who do not belong to a particular faith or tradition, it has an effect on public opinion for those that are religious regardless of their religious affiliation.

For those interested in exploring the correlations listed above, a multivariate analysis is included in Appendix 4.1 as Table 4.7. This analysis shows that these correlations hold with appropriate control variables in place. So, what can we conclude about this analysis, and what are the implications for the findings in Tables 4.1–4.7?

Stepping back, the overall pattern of results has at least two major implications. First, it is impossible to understand why mass publics so frequently take opposing views on stem cell research without looking to religion. Second, religion matters in very specific ways for stem cell opinion. Those who simply affiliate or identify as Catholic or Evangelical are substantially less apt to favor stem cell research. They are more apt to mirror the stated, and highly politicized, preferences of their church leaders in this regard. By contrast, those who affiliate with religious traditions who have not taken such defining views on the stem cell debate do not, on average, have their religious tradition influence their opinions on this issue. But there is substantially more to the story than the effect of just affiliating with a particular religious tradition. The more one attends any religious service, and the more important one reports religion is in their life, the less likely they are to support stem cell research. Devotional activities, like praying, and heavy involvement in the activities of one's house of worship (social or service) impact support for stem cell research as well. *This indicates that it is a combination of the doctrinal aspects of religious involvement as well as the more informal social networking and personal devotional activities that drive policy opinions as it pertains to stem cell research.* We now have answers to the question of how, exactly, religiosity influences opinion on stem cell research. It is through regular exposure to formal religious views and the prioritization of religion in one's life coupled with religious doctrine and

Table 4.7 Dimensions of Religiosity and Support for Stem Cell Research

	Beta	Standard Error	P > |z|	Exp (B)
Affiliation Dimension				
Catholics	−.392	.174	.024	.676
Mormons	−.977	.540	.070	.377
Jews	−.298	.277	.283	.743
Others	−.913	1.568	.560	.401
Control: *Protestants*				
Evangelical (Born Again)	−.716	.170	.000	.489
Theological Dimension				
Importance of Religion	−.508	.205	.013	1.057
Participatory Dimension				
Frequency of attendance	−.412	.090	.000	.662
Involved in Church	.055	.179	.758	1.057
Devotional Dimension				
Frequency of Prayer Ritual	−.059	.083	.473	.942
Other Variables				
Age	−.084	.223	.705	.919
Age^2	.019	.030	.530	1.019
Married	−.130	.153	.395	.878
Education	**.339**	**.080**	**.000**	**1.403**
African American	.286	.254	.260	1.331
Minority, Not African Am.	−.083	.345	.811	.921
Income	.030	.070	.663	1.031
Political Conservatism	**−.322**	**.087**	**.000**	**.724**
Female	−.054	.147	.711	.947
Constant	**2.983**	**.591**	**.000**	**19.747**
−2 log likelihood	1184.087			
Nagelkerke R-Square	.220			
N	2002			

Note: Binary Logistical Regression Analysis. All test results are for a two-tailed test. *Data Source:* Politics and Religion Survey. 2002. Pew Center for the People and the Press.

religious social networks or private activities that significantly impact views on stem cell research.

CONCLUSION

Religion has always played a central, if contested, role in American politics and public policy.[39] This chapter has examined how, exactly, religion matters in the debate surrounding stem cell research. We saw how the stem cell debate has moved firmly into the political consciousness of everyday Americans and its prominence in the defining political discourse of the day.

In both instances, the division between supporters and non-supporters of stem cell research is firmly rooted in religion. Non-supporters were substantially more likely to rely on their religious beliefs when formulating their views on the issue. Cross-tabulation analysis allowed for ascertaining precisely what dimensions of religiosity influence views on stem cell research. Affiliating as Catholic or Evangelical, regular attendance of church services, and the prioritization of religion were what mattered. Thus, it was the affiliation with religious traditions that took prominent stances against stem cell research and the formal, doctrinal aspects of religiosity that mattered for stem cell opinion. The social networks that develop out of volunteering in one's house of worship and the private activities taken to affirm one's faith or religious beliefs also play an important role in forming opinions about stem cell research. Our analysis thus makes clear that religion matters for public policy opinion and matters in specific ways associated with simple religious affiliation *as well as* internalization/exposure to the formal, doctrinal aspects of one's house of worship.

All this has very real implications for politics and public policy. For example, it is clear that statements noting that particular religious groups are apt to feel one way or another on a policy issue fall somewhat short. The story is often in how these groups came to feel differently, as this is where the political possibilities lie. As various religious denominations and groups galvanize around "matters as central as procreation, family, human identity formation, and the meaning of life and death," much of what many Americans "think and feel springs from . . . religious and spiritual sources."[40] A lesson from our analysis is that policy entrepreneurs attempting to mobilize these forces toward various sides of an issue would do well to frame their attempts in language that resonates with doctrinal aspects of the religious group they are targeting. It is not a foregone conclusion that doing so denotes moving to the "right" or "left" of the political spectrum. It does, however, suggest that mobilizing (or shifting) those who rely heavily on their religious beliefs for opinion formulation requires making salient the ways a particular policy position can be rectified with doctrinal aspects of particular religious traditions. There is room for multiple policy positions in these traditions. Our analysis simply indicates that these positions must be shown to resonate within church doctrines for a sizable percentage of the American populace.

This does not mean that secular voices should not be appealed to. Far from it. As Nagel argues, "in a democracy, the aim of the procedures of decision-making should be to secure results that can be acknowledged as legitimate by as wide a portion of the citizenry as possible."[41] This requires acknowledging an array of views—those that pull on secular as well as religious traditions. Our analysis demonstrates how religion is far from a mere undercurrent in the stem cell debate and that doctrinal and affiliative aspects of religiosity are major divisions between supporters and non-supporters. Each merits voice and attention.

APPENDIX 4.1: GROUPS ASSOCIATED WITH VARIOUS RELIGIOUS TRADITIONS AND VIEWS ON STEM CELL RESEARCH

Against Stem Cell Research

Focus on the Family Focus on the Family opposes stem cell research using human embryos. They argue that in order for scientists to isolate and culture embryonic stem cells, a living, human embryo must be killed. It is never morally or ethically justified to kill one human being in order to benefit another. By requiring the destruction of embryos, the tiniest human beings, embryonic stem cell research violates the medical ethic of "Do No Harm."[42] Focus on the Family's mission is to cooperate with the Holy Spirit in sharing the Gospel of Jesus Christ with as many people as possible by nurturing and defending the God-ordained institution of the family and promoting biblical truths worldwide. As such, Focus on the Family has strong ties to the Christian evangelical movement.

Catholic Bishops The U.S. Conference of Catholic Bishops strongly opposes the destruction of embryos for medical research. Having called the August 2000 guidelines for destructive human embryo research immoral and illegal, the bishops excoriated President Bush's "accommodation" of destructive research already performed on existing embryonic stem-cell lines as "morally unacceptable" and urged him to "return to a principled stand." The bishops' position is based on the Church's commitment to preserving human life, which they believe occurs at the moment of conception.[43]

Christian Coalition The Christian Coalition contends that embryonic stem cell research is a violation of human rights. If the U.S. government were to place its stamp of approval on the destruction of living human embryos in order to obtain stem cells, it would be the first time that our government has declared that a non-consenting human being may be exploited and killed for experimental research purposes. The killing of human beings is never justified for research ends.[44] Christian Coalition of America is a political organization, made up of pro-family Americans who care deeply about becoming active citizens for the purpose of guaranteeing that government acts in ways that strengthen, rather than threaten, families. As such, they work together with Christians of all denominations, as well as with other Americans who agree with their mission and ideals.[45]

Concerned Women for America   Concerned Women for America objects to the process by which embryonic stem cells are obtained by killing embryos and argues that these embryos are too unstable to even begin human trials. They argue that we do not have to choose between curing lives and preserving lives of embryos; we can do both.[46] The mission of CWA is to protect and promote Biblical values among all citizens—first through prayer, then education, and finally by influencing our society—thereby reversing the decline in moral values in our nation.[47]

Southern Baptist Convention   The Southern Baptist Convention is on record for its enduring, consistent, and vigorous opposition to 1) elective abortion, 2) the use of fetal tissues harvested from elective abortions for research, and 3) experimentation using human embryonic stem cells obtained from electively-aborted embryos.[48]

Greek Orthodox Archdiocese of America   In vitro fertilization is looked upon with great doubt by the Greek Orthodox Archdiocese of America because present methods cause the destruction of numerous human fertilized ova and even developing fetuses; this is still a form of abortion. Genetic counseling and screening cannot be objected to in principle and in fact should be encouraged.[49]

For Stem Cell Research

Union of American Hebrew Congregations (Reform Jews)   There is an emerging consensus of Reform Jewish authorities that tissue obtained from either therapeutic or spontaneous abortions may be used for purposes of life-saving or life-enhancing research and treatment. Jewish requirements that we use our God-given knowledge to heal people, together with the concept of *pikuach nefesh* (the primary responsibility to save human life, which overrides almost all other laws), has been used by Jewish legal authorities to justify a broad range of organ transplants and medical experimentation. These requirements likewise justify the use of fetal tissue transplants.[50]

Episcopal Church   A task force reporting to the Episcopal Church's 2003 General Convention concluded that "it is in keeping with our call to heal the afflicted" to make use of embryos already held in fertility clinics, but took a "conservative and balanced approach," its chairman said, in stressing that the task force "does not recommend that embryos be created for this research."[51]

NOTES

1. Rupert Cornwell, "Fear and Loathing on the Road to the White House," *The Independent*, July 19, 2004, available at www.independent.co.uk, Peter S. Canellos, "Stem-Cell Vote Blurs Religion Based Politics," *The Boston Globe*, November 9, 2004.

2. Matthew Most, "Michael J. Fox Records Ad for Cardin: Actor Questions Steele's Stance on Funding for Stem Cell Research," *The Washington Post*, October 24, 2004.

3. Ronald Cole-Turner, "Religion Meets Research," *God and the Embryo: Religious Voices on Stem Cells and Cloning* (Washington, D.C.: Georgetown University Press, 2003), 7.

4. Pui-Yan Lam, "As the Flocks Gather: How Religion Affects Voluntary Association Participation," *Journal for the Scientific Study of Religion* 41, no. 3 (2002): 405–22.

5. John Green and James Guth, "From Lambs to Sheep: Denominational Change and Political Behavior," in *Rediscovering the Religious Factor in American Politics* (Armonk, NY: M.E. Sharpe, 1996).

6. Cole-Turner, "Religion Meets Research," 7.

7. Ibid., 11.

8. "Is the Ban on Federal Funding of Human Stem Cell Research Justified?" in *Taking Sides: Clashing Views on Bioethical Issues* (Dubuque, IA: McGraw-Hill Co. 2007), 206.

9. President's Council on Bioethics, "Monitoring Stem Cell Research," in *Taking Sides: Clashing Views on Bioethical Issues* (Dubuque, IA: McGraw-Hill Co. 2007), 209.

10. President George Bush, *President Discusses Stem Cell Research*, Crawford, TX, August 9, 2001; available at http://www.whitehouse.gov/news/releases/2001/08/20010809-2.html.

11. The Pew Forum on Religion and Public Life, "A Fact Sheet," January 2007, available at http://pewforum.org/docs. Survey utilized random sampling procedures and thus can be generalized to the population.

12. William T. Gormley Jr., "Regulatory Issue Networks in a Federal System," *Polity* 18, no. 4 (Summer 1986): 595–620.

13. Miriam Brouillet and Leigh Turner, "Bioethics, Religion, and Democratic Deliberation: Policy Formation and Embryonic Stem Cell Research," *HEC Forum* 17, no. 1 (2005): 49–63.

14. Richard M. Doerflinger, "The Ethics of Funding Embryonic Stem Cell Research: A Catholic Viewpoint," *Kennedy Institute of Ethics Journal* 9 (1999): 138.

15. Gene Outka, "The Ethics of Stem Cell Research," in *God and the Embryo:*

Religious Voices on Stem Cells and Cloning, ed. Brent Waters and Ronald Cole-Turner (Washington, D.C.: Georgetown University Press, 2003).

16. President George Bush, "White House News Release," as printed in *God and the Embryo: Religious Voices on Stem Cells and Cloning* (Washington, D.C.: Georgetown University Press, 2003), 7.

17. Doerflinger, "The Ethics of Funding Embryonic Stem Cell Research," 137.

18. Steve Parker, "Bringing the Gospel of Life to American Jurisprudence: A Religious, Ethical and Philosophical Critique of Federal Funding for Stem Cell Research," *Journal of Contemporary Health Law* 7 (2002): 771.

19. Brouillet and Turner, "Bioethics, Religion, and Democratic Deliberation," 53.

20. John A. Robertson, "Ethics and Policy in Embryonic Stem Cell Research," *Kennedy Institute of Ethics Journal* 9, no. 2 (1999): 117–118.

21. Numerous articles present primers that explain and expand upon stem cell research terminology. For a closer examination visit the National Institutes of Health at http://stemcells.nih.gov.

22. For further information related to how stem cells are formed, see Michael Ruse and Christopher Pynes, *The Stem Cell Controversy: Debating the Issues* (Amherst, NY: Prometheus Books, 2003) or Michael Bellomo, *The Stem Cell Divide* (New York: AMACOM, 2006).

23. On January 12, 2007, researchers announced that they had obtained viable pluripotent stem cells from the embryonic fluid surrounding the embryo. If proven to be viable, this research generates a new area of interest for stem cell research. See http://www.msnbc.msn.com/id/16514457.

24. Brouillet and Turner, "Bioethics, Religion, and Democratic Deliberation," 51. See also, I.N. Rich, "In Vitro Hexatotoxicology Testing in Drug Development," *Current Opinion in Drug Discovery and Development* 6, no. 1 (2002): 159–163.

25. Brouillet and Turner, "Bioethics, Religion, and Democratic Deliberation," 53.

26. T.L. Limke, "Neural Stem Cells in Ageing Disease," *Journal of Cellular and Molecular Medicine* 6, no. 4 (2002): 475–496.

27. Pew Forum on Religion and Public Life, August 2005, available at www.pewforum.org/bioethics/.

28. Brent Waters, "What is the Appropriate Contribution of Religious Communities in the Public Debate on Embryonic Stem Cell Research," *God and the Embryo: Religious Voices on Stem Cells and Cloning* (Washington, D.C.: Georgetown University Press, 2003), 19.

29. Lam, "As the Flocks Gather," 405–422.

30. Alexis de Tocqueville, *Democracy in America* (New York: Alfred A. Knopf, [1840] 1945).

31. Green and Guth, "From Lambs to Sheep"; Brian Lazerwitz, "Membership in Voluntary Associations and Frequency of Church Attendance," *Journal for the Scientific Study of Religion* 2, no. 1 (1962): 74–84. See also Robert Stark and

Charles Glock, *American Piety: The Nature of Religious Commitment* (Berkeley, CA: University of California Press, 1968).

32. John Paul II, *Evangelium Vitae*, quoted in Steve Parker, "Bringing the Gospel of Life to American Jurisprudence: A Religious, Ethical and Philosophical Critique of Federal Funding for Stem Cell Research," *Journal of Contemporary Health Law* 7 (2002): 771.

33. This variable is identified as a variable that separates conservatism from liberalism in many of the religious traditions today.

34. James Wilson and T. Janoski, "The Contribution of Religion to Volunteer Work," *Sociology of Religion* 56, no. 2 (1995): 138.

35. Nancy Ammerman, "Organized Religion in a Voluntaristic Society," *Sociology of Religion* 58, no. 3 (1997): 202.

36. Lam, "As the Flocks Gather," 407.

37. L.D. Nelson and R.R. Dynes, "The Impact of Devotionalism and Attendance on Ordinary and Emergency Helping Behavior," *Journal for the Scientific Study of Religion* 15, no. 1 (1976): 52.

38. Lam, "As the Flocks Gather," 408.

39. Carla Messikomer, Renee Fox, and Judith Swazey, "Presence and Influence of Religion in American Bioethics," *Perspectives in Biology and Medicine* 44, no. 4 (2001): 505.

40. Harold Shapiro, "Ethical Considerations and Public Policy: A Ninety Day Exercise in Practical and Professional Ethics: Cloning Human Beings," *Science and Engineering Ethics* 5 (1999): 3–16; see also Messikomer et al., 501.

41. Thomas Nagel, "Moral Epistemology," in *Society's Choices* (Washington, D.C.: National Academy Press, 1995), 201–214.

42. Available at http://www.citizenlink.org/FOSI/bioethics/cloning/A000002295.cfm.

43. Available at http://www.americancatholic.org/News/StemCell/default.asp.

44. Available at http://www.cc.org/content.cfm?srch=stem+cell+research.

45. Available at http://www.cc.org/.

46. Available at http://www.cwfa.org/articledisplay.asp?id=6087&department=CWA&categoryid=life.

47. Available at http://www.cwfa.org/about.asp.

48. Available at http://www.sbcannualmeeting.org/sbc99/res7.htm.

49. Available at www.goarch.org.

50. Available at http://urj.org/index.cfm?.

51. Available at http://www.episcopalchurch.org/3654_75220_ENG_HTM.htm.

FURTHER READING

There are numerous recently published articles and books dealing with the relatively new public policy issue surrounding stem cell research. The President's Council on Bioethics offers numerous views on the experimentation issues surrounding stem cell research and can be accessed by visiting http://www.bioethics

.com. When you visit this site, make sure and read the report entitled "Monitoring Stem Cell Research" (January 2004). You can also visit the website of the International Society for Stem Cell research at http://www.isscr.org, which highlights opposing views of the stem cell debate and offers valuable insight into the moral and ethical debate of using embryonic stem cells for research purposes. An additional excellent reference for understanding the debates surrounding stem cell research is *Taking Sides: Clashing Views on Bioethical Issues*, Issue 12, "Is the Ban on Federal Funding of Human Stem Cell Research Justified?" (2004, McGraw-Hill Companies). Numerous scholarly journals are available that address the question of stem cell research, including the *Kennedy Institute of Ethics Journal* (March 2004) and the January-February 2006 issue of the *Hastings Center Report*, which contain a series of articles on questions related to stem cells. For views supporting the experimentation on and use of stem cells in medical research, see "Embryonic Stem Cell Research: An Ethical Justification," *Georgetown Law Journal* 90 (2002), and website for the Union of American Hebrew Congregations (Reform Jews) at http://urj.org/index and the website of the Episcopal Church at http://www.episcopalchurch.org.

For views opposing stem cell research, see the website for Focus on the Family (http://www.citizenlink.org) and the Christian Coalition (http://www.cc.org). See also "Are We Killing the Weak to Heal the Sick? Federally Funded Embryonic Stem Cell Research," in *Health Matrix: Journal of Law-Medicine* (Summer 2002).

5

Tracing Sanctuary and Illegal Immigration as a Church and State Issue

Samuel S. Stanton Jr.

On August 16, 2006, Elvira Arellano refused to comply with an order from the U.S. Office of Immigration and Customs Enforcement directing her to return to her home country—Mexico. Instead, she has taken sanctuary in Adalberto United Methodist Church in Chicago, Illinois, resurrecting memories of the Sanctuary Movement of the 1980s when churches sheltered undocumented aliens who they claimed should have been protected refugees from civil wars in El Salvador and Guatemala. Ms. Arellano, by her own admission, came to this country from Mexico to make a better life for herself.[1] She entered the country illegally in 1997 using false documents and was caught and returned to Mexico. She returned shortly with a different set of false documents and found work in Washington State—where she gave birth to her son, Saul (who is now 7 years old). Ms. Arellano moved to Chicago in 2000, took a job at O'Hare International Airport using false documents, and was arrested in 2002. Senators Durbin and Obama previously secured stays of deportation for Ms. Arellano, but they have expired. Both of these senators are now on record saying that Ms. Arellano must obey current immigration laws.[2] Her legal entry into this country aside, the case of Ms. Arellano has little in common with the provision of sanctuary for Central Americans fleeing violence in their countries of origin.

In the late 1970s and early 1980s, churches, primarily in the southwestern United States but supported by churches found in every region of the country, provided sanctuary to people from Central America and South America who entered the United States illegally. Unlike the case of Elvira Arellano, the majority of these recipients of sanctuary came to the United States seeking asylum as political refugees from the civil wars and violence that marked Central America and South America during that time period. But as in the case of Elvira Arellano, regarding the provision of sanctuary to illegal entrants to the country, hereafter referred to as illegal immigrants, most people in the United States are unaware of the history and philosophy of religious sanctuary.

So, what is this practice to which Ms. Arellano appeals? What place does it hold in the relations of church and state? To answer these questions, this chapter is organized in three sections. First, the definition of the current understanding of sanctuary is developed. This is done by examining the Judeo-Christian tradition regarding sanctuary by tracing the practice of sanctuary from its biblical inception to the present day. Particular attention is given in this section to understanding the current status of sanctuary as providing asylum. Second, consideration is given to how theories regarding the relationship between asylum/sanctuary and immigration should be applied by states. Third, this chapter examines how the practice and theory of sanctuary bring church and state into confrontation.

SANCTUARY

Biblical Roots

The biblical inception of sanctuary is found in the books of law attributed to Moses. In the book of Numbers, there are two passages in the 35th chapter that delineate the Jewish legal system's creation of sanctuary:

Then you shall appoint cities to be cities of refuge for you; that the manslayer who kills any person accidentally may flee there. They shall be cities of refuge for you from the avenger, that the manslayer may not die until he stands before the congregation in judgment. And of the cities, which you give, you shall have six cities of refuge. You shall appoint three cities on this side of the Jordan, and three cities you shall appoint in the land of Canaan, which will be cities of refuge. These six cities shall be for refuge for the children of Israel, for the stranger, and for the sojourner among them, that anyone who kills a person accidentally may flee there.[3]

Sanctuary in its Biblical context is God's command to Moses to create safe havens for people fleeing from the commission of manslaughter. There were specific limits on the location and number of havens to be provided for those who "killeth any person unawares." Traditional Judeo-Christian theological writing suggests that sanctuary, as described in Numbers, was to provide protection from vigilante justice.[4] The safety of these places was provided both for the citizens of Israel and for visitors in the country. But no distinction is made in the Biblical ideal of sanctuary between a legal visitor to the country and an illegal visitor to the country. There is a contextual understanding that visitors were family and relatives of people living in the country as subjects of the king, or that they were visitors in the country at the request of the king or his ministers. Anyone else in the country who did not declare their presence to the local authorities would be considered a spy—a livelihood punishable by death if caught.

Sanctuary is not, however, in its Biblical roots, protection from trial. A person found guilty of murder is still condemned to death. Also, as seen in the passage that follows, any person found guilty of manslaughter is forced to remain inside the boundaries of the city of refuge until the death of the current high priest, at which time the individual may return to their original home. At any time that the person seeking sanctuary left the city of refuge, a blood relative of the slain could kill the person without being guilty of murder.

Then the congregation shall judge between the manslayer and the avenger of blood according to these judgments. So the congregation shall deliver the manslayer from the hand of the avenger of blood, and the congregation shall return him to the city of refuge where he had fled, and he shall remain there until the death of the high priest who was anointed with the holy oil. But if the manslayer at any time goes outside of the limits of the city of refuge where he fled, and the avenger of blood finds him outside of the limits of his city of refuge, and the avenger of blood kills the manslayer, he shall not be guilty of blood, because he should have remained in his city of refuge until the death of the high priest. But after the death of the high priest the manslayer may return to the land of his possession.[5]

Sanctuary applied in this standard does provide a form of punishment to a manslayer, namely, a form of house arrest. It is a punishment from which there is no reprieve and to which there is no end, except the death of the high priest. This form of punishment for the sanctuary seeker is repeated in historical uses of sanctuary and in no use prior to that in the United States during the last few decades was there any hope that the recipient of sanctuary might one day walk free among the population of the country without the death of a high priest, pope, or king.

Sanctuary in Historical Context

Sanctuary as we understand it in a more modern context is devoid of the scriptural references of Mosaic times. Instead, it is in reference to the inviolability of all things sacred in the Holy Roman Church. There is little record of the application of sanctuary during the first three centuries C.E. We do know that it was generally in use in the Holy Roman Church, and that it was applied by bishops of the Church. The problematic way in which the right of sanctuary was meted out by local bishops actually led Theodosius the Great to outlaw the practice in the late 390s C.E., but it was resurrected in the first decade of the fifth century.[6]

It was determined and accepted by Clovis I at the First Council of Orleans (511 C.E.) that refuge (sanctuary) could be claimed in a church or the ecclesiastical residences. This sanctuary was for adulterers, murderers, and thieves. Also, the right of sanctuary was to be given to fugitive slaves, with the stipulation that a slave be returned to his master if the master swore on the Bible not to treat the slave cruelly.[7] This decree gives a delineation of sanctuary above and beyond the strict application of it as given in the Jewish law.

The earliest mentions of the practice of sanctuary in England trace to the reign of King Ethelbert and his 600 C.E. codifications. The practice was very limited and very structured, demanding that the offender be within the sanctuary zone surrounding the church building prior to declaring sanctuary. Ethelbert's codifications required a claimant to sanctuary declare in detail the guilt of the crime for which sanctuary was sought within 40 days of entering sanctuary. A fee was paid to the church for sanctuary and after admitting guilt the claimant had to enter exile by traveling a prescribed route within a set (and brief) period of time to the nearest port city and never return to England. If after forty days you did not confess, you were handed over to the civil authorities.[8] Henry VIII limited the number of sanctuary cities in England to 7 in 1540 and in the same act limited it to murderers and felony level thievery. James I formally abolished sanctuary in England and English Common Law in 1623.[9] For the United States, this is an important factor to remember, as most of the laws and legal practices in the United States today trace their roots to English Common Law (with the notable exception of the state of Louisiana, which traces its legal system to the Napoleonic Codes).

Sanctuary in U.S. History

In the United States, sanctuary as an organized practice prior to the 1900s finds it roots in the abolitionist movement. It was a means of smuggling escaped slaves into free states or out of the United States entirely. The religious aspect of this practice was exemplified by the involvement of the Society of Friends, or Quakers. Pennsylvania as a colony was formed to provide a sanctuary (safe haven) for Quakers, and Quakers have been deeply involved in every Sanctuary Movement in the United States. This participation by members of a church represents a direct link between the practice of religion by members of a church and violation of laws of this country. With the passage of the Thirteenth Amendment to the Constitution in 1865, slavery was abolished in the United States. The organized practice of sanctuary as a means of protecting and promoting the freedom of slaves was no longer necessary.

Sanctuary in the United States in its early practice became the protection not of adulterers, murderers, and thieves, as it was in England, but the protection of the freedom and liberty of individuals. It also became a movement in opposition to the legal system of the country and not a surrogate part of the legal system by common practice. Where sanctuary before had meant the harboring of fugitives with justice to be applied by trial in the church or by admission of guilt by the fugitive and punishment meted by the church, in the United States it has become the harboring of fugitives from the sanction of law. Or, as argued by the defendants in the most renowned case dealing with sanctuary in the United States in the last 30 years, sanctuary has become the enforcement of laws by the people when the state has failed in its duty.[10] Clearly, sanctuary in the United States as currently practiced is tied to the idea of the status of individuals seeking asylum in this country.

Before examining the specifics of the Sanctuary Movement in the southwestern United States and its current resurrection in connection with illegal immigration issues, it is necessary to look at how the practice of sanctuary came to be tied to the question of political asylum. The first subject to be addressed is what is political asylum? It is also necessary to address theoretically how states make determinations about the application of political asylum—which in turn better allows us to understand the decision of churches and their members to offer sanctuary in violation of the laws of the United States.

Sanctuary and Asylum, International Law

During the first half of the twentieth century, violent conflicts and political issues that arose in many areas of the world caused the displacement of many people. The League of Nations did what it could to provide ad hoc answers and negotiate solutions to specific situations, but no general definition of refugee was created, nor was a standardized procedure adopted for handling refugees. The contemporary understanding of sanctuary, namely as a form of asylum, finds its roots in the post WWII development of the Cold War. It is a natural continuation both in language and practice to apply the idea of hosting refugees as providing a sanctuary for them.

In July 1951, the Convention Relating to the Status of Refugees was adopted by a special United Nations Conference.[11] Drafted between 1948 and 1951, and involving the participation of 26 states, it gave the first general definition of refugee. Additionally, it lists five reasons to consider a person as a refugee—race, religion, nationality, social group membership, and political opinion. If such categories were reason for a person to have a well-grounded fear of being subject to serious harm if they returned to their state of origin, then they could seek sanctuary in a foreign land.[12] The 1951 Convention also provides a guarantee of not returning a refugee to their country of origin if doing so would subject them to persecution.[13] One shortcoming of the 1951 Convention is that it limited the status of refugees to persons who feared for their well being because of events prior to January 1, 1951. Anyone seeking refuge for an event after that date was not covered by the UN Convention. In 1967 a Protocol was adopted, affirming the primary details of the 1951 Convention but eliminating the time constraints, making refugee status universally applicable regardless of the date of the event. As of 2005, over 140 states have signed the Convention and Protocol.[14]

We must recognize that some serious limitations exist pursuant to the Convention and Protocol. First, the fact is that refugee status is limited to the civil and political status of an individual caused by race, religious affiliation, national origin, membership in a social group, or expressed political opinion. There is no concern for the quality of life expressed in the legal definition of a refugee. What if events simply overtake a person, forcing this person to flee their country of origin, not because of some classification, but because natural and man-made disasters occur? By the language of the Convention and Protocol this person has no claim to refugee status. What this means is that a person fleeing a civil war does not have the right of refugee status unless they can demonstrate successfully that fitting into one of five categories provides a well-founded fear that they will be persecuted if returned to their country of origin. This is not readily demonstrable in most cases. It also means that simply wanting a better life is not cause for granting refugee status to individuals.

The second limitation that we must recognize is that the Convention and Protocol make individual states responsible for determining if a person qualifies under the provisions of the Convention to be considered a refugee. There is no international right of immigration or to refugee status. This is in keeping with the idea that no supra-national government exists that can dictate behavior to states. States themselves are responsible for maintaining the international system, according to realist theories. Many competing theories of international relations attribute to non-state actors in the system equal or partial responsibility along side states for maintaining the international system. Examples of those non-state actors include civic/social organizations (churches, interest groups, non-governmental organizations).

However imperfect and arguable the Convention and Protocol are, they remain the authoritative source for most states trying to determine refugee status.[15] It is these definitions that are employed in U.S. laws regarding the status of refugees and immigration. In bringing sanctuary back to the foreground of issues in the United States, it is opposition to the application of the 1980 U.S. Refugee Act that led many people to participate in the Sanctuary Movement of the 1980s prominent in the southwestern United States.

The United States obligated itself to recognize valid claims for asylum (refugee status) as a signatory to the Convention and Protocol. This commitment was codified by the passage of the Refugee Act of 1980 and further affirmed and developed in the U.S. Immigration and Nationality Act (1996). No fewer than three U.S. offices in 3 different departments take part in determining refugee status, proper procedure in application, and resettlement of refugees in the United States.[16] Figures available through the United Nations High Commissioner for Refugees (UNHCR) office show that the United States accepts more refugees seeking asylum than any other country in the world and that the United States is the number one destination for general immigration as well.[17]

THEORIES

Security and Economics

There are two primary theoretical sides to the issue of admitting immigrants and refugees into a country. One side argues that the state (government) of a country must consider the general welfare of its own population as its top priority. The other believes that the primary duty of all mankind is to be humanitarian to all people and that by extension so should the state act in as humanitarian a manner as possible.

Myron Weiner correctly points out that migration creates security and policy issues for states.[18] Consider the fact that Palestinian immigrants in

Kuwait collaborated with Iraqi forces in 1990. Consider also that the United Kingdom feared that an influx of Vietnamese refugees in the mid- to late-1970s would jeopardize the security of Hong Kong and ordered them returned to Vietnam despite international protest. In the current world climate, with its robust fear of terrorism, it must be recognized that when a state's security is at stake, it is easily justifiable to create preferences in admissions policy for immigrants and refugees.

But all admissions policies cannot be predicated on fear and security. After all, not even the current executive branch of the U.S. government considers all states to be progenitors of future terrorists. In fact, most admissions of immigrants into the United States are based on economic concerns. Both concerns for those less fortunate than our average citizens and concerns for the employment needs of U.S.-based firms affect government decision-making in regard to target immigration numbers. It also affects the type of immigrant that is targeted. Most immigrant visas granted today are issued for people seeking to work in technologically-advanced fields of industry and in the public healthcare sector of the U.S. economy.

There is widespread recognition that globalization and free trade are not beneficial to all people. Some people gain; others lose. The losers are often disadvantaged minorities within their country of origin. These people are compelled by economic conditions to seek a better situation. Often that better situation will only be available to them in another country. But what about that receiving country? Can the receiving country support the influx of migrants?

Citizens of countries such as the United States, in which the state takes responsibility for provisions of services and resources to all or portions of the population, must recognize the economic cost associated with acceptance of immigrants. By accepting refugees in the United States, we accept them into a society that provides more service and infrastructure at no cost or reduced cost to individual users than most countries in the world. To what extent can states afford to keep offering these benefits when increasingly large parts of populations may not be providing revenue for state action? One reason a state sets limits upon immigration is the recognition of the costs of assimilating those people into the society.

In fact, any state that opens its borders readily to immigration "might soon find other states taking advantage of its beneficent policy."[19] Many states are perfectly willing to allow parts of their population to leave if it means financial savings for the state. If a neighboring state is lax in immigration control or readily admitting large numbers of immigrants, it is not unheard of for a state to encourage citizens to consider migrating. Not all decisions, however, are based on bureaucratic and economic judgment; many are made based on political and moral bases.

In dealing with the question of granting refugee status to individuals or to groups, a state is making a moral and political judgment. Given the Convention and Protocol definition of who qualifies as a refugee, making that decision means passing judgment against another state. When the U.S. government grants asylum to a Cuban, saying that this person can reasonably expect to be persecuted for political opinion if they return to Cuba, a statement is being made on behalf of all citizens of this country about Cuba's government. On the public's behalf, the government is saying that another sovereign state is mistreating its own citizens. This is a strong statement to make, and it implies strong criticism of the state in the refugees' country of origin.

When State A declares asylum for citizens of State B, State B will most often see this as interference in their internal matters. State A is after all saying that State B has mistreated or might mistreat these citizens if they are returned to their nation of origin. The long-term effects of such blatant statements about the moral, ethical, and sovereign behavior of State B can be politically taxing. Consider too that most refugees receive asylum in openly democratic states that allow them to speak out against the state in their country of origin. Do citizens of State A really support the overthrow of the government of State B? This will appear to State B to be affirmed when those granted asylum speak out openly and loudly against their homeland.

Immigration and asylum policy considered in this light is inherently a political decision. It is not made out of concern for all people in the world, but out of concern for the quality of life of citizens in this country. A government that represents its citizens must first and foremost make decisions about how to best protect those citizens. Secondly, this government must make decisions about how to promote the economic well being of the greatest number of its citizens. All decisions of immigration and asylum must consider how it will affect the security of the country and the economy of the country, which are understood as the primary responsibilities of modern states.

In a globalized world, a great deal of the security and economy of the country is tied to foreign trade, investment, security arrangements, and so on. This requires a country to be extremely cautious in making moral and political judgments regarding any other country. It also means that asylum and immigration policies are tied to foreign policy goals, affecting from which areas of the world and from which specific countries of the world governments will accept people.

Equality and Human Rights

Opposed to the idea that states must be concerned about implications made about the quality of other states is the support for open immigration as a means of providing the best quality of life for the most people. The fact that some people lose and others gain from globalization and free trade is a show of the inequalities of life. According to John Rawls' difference principle, these inequalities should be acceptable only if they ultimately benefit those who are least well off.[20] Joseph Carens takes this even further by pointing out that it is only a matter of chance that people are born in democratic, peaceful, prosperous countries versus being born in poor, authoritarian, conflict-torn countries.[21] The great necessity addressed by immigration is providing a better quality of life to a maximum number of people. The overriding question is as follows: is it more moral to preserve a particular way of life or to promote the welfare of every individual of the human race?

Andrew Shacknove argues that a claim to refugee status exists whenever a state does not protect the basic needs of citizens.[22] This is a moralistic and a very broad claim. What are the basic needs of citizens? Does this include a job? Does a government owe a person protection of their employment? Does this mean protection of access to fresh water (a necessity for life) and arable land (needed to grow food or raise livestock)? Human rights activists claim that any discrimination against human rights is grounds for asylum. Liberal democracies thus ought to admit all individuals whose human rights are violated by the own governments. But what are human rights? Does government have a right to put limitations on things that are generally considered rights by most people? For instance, does a government have a right to impose a one child per family limit? Is this a violation of human rights that should cause the states to give asylum to any family asking for protection on grounds of desiring to have two or more children? Should a country grant asylum to a man from Brazil because he is openly homosexual and in Brazil the society rejects this behavior and the government does not openly protect him from social derision? In the end, it would still be a government decision as to what human rights are basic and justify granting asylum if violated.

Egalitarian arguments dismiss the notion of community as an impediment to a just world. The predominant idea is distributive justice. Proponents of this ideal argue that we should not consider immigration's impact on welfare, employment, educational benefits, healthcare, the environment, and community relations. Instead, we must make life as quality as possible for the most people regardless of political and economic costs to individual states. This is not just a humanitarian act, it is a moral imperative.

Further complicating a simple understanding of state-centric versus open border arguments surrounding asylum is the question of whether or not sovereignty resides on more than one level. Previously, I discussed sovereignty in relation to the actions of the state in pursuit of a range of policies that are designed to maximize the outcomes for the population represented while protecting the right of a government to determine what is best in dealing with its own citizens free from encroachment by foreign powers. However, another matter to be decided is whether sovereignty is held at multiple levels within a country.

Federalism

A final theoretical consideration is based on federalism. Federalism represents power sharing between more than one level of government in a country. In the United States, this refers to cities and counties (local government), states, and the federal or U.S. national government. Which of these is sovereign? Based on the U.S. Constitution and numerous court decisions, in the United States federal laws are the supreme law of the land. State and local laws may add to federal law but cannot take away or negate sections of federal law. In this legalistic sense, sovereignty ultimately rests with the federal government.

Recent scholarship seeks to challenge this idea. Randy Lippert examines sanctuary cases in Canada and applies a definition of sovereignty existing within multiple spheres.[23] Sovereignty is held as the ability to coerce and the ability to make and suspend laws. Lippert argues that this is exactly what churches did in Canada and in the United States by offering sanctuary, because the churches did not have to offer sanctuary and could remove sanctuary at any time of their choosing. Also, the churches were seeking to coerce the government to take action.[24]

At its fullest extent, this reasoning leads us to ask the question of who determines the sovereignty of the government and/or other actors within a country? As the source of ultimate authority for the Constitution and for the government that it creates, are the citizens of the United States the last arbiters in determining where sovereignty resides? The argument can be made to favor this position for the population. However, as mentioned before, there are legal and historical precedents that dispute this argument. Nevertheless, this line of reasoning is alive and well for some Christians in the United States. The next section of this chapter will explore in more detail the Sanctuary Movement of the 1980s and the modern progeny of this movement—namely, the offering of sanctuary to illegal immigrants who are facing expulsion after legal decisions have been rendered.

SANCTUARY, REDUX

The 1980s Sanctuary Movement

As previously mentioned, in 1980 the U.S. government enacted a policy regarding refugees and resettlement of the same within the United States based on following the principles of the UN Convention and Protocol. The act was to systematically create a process by which a target number of refugees as recognized by the Convention and Protocol would be admitted into the United States and be given official asylum or sanctuary.

In November 1980, Ronald Reagan was elected President of the United States, bringing to office a conservative outlook that included tougher measures to defeat Communism throughout the world. One area of the globe where the growth of Communism was of particular concern to President Reagan was Central America. The decision was made to support right-leaning and conservative governments in Central America economically and militarily where they were engaged in often violent conflict with portions of their populations that advocated socialist and communist ideals.

As a political matter, this meant that the U.S. government could not make negative statements about these governments in regard to their treatment of their populations. In realistic perspective, if the U.S. government had made a negative statement about one of these governments it could have caused that government to fall and the fears existed in this Cold War era that if a conservative government fell, it would be replaced with a socialist or communist government. In this vein of reasoning, a decision was made to deny most asylum applications from this region.

In truth, some of the asylum seekers were true refugees as defined by the Convention and Protocol. They had well founded fear of persecution if they returned to their countries of origin based on race, religion, nationality, social group membership, and political opinion. In criticism of the policy adopted by the Reagan Administration, several churches and individuals began in the early 1980s to create an underground network to bring people from these Central American countries illegally across the U.S.-Mexico border and provide them with "sanctuary" in their churches and in their homes. It became a classic clash between church and state over "who and what interests defined U.S. sovereignty."[25]

James A. Corbett and Rev. John Fife, pastor of Southside Presbyterian

Church (Presbyterian Church United States of America), are recognized as the co-founders of the Sanctuary Movement of the 1980s in the southwestern United States. Corbett, who passed away in early August 2001, is credited with having personally guided hundreds of Salvadorans and Guatemalans from Mexico to Tucson.[26] Fife stated in 2001 that Corbett was "the intellectual and spiritual architect of the Sanctuary Movement."[27] Both Corbett and Fife have stated that what they were doing was the ethical thing to do, because the United States was not accepting Central American refugees.

The Sanctuary Movement was contested among churches and among church leaders. Obvious questions arose over the religious correctness of liberation theology, as well as the proper role for churches in contesting laws.[28] Liberation theology emphasizes Jesus Christ as the redeemer and goes further to proclaim Jesus Christ as the liberator of the oppressed. In its inception this theology was predominantly fostered in the Roman Catholic Church and primarily in Central America and South America. Ironically, Pope John Paul II admonished such teachings and led to it being curtailed. However, among liberal theological circles, it finds a greater place in what they interpret as social justice as taught in scripture. This position is one of many points of theological controversy that still exists among Christian denominations to this day.

On March 24, 1982, a dozen congregations—primarily in southern Arizona—declared themselves open sanctuaries for illegal immigrants seeking asylum in the United States. While the fact that it was church-based gets most of the attention regarding the Sanctuary Movement, we must not ignore the fact that it was very politically motivated. Robert Tomsho, an apologist for the movement, writes that the "political goals of sanctuary were never clandestine. The movement was not smuggling refugees merely to satisfy religious commandments or provide the press with a few good headlines ... the movement hoped to persuade Americans to reconsider their government's support of regimes the refugees were fleeing."[29]

Tomsho's assessment is echoed in statements made in 2002 by Fife, who stated in 2002 that it was gratifying to see that the movement "seems to have been a significant moment in the whole history of human rights and refugee rights."[30] It was even reasoned by some of those involved in the movement that they were actually enforcing United States law that the government was failing to enforce, and should therefore not be considered in violation of the law. Indeed, the term civil initiative was used to express the actions of the movement to recognize that they were carrying out existing law. This differs from civil disobedience, which means to disobey law that is determined to be morally reprehensible by individuals.[31]

More than 40 churches gave sanctuary to illegal aliens from Central America during the height of the movement. According to one report, "some church leaders say the churches are taking a humanitarian stand and calling attention to what they consider the unfair application of the Refugee Act of 1980."[32] Among those churches in the United States that extended sanctuary to refugees were congregations from a wide range of denominations, including American Baptist, Episcopalian, Lutheran (ELCA), Mennonite, Methodist, Presbyterian (PCUSA), Quaker, and Roman Catholic.[33]

The response of the political authorities was twofold. First, the government made regular statements to point out that no right of sanctuary was recognized by the United States. The second was to begin investigating and collecting information regarding the exact activities of members of the movement. The second area represented active infiltration of the churches involved by informants and actual agents of the U.S. government. Reagan administration officials defended the "indictments of American church workers—and the use of infiltrators with concealed tape recorders—as part of their obligation to pursue people suspected of breaking laws concerning illegal aliens."[34]

Does the infiltration of a church by government agents represent a violation of the separation of church and state? Do individuals have the right to contest the source of a state's sovereignty? Do individuals have the right to carry out law for the government? In *United States v. Aguilar* (1986), pretrial motions and the decision of the case found the answers to these questions to all be no. The government sees it as no infringement on the activities of a church for a government representative to participate and report on those activities.

However, the defendants certainly felt otherwise. Stephen Cooper, attorney for two church workers who faced trial in Texas for harboring and smuggling illegal aliens stated, "I do see it as church versus state, but in a very much different way than we normally see church versus state. I can't remember any time in the past when the Government has tried to invade the churches, tried to tell the churches they can't do things that have always been recognized as within the province of the churches, tried to turn church people into criminals for nonviolent behavior."[35]

It is an intriguing proposition. The church and Christians are to be honest, open, and truthful according to teachings of the Bible. But a certain amount of secrecy was required by the Sanctuary Movement. This is one of the many points of disagreement between congregations that were supportive of the Sanctuary Movement and those who opposed it. In the words of one Southern Baptist minister, "I could not support such interpretation of scripture and Christian duty that would require me to be dishonest to the authorities. But it remains my dilemma to consider how to serve God and assist those in need as scripture teaches and not violate the laws of this country, which tell me to report and turn-in illegal aliens."[36]

The ruling in the *Aguilar* case was that sanctuary was not a matter of religious practice, since millions of Christians never engage in it and openly oppose it. Since the practice of sanctuary is not a religious practice, but a political practice, infiltration of the Sanctuary Movement was not infiltrating a church.

Interestingly, the insistence that they were carrying out the law for the state smacks of vigilante justice. Protection from vigilante justice appears to have been one of the important reasons for the creation of sanctuary in the first place. This is the most ironic aspect of the modern movement: it seeks to give sanctuary, which is supposed to protect people from vigilante justice, by way of exercising vigilante justice.

In the sanctuary debate, the sticking point for Christians is that Christianity teaches both obedience to authority as well as kindness and humanitarianism. Which of these is to be the guiding principle for behavior? Many denominations teach that the Bible is infallible and the ultimate source of authority. For the members of these churches, the answer to the question is the conundrum of both obedience to authority and human kindness, though it's not always clear how this works out. More liberal churches teach that the Bible needs to be interpreted in a more socially relevant manner. For members of these churches and adherents of their theological offering, it is more difficult to both obey the law and follow through with teachings of social justice—which they see as often contradictory.

The Current Sanctuary Movement

The government of the United States remains adamant that no right to sanctuary exists. The modern version of sanctuary is more concerned with distributive justice and humanitarian values than with legal and political questions concerning refugee status. Rather, contemporary practitioners of sanctuary focus on stories like that of Elvira Arellano related in the opening of this chapter.

Modern sanctuary does not care that Arellano openly admits she came here to find a better life, meaning economic opportunity. In this regard, the modern movement is more tied to the open borders philosophy than the movement was in the 1980s. She has become a celebrity for the new movement to support. *Time* named her as one of the "People Who Mattered in 2006."[37]

Statements made by Arellano's supporters say nothing about any fear of persecution if she is returned to Mexico. Most of them focus on the fact that her son Saul was born in the United States and as such is guaranteed United States citizenship. Pastor Walter Coleman said his congregation offered Arellano refuge after praying about her plight. Coleman said he does not believe Arellano should have to choose between leaving her son behind or removing him from his home. "She represents the voice of the undocumented, and we think it's our obligation, our responsibility, to make a stage for that voice to be heard," he said.[38]

The government's statements in regard to Ms. Arellano sound the same as their statements regarding Central Americans denied their asylum petitions in the 1980s. In fact, the government has said it has every right to enter the Adalberto United Methodist Church and arrest her and will do so "at a time of their choosing."[39] In response to the government's position, Arellano has said, "If Homeland Security chooses to send agents to a holy place, I would know that God wants me to serve as an example of the hatred and hypocrisy of the current administration."[40]

DILEMMA

The remarks of this paper have been confined to sanctuary and illegal immigration as a church and state issue for Christians, largely because Christian churches predominate the religious landscape of the United States. Furthermore, the Sanctuary Movement in the 1970s and 1980s involved Christian churches, as does the revived movement in the first decade of the second millennium. That is not to say that there are no other religious institutions recognized in the United States for whom this is also an issue. Based on the premises of their belief systems, it is highly probable that this becomes an issue for Buddhist and Hindus. It would be less of an issue for stalwart Muslims for whom there is little or no separation between church and state.

Sanctuary is humanitarian. Christianity recognizes a necessary duty to preserve and defend human life and an adherence to a belief system that routinely suggests provision of aid to those in need. If people are unable to provide for the protection of their own life, sanctuary should be provided for them. This was evidenced in the movement of the 1970s and 1980s, where the concern for the physical safety of the illegal immigrants in question was repeatedly voiced.

Sanctuary is also political. The Sanctuary Movement in 1980s was a political confrontation with President Reagan's anti-communist Central American policy. Reagan policy supported governments with abysmal human rights records on the basis that these governments were at least not communist. Sanctuary providers were challenging the legality of supporting human rights abusers in the name of fighting Communism. While good humanitarian assistance was offered, would the same assistance have been offered under different political circumstances? Remember that most sanctuary declarations included a statement that the actions were taken because of the illegal and immoral policy of the U.S. government concerning Central America. If it were truly about the moral issues of the preservation and sanctity of life, why would it be necessary to include a statement concerning the legality of U.S. policy in Central America? That it is political is certainly evidenced in the case of Elvira Arellano, where no concern exists for her safety, but plenty of concern is voiced over her possible deportation and the status of her son, Saul.

But is it really a matter of church and state relations? It is when certain churches and congregations choose to make it an issue. The state certainly has shown that it does not recognize it as a church/state issue. But the delay in violating the Adalberto United Methodist Church to seize Arellano suggests that they recognize that the image of federal agents forcibly entering a house of worship makes many Americans uncomfortable. However, some denominations continue to issue proclamations that they will support sanctuary and disobedience of the laws of the United States in answering to a higher calling.[41] Most churches have taken an approach that says illegal immigration is a problem that needs to be dealt with humanely and legally, but not in a manner that penalizes people for acting on Christian values.

POSTSCRIPT

On August 19, 2007, while this book was in process, Elvira Arellano, the face of the modern sanctuary movement, was arrested in Los Angeles, CA, and deported to Tijuana, Mexico. Arellano had decided to leave sanctuary in Chicago to lobby U.S. lawmakers. She was arrested outside of a church in Los Angeles where she had just spoken. Arellano has decided to send her son to live in Chicago with his godmother, so he can attend school, despite her claims that she did not want to be separated from her son.

NOTES

1. Notes from speech by Elvira Arellano given at the University of Wisconsin-Stevens Point on May 3, 2006. Ms. Arellano spoke in Spanish throughout the presentation and the notes are based on interpretation by an unnamed associate at the event.

2. P.J. Huffstutter, "Sanctuary Movement Still Has a Heartbeat," *Los Angeles Times*, Nov. 24, 2006, Home Edition.

3. Numbers 35: 11–15, *Bible*, New King James Version.

4. One such theological discussion can be found in the Matthew Henry Complete Commentaries. The commentaries are available online and this particular passage of the *Bible* are archived at: http://bible.crosswalk.com/Commentaries/MatthewHenryComplete/mhc-com.cgi?book=nu&chapter=035

5. Numbers 35: 24–28, in *Bible*, New King James Version.

6. "The Sanctuary," *Luminarium Encyclopedia*, available at http://www.luminarium.org.

7. "Councils of Orleans," *Catholic Encyclopedias*, available at http://www.newadvent.org

8. Numbers 35: 24–28, in *Bible*, New King James Version.

9. Ibid.

10. Susan Biber Coutin, "Smugglers of Samaritans in Tucson, AZ: Producing and Contesting Legal Truth," *American Ethnologist* 22, no. 3 (August 1995): 549–71. See also pretrial motions in *United States v. Aguilar* (1986), no. CR-85–008-PHX-EHC (D. Ariz).

11. John Vrachnas et al, *Migration and Refugee Law* (New York: Cambridge University Press, 2005), 173.

12. Article 1A (2), *Convention Relating to the Status of Refugees* (1951).

13. Article 33, *Convention Relating to the Status of Refugees* (1951).

14. John Vrachnas, *Migration and Refugee Law*. 174.

15. I say most states because in 1969 the Organization of African Unity (OAU) adopted a broader definition of refugee applicable to its member states. Also, the 1984 Cartagena Declaration incorporates a definition similar to that of the OAU signed by many Latin American states. John Vrachnas, *Migration and Refugee Law*, 173.

16. The Office of Refugee Resettlement (Department of Health and Human Services), Bureau of Population, Refugees, and Migration (Department of State), and Citizenship and Immigration Services (Department of Homeland Security).

17. Available at http://www.unhcr.org.

18. Myron Weiner, "Security, Stability and International Migration," in *International Migration and Security*, ed. Myron Weiner (Boulder, CO: Westview Press, 1993).

19. Myron Weiner, "Ethics, National Sovereignty and the Control of Immigration," *International Migration Review* 30, no. 1 (Special Issue: Ethics, Migration, and Global Stewardship) (Spring 1996): 173.

20. This idea emanates from Rawls' "difference principle," which is the primary basis for much of social justice theory among human rights scholars. John Rawls, *A Theory of Social Justice* (Cambridge, MA: Harvard University Press, 1971).

21. Jospeh Carens, "Aliens and Citizens, the Case for Open Borders," *The Review of Politics* 49, no. 2 (Spring 1987): 261.

22. Andrew Shacknove, "Who is a Refugee?" *Ethics* 95 (1985): 274–284.

23. Randy K. Lippert, *Sanctuary, Sovereignty, Sacrifice: Canadian Sanctuary Incidents, Power and Law* (Vancouver: UBC Press, 2005).

24. Ibid., 69–74.

25. Hillary Cunningham, "Sanctuary and Sovereignty: Church and State Along the U.S.-Mexico Border," *Journal of Church and State* 40, no. 2 (Spring 1998): 370–86. Quote on 370.

26. "Sanctuary Movement Co-Founder Dies," *Associated Press State and Local Wire*, August 7, 2001, BC Cycle.

27. Ibid.

28. Renny Golden and Michael McConnel discuss the contest and the eventual size and scope of the Sanctuary Movement in *Sanctuary: The New Underground Railroad* (Maryknoll, NY: Orbis Books, 1986). Eventually the movement involved approximately 70,000 members. William K. Tabb, *Churches in Struggle: Liberation Theologies and Social Change in North America* (New York: Monthly Review Press, 1986) discusses the ideas of liberation theology and its impact on the Sanctuary Movement.

29. Robert Tomsho, *The American Sanctuary Movement* (Austin, TX: Texas Monthly Press, 1987), 94.

30. Arthur Rotstein, "Sanctuary Movement Marks 20th Anniversary of Aiding Refugees," *Associated Press State and Local Wires*, March 22, 2002.

31. Susan Biber Coutin. "Smugglers or Samaritans in Tucson, Arizona," 553.

32. George Volcky, "U.S. Churches Offer Sanctuary to Aliens Facing Deportation," *New York Times*, April 8, 1983.

33. Ibid. It is not totally clear whether or not any Missouri Synod Lutherans participated in the movement, but the ELCA issued a denominational level statement in support of the movement. The same may be said of the different variants of Presbyterian Churches, and the PCUSA did issue a denominational statement in support of the movement.

34. "Sanctuary Leaders Assail U.S. for Ousting Central American Refugees," *Los Angeles Times*, March 2, 1985, Home Edition.

35. Wayne King, "Leaders of Alien Sanctuary Drive Say Indictments Pose Church-State Issue," *New York Times*, February 3, 1985.

36. Samuel S. Stanton is pastor of First Southern Baptist Church in Fallon, NV. This excerpt is from a personal conversation with the author which took place on December 29, 2006.

37. Wendy Cole, "Elvira Arellano, An Immigrant Who Found Sanctuary," *Time*, available at http://www.time.com/time/personoftheyear/2006/people/3.html.

38. Don Babwin and Karla Johnson, "Immigrant Takes Refuge in Chicago Church," *Associated Press*, August 16, 2006, available at http://www.breitbart.com/article.php?id=D8JHRKAO2&show_article=1.

39. Editorial, "Elvira Arellano and the Law," *Chicago Tribune*, August 17, 2006, available at http://www.chicagotribune.com/news/local/chi-0608170087aug17,1,2309585.story?coll=chi-photo-front.

40. "Illegal Alien Activist Elvira Arellano Hides out in Church to Avoid Deportation," available at http://www.diggersrealm.com/mt/archives/001790.html.

41. See for instance the statement of the Presbyterian Church-USA 217th General Assembly (2006) on Advocacy for All Immigrants.

FURTHER READING

If you are interested in finding out more about the Sanctuary Movement of the 1970s and 1980s, several good works exist. Biber Coutin's "Smugglers or Samaritans in Tucson, Arizona: Producing and Contesting Legal Truth" in *American Ethnologist* provides good insight in the defendants' position in *Aguilar* (1985). Similarly, Hillary Cunningham's "Sanctuary and Sovereignty: Church and State Along the U.S.-Mexico Border" in *Journal of Church and State* investigates the religious belief and political motivations of participants in the Sanctuary Movement. Robert Tomsho's *The American Sanctuary Movement* provides an accurate account of the activities of pioneers in the movement. To improve understanding of the legalities of immigration into the United States, readers should look at the U.S. Refugee Act (1980). Similarly, for information regarding the international law regarding asylum and refugee status, readers should consult the *Convention Relating to the Status of Refugees* (1951) and the subsequent *Protocol Relating to the Status of Refugees* (1967). Many works exist for understanding the theoretical issues surrounding immigration policy. Among the best for consideration are Myron Weiner's "Ethics, National Sovereignty and the Control of Immigration," in *International Migration Review* and Andrew Shacknove's "Who is a Refugee," in *Ethics*. No full accounting for a study involving ideas of social justice would be complete without considering John Rawls' *A Theory of Justice*. Finally, turning to the understanding of the nexus between Christian theology and immigration issues, works by William Tabb, such as *Struggle: Liberation Theologies and Social Change in North America*, and Luke Bretherton's "The Duty of Care to Refugees, Christian Cosmopolitanism, and the Hallowing of Bare Life," in *Studies in Christian Ethics* provide excellent background.

6

Native American Sacred Sites under Federal Law

S. Alan Ray

As Indians we don't have many responsibilities, but one of them is to fix the world.
—Julian Lang, Karuk Indian scholar,
author and performance artist[1]

INTRODUCTION

Across the United States today, thousands of Native Americans engage in traditional spiritual practices. Conducted for centuries or even millennia, these diverse practices serve to renew profound communal and personal bonds between indigenous communities and the land. For these Americans, land announces their emergence as peoples, signifies their origin and place in the cosmos, and provides the source of the sacred medicine that keeps in balance all life on earth. The displacement of many Indian communities from their aboriginal homes during the long history of European conquest and American expansion means that frequently these sacred places, which comprise millions of acres in all, are located on tracts owned by the United States and therefore are subject to its laws and policies for public lands management. When land-based spiritual practices and public land uses collide, the federal government is forced to arbitrate.

Traditional Native American practices on sacred lands are challenged daily by a legal regime formed under the influence of Euro-American norms of property and personhood and the historically powerful force of Christianity. Like other practitioners of non-mainstream religious traditions in the United States, Native Americans struggle to establish legal entitlements in the face of assertions that permitting them to pursue their particular spiritual imperatives would harm the common good. Differences between Euro-American and Native American sensibilities about the common good run long and deep.

MANY CULTURES IN ONE COUNTRY

Native Americans Today

Native Americans in 2007 are a diverse and growing population.[2] According to the 2000 census, 2.5 million U.S. citizens claim an American Indian identity, and an additional 1.6 million identify as American Indian and at least one other race. In all, 4.1 million people, or 1.5 percent of the total U.S. population, assert an Indian identity. This figure is especially remarkable, given that in 1950, the Native American population stood at 357,499. Yet many factors combine to undermine any notion that the rapid and substantial growth of the American Indian population represents the expansion of a homogenous and uniform culture.

The 562 federally recognized tribes, including 320 Alaska village communities, plus thousands of Native Hawaiians and hundreds of non-federally recognized tribes and bands, share the distinction of being among North America's indigenous communities. They are linked by a history of conflict with and colonization by the powers of Europe and later the United States, but they experience, organize, and represent the world in very different ways. There is no single "Native American culture" and no foundational "real Indian." There are many ways of being Native American, and many kinds of indigenous cultures in North America.[3] About half of today's Native Americans live on reservations: geopolitical regions "reserved" by the tribes when the rest of their ancestral lands were ceded to the United States under treaties in the eighteenth and nineteenth centuries. The rest of the American Indian population lives in cities and towns, suburbs and exurbs, across the United States. Further, the trend toward out-marriage—the phenomenon of tribal members marrying non-tribal members, often non-Indians—is increasing and means that biological interrelation, to the extent it was ever a meaningful proxy, is an increasingly unreliable indicator of Native self-identification and traditional cultural proficiency. Finally, it is difficult to underestimate the devastating and continuing impact of European and American colonialism on indigenous communities and their distinctive cultural and religious forms.

Faced with destabilizing social forces, Native communities are acutely aware of the need to preserve their cultures.[4] Many tribes have implemented effective and broad-ranging programs of tribal language instruction, celebration of traditional skills, tribal history instruction, and traditional methods of conflict resolution. Tribes seek to preserve and develop their cultural forms from *within* by promoting postcolonial historical research and stimulating their distinctive lifeways among community members. They also protect themselves against threats from *without* by self-regulating under tribal codes, filing legal actions to fight encroachments by non-tribal interests, and building coalitions to exploit opportunities in the political process. Many tribal communities are especially focused on revitalizing or protecting their indigenous spiritual traditions: those core ritual practices that celebrate and renew their bonds with the cosmos and allow them to fulfill their obligations to humankind.

Sacred Texts and Sacred Sites

Religions of the book—Judaism, Christianity, and Islam—find their source and touchstone in divine revelations contained in sacred texts. Religions of the land, such as traditional Native American spiritualities, recur to sacred sites for stories of human origin and the renewal of their communities.[5]

The religion of the book that has had the greatest historical impact on Native Americans is Christianity. Christianity focuses on *right belief*, literally orthodoxy: Christians profess Jesus as their Lord and Savior, and in that profession receive God's salvation. The various creeds that Christians have professed through their long history strive to state with precision—though not explain—the mysterious nature of God (a trinity of Father, Son, and Holy Spirit) and the relationship between God and humankind. For Christians, the Bible is the primary repository of God's unique revelation. As a religion of the book, Christianity is not tied to a specific place, but rather to an authoritative text, which is immanently portable and translatable to all whom the religion's missionaries encounter. Indeed, it is enjoined upon Christians to share the good news, or Gospel, of their beliefs with all, as the salvation of non-Christians depends on it. When explorers of the 15th and 16th centuries came to North America, they claimed the land for Christian rulers, even as the missionaries who accompanied them proclaimed God's salvation to the "heathen" inhabitants of the New World.[6]

Religions of the book and religions of the land differ greatly in their understanding of space. For the former, space is an emptiness that an all-sufficient God gratuitously fills with creation and over which God has set human beings as rulers and stewards.[7] The European colonists of the first centuries after contact, who were, of course, Christians, conceived of North American space as wilderness—an unredeemed waste filled with savage animals and Indians where the power of the devil went unchecked.[8] As scholar Lloyd Burton has observed of the Puritans, "[t]heir disregard for uncultivated land and fear of all things wild was itself a product of their religious training."[9] Breaking the forests and subduing the wilderness, and converting the land's aboriginal inhabitants to Christianity were religious obligations of the colonists.

Detached from an overt commitment to Christianity, the Western experience of space perceives a Newtonian emptiness, a vacuum to be filled by objects. On this model, nature is like a finely operating machine, moving within space according to its own laws.[10] However, because of the way Western society makes use of nature, these laws are inevitably economic as well as physical. The Western notion of space finds its logical end in the commodity of real estate: the legal delineation of physical space according to the rights of ownership. Real property is a fungible commodity or resource best suited for development to its economic "highest and best use."[11]

In contrast to the Christian emphasis on right belief, Native American spirituality focuses on *right conduct*—literally, orthopraxis. Indigenous peoples feel a kinship with specific, sacred places to which, or, more precisely, to whom they feel profound responsibility and seek to honor through correct ceremonial performance. Traditional Native American spiritual practices and cultures often are grounded in worldviews that do not distinguish between spiritual and material worlds. Rather, the world is the home of many kinds of interrelated beings, including humans, animals, human-like beings including but not limited to gods, and what Euro-Americans would call inanimate objects, such as geological formations, but many of which traditional Indians know to be living entities. Given this interrelatedness, it should not be surprising that Native communities typically do not distinguish between religion and culture. Indeed, as religion scholar Phil Cousineau has observed, the concept of "religion," as institutionalized spirituality, was unknown to Native Americans before contact with Christians. Cousineau states, "Traditionally, Indians had no institutions, no dogma, no commandments, and no one idea about how to worship, or even what to call the great force at the heart of all life that was perceived by all the tribes in their own way." Pre-contact peoples experienced, and many still enjoy, "a way of life that encompassed a rich variety of ceremonies, a mosaic of myths, legends, and poetry, together forming a complex heritage and a deep spiritual force."[12]

Native American experience of space is specific to particular places. Places are sites of tribal self-representation according to tribal myths—not just "land," but *this* land for *this* people in *this* way. In his study of the Western Apache, linguistic anthropologist Keith Basso has observed that "what matters most to the Apaches is *where* events occurred, not when, and what they serve to reveal about the development and character of Apache social life."[13] What Basso describes as place-making—the investment of meaning in specific geological locations through communal story-telling and ritual—provides the Western Apache with a powerful moral compass and an irreplaceable sense of their identity.

Basso's analysis underscores the role of human agency in delineating sacred places. As religion scholars David Chidester and Edward Linenthal have noted, the production of sacred space by human actors is marked by several key features. First, sacred space is ritualized, which means that sacred places are set apart as locations "for formalized, repeatable symbolic performances."[14] Second, sacred places are sites where meaning is made: they tell us "what it means to be a human being in a meaningful world."[15] Finally, "sacred space is inevitably contested space, a site of negotiated contests over the legitimate ownership of sacred symbols."[16] As American settlers blazed trails and cleared the North American wilderness, expanding across the Great Plains to the Pacific, the use of this land became contested in a new way. For example, where the Lakota once controlled the physical area and symbolic meaning of the Black Hills, once gold was discovered there in the late 1800s, Lakota communities fought for both their right to physically occupy their ancestral lands and their obligation to perform their sacred ceremonies.

The example of the Lakota points to an important dimension of land-based spiritualities. Ritual performance attempts to fulfill a sacred responsibility to the world. In performing the world renewal dance called the Jump Dance, for example, the Yurok, Karuk, Tolowa, and Hupa of northwestern California act ritually on behalf of everyone.[17] Failure to perform the Dance in a ritually correct way may endanger the balance not only of the tribe, but also of the entire world. Sickness, death, war, and other catastrophes, practitioners believe, will surely result.

The incongruities of religions of the book and religions of the land are more than merely formal: they are historical. Throughout his life's work, the late Lakota attorney, activist, and religion scholar, Vine Deloria, Jr., criticized the spread of Christianity among indigenous communities, not because Christianity is a false religion, but because he believed it historically has sought to be the exclusive source of truth about ultimate reality. As a result, "what has been the manifestation of deity in a particular local situation is mistaken for a truth applicable to all times and places, a truth so powerful that it must be impressed upon peoples who have no connection to the event or to the cultural complex in which it originally made sense."[18] Deloria observed that in contrast to the religious belief-systems of Christians, for American Indians,

> The structure of their religious traditions is taken directly from the world around them, from their relationships with other forms of life. Context is therefore all-important for both practice and the understanding of reality. The places where revelations were experienced were remembered and set aside as locations where, through rituals and ceremonials, the people could once again communicate with the spirits. Thousands of years of occupancy on their lands taught tribal peoples the sacred landscapes for which they were responsible and gradually the structure of ceremonial reality became clear.[19]

In summary, religions of the book tend to view space instrumentally, as a help or hindrance to the spread of sacred doctrine. Religions of the land see space as place: unique sites where the community renews its relationship with the sacred through ritual action. As historian Andrew Gulliford explains:

> For most tribes, a sacred place is where the Great Creator or spirits, both good and evil, communicate with the living. Most Anglo Americans consecrate a church as a sacred place, and it remains sacred as long as the congregation meets there. But when congregations outgrow a building, they may well sell it and purchase a new space to make holy. By contrast, what is important for traditional Indian religious believers is not the sacred space of a church or cathedral but rather a location made holy by the Great creator, by ancient and enduring myth, by repeated rituals such as sun dances, or by the presence of spirits who dwell in deep canyons, on mountaintops, or in hidden caves ... Sacred sites remain integral to tribal histories, religions, and identities.[20]

America's founding religion of the book, Christianity, has operated from assumptions about the world radically different than those of the place-based spiritualities of traditional Native Americans. These assumptions have informed judicial understandings of the guarantees and limits of religious liberty in the Constitution. When Native Americans have turned to the courts to try to protect the sacred character of their traditional places, they have encountered these same underlying beliefs.[21]

THE FREE EXERCISE CLAUSE AND "SOME RATHER SPACIOUS TRACTS" OF PUBLIC LAND

The Free Exercise Clause of the First Amendment of the Constitution provides that "Congress shall make no law . . . prohibiting the free exercise [of religion]."[22] The Free Exercise Clause, which applies to the states through the Fourteenth Amendment,[23] is the cornerstone of American religious liberty. Over the years, the courts have developed a constitutional jurisprudence based on three assumptions: that religion is primarily a matter of individual conscience not collective behavior; that religion can be protected against unreasonable governmental interference because religion can be distinguished from non-religion; and that religion is characteristically a set of beliefs about a Supreme Being or ultimate reality.

Three Assumptions of Constitutional Jurisprudence

The Supreme Court has consistently interpreted the Free Exercise Clause to prohibit government from constraining what people *believe* in matters of religion, even as the Court has upheld governmental regulation that burdens religiously motivated *conduct*.[24] In the early free exercise case of *Reynolds v. United States*, the Court in 1878 upheld a federal law criminalizing polygamy, even though the law burdened the religious practices of Mormons at the time.[25] The Court said that Mormons were free to believe whatever they liked about the sacrality of plural marriage; however, the justices added, the government has a legitimate interest in protecting the public against behavior such as polygamy that poses a threat to public safety, peace, or order.[26] Though in the twentieth century, the Court raised the bar that government would have to meet to constitutionally regulate religiously motivated conduct, the faith-conduct distinction expressed in *Reynolds* remains a bedrock principle of American jurisprudence.

Moreover, the Supreme Court has consistently expressed support for a constitutional distinction between religion and culture and held that the Free Exercise Clause protects *religious* beliefs and (to a qualified degree) *religious* practices but does not protect the *cultures* in which these beliefs and practices occur. Stated differently, the "quality of the claim" brought by those seeking protection must be "rooted in religious belief" and not in culture alone, to be recognized under the Free Exercise Clause.[27] Thus, the adverse impacts of government regulation on the well-being of a community do not by themselves raise Free Exercise issues, even though the impacts may be deleterious to the survival of the community and therefore to the religious beliefs and practices of its members. Government actions that only impact culture are usually held to the lowest standard of judicial review—they must merely be rationally related to a legitimate governmental end to pass muster.

Finally, when the Supreme Court has taken up the question of what "religion" is for purposes of the Free Exercise Clause, it has focused on the beliefs, not the behavior, of religious adherents. The Court's first efforts to define "religion," in 1890, reveal the justices' debt to Christianity when they state, "The term 'religion' has reference to one's views of his relations to his Creator, and to the obligations they impose of reverence for his being and character, and of obedience to his will. It is often confounded with the *cultus* or form of worship of a particular sect, but is distinguishable from the latter."[28] Here, "religion" is distinguished by what one thinks ("one's views"), not by what one does as part of a community (the "form of worship"). More recently, in a case involving conscientious objectors to the Vietnam War, the Court broadened its definition of "religion" to include "a given belief"—again, not a practice—"that is sincere and meaningful [and] occupies a place in the life of its possessor parallel to that filled by the orthodox belief in God."[29] Each time it has defined religion, the Court has focused on the cognitive—not the performative—aspect of spiritual engagement. This means that the Court has assumed the *beliefs* of religious adherents—*not ritual behaviors*—were the constitutionally relevant tokens of religious engagement.

In summary, (1) the faith-conduct distinction, (2) the religion-culture distinction, and (3) the notion of religion as a body of beliefs about ultimate reality reflect the power of America's religious history and culture to shape judicial assumptions about what it means to be religious. Lawmakers and courts steeped in the rhetoric, if not the beliefs, of Christianity assume that religion is primarily an act of assent of the mind or heart to divinely-revealed truths about ultimate reality (faith); that this interior disposition calls upon the will to act in conformity with these truths (conduct); and that collective behavior inspired by faith (religion) can be distinguished from collective behavior that seeks to further non-religious or "secular" ends (culture).

These three foundational assumptions of American law are, point for point, at odds with the experience and practice of traditional Native Americans. For the latter, religion is not primarily a body of beliefs with secondary ritual behavior. Indians do have belief-systems about the origin and nature of the world, of course, and these systems can be as sophisticated as any Western theology. However, there are no orthodoxies. There are sacred places that must be attended to for the good of all. For Native traditionalists, ritual comes before belief because place comes before theology.

Similarly, for indigenous communities, religion is not distinct from culture. Under the second assumption, religion can be distinguished from culture because religion is conceived-of primarily as a body of beliefs that can, indeed, for Christians should, travel freely from culture to culture, independent of all cultures in order to achieve salvation for as many people as possible. In contrast, for traditional peoples, because sacred places organize and orient their communal lifeways, there is simply no social or psychological "place" for culture to exist apart from religion.

Third, the notion that religion refers to a body of beliefs about a Supreme Being or ultimate reality misses the Native American traditional insistence that religion as practice (ritual) is directed to maintaining or restoring right relations between the tribe or humankind and the rest of reality, which is experienced as being infused with or populated by innumerable non-human but personal forces. Even where Native American spirituality includes reference to a Supreme Being—and here one must be alert to the Christianizing influence of missionaries on indigenous myths—beliefs about the Supreme Being or Great Spirit are subordinated to the performance of site-specific ritual practices that are believed to restore balance to the tribe and world.

Given such basic differences between federal constitutional jurisprudence and traditional Native American spirituality, it was perhaps inevitable that when clashes occurred over public land use and Indians called upon American constitutional law, the Free Exercise Clause would offer them little relief.

The Modern Context for Analyzing Native American Religious Liberty Claims

In the 1960s and 1970s, a series of cases in the Supreme Court expanded the scope of protection under the Free Exercise Clause while making it more difficult for the government to take actions that harmed religious practitioners. *Sherbert v. Verner* (1963) set the modern standard for constitutional analysis in this area.[30] Adeil Sherbert was a Seventh Day Adventist whose religion required her not to work on Saturday, her sabbath. Her employer demanded she work on Saturday, and when she refused, she was fired. When the state denied her request for unemployment benefits, she sued, claiming the Free Exercise Clause protected her from being forced to choose between violating her conscience and getting benefits, on the one hand, or remaining steadfast in her religion and being denied compensation, on the other. Such a choice, she argued, amounted to a constitutionally significant indirect burden on her religious liberty. An "indirect burden," in this context, refers to a government action which does not overtly criminalize or prohibit religiously motivated conduct, but nonetheless coerces a believer to betray his or her religious convictions in order to obtain a government benefit.

The Court ruled in Sherbert's favor, holding that indirect burdens like hers implicated the Free Exercise Clause just as much as direct burdens, such as outright religious prohibitions. Replacing the low standard set by *Reynolds* (a threat to public safety, peace, or order), the Court held that where a burden was found, the government must identify a compelling interest for its actions which could be served by no less restrictive means. If, on balance, the harm to a claimant's religious liberty was greater than the interest of the government in pursuing its project or program, the religious claimant won. In Sherbert's case, the Court found that the state's denial of unemployment compensation did constitute an indirect burden on her religious beliefs, and outweighed the government's interest in advancing an efficient, fraud-free system of unemployment compensation. "*Sherbert* balancing," as the method of judicial analysis came to be known, led to a series of victories for religious adherents.[31]

In addition to judicial expansion of the scope of Free Exercise protection and the development of a method of analysis more favorable to religious claimants, federal legislation gave American Indians new hope that their land-based spiritual traditions could successfully resist government land development projects. The federal law, called the American Indian Religious Freedom Act of 1978, or "AIRFA," stated:

It shall be the policy of the United States to protect and preserve for American Indians their inherent right to freedom to believe, express, and exercise the traditional religions of the American Indian, Eskimo, Aleut, and Native Hawaiians, including but not limited to access to sites, use and possession of sacred objects, and the freedom to worship through ceremonial and traditional rites.[32]

The appearance of AIRFA in 1978 represented in the domain of religion the federal government's endorsement of tribal self-determination.[33] This marked a shift in U.S. policy, which, with some significant exceptions, had long favored eliminating the distinctively "Indian" features of indigenous life in order to improve the lot of individual Native Americans. From 1883 until the early 1920s, for example, the federal government outlawed and sought to suppress Indian religious practices, especially sacred dances, on grounds similar to those invoked in the *Reynolds* case—namely, that the dances were offensive to public health, decency, and good order. The suppression of traditional Indian dances also served the government's avowed purpose of "civilizing" and Christianizing the Indians.[34] Though official suppression ended with the 1934 Indian Reorganization Act, hostility to tribalism returned after 1945, when the government instituted a policy of legally terminating tribes in hopes of "mainstreaming" Indians into postwar American society. The policy failed miserably, and by 1970, the pendulum of national politics had swung again, from assimilation of individual Indians to empowerment of Indian nations.

Encouraged by the government's embrace of tribal self-determination and the adoption of AIRFA, as well as by the federal courts' newly expansive elaboration of Free Exercise Clause rights in non-Indian cases, tribes fought back against a series of federal projects in the 1980s. The results of the litigation in four pivotal cases reveal how deeply the three assumptions of Free Exercise Clause jurisprudence have informed judicial analyses of Native American life.

Sequoyah, Badoni, Crow, and *Wilson*: Judicial Struggles with Sacred Sites

In *Sequoyah v. TVA* (1980),[35] the Eastern Band of Cherokee sought an injunction to stop the federal government from completing the Tellico Dam as part of a vast hydroelectric generation project. Flooding from the dam would inundate the Cherokee homeland and destroy sacred sites, medicine gathering areas, and the graves of ancestors, who Cherokee believe possess sacred knowledge for future generations. The dam's operation would flood the town of Chota, called the "birthplace" of the Cherokee and the location connecting the Cherokee "with the Great Spirit."[36] Reflecting the assumptions that religion and culture are distinguishable and that religion is protected by the Constitution but culture is not, the U.S. Court of Appeals for the Sixth Circuit held that the Cherokee had no *religious* interest in preserving their homeland. The majority asked whether the Valley was "central" or "indispensable" to Cherokee religious observances, and concluded it was not. The damage to the Cherokee would be "to tribal and family folklore and traditions, more than particular religious observances."[37] Concluding that the quality of the claim was not religious, the court said, "[t]hough cultural history and tradition are vitally important to any group of people, these are not interests protected by the Free Exercise Clause of the First Amendment."[38]

The *Sequoyah* court noted that the fact that the land in question was owned by the government, not the Cherokee, while not conclusive, was a "factor" to be considered.[39] Further, the bill creating the Tellico Dam had trumped AIRFA and any other competing legislation.[40] The Tellico Dam was built, residents of the southeastern United States received reliable electrical power, and the Cherokee homeland—millions of acres—was lost to the Cherokee people forever.

Soon after *Sequoyah* came *Badoni v. Higginson* (1980), a decision of the Tenth Circuit Court of Appeals.[41] Seeking to increase the supply of water to Western states, the federal government raised the elevation of water behind Glen Canyon Dam on the Colorado River. The Dam's reservoir (Lake Powell) flooded a canyon of federal land beneath Rainbow Bridge, an immense sandstone arch sacred to the Navajo as the incarnation of two of their gods. The bridge, along with 160 acres, constitutes the Rainbow Bridge National Monument. Navajo plaintiffs claimed the rising waters had drowned the gods who lived in the canyon adjacent to the bridge and prevented Navajo medicine men from performing vital religious rituals at the site. Further, as the water encroached on the canyon, pleasure boaters arrived in large numbers, trashing the site with refuse and marring the bridge itself (the gods) with graffiti.

Like the *Sequoyah* court, *Badoni* rejected "the conclusion that plaintiffs' lack of property rights in the Monument is determinative."[42] The *Badoni* court acknowledged the relevance of *Sherbert* balancing to the claims of drowned gods and denial of access to a sacred site, but jumped straight to a finding that the government had a compelling interest in supplying Western states with water, which could not be served by a less restrictive means. As to restricting public access to the bridge, the court, relying on the belief-conduct distinction, held that the tribe had no recourse under the Free Exercise Clause, since the government had done nothing to coerce the Navajo to violate their religious beliefs and had left the medicine men free to enter the area, although the court was "mindful of the difficulties facing plaintiffs in performing solemn religious ceremonies in an area frequented by tourists."[43] For the government to do more would implicate the Establishment Clause and turn the Monument into "a government-managed religious shrine."[44] The court turned aside plaintiff's claim that AIRFA warranted relief, ruling that the pleadings were inadequate to state a cause of action.[45] The court denied the Navajos' request, the waters beneath the sandstone gods continued to rise, and tourists enjoyed enhanced access to the Monument.

Two years later, in *Crow v. Gullet* (1982),[46] the South Dakota district court ruled that the state's construction activities near ceremonial grounds on Bear Butte had not violated the constitutional rights of the Lakota and Tsistsistas. Bear Butte was both the site of Vision Quest ceremonies, requiring solitude and silence, and a popular site for hiking and camping by tourists. The plaintiffs claimed the construction activities unconstitutionally diminished the spiritual power of Bear Butte. The court rejected this claim, observing, "It is clear . . . that plaintiffs have no property interest in Bear Butte or in the State Park," and holding that the Constitution does not require government "to provide the means or the environment for carrying . . . out [religious actions]."[47] The court, citing *Badoni*, rejected the claim that the state had a constitutional duty to prevent tourists from acting in ways that interfered with religious practices.[48]

Because the *Crow* plaintiffs were denied use of their usual ceremonial area because of the construction, they were obliged to camp overnight at Bear Butte Lake, where they were subject to the Lake's prohibition on building sweat lodges, used for spiritual purification and awakening. Invoking the belief-conduct distinction, the court concluded that the state's "minimal" restriction with respect to "time and place" of conducting a sweat lodge ceremony failed to constitutionally burden plaintiffs' religion.[49] The court held that AIRFA did "not create a cause of action in federal courts for violation of rights of religious freedom" and represented "merely a statement of policy of the federal government with respect to traditional Indian religious practices."[50] Defeated in court, the Lakota and Tsistsistas watched as the construction projects on their sacred mountain were completed.

Soon after *Crow*, the Court of Appeals for the District of Columbia Circuit decided *Wilson v. Block* (1983).[51] The federal government had approved permits for increased private development of a ski resort on the San Francisco Peaks. These mountains—living deities—are sacred to the Navajo and Hopi and, for the Hopi, are the home of the Kachinas, spirit beings and emissaries of the Creator. Seeking an injunction, plaintiffs argued that the act of additional commercial development would be a sacrilege offensive to the Kachinas and the Creator and would result in the peaks losing their beneficial powers. Development would also impair the plaintiffs' ability to pray and conduct religious ceremonies on the peaks and to gather necessary medicine.

The *Wilson* court rejected plaintiffs' argument that under *Sherbert* and its progeny, the Free Exercise Clause prevented "governmental actions which strongly, if indirectly, encouraged religious practitioners to modify their beliefs."[52] Instead, the court ruled narrowly to hold that "the government may not, by conditioning benefits, penalize adherence to religious beliefs."[53]

If not religious *beliefs*, might the proposed development indirectly burden the plaintiffs' religious *practices* in a constitutionally relevant way, thus putting the government to the test of showing a compelling interest? The court initially recognized that *Sherbert* and the unemployment compensation cases "did not purport to create a benchmark against which to test all indirect burden claims."[54] Instead, the court looked to *Sequoyah* and announced, "If plaintiffs cannot demonstrate that the government land at issue is indispensable to some religious practice, whether or not central to their religion, they have not justified a First Amendment claim."[55] The proposed government land use must be one that "would impair a religious practice that could not be performed at any other site."[56] The *Wilson* court found that while the peaks were indispensable for plaintiffs' religious practices, the specific section of the peaks where the development would occur was not: medicine could be collected in many other locations on the peaks. Though plaintiffs failed to state a claim under the First Amendment, the court rejected any contention that the absence of property rights by the Navajo or Hopi in the Peaks was determinative, saying that "we see no basis for completely exempting government land use from the Free Exercise Clause."[57] This is consistent with the court's analysis that had the plaintiffs been able to show the indispensability of the affected portion of the Peaks for their religious practices, an indirect constitutional burden on their religion could have been stated, and the government would be forced to try to establish a compelling interest in its project, one that would be served by the least restrictive means.

The *Wilson* court also announced that an agency would be in compliance with AIRFA if, in deciding whether to undertake a land use project, decision-makers considered "the views of Indian leaders, and if, in project implementation, it avoids unnecessary interference with Indian religious practices."[58] Because the Forest Service had "held many meetings with Indian religious practitioners and conducted public hearings on the Hopi and Navajo reservations," AIRFA was satisfied.[59] Defeated in court, the Navajo and Hopi had no choice but to suffer the impact of the expansion of the ski resort on the living deities, the San Francisco Peaks.

As the end of the 1980s approached, decisions of the lower courts reflected an emerging set of conclusions regarding Native American rights to religious liberty, but no clear set of theories. Many questions swirled through the decisions of the federal courts: Should analysis under the Free Exercise Clause give any special weight to the land-based nature of Native American spirituality? How could such an analysis proceed without asking whether tribal religious beliefs were true or false? Could some practices be deemed central or indispensable to Indian spiritual traditions, and, if so, should these practices be constitutionally protected? Should the *Sherbert* balancing test—developed largely in the context of unemployment benefits claims—be extended to sacred sites? When, if ever, can the Free Exercise Clause be used as a sword to demand government cooperation with Indian religious practices, and when can it be used as a shield to prevent government from acting to harm, even indirectly, these same practices? When should the *Sherbert* test take cognizance of government actions that do not coerce or penalize Native Americans for their worldview but simply make it harder for them to practice their religion? Could the government constitutionally accommodate Indian religious practices on public lands if it wished? What weight should be given to AIRFA? And looming behind all of these questions: what weight should be given to the government's ownership rights in public lands?

Finally, the U.S. Supreme Court provided answers to many of these questions in 1988 through the landmark case *Lyng v. Northwest Indian Cemetery Protective Association*.[60]

LYNG AND THE INSTATEMENT OF GOVERNMENT PROPERTY RIGHTS

For centuries, if not longer, tribes of remote northwestern California have been fixing the world. Through regular participation in world-renewal dances, members of the Yurok, Karok, Hupa, and Tolowa nations restore balance to the universe and thus to themselves. Their dances, which are put up at two-year intervals, last for ten days in September and involve hundreds of tribal members, men and women alike, who take part in strenuous discussion, cultural and political debate, storytelling, food, and, of course, dance, all focused on restoring the right relation of the tribes with the universe.[61] The world-renewal dances of the northwestern California Indians are part of a complex set of lifeways that depend upon access to the prehuman spiritual powers believed to be immanent in the mountains surrounding the people. The High Country, as it is known, is especially sacred and consists of twenty-five square miles of the highest peaks of the Siskiyou mountains in the Blue Creek Unit of Six Rivers National Forest—the aboriginal lands of the tribes but now property owned by the federal government. Native spiritual leaders—medicine men—make frequent pilgrimages to the High Country. Seated alone and surrounded by silence, the medicine men acquire the spiritual power needed to sustain their communities. Without their connection with the sacred forces resident in the High Country, the tribes believe their communal integrity would fail and their responsibility to fix the world would go unmet, with dire consequences for all.

In the late 1970s, the Forest Service planned to create a paved road through Six Rivers National Forest which would run 75 miles and link two small California towns, Gasquet and Orleans, for use by logging trucks and cars. However, deep in the High Country, construction of the "G-O road" halted with six miles left to complete when the project approached the foot of Chimney Rock. As determined by the government's own study of Indian cultural and religious sites, commissioned at the outset of the project, the entire Chimney Rock area "is significant as an integral and indispensible [sic] part of Indian religious conceptualization and practice . . . [S]uccessful use of the [area] is dependent upon and facilitated by certain qualities of the physical environment, the most important of which are privacy, silence, and an undisturbed natural setting."[62] The government's study concluded that constructing the G-O road "would cause serious and irreparable damage to the sacred areas which are an integral and necessary part of the belief systems and lifeway of northwest California Indian peoples."[63] Notwithstanding this advice, the Forest Service pursued the project, and when the road reached Chimney Rock, individual Indians and groups representing the tribes went to court, claiming completion of the G-O road would constitute an indirect burden on their religious practices that was impermissible under the First Amendment. A federal district court agreed, and issued an injunction to stop the road. A panel of the Ninth Circuit affirmed. By a majority of 5–3, the Supreme Court reversed.[64]

Writing for the majority, Justice Sandra Day O'Connor agreed that the G-O road would have "severe adverse effects on [the tribes'] practice of their religion";[65] "could have devastating effects on traditional Indian religious practices";[66] and that "the threat to the efficacy of at least some religious practices is extremely grave."[67] Nevertheless, O'Connor stated, "the incidental effects of government programs, which may make it more difficult to practice certain religions but which have no tendency to coerce individuals into acting contrary to their religious beliefs, [cannot] require government to bring forward a compelling justification for its otherwise lawful actions."[68] With this move, the Court made clear that the Free Exercise Clause's protection against indirect burdens on religion was limited to protection from coercion of religious conscience and penalization by denying benefits or rights enjoyed by other citizens.

In so doing, the Court closed the door opened ever so slightly by *Wilson* that government land use might implicate the Free Exercise Clause if it denied religious adherents the use of land "indispensable" for religious practices. Also precluded was *Crow*'s implication that if government denial of access to a sacred site was more than "minimal" and other than a reasonable "time and manner" restriction, Free Exercise Clause rights might be at stake. The Court's reasoning made irrelevant *Sequoyah*'s deliberations over the "centrality" or "indispensability" of a site to religious observances. Like *Badoni*, the Court hued closely to coercion and penalization as the only legitimate Free Exercise indirect burdens, while (as *Badoni* had put it) "mindful of the difficulties facing plaintiffs in performing solemn religious ceremonies" in the presence of intrusive third parties. After *Lyng*, the Free Exercise Clause would clearly be a shield, not a sword, against government, and a small shield at that: indirect adverse impacts on religious practices would raise no constitutional question, even if the effects would virtually destroy a religion.

While *Lyng* could have been decided simply by clarifying the scope of indirect burdens recognized under the Free Exercise Clause, Justice O'Connor added a second, highly significant ground for the Court's decision. The majority expressed great concern that if the Court acceded to the tribes' request, it would be allowing the Indians to impose a "religious servitude" on the government's land: a legal right-of-way exclusive to the tribes, in the service of their religious beliefs, which would entitle them to deny anyone—"recreational visitors, other Indians, or forest rangers"—access to the Chimney Rock area.[69] O'Connor added that accommodating the Indians' religious beliefs "could easily require *de facto* beneficial ownership of some rather spacious tracts of public property . . . [T]he diminution of the Government's property rights, and the concomitant subsidy of the Indian religion, would in this case be far from trivial."[70] Concluding her point, O'Connor stated, "Whatever rights the Indians may have to the use of the area, however, those rights do not divest the Government of its rights to use what is, after all, *its* land."[71] With these words, the *Lyng* majority went further than any previous federal court in making government property ownership an absolute standard for adjudicating constitutional rights under the Free Exercise Clause. *Sequoyah*'s "factor" analysis of property rights, in comparison, appears as so much judicial handwringing.

Neglected by many commentators at the time, the majority's opinion contained an admonition that would come to be a lynchpin of policymaking in subsequent years. As Justice O'Connor wrote, "Nothing in our opinion should be read to encourage governmental insensitivity to the religious needs of any citizen. The Government's rights to the use of its own land, for example, need not and should not discourage it from accommodating religious practices like those engaged in by the Indian respondents."[72]

The Court endorsed the interpretation of AIRFA presented by *Crow* and *Wilson*: that AIRFA was a sense of Congress resolution that created no private rights of action—it conferred no "special religious rights on Indians," as the bill's sponsor, Representative Morris Udall, had said. Quoting Representative Udall, the Court observed that AIRFA would "not change any existing State or Federal law" and, in fact, "has no teeth in it."[73]

In a scathing dissent, Justice Brennan, joined by Justices Marshall and Blackmun, attacked the majority's view that the government's "prerogative as landowner should always take precedence over a claim that a particular use of federal property infringes religious practices."[74] The dissenting justices rejected the majority's reading of precedent to diminish the scope of free exercise protection for indirect burdens to coercion and penalization, stating that "we have never suggested that the protections of the guarantee are limited to so narrow a range of governmental burdens."[75] Arguing passionately for an effects-based analysis of constitutional rights, Justice Brennan wrote, "Today, the Court holds that a federal land-use decision that promises to destroy an entire religion does not burden the practice of that faith in a manner recognized by the Free Exercise Clause."[76] Responding to the majority's averment that nothing in its opinion should be read as insensitivity to religion, he said, "I find it difficult, however, to imagine conduct more insensitive to religious needs than the Government's determination to build a marginally useful road in the face of uncontradicted evidence that the road will render the practice of respondents' religion impossible."[77] As to the majority's claim that after their ruling the tribal claimants remained free to believe whatever they liked, "Given today's ruling, that freedom amounts to nothing more than the right to believe that their religion will be destroyed."[78]

While the *Lyng* majority can be faulted for attenuating the *Sherbert* test, the test itself is not unproblematic. Recall that under *Sherbert*, once sincere religious claimants establish that the government has imposed an indirect burden on their religious observance by putting them to a choice between violating their beliefs or foregoing a generally available benefit, the onus shifts to the government to show a compelling interest for its actions, one that is achieved by the least restrictive means possible. Given the reticence of courts to challenge the sincerity of religious beliefs, under *Sherbert* a sincere religious adherent "may force government to show how almost any law serves a compelling interest and is narrowly tailored to that interest."[79] Further, balancing tests like the *Sherbert* test require courts to make value judgments, to identify the common good implicitly or explicitly with the government's interest, and to "weigh" it against what is by definition a parochial (and often culturally unfamiliar) good. The results can be idiosyncratic.

The four federal cases in the 1980s that engaged Indian use of sacred lands, for example, struggled to develop a balancing test for sacred sites claims, and their failure to produce a coherent method of analysis may well have influenced the Court's decision to take up *Lyng* in the first place. Land-based spiritual practices, intimately tied to indigenous peoples' cultures, were foreign to the experience of the courts and at odds with Euro-American assumptions about constitutional jurisprudence. Further, as to the government's rights as property owner, it is worth considering what limitations could fairly be placed on plaintiffs, Indian or other, who claim that their religious well-being depends on certain uses of federal property. How are courts to draw lines that might prevent the destruction of a religion by conceding certain uses of land at the expense of the common good, while denying uses by others whose practices are deemed to be (by whom?) less critical to their religion's survival? According to emerging sources in international law and a growing number of legal scholars, the answer may lie in a fundamental reassessment of Euro-American notions of "property" and "property rights" in order to recognize indigenous peoples' rights to ancestral lands—cutting the Gordian knot, in effect, in favor of indigenous peoples' lifeways.[80] Clearly, *Lyng* yielded a harsh result for the tribes of northwestern California, but under the existing federal legal regime restricting government property rights in the interest of religious groups presents constitutional challenges, leading some to argue that Congress, the President, and federal agencies, not the courts, are best situated to make such determinations.[81]

From the Courts to Congress: Legislative Resources after *Lyng*

Two years after *Lyng*, the U.S. Supreme Court in *Employment Division v. Smith* (1990)[82] held that where the intent of a law is not to prohibit or burden a religion, the government may apply its law to religious practitioners, even if the incidental effect of the law is to make it harder for believers to pursue their faith. The case centered on members of the Native American Church, who had been fired from their jobs and denied unemployment compensation after using peyote for sacramental purposes. The use of peyote violated Oregon drug laws, which were neutral as to religion. In ruling for the state, the *Smith* Court put an end to *Sherbert* balancing: unless a law outright attacked religion, the state, to survive a Free Exercise challenge, had only to show that its law was reasonably related to a legitimate governmental purpose. In effect, *Smith* brought Free Exercise Clause jurisprudence back to the nineteenth century and *Reynolds*, where any law furthering public safety or good order would be sustained.

Congress responded aggressively to *Smith* by passing the Religious Freedom Restoration Act (RFRA), which expressly reversed *Smith* and restored the compelling-interest test (i.e., *Sherbert* balancing) for judicial analysis of Free Exercise claims. RFRA states, "Government shall not substantially burden a person's exercise of religion even if the burden results from a rule of general applicability," unless the government shows a compelling interest in the application of its law, which can be served by no less restrictive means.[83]

Although the Supreme Court later held RFRA unconstitutional as applied to the states, RFRA remains good law as to the federal government.[84]

Does the validity of RFRA for the federal government mean that *Lyng* is also reversed and *Sherbert* balancing restored to sacred sites cases? The answer appears to be that *Lyng* remains the law of the land. The legislative history of RFRA reveals that "Congress was assured that RFRA would not create a cause of action on behalf of Native Americans seeking to protect sacred sites. The Senate report stated that RFRA would not overrule *Lyng*."[85] Federal courts considering RFRA's applicability in the sacred sites context have agreed that *Lyng* lives. In the recent case of *Navajo Nation v. U.S. Forest Service* (2006),[86] the district court of Arizona heard claims by tribal members that the government's plan to use polluted water for snow-making on the sacred San Francisco Peaks would violate their free exercise rights. The court found that while RFRA had reversed *Smith* and restored *Sherbert* balancing, RFRA had made no changes to what constitutes a constitutionally cognizable burden on religious practices. Since *Lyng* had rejected considering the adverse impacts of government development projects on the spiritual well being of practitioners, the *Navajo Nation* court declined to so as well. Because the tribal plaintiffs could not establish that the waste-water snowmaking project would damage their shrines, nor that the project would deny individual Indians access to the mountain, the court ruled that plaintiffs had stated no constitutional burden.

In addition to RFRA, Congress's post-*Smith* responses included RLUIPA, the Religious Land Use and Institutionalized Persons Act of 2000.[87] Like RFRA, RLUIPA also restores *Sherbert* balancing to judicial analysis of certain actions by state and local governments. In the land use context, RLUIPA has been helpful to churches and synagogues seeking to resist municipal zoning laws and other land use decisions that would adversely impact them, often by limiting their physical expansion. However, RLUIPA has not been an asset to Native Americans seeking to protect sacred sites, because RLUIPA stipulates that the religious adherents must have an ownership interest in their land—a property right that would be negatively affected by government regulation—and tribes often lack such rights in their sacred lands.

As tribes struggled to find legislative or judicial help to state claims under the Free Exercise Clause, they received support for their use of sacred sites from an unexpected quarter—the political process and federal agencies. When the political winds shifted in the 1990s, Congress and the president provided new assistance to land-based religions. The result was a series of judicial challenges testing the limits of government accommodation of Native American spiritual traditions.

THE ESTABLISHMENT CLAUSE AND ACCOMMODATION OF NATIVE AMERICAN SPIRITUALITY

The Establishment Clause of the First Amendment provides, "Congress shall make no law respecting an establishment of religion . . . ."[88] The Establishment Clause, intended by the Framers to protect the Christian denominations of the former colonies from control by the federal government, today operates largely as a restraint on both state and federal government from favoring one religion over another, or religion over nonreligion.[89] Even as the Establishment Clause has been called upon throughout its modern history to keep strong the metaphorical wall of separation between "church and state," for the well-being of both, the Supreme Court and scholars of the Constitution have recognized that government has an obligation to try to accommodate religious beliefs and actions.[90] Indeed, as Justice O'Connor wrote for the *Lyng* majority, the government's ownership rights in its lands should not discourage it from accommodating Native American religious practices on those lands. How far state and federal actors may go to make such accommodations, consistent with the Establishment Clause, remains a challenge for courts in the twenty-first century.

When Streams Converge

Public law and policy today reflect an increased governmental willingness to accommodate traditional Native American practices, including religious practices. Much as *Smith* in 1990 became a call to arms for mainstream religious leaders and politicians sympathetic to their viewpoints, resulting in RFRA and RLUIPA, *Lyng* in 1988 prompted outrage in Indian Country at what was perceived as the end of judicial tolerance for indigenous religions in the United States. Immediately after *Lyng*, the American Indian Religious Freedom Coalition was formed, and through its advocacy, Congress passed legislation in 1990 that designated the sacred High Country part of a permanent wilderness area, thus denying completion of the G-O road.

Throughout the 1990s, many accommodations of traditional Indian culture were achieved through the political process. After years of work by tribal leaders, Congress passed the Native American Graves Protection and Repatriation Act (NAGPRA) of 1990,[91] an important initiative which provides for protection of unmarked Indian burials on public lands and repatriation of Indian remains and certain classes of artifacts found on federal land or in museums receiving federal funds—sacred remains and artifacts likely numbering in excess of a million.[92]

Congress also acted to protect the cultural resources of Native Americans in 1992, when, after lobbying by the Coalition and other Indian groups, it amended the National Historic Preservation Act (NHPA). The amendments allow "properties of religious and cultural importance for an Indian tribe" to be included on the National Register of Historic Places and require federal agencies to consult with tribes before undertaking development projects that could affect sensitive sites.[93] The NHPA amendments also acknowledge that tribes have the right not to disclose sensitive information about sacred sites, create the option of establishing tribal preservation offices separate from those of the state, and give tribes legal authority over administering sacred sites on their reservations.

Amendments to existing legislation also served to reverse the effects of one of the most objectionable judicial decisions of the previous decade. Angered by the outcome of *Smith*, which had upheld the criminalization of sacramental peyote use by members of the Native American Church, Native leaders worked closely with legislators to change the law. As a result, Congress passed the American Indian Religious Freedom (AIRFA) Amendments of 1994.[94] Today, federal law prohibits states from penalizing Indians who ingest peyote for traditional religious purposes.

Taken together, NAGPRA and the amendments to the NHPA and AIRFA represent some of the most significant legislation that has come to mark what one scholar calls the "era of atonement" in federal policy-making toward Indian cultures.[95] Finally, in 1996, President Clinton signed Executive Order 13,007, which directs agencies administering federal lands to accommodate access to and ceremonial use of Indian religious sites to the extent practicable and not inconsistent with essential agency functions.[96] The Implementation Report on E.O. 13,007 requires agencies to consult with tribes on a government-to-government basis, requires agencies to use tribal standards to identify sacred sites and to allow tribes to maintain control over information about sites, and requires agencies to recognize that tribal culture is dynamic, that tribal religion is practiced in the present, and that not all sacred sites are historical—some are recent in origin.

In summary, after *Lyng* and *Smith* appeared to foreclose recourse to the Free Exercise Clause, advocates of religious liberty—Indian and non-Indian—engaged in parallel and sometimes cooperative political behavior to expand the procedural and substantive scope of protection for religiously motivated conduct. Two streams, one broad and propelled by the concerns of majority-American religions and the other narrow and targeted to the exceptional characteristics of traditional Native American spirituality, converged with force. Congress and the executive branch responded, and by the start of the twenty-first century, the question for the courts had become not whether federal agencies could devise land use plans to accommodate Native American uses of sacred sites, but how far they could go without establishing religion in violation of the First Amendment. The stage was quickly set for a contest between, on the one hand, Native American cultural and religious traditionalists, and, on the other, tourists, hikers, climbers, campers, commercial interests, and other users of public lands sacred to tribes.

Close Encounters at Devil's Tower

Devil's Tower National Monument in Wyoming rises like an immense cylinder of rock above the Great Plains that surround it. Made famous by the film *Close Encounters of the Third Kind* as the site of alien-human contact, in the last twenty years Devil's Tower has become a destination for a different kind of encounter: it is one of the world's premiere rock climbing destinations. More than 6,000 climbers scale the Tower each year, especially during the summer. Many have described their ascents of Devil's Tower in terms of respect and awe, and even in the vernacular of religious or spiritual experience. A lively industry has sprung up supporting the needs of the climbers and their families, as well as the half-million tourists a year who simply wish to visit one of "nature's miracles" in the first national monument created by President Theodore Roosevelt in 1906 and now managed by the National Park Service (NPS).

The same edifice is called *Mato Tipila*, or "Bear's Lodge," in Lakota. Since at least 1000 C.E., *Mato Tipila* has played a central role in the myths of origin for tribes including the Lakota, Arapahoe, Crow, and Kiowa. For the Lakota, at the beginning of creation, the spiritual intermediary White Buffalo Calf Woman emerged from *Mato Tipila* to give the people their most sacred religious artifact, the White Buffalo Calf Pipe. *Mato Tipila* remains one of the most sacred sites in Indian Country. It is the site of annual pilgrimages, Sun Dances, Vision Quests (requiring prayer, fasting, solitude, and sweat lodge purification), and other liturgical activity. Though active throughout the year, the most intensive use of the mountain by tribes is during the summer, especially the month of June, when the summer solstice occurs. As the number of seasonal climbers soared, run-ins between Indian spiritual practitioners and the public became frequent, tensions rose, and the NPS was forced to formulate a plan that would ameliorate antagonisms and try and suit all concerned.

The NPS was not working from whole-cloth. In the background were the federal laws enacted for the benefit of Native American culture. Accordingly, starting in the early 1990s, the NPS nationwide adopted management policies intended to maximize traditional Indian utilization of sacred sites and minimize interference with Indian religious practitioners by third parties, whether recreational or commercial. Applying these policies to Devil's Tower, the NPS issued a management plan in 1995 which included prohibiting new fixed pitons on the mountain (considered an affront to its sacred quality), rehabilitation and maintenance of access trails, camouflaging of climbing equipment, and seasonal closing of climbing routes to protect raptors' nests. The NPS also placed signage encouraging tourists to stay on the trails around Devil's Tower ("The Tower is sacred to American Indians. Please stay on the trail.") and adopted an interpretive education program to explain to tourists the religious and cultural significance of the site for certain Native Americans. Initially, the NPS plan banned commercial climbing licenses during June in deference to Native American uses associated with the solstice. A group of commercial climbers obtained an injunction against the ban, and the NPS relented, replacing the prohibition with a "voluntary ban" on climbing for June. NPS staff would ask potential climbers to choose to refrain from their sport "out of respect for American Indian cultural values"; those who chose to climb anyway would be issued licenses without further ado.

Unsatisfied, the climbers sued the NPS, claiming that its plan even as modified with the voluntary ban violated the Establishment Clause, and in 1998 the federal district court for Wyoming, in *Bear Lodge Multiple Use Association v. Babbitt*, rejected the climbers' arguments.[97] Applying the traditional test of *Lemon v. Kurtzman*, the court found that the NPS plan had a secular purpose; did not have the primary effect of advancing religion; and would involve no excessive entanglement of government with religion.[98] First, the court accepted the NPS's argument that its plan served the valid purposes of helping to "eliminate barriers to American Indians' free practice of religion," a special concern where, as here, "impediments to worship arise because a group's sacred place of worship is found on property of the United States."[99] Further, the plan served to foster "the preservation of the historical, social and cultural practices of Native Americans which are necessarily intertwined with their religious practices."[100] Second, the court found that the voluntary ban did not have the primary effect of advancing religion, where the climbers were not improperly coerced from their activity—a proper and traditional use of the monument—and were allowed meaningful access to the Tower. While an outright ban on climbing, the court hinted, would cross the line into unconstitutional coercion, the voluntary ban did not.[101] Third and finally, the court held that enforcing the voluntary climbing ban would entail little if any governmental involvement in Native American religion (noting that tribes "are not solely religious organizations, but also represent a common heritage and culture"[102]) and therefore pose no significant risk of excessive entanglement. In short, the court held that the National Park Service's land management plan was an appropriate accommodation of Native American religious practices. The Tenth Circuit Court of Appeals affirmed the decision in 2002 without reaching the Establishment Clause issues, holding that plaintiff climbers had suffered no injury in fact and therefore lacked standing.[103]

An Emerging Jurisprudence of Accommodation?

Bear Lodge has proven to be the "myth of origin" for other federal decisions upholding government land management plans which sought to accommodate Native American practices at sacred sites through voluntary compliance by the public. In 2002, at Rainbow Bridge in Utah—the subject of the *Badoni* litigation of the 1980s—a comprehensive plan that included discouraging, though not prohibiting, visitors from approaching or passing under the arch formed by the sandstone edifice "[out of respect] for the sacred nature of this area to American Indians" was upheld against an Establishment Clause challenge brought by a tourist.[104] The water level has receded from beneath Rainbow Bridge and policies of the NPS favorable to the accommodation of Navajo cultural values and religious beliefs, as well as the preservation of the site from degradation by overuse or misuse by tourists, have brought a measure of relief, though not satisfaction, to those who hold the site sacred.

Federal courts since *Bear Lodge* have rejected Establishment Clause challenges in two cases and found violations in none. In 2004, the Tenth Circuit Court of Appeals held that the Forest Service's historic preservation plan for the Medicine Wheel National Historic Landmark—an ancient, highly complex site in Bighorn County, Wyoming, used for centuries by innumerable tribes for religious observances—did not violate the Constitution by requiring the closing of roads used by commercial loggers, and stopping a planned timber sale in deference to Native religious sensibilities.[105] Also in 2004, the Ninth Circuit Court of Appeals upheld Arizona's Department of Transportation policy against issuing permits to private landowners that would allow them to sell the state materials mined from sites on their land (Woodruffe Butte) that were sacred to the Hopi, Zuni, and Navajo.[106] Taken together, *Bear Lodge* and its progeny may represent an emerging jurisprudence of accommodation of sacred sites, one grounded in a court-recognized policy of religious accommodation under the First Amendment and informed by federal statutory and executive commitments to preserving and fostering traditional Native American culture, history, and tradition. Whether such politically generated commitments by the non-judicial branches can sustain Native American spiritual practices "to the seventh generation," however, remains a profoundly unsettling and unsettled question to many.[107]

THE FUTURE OF NATIVE AMERICAN SACRED SITES UNDER FEDERAL LAW

Today federal courts are not disposed to recognize that government actions that unintentionally harm or even destroy tribal religious practices and cultures amount to constitutional burdens on the freedom of religion, at least where the practices require certain uses of government-owned land. Despite RFRA, sacred sites have no more constitutional protection than after *Lyng*. The Free Exercise Clause offers no sword to land-based religions. However, neither has the Establishment Clause provided a sword to the opponents of land-based religions, as long as federal land managers seek to accommodate Indian religious practices in ways that do not coerce the public's voluntary compliance with land use restrictions.

The Supreme Court may be willing to consider expanding the notion of indirect constitutional burdens beyond government coercion or penalization. In *Gonzales* (2006),[108] customs inspectors seized a quantity of a plant containing an illegal drug that was bound for an indigenous peoples' church to be used sacramentally in a tea called *hoasca*. The government and church members agreed that the confiscation burdened members' religion for purposes of RFRA—without its sacrament, the church's religious practices would be harmed. The Court ruled that the government had failed to show a compelling interest in enforcing its drug laws against church members, or that seizure was the least restrictive means of doing so. Might the Court be receptive to other kinds of indirect burdens, such as those in *Navajo Nation*, which also make it harder for Indians to practice their religions, without coercing or penalizing them? Probably not. The *Gonzales* Court noted that the facts behind the *Smith* case, which RFRA expressly reversed, were very much like the facts of *Gonzales* (peyote instead of *hoasca*), thus showing congressional willingness to make exceptions for sacramental drug use by indigenous communities. Also, with amendments to AIRFA in 1994 that allow sacramental peyote use by Indians, Congress had shown its support for this type of exception to generally applicable drug laws. Perhaps most significantly, in *Gonzales* the government agreed from the outset that its conduct "burdened" members' religion in a legally relevant way—a stipulation unusual if not unique for the United States. Thus, while *Gonzales* may indicate greater judicial sympathy for Indian religious practices that are *not* land-based (like consuming peyote or other drugs in traditional religious ceremonies), the opinion does not provide a basis for optimism that *Lyng* will be overturned soon.

As long as property ownership remains conclusive for establishing a right to worship at sacred sites, Native Americans may benefit from recent work by legal scholars who are exploring new theories of property rights that Indians may assert. As law professor Kristen Carpenter has argued, "Indians have the longest and deepest relationship with sacred sites of any peoples in North America, and in some instances, some of those relationships may be cognizable under property law."[109] Easements—rights of land use— which Indians may have retained in treaties or established through long and open conduct may provide help. A federal district court has recognized such a right of use in the Zuni, holding that under Arizona law, the tribe was entitled to an easement over private property for the purpose of making a quadrennial pilgrimage to a mountain region, Kohlu/wala:wa, which the Zuni believe to be their place of origin.[110] While an easement is less than a fee simple estate (which gives the possessor all of the rights in the "bundle" that goes with ownership), it is nevertheless a powerful interest that would be familiar to judges and a legal system indebted to conventional Euro-American notions of property.

Until such time, if any, that the Supreme Court expressly overrules *Lyng* or permits judicial interpretations of "burdens" under RFRA that reach government acts affecting sacred sites, or until federal courts consistently recognize Native American relationships to land as falling within the conventional tenets of property law, or until Congress acts, the future of sacred sites on public lands may depend upon the ingenuity and "beneficence" of federal agents. Consistent with federal policies, National Park Service employees and other land managers must craft plans that aim to strike a balance between "multiple uses" by the public and religious or cultural uses by Native Americans. Allowing federal land managers to determine how sacred sites will be impacted by third parties permits those closer to the "grass roots" than judges to make decisions in dialogue with stakeholders such as Native Americans, tourists, and business owners. Land managers also are empowered by more than a decade of express federal policies favoring accommodation of Indian religious practices. Federal agents can sometimes be informed, flexible, and sensitive to all sides of a land-use issue. On the other hand, allowing land managers to determine whether a tribe has "enough" access to its sacred sites, or whether an impact will have "minor" effects, may place them in awkward, perhaps inappropriate, roles as quasi-experts in anthropology, sociology, or religion. When trying to create plans that approach but do not violate the Establishment Clause, land managers may operate as de facto legal scholars, or even as judges. The plans themselves may please no one, or lead to litigation in any event. Individual planners may be gifted with interpersonal skills, organizational abilities and sensitivity to their constituencies—or not. Finally, even where land management plans are deemed successful enough by stakeholders, as creatures of federal agencies, they rely upon the political process for their longevity and thus rest on the shifting sands of the executive and legislative branches of government.

The future of Native American sacred sites may depend on the ability of tribes to form politically effective coalitions to persuade lawmakers and the non-Indian public that they seek no special rights but only legal protection for uses of land that have gone on for at least centuries. Whether sacred sites endure will also depend on whether Native peoples can maintain their cultural integrity—not just acquire the legal use of public land, but continue to grow and develop the languages and lifeways that sprang from their relationships with the land, in ways responsive to the difficulties and opportunities of the present day. For over five centuries Euro-Americans and Native Americans have been challenged to articulate and demonstrate their right relationship with each other. Euro-Americans may call this dialogue negotiating the common good. For many Native Americans, achieving this balance of interests is called, simply, fixing the world.

NOTES

1. Thomas Buckley, "Renewal as Discourse and Discourse as Renewal in Native Northwestern California," in *Native Religions and Cultures of North America: Anthropology of the Sacred*, ed. Lawrence E. Sullivan (New York: Continuum, 2003), 34.

2. Population and tribal statistics cited in this section appear in David H. Getches, Charles F. Wilkinson, and Robert A. Williams, Jr., *Cases and Materials on Federal Indian Law*, 5th ed. (St. Paul, MN: West, 2005), 9, 14–15.

3. See Eva Marie Garroutte, *Real Indians: Identity and the Survival of Native America* (Berkeley, CA: University of California Press, 2003), 1–98. Garroutte, a sociologist, analyzes present-day notions of American Indian identity according to law, biology, culture, and self-identification.

4. See Michael F. Brown, *Who Owns Native Cultures?* (Cambridge, MA: Harvard University Press, 2003); and Angela R. Riley, "'Straight Stealing': Towards an Indigenous System of Cultural Property Protection," 80 *Washington Law Review* 69 (2005).

5. Readers interested in Native American spiritual traditions may wish to consult Vine Deloria, Jr., *God Is Red: A Native View of Religion*, 30th Anniversary ed. (Golden, CO: Fulcrum Publishing, 2003); Huston Smith and Phil Cousineau, *A Seat at the Table: Huston Smith in Conversation with Native Americans on Religious*

Freedom (Berkeley, CA: University of California Press, 2006); Winona LaDuke, *Recovering the Sacred: The Power of Naming and Claiming* (Cambridge, MA: South End Press, 2005); and *Seeing with a Native Eye: Essays on Native American Religion*, Walter Holden Capps, ed. (New York: Harper & Row, 1976).

6. On the role of Christianity in the colonization of the Americas, including its theological antecedents in the Middle Ages, see Robert A. Williams, Jr., *The American Indian in Western Legal Thought: The Discourses of Conquest* (New York: Oxford University Press, 1990).

7. Genesis 1: 1–2 ("In the beginning God created the heavens and the earth. The earth was without form and void, and darkness was upon the face of the deep . . ."), in *Bible* Revised Standard Version. On the philosophy of creation in the Jewish, Christian and Islamic traditions, see David B. Burrell, *Freedom and Creation in Three Traditions* (Notre Dame, IN: Notre Dame Press, 1993).

8. See Catherine L. Albanese, *Nature Religion in America: From the Algonkian Indians to the New Age* (Chicago, IL: University of Chicago Press, 1990), 35 (For Puritans, "[t]he wilderness was the territory of the devil and the powers of evil. Wild beasts and wild men who dwelled there could only be his emissaries and servants").

9. Lloyd Burton, *Worship and Wilderness: Culture, Religion, and Law in Public Lands Management* (Madison, WI: University of Wisconsin Press, 2002), 55.

10. Albanese, *Nature Religion*, 53 (Beginning in the Enlightenment, "[w]ith the order and regularity of the Newtonian universe, the harmony of the spheres moved from ancient Greek philosophy to modern scientific laws").

11. Barron's defines "highest and best use" as a real estate appraisal term referring to the "legally and physically possible use that, at the time of appraisal, is most likely to produce the greatest net return to the land or buildings over a given period." *Dictionary of Business Terms*, Barron's Educational Series, Inc, 2000. See also *Answers.com*, available at http://www.answers.com/topic/highest-and-best-use.

12. Smith and Cousineau, *A Seat at the Table*, xix.

13. Keith H. Basso, *Wisdom Sits in Places: Landscape and Language among the Western Apache* (Albuquerque, NM: University of Albuquerque Press, 1996), 31.

14. *American Sacred Space*, ed. David Chidester and Edward T. Linenthal (Bloomington, IN: Indiana University Press, 1995), 9.

15. Ibid., 12.

16. Ibid., 15.

17. Buckley, "Discourse as Renewal," 33.

18. Vine Deloria, Jr., *God Is Red*, 65.

19. Ibid., 65–66.

20. Andrew Gulliford, *Sacred Objects and Sacred Places: Preserving Tribal Traditions* (Boulder, CO: University Press of Colorado, 2000), 68–69. The contrasts I draw between the two types of religion for the sake of highlighting their differences should not elide the fact that religions of the book also have sacred places (e.g., Jerusalem, Mecca) and routinely engage in ritual actions, and religions of the land have complex belief systems that explain the universe to adherents.

21. The poet Audre Lorde, speaking in a different context, famously claimed "the master's tools could never dismantle the master's house." Native Americans who have spun arguments for sacred sites protection based on American constitutional law may have reached the same conclusion. Audre Lorde, *Sister Outsider* (Berkeley, CA: Crossing Press, 1984), 112.

22. U.S. Constitution, Amendment 1.

23. *Cantwell v. Connecticut*, 310 U.S. 296 (1940).

24. Ibid., 303; *Braunfeld v. Brown*, 366 U.S. 599, 603 (1961).

25. *Reynolds v. United States*, 98 U.S. 145 (1878).

26. *Reynolds*, 98 U.S. at 164 ("Congress was deprived of all legislative power over mere opinion, but was left free to reach actions which were in violation of social duties or subversive of good order").

27. *Wisconsin v. Yoder*, 406 U.S. 205, 215 (1972). Another threshold criterion for stating a Free Exercise Clause claim is that the religious basis for the assertion be "sincere," not feigned. Courts have tended to accept the sincerity of claimants rather than engage in second-guessing their motives. See Michael W. McConnell, John H. Garvey, and Thomas C. Berg, *Religion and the Constitution* (New York: Aspen Publishers, 2002), 237–45.

28. *Davis v. Beason*, 133 U.S. 333, 342 (1890).

29. *United States v. Seeger*, 380 U.S. 163, 165 (1965). See also *Welsh v. United States*, 398 U.S. 333 (1970).

30. *Sherbert v. Verner*, 374 U.S. 398 (1963).

31. *Shebert*'s mode of analysis led to invalidations of governmental actions in the following Free Exercise Clause cases: *Wisconsin v. Yoder*, 406 U.S. 205 (1972) (fine on Old Order Amish for failing to send children to public schools); *Thomas v. Review Board*, 450 U.S. 707 (1981) (unemployment compensation denied Seventh Day Adventist for refusing to work in a munitions factory); *Hobbie v. Unemployment Appeals Commission*, 480 U.S. 136 (1987) (unemployment compensation denied Seventh Day Adventists who refused to work on Saturday); *Frazee v. Ill. Dep't of Employment Security*, 489 U.S. 829 (1989) (unemployment compensation denial to Sabbatarian).

32. 42 U.S.C. § 1996.

33. AIRFA and subsequent Indian legislation and executive branch actions, discussed below, can be viewed as attempts by the federal government to fulfill its trust responsibilities to the tribes. On the Trust Doctrine, see Rebecca Tsosie, "The Conflict Between the 'Public Trust' and the 'Indian Trust' Doctrines: Federal Public Land Policy and Native Nations," 39 *Tulsa Law Review* 271 (2003).

34. On the history of federal policies outlawing and suppressing Indian religious practices in the late-nineteenth and early-twentieth centuries, see Allison M. Dussias, "Ghost Dance and Holy Ghost: The Echoes of Nineteenth-Century Christianization Policy in Twentieth-Century Native American Free Exercise Cases," 49 *Stanford Law Review* 773–852 (1997), esp. 788–805 (on federal policies of Christianization of Indians and suppression of indigenous religious rituals), and Ronald Niezen, *Spirit Wars: Native North American Religions in the Age of Nation Building*

(Berkeley, CA: University of California Press, 2000), 46–87 (on Indian boarding school phenomenon in United States and Canada).
35. *Sequoyah v. TVA*, 620 F.2d 1159 (6th Cir. 1980).
36. Ibid., 1162.
37. Ibid., 1164.
38. Ibid., 1165.
39. Ibid., 1164.
40. Ibid., 1161.
41. *Badoni v. Higginson*, 638 F.2d 172 (10th Cir. 1980).
42. Ibid., 176.
43. Ibid., 178.
44. Ibid., 179.
45. Ibid., 180.
46. *Frank Fools Crow v. Gullet*, 541 F. Supp. 785 (D. South Dakota 1982).
47. Ibid., 791.
48. Ibid., 792.
49. Ibid., 793.
50. Ibid.
51. *Wilson v. Block*, 708 F.2d 735 (D.C. Cir. 1983).
52. Ibid., 741.
53. Ibid.
54. Ibid., 743.
55. Ibid.
56. Ibid., 744.
57. Ibid., 744 fn. 5.
58. Ibid., 747.
59. Ibid.
60. *Lyng v. Northwest Indian Cemetery Protective Association*, 485 U.S. 439 (1988).
61. Buckley, "Renewal as Discourse," 33–52.
62. Ibid., 442.
63. Ibid.
64. Justice Kennedy, who was new to the Court, took no part in the case.
65. Ibid., 447.
66. Ibid., 451.
67. Ibid.
68. Ibid., 450–451.
69. Ibid., 452.
70. Ibid., 453.
71. Ibid. (italics in original).
72. Ibid., 453–454.
73. Ibid., 455.
74. Ibid., 465.
75. Ibid.
76. Ibid., 476.

77. Ibid., 477.

78. Ibid.

79. Charles Fried, *Saying What the Law Is: The Constitution in the Supreme Court* (Cambridge, MA: Harvard University Press, 2004), 152.

80. See, e.g., the Draft United Nations Declaration on the Rights of Indigenous Peoples, the Proposed American Declaration on the Rights of Indigenous Peoples, and related international law initiatives and documents discussed in Patrick Thornberry, *Indigenous Peoples and Human Rights* (Manchester, UK: Manchester Univ. Press, 2002). See also S. James Anaya, *Indigenous Peoples in International Law* (2000) (important theoretical discussion of the basis for indigenous rights) and S. James Anaya and Robert A. Williams, Jr., "The Protection of Indigenous Peoples' Rights over Lands and Natural Resources Under the Inter-American Human Rights System," 14 *Harvard Human Rights Journal* 33 (2001).

81. Marcia Yablon, "Property Rights and Sacred Sites: Federal Regulatory Responses to American Indian Religious Claims on Public Land," 113 *Yale Law Journal* 1623 (2004).

82. *Employment Division v. Smith*, 494 U.S. 872 (1990).

83. 42 U.S.C. §§ 2000bb-1(a) and (b).

84. *City of Boerne v. Flores*, 521 U.S. 507 (1997) (RFRA invalid as to the states); *Gonzales v. O Centro Espirita Beneficente Uniao Do Vegetal*, 126 S. Ct. 1211, 1216–17 (2006) (RFRA valid as to the federal government).

85. Anastasia P. Winslow, "Sacred Standards: Honoring the Establishment Clause in Protecting Native American Sacred Sites," 38 *Arizona Law Review* 1291, 1315 (1996).

86. Navajo Nation v. U.S. Forest Service, 408 F. Supp. 2d 866 (D. Ariz. 2006).

87. 42 U.S.C. §§ 2000cc.

88. U.S. Constitution, Amendment 1.

89. The Establishment Clause applies to the states through the Fourteenth Amendment. *Everson v. Board of Ed.*, 330 U.S. 1 (1947).

90. See, for example, *Lynch v. Donnelly*, 465 U.S. 668, 673 (1984) (The Constitution "mandates accommodation, not merely tolerance, of all religions, and forbids hostility toward any"); *Hobbie v. Unemployment Appeals Commission*, 480 U.S. 136, 144 (1987) (The Supreme Court "has long recognized that the government may (and sometimes must) accommodate religious practices and that it may do so without violating the Establishment Clause"); and Michael W. McConnell, "The Origins and Historical Understanding of Free Exercise of Religion," 103 *Harvard Law Review* 1409 (1990).

91. 25 U.S.C. §§ 3001–3013.

92. The National Park Service reports that as of November 30, 2006, the total of number of remains and artifacts reported and eligible for repatriation under NAGPRA amounted to 824,405. Available at http://www.cr.nps.gov/nagpra/FAQ/INDEX.HTM#How_many.

93. 16 U.S.C. § 470a (d)(6)(A) & (d)(6)(B).

94. 42 U.S.C.A. § 1996a.

95. Burton, *Worship and Wilderness*, 107.

96. Related Executive Orders of the Clinton presidency include E.O. 12,898, "Federal Actions To Address Environmental Justice in Minority Populations and Low-Income Populations" (1994), and E.O. 13,175, "Consultation and Coordination With Indian Tribal Governments" (2000).

97. *Bear Lodge Multiple Use Assn. v. Babbitt*, 2 F. Supp. 2d 1448 (D. Wyo. 1998).

98. *Lemon v. Kurtzman*, 403 U.S. 602 (1971).

99. *Bear Lodge*, 2 F. Supp. 2d at 1454.

100. Ibid.

101. Ibid., 1455 fn. 7 ("In fact, a complete elimination of climbing from the Tower in the month of June would serve as powerful evidence of actual coercion").

102. Ibid., 1456.

103. *Bear Lodge Multiple Use Assn. v. Babbitt*, 175 F.3d 814, 816 (10th Cir. 1999).

104. *Natural Arch and Bridge Society v. Alston*, 209 F. Supp. 2d 1207, 1214 (D. Utah 2002).

105. *Wyoming Sawmills, Inc. v. U.S. Forest Service*, 383 F.3d 1241 (10th Cir. 2004).

106. *Cholla Ready Mix, Inc. v. Civish*, 382 F.3d 969 (9th Cir. 2004).

107. Even in the so-called "age of atonement," federal courts have rejected Indian challenges to the siting of telescope complexes on an Apache sacred mountain (Mt. Graham in Arizona) and requests by tribes for return of the bones of ancient ancestors (the "Kennewick Man" case), to name but two high-profile cases. See Robert A. Williams, Jr., "Large Binocular Telescopes, Red Squirrel Pinatas, and Apache Sacred Mountains: Decolonizing Environmental Law in a Multicultural World," 96 *West Virginia Law Review* 1133 (1994); and S. Alan Ray, "Native American Identity and the Challenge of Kennewick Man," 79 *Temple Law Review* 89 (2006).

108. *Gonzales v. O Centro Espirita Beneficente Uniao Do Vegetal*, 126 S. Ct. 1211 (2006).

109. Kristen A. Carpenter, "Old Ground and New Directions at Sacred Sites on the Western Landscape," 83 *Denver University Law Review* 981–1002, 997 (2006); see also Kristen A. Carpenter, "A Property Rights Approach to Sacred Sites: Asserting a Place for Indians as Non-Owners," 52 *UCLA Law Review* 1061 (2005).

110. *United States on Behalf of Zuni Tribe of New Mexico v. Platt*, 730 F. Supp. 318 (D. Ariz. 1990).

FURTHER READING

Every study of American Indian spiritual traditions should begin by consulting Lakota author Vine Deloria, Jr.'s work, *God Is Red: A Native View of Religion* (30th anniversary ed., Golden, CO: Fulcrum Publishing, 2003). First published in 1973, this seminal text on Native spirituality in the modern West from an Indian perspective remains relevant to all students of history, politics, law, and religion. Complementing Deloria's classic is the recent work by Huston Smith and Phil Cousineau, *A Seat at the Table: Huston Smith in Conversation with Native Americans on Religious Freedom* (Berkeley, CA: University of California Press, 2006). Smith, a noted scholar of religion, engages in a series of well-edited dialogues with Native traditional leaders, activists, legal experts, and religionists on the challenges facing indigenous spirituality in the United States.

Readers interested in comparative cultural analysis of land-based religious practices should consult Lloyd Burton, *Worship and Wilderness: Culture, Religion, and Law in Public Lands Management* (Madison, WI: University of Wisconsin Press, 2002). Burton explores the profound differences between Euro-American and Native American experiences of nature to illuminate and challenge the ethnocentrism of U.S. laws and policies governing public lands.

The unique relationship with the land enjoyed by many Native American communities is explored in linguistic anthropologist Keith Basso's award-winning book, *Wisdom Sits in Places: Landscape and Language among the Western Apache* (Albuquerque, NM: University of Albuquerque Press, 1996). Places—sacred and otherwise—are made, not found, as Basso demonstrates in this outstanding study of the Cibecue Apache and their relationship with their land, language, and social world.

Another fine study of present-day sacred sites and their meaning for Native communities is Peter Nabokov, *Where the Lightning Strikes: The Lives of American Indian Sacred Places* (New York: Viking, 2006). Through first-person narratives and scrupulous research, Nabokov, an anthropologist and Native studies scholar, describes his encounters with indigenous communities and their sacred sites across America in this fascinating ethnographic study.

The complex story of federal law and the suppression of indigenous religious traditions in the United States is well told by legal scholar Allison M. Dussias in "Ghost Dance and Holy Ghost: The Echoes of Nineteenth-Century Christianization Policy in Twentieth-Century Native American Free Exercise Cases" (49 *Stanford Law Review* 773 (1997)). Dussias provides a compelling argument that present-day jurisprudence carries forward the nineteenth century's bias toward Christianity in this foundational article on the history of Indian law and religious liberty.

For a comprehensive exposition and analysis of federal Indian law and its impact on real world issues, including access to and protection of Native American sacred sites, see Felix Cohen, *Cohen's Handbook of Federal Indian Law* (Newark, NJ: LexisNexis Matthew Bender, 2005). This recent edition of the classic treatise contains contributions by leading scholars in all areas of Indian law, including chapters devoted to Civil Rights and Tribal Cultural Resources.

The future of sacred sites protection will depend in part on ingenious legal strategies that move beyond constitutional law and the Free Exercise Clause. In her ground-breaking article, "A Property Rights Approach to Sacred Sites Cases: Asserting a Place for Indians as Non-Owners" (52 *UCLA Law Review* 1061 (2005)), law professor Kristen A. Carpenter criticizes the legal definitions of ownership and offers an important approach to protecting indigenous spiritual practices based on Indian rights in land under principles of Euro-American property law. Are land-based religious practitioners actually better off under the authority of federal agencies and Congress than under the protection of the Constitution? Legal scholar Marcia Yablon says yes, in her controversial perspective on Indian sacred sites and public lands, "Property Rights and Sacred Sites: Federal Regulatory Responses to American Indian Religious Claims on Public Land" (113 *Yale Law Journal* 1623 (2004)).

Readers interested in any dimension of Native American religions and the law should consult the DVD, *In the Light of Reverence: Protecting America's Sacred Lands* (Bullfrog Films, 2001). Director Christopher McLeod's award-winning documentary offers a highly engaging set of narratives focused on three tribes—the Hopi, Lakota, and Wintu—who are struggling to maintain their traditional spiritual practices in the context of non-Native values and the U.S. legal system. Information on this DVD and the Sacred Land Film Project of which it is a part is available at www.sacredland.org.

7

Consecrating the Green Movement

Nadra Hashim

Upon entering office, the Bush Administration withdrew the United States from the Kyoto Protocol. Ironically, this may have been the best thing that ever happened to the modern environmental movement, as it seems to have galvanized a community of scientists, an assortment of grass roots organizations, and a variety of politicians.[1] The Kyoto debacle specifically invigorated a lingering debate over the issue of greenhouse gases, particularly carbon dioxide emissions, and its relationship to global warming, as well as the relationship between international economic competition and American and international laws governing environmental protection.

Along with usual parties to the debate—the left-centrist greens and their opponents, the Wise Use advocates—at least one new faction has joined the fray. Recently, evangelical environmentalists, in a growing network of church-based grassroots organizations, have formed a loose coalition based on their shared interest in nature and on the doctrinal strategy of lobbying the government in the name of God. In the last two decades and in many areas of government, the Evangelical Right has enjoyed a rather swift and especially powerful influence in the Republican Party. This is especially true where matters of social policy are concerned. In light of this history, it stands to reason that the Evangelical Greens might expect similar results in the realm of regulatory protection, especially given the rather dramatic and apocalyptic melting of the polar ice caps.[2]

When George W. Bush ran for president, he made his faith, and more specifically his spiritual re-awakening, a central feature of his campaign. Once elected, President Bush created the Office of Faith-Based Initiatives, which formulates social welfare policy, coordinating and funding various advocacy and charity organizations. The president drew appointees to his faith-based initiatives from a pool of leaders within America's growing evangelical movement. In almost all areas of social policy, these evangelical leaders, both those in the White House as well as others associated with national think tanks, supported Bush Administration policy. However, in the past few years some evangelical leaders have broached topics outside the scope of the faith-based initiative. More specifically, a coalition of maverick evangelicals is pressing the Bush Administration to reconsider the Kyoto Protocol and formulate legislation which would regulate America's reliance on forms of energy that cause global warming. Like many Americans who have waged a campaign to advance regulatory law, Evangelical Greens may be aware that such a victory will be hard won.[3]

Depending on your perspective, the history of the American Green Movement can be characterized by its waves of relative popularity or obscurity. Many historians cite Rachel Carson's 1962 publication of *Silent Spring* as the epiphanic moment in modern environmental consciousness. Others suggest that the 1960s and 1970s were merely the second wave of environmental activism.[4] They assert that the first wave of environmental awareness occurred in the nineteenth century, when the early evidence of smoky fog, dubbed "smog," was detected in industrialized metropolises such as London.[5]

In this, the third wave of environmental consciousness, many scientists argue that the melting of the glaciers and ice caps requires immediate and sustained attention.[6] A far smaller group of scientists suggests that global warming is not imminent, and if it is, its effects may be self-correcting. The debate between these two scientific communities is highly charged, because most nations who signed the Kyoto Protocol argue that global warming is the leading cause of climate change.[7] The latest ripple in the current environmental debate has emerged because America's various scientific communities are discussing their differences very publicly. Due to the fact that some scientists are disputing what others believe to be verifiable facts, the focus of the political debate has shifted from formulating environmental policy to interpreting scientific data. More proverbial fuel has been added to the incendiary debate because most of the industrialized nations who signed the Kyoto Protocol are intrigued by this uniquely American debate. In a further and highly unusual departure from American environmental history, twelve states sued the Bush Administration EPA in an effort to induce the agency to acknowledge the link between carbon dioxide emissions and global warming/climate change and to formulate policy accordingly.[8]

The study of carbon dioxide emissions and their effect on air pollution stretches back to the late-nineteenth century. However, the recent and highly dramatic effects of global warming are making the solitary study of carbon dioxide a decisive element in the strategy of interest group political activity. Whereas in previous decades environmental protection was a grassroots effort, the activism of Third Wave Greens has developed into a legal struggle concerning the science of conservation, one that is being contested at the highest levels of government.[9] Meanwhile, Evangelical Greens have begun lobbying the presidential administration to reconsider its position on global warming.

This continuing dispute over environmental science, the role of the government in promoting conservation, and the recent emergence of religious environmentalists are intriguing developments. In the latter instance, evangelical activism has caused some to fear that the wall between church and state is being breached. However, these trends also suggest that some evangelical Christians, disenchanted with scientific inquiry since the emergence of Darwinian evolution and the triumph of academic and political agnosticism, may have finally made their peace with scientific inquiry. In order to understand how the historic tensions between scientific analysis and religious study have influenced current environmental policy, it is necessary to measure the breadth of antagonism toward Darwinian evolution. This aversion has helped promote not only Creationism and Intelligent Design, but it has also sustained a vague suspicion of the environmental sciences. Evangelical Greens, with their interest in natural sciences and environmental protection, find themselves outside the mainstream of their community. Their new political activism begs the question: are the tentative efforts by evangelical Greens a passing fad or an enduring trend? If Evangelical Greens institutionalize their position within their respective religious communities, will scientific inquiry finally enjoy a more laudable position in evangelical circles, or will the legacy of the Scopes Trial continue to keep evangelical Protestants cast out of the province of scientific inquiry into the twenty-first century? Ironically, the tension between the advancement of science and the promotion of religion is not a conflict born of America's Puritan history. Rather, this cleavage emerged once the wall between church and state had been firmly established.

THE FIRST WAVE: RELIGIOUS INNOVATION, INDUSTRIAL PROGRESS AND NATURAL THEOLOGY

By the mid-nineteenth century, scientific innovation made America the world's leading economic superpower. Americans inherited an enthusiasm for the study of science from their seventeenth-century Puritan forebears, who were beneficiaries of Enlightenment scholarship. According to Robert Merton, "Experiment was the scientific expression of the practical, active and methodological bents of the Puritan. This is not to say, of course, that experiment derived in any sense from Puritanism. But it serves to account for the ardent support of the new experimental science by those who had their eyes turned towards the other world and their feet firmly planted on this one."[10]

In seventeenth-century England, Sir Francis Bacon, the father of empiricism, and Robert Boyle and Isaac Newton, Enlightenment innovators in the physical sciences, were all associated with the Puritan faith, even if they did not practice their religion publicly.[11] Boyle and Newton were distinguished not only by their intellectual discovery, but also by their willingness to incorporate their faith in the language of their discovery. Newton argued that "[God] being in all places is more able by his will to move the Bodies within his boundless uniform Sensorium and thereby form and reform the parts of the Universe, than we are by our will to move the parts of our own bodies."[12]

Like Newton, Robert Boyle implied that his laws of science were fashioned by God, "since motion does not essentially belong to matter, as divisibility and impenetrableness are believed to do; the motions of all bodies, at least at the beginning of things . . . were impressed upon them, either by an external immaterial agent, God; or by other portions of matter acting upon them."[13]

Whether the Protestant Reformation in general or Puritanism more specifically was responsible for indulging an enlightened pursuit of scientific inquiry is a matter of significant dispute. By the eighteenth century, Puritan religious authority in America was being displaced by the proliferation of less rigidly religious political communities. In the eighteenth century, among the leadership of prominent intellectual communities, there was even a movement away from organized religion. One significant manifestation of this trend was the emergence of Deism.

Like Puritanism, Americans inherited Deism from the British.[14] The controversial aspects of Deist thought included its skeptical attitudes regarding the divinity of Jesus Christ, the existence of hell, and the authenticity of some portions of the New Testament. Many Deists believed that organized religion was extraneous to these revelations and as such should have little role in determining the ethical, legal, and political design of common law or national institutions.[15] As Deists and disciples of the European Enlightenment, Paine and Jefferson wanted secular law and rational philosophy to govern public discourse and civic life, so they argued that church and state should remain separate.[16] In his drafts of the Virginia Constitution, Jefferson stipulated that all citizens should have religious liberty and be freed from the compulsion of attending religious institutions. These sentiments found their highest ultimate expression in the Bill of Rights.[17] Thomas Jefferson's apprehension with the role of organized religion in civic life sprang from his knowledge of the turmoil caused by Europe's Thirty Years War, a feeling that was confirmed by the upheavals of America's nascent spiritual revival.

Spanning the years 1720–1750, America's First Great Awakening created a sustained schism in the ranks of various Protestant denominations over the appropriate means of interpreting the Bible.[18] In the Presbyterian Church, revivalists sought a literal interpretation of the Bible. Anti-revivalists championed a different approach to Biblical interpretation, one that drew from Enlightenment philosophy and scientific reasoning. This schism between the so-called "old" and "new" sides in the Presbyterian Church reflected a larger trend in various Protestant denominations and in the broader American society. The core dispute in most First Great Awakening communities concerned a tension over two facets of the Bible—its "inspirational" value and its "genuineness."[19] In the first instance, theological scholars were interested in determining which aspects of the Bible were wholly divine and what constituted divinely inspired human activity. The debate over inspiration often took place in the higher realms of theological discourse.[20] The second area was more mundane and concerned matters of "authorship, date and canonicity."[21]

In response to this intellectual revival, more traditional evangelical scholars, such as Samuel Tyler, led the "anti-revivalist" charge. Tyler argued that the Bible should be read for its overall message and should not be subjected to speculative criticism or reductionism.[22] This debate would reemerge in the late nineteenth century, when Darwin's focus on the mundane laws of the environment would challenge the biblical narrative of the earth's miraculous creation. Meanwhile, the political impact of the First Great Awakening and the debates it spawned between men of faith and men of reason pushed Americans toward scientific realism and political independence from England.[23] The struggle between revival and anti-revivalists in the late-eighteenth and early-nineteenth century also began to reflect a change in cultural and political norms brought about by the growing impact of the industrial revolution.

In the eighteenth century, promising scientific innovations such as the invention of the steam engine and electricity determined how modern society would be organized. These innovations permanently altered migration and improved employment opportunities. In England the industrial innovation also began to influence theological thought. In 1802, William Paley wrote a treatise recalling St. Thomas Aquinas' effort to prove the existence of God. Paley's *Natural Theology* placed God's works into various precise categories, which he called natural, supernatural, and miraculous.[24] In the years following the Civil War, Paley's natural theology became popular among American scholars who thought they might reconcile evolution with creation.[25] In the years between the First and Second Great Awakenings, the social developments that accompanied industrialization shifted national attention from religion and politics to science and industry. Americans belonging to a range of religious denominations grew enamored of modern scientific innovation, even if they remained leery of progressive scientific reasoning, a development that promoted economic expansion at the expense of environmental protection.

During the eighteenth century, the most important development in the world of commercial manufacturing and the harbinger of the Industrial Revolution was the "harnessing" of steam power.[26] This led to further experimentation with coal, rubber, and steel, which gave way to the first generation of British and American coal-burning factories.[27] These so-called "smog producers" displaced rural cottage industries, becoming the dominant feature of urban London by the mid-nineteenth century.[28] During the decade of the 1840s, at the height of the Industrial Revolution in Europe, the British parliament passed a city ordinance to control smoke emitted by local factories.[29] The law had little effect, and by the 1870s smog covered most of London, especially trees and tall buildings, obscuring the horizon. In 1873 an emission of pale, highly toxic smog led to citywide respiratory failure and caused as many as seven hundred deaths in the span of two days.[30] This particularly virulent smog attack, and one that followed it in the 1880s, may have not been carbon dioxide alone, as carbon dioxide is not observable, but they were warnings of the pernicious side effects of industrial development.[31]

In 1870s London, Charles Darwin's research on the environment was a central feature of most intellectual and political discourse. The concept of adaptation and survival, lexicon intended for analyzing animals experiencing biological evolution over millennia, was often used to justify the maladies and dislocations caused by the ever-expanding industrial economy. This was especially true in the case of a phenomenon known as "industrial melanism" observed in a moth named *B. betularia*.[32] By the 1860s, R.S. Edelson, a naturalist and moth enthusiast, noticed that some *B. betularia* had mutated. Unlike the original grey- and white-flecked moths, the new *B. betularia* were dark like the soot that covered most surfaces in urban London. In 1864, Edelson published his findings and named the new moth *carbonaria* in honor of the chemical element that furnished this adaptation.[33] As if to forewarn future environmentalists of an enduring trend, by 1900 the speckled moths had virtually "died out," and a full 90 percent of *B. betularia* were *carbonaria* moths.

The concepts of adaptation, evolution, and extinction were radical ideas outside the mainstream of much of nineteenth-century public discourse, as was the notion of environmental protection.[34] Even more problematic, Darwinian philosophy, one of the few scientific fields that addressed the function of the environment, was viewed in many circles as heretical. It seemed to directly contradict the sacred chronicle of biblical creation. In the era before industrialization—the early years of the Enlightenment—mathematicians and scientists such as Isaac Newton and Robert Boyle took pains to emphasize the harmony of their research with divine law. American scholars of the eighteenth and early nineteenth century followed suit, often quoting religious doctrine as they advanced their scientific inquiry.

In the 1840s, several religious scholars began to blend science and faith in an effort to challenge Deism, Materialism and Agnosticism, philosophies that juxtaposed science and faith and often disparaged organized religion.[35] Like their American counterparts, British theologians sought to establish a rapport between religious study and empirical research. In the 1820s, the Earl of Bridgewater asked that a conference of notable scholars work in residence on his estate and demonstrate the use of scientific constructs to describe the "Power, Wisdom and Goodness of God" in nature.[36] The *Bridgewater Treatises* were published after the Earl's death and included analysis from the fields of physics, the natural sciences, and human anatomy. By various accounts, one essay in particular, that of William Whewell's treatise on natural theology, made the most profound impact on a community of scholars interested in theology and the natural sciences. Whewell used his own observations of biological adaptation in nature to argue that there was a divine "cosmic mechanism" at work in the universe.[37] *The Treatises* became very popular reading in rarefied circles of academia and theological study.[38]

In an attempt to bring natural theology to a broader community and to lay evangelicals in particular, the University of Virginia sponsored a public lecture series to provide "Evidences of Christianity." The Virginia lectures were delivered and published as a complement to the *Bridgewater Treatises*.[39] One lecture in particular, that of Pastor Thomas Moore of Richmond's First Presbyterian Church, spoke of the unity of the human race and suggested that creation as revealed by the book of Genesis was consistent with science. Moore maintained that only "false" science would promote the notion of separate creations and different races.[40]

Once Darwin published the *Origin of the Species*, British discord over religion and science spread to America, but due to the distractions of the impending Civil War—and the Reconstruction period that followed—the debate was somewhat muted. Political and religious tensions in Reconstruction-era American society included disagreements about western expansion, immigration control, the impending conflict between agricultural and mercantile states, and the slave dilemma.

The Second Great Awakening reflected these concerns especially during the first half of the nineteenth century. In various parts of the country, the Second Great Awakening became both a social and religious movement. It counted among its leaders Calvinists who tried once again to reconcile conservative Protestantism with Enlightenment ideas such as free will and analytical reasoning—ideologies that were not averse to academic inquiry.[41] On a more popular level, the mass revival of evangelical Protestantism promoted both personal salvation as well as religiously sanctioned political activism. These Second Great Awakening activists represented large portions of American society dissatisfied with the influence of alcohol and slavery on national culture. These groups drew strength from a broad association with other Second Great Awakening factions and their ideas became influential even as the revival began to wane in the 1840s and 1850s.[42]

In 1859, on the eve of the American Civil War, Charles Darwin published his *Origin of the Species*. It was for a time largely ignored by the vast majority of the population, but it received more urgent and considerable attention in academia. In many cases, nearly all theologians, and even the majority of secular scholars, took a rather dim view of natural selection. Several issued written and verbal refutations of evolution within the first years of Darwin's publication.[43] Darwinian evolution, unlike Newton's laws of math and physics, seemed to be in direct conflict with the narrative of the Bible. Biblical literalists, many of them evangelical, began to promote creationism as an alternative theory to the science of evolution.

According to Bertrand Russell, Darwinian evolution was as severe a shock to nineteenth century religious orthodoxy as Copernican gravity had been in the sixteenth century. According to Russell:

Not only was it necessary to abandon the fixity of species and the many separate acts of creation which Genesis seemed to assert; not only was it necessary to assume a lapse of time, since the origin of life was shocking to the orthodox, not only was it necessary to abandon a host of arguments for the beneficence of providence, derived from the exquisite adaptation of animals to the environment which was now explained as operation of natural selection—but worse than any or all of these, evolution ventured to affirm that man was descended from lower animals . . . As often happens, the theologians were quicker to perceive the consequences of the new doctrine than were its advocates, most of whom, though convinced by the evidence, were religious men and wished to retain as much of their former beliefs.[44]

Scholarly theologians, lay preachers, and other defenders of the faith tried a variety of tactics to blunt the impact evolution would have on popular thought. For a large group of American Christians, mainline Protestants, Catholics, and many Second Great Awakening evangelicals, the church took a firm stand against evolution and by extension other fields in the natural sciences, including the study of man's impact on the environment.[45] Even many liberal churches turned from science, concentrating on historical, existential, and psychological analysis in an attempt to address modern alienation. In academic circles, a variety of theologians and philosophers tried to challenge evolution. Others tried to modify this scientific theory so it harmonized with religious orthodoxy. Still others tried to co-opt Darwinism in order to promote science or to further political purposes. A large portion tried to ignore evolution, hoping it would go away.[46]

Among those who promoted science and thought it was incompatible with religion were the scientific naturalists. Among the most notable examples of this approach were Thomas Huxley and Herbert Spencer. Huxley was an agnostic and simply argued that evolution was real and that Creationism was largely mythology.[47] Unlike Thomas Huxley, who primarily promoted the biological component of evolution, Spencer believed that natural selection was a social construct as well as a biological phenomenon. Spencer suggested that some men were biologically "fitter" than others. He promoted a Malthusian interpretation of Darwinian evolution, including an idea later dubbed *multiple creations*, which suggested that the races were distinct species in competition with one another, thereby reducing Darwinism to political opinion rather than scientific fact. This sensationalized view of evolution—often called Social Darwinism or *eugenics*—came to characterize popular understanding of Darwin's theories, set the stage for the Scopes Trial, and caused a sustained reaction to or aversion of the natural sciences among many lay evangelicals.[48]

THE SECOND WAVE: ANOTHER AWAKENING, DISCOVERING HEAT, AND CONSERVING NATURE

Perhaps in reaction to the politicization of evolution, an emerging group of scholars tried to reconcile the science of evolution with the truth of religion. This struggle was best characterized by the Hodge-Gray debate of 1870s. Professor Hodge was Professor of Theology at Princeton. He believed the best way to defeat the implicit atheism of evolution was to promote an unwavering commitment to Biblical literalism.[49] Asa Gray, a scientist and theologian in the tradition of William Paley and Edward Hitchcock, believed that the facts of the natural sciences could inform and support the truths of faith. Like Paley, Gray was interested in helping reveal a greater number of Thomist evidences found in nature as further proof of God's existence. More specifically, Gray's primary occupation in the sciences was promoting natural theology and refining the taxonomy of various living creatures. When Darwin published his thesis, Gray found that it resonated with his own religious ideology in that all living creatures had a common, if divine, origin.[50] Though both pursued the study and classification of animals, Darwin's study soon garnered more attention than Gray's analysis. Many years after the publication of all these studies, theologians with an interest in promoting creationism would revisit Paley and Gray's formulations when articulating the concept of intelligent design.[51] Ultimately, throughout many political and social circles in Europe and America, various pseudo-scientific views of evolutionary biology began to prevail, thereby polarizing political camps into those who promoted Social Darwinism and those, including Second Awakening evangelicals, who fought it.

Often applied to social policy, sometimes to regulatory law, Social Darwinism became the rallying cry of many elite industrialists who directed their political rhetoric to other members of their class.[52] Paradoxically, many working class men and women, eager for wealth—and confident in America social mobility—answered the summons. They began a mass migration from country to city, which was unknown in previous centuries, and symbolized the beginning of the modern age. By the end of the nineteenth century, Britain was the world's leading industrial power, but Germany and America were quickly "evolving" into economic rivals. Although Britain had the "head start," the American adaptation of coal and steel to a variety of industries, including the mass production of automobiles, soon catapulted the United States ahead of the world's other leading economic powers.[53] In industrial Europe and in America, two distinct scientific communities emerged. There were those who pursued knowledge to advance industry, and there were those scholars who researched science for the pure love of inquiry. Among the latter group was a tiny faction who studied the environment. Whereas scientific communities in Europe were rather small, in America a larger number of learned men pushed the Industrial Revolution ever forward. Those who worked for industry often enjoyed wealth and notoriety, while those pursuing a more personal form of inquiry often toiled in relative obscurity. The technology of the industrial era was in its infancy and the danger of carbon dioxide was not widely understood.

Many of the discoveries that addressed possible changes in the environment were discovered because of the work of a few solitary academics scattered throughout Europe and America.[54] Initial research into the properties of carbon dioxide conducted by Joseph Black, Humphry Davy, Michael Faraday, and Charles Thiloreir paved the way for the era's most rigorous study of the environment. Building on earlier research, Svante August Arrhenius declared that the atmosphere functioned like a "hot-house," or greenhouse, and human enterprise was inherent to this type of environmental transformation.[55] In the early months of 1894, Arrhenius began a study of daily changes in the local climate until at the end of the year he arrived at his various mathematic and scientific models, which tested the relationship between carbon dioxide emissions and climate change. Arrhenius argued that water vapor and carbon dioxide warm the atmosphere. Being a native of a Scandinavian region where the winters could be arctic, and like so many men of his age, Arrhenius was disinclined to see the hazards of industrialization. He praised the increase of carbon dioxide in the atmosphere as a boon to agriculture.[56]

The mere discovery that greenhouse gases such as carbon dioxide captured and stored heat stunned and impressed the scientific community. Any negative impact carbon dioxide may have—including the possibility of cataclysmic climatic reversals, such as a rash of hurricanes, flooding, or even a creeping ice age—did not worry Arrhenius. Like other scientists of that era, Arrhenius was captivated by the promise of what modernity would bring.[57]

The Second Wave Crests: Mass Production, Secular Law, and Their Discontents

Modern enterprise expanded between the mid-eighteenth century and the late-nineteenth century, and carbon dioxide emissions swelled. The dawning twentieth century marked the beginning of a new phase of industrialization, one that was characterized by an adaptation of fossil fuels, innovations in technology, and the emergence of a scientific approach to industrial management. The decades stretching from the end of the Civil War to the turn of the century were devoted to the building and financing of railroads. Between the years 1860 and 1910, the network of railroads multiplied eightfold.[58] Once electrical mechanization was added to the industrial mix, the volume or scale of production increased exponentially, and for a time industry needed an ever-increasing number of skilled managers and semi-skilled workers.

The expansion of production and the demand for workers was especially high in newly-emerging firms, such as the commercial oil and automobile industries, where electricity and steel where utilized and where there was a convergence of new innovations and new managerial methodologies.[59] Petroleum became even more important with the invention of the internal combustion engine that emerged in the United States and Germany during the 1880s.[60] Utilizing the abundance of petroleum, the Ford Company, the world's largest car manufacturer, began promoting the internal combustion engine.[61]

Ironically, Henry Ford almost abandoned the internal combustion engine when the nation was facing a shortage of crude oil and he learned that petroleum was causing groundwater contamination. During the years 1912–13, Henry Ford thought that electricity might one day be more efficient and environmentally friendly than gas cars. Ford and Thomas Edison began working on the Edsel, their version of an electric car. They constantly improved the electrical batteries during those years, trying to make them dependable and safe. In reality, the technological innovation that would make electric cars truly reliable was at least a generation away. By 1914, the gathering war made the demand for gas-powered automobiles a national cause, which rendered efforts at improving electric cars seem truly irrelevant.[62]

In 1915 the U.S. government created the War Industrial Board in order to increase production and supply a massive amount of weaponry to the military. During World War I, War Board industries produced hundreds of warships and began tentative efforts to mass-produce fighter airplanes.[63] These new forms of transportation required carbon dioxide-emitting gasoline. The oil-refining/gas-producing industry experienced another surge a mere twenty years later when America entered the Second World War. By then, the United States was the world's undisputed military and economic leader. In 1938, President Roosevelt and Congress approved a total of three billion dollars for industrial production of warships, airplanes and vast amounts of weaponry. That same year, in what was a swell of this vast commercial optimism, a British engineer working for the British Electrical and Allied Research Association published an article confirming Svante Arrhenius's conclusion.[64] Vast and rapid industrialization was changing the climate. Like Arrhenius, Callendar wistfully concluded that global warming was a positive development, as it would probably increase the number and variety of agricultural products.[65]

Less interested in farm production than manufactured products, by the beginning of the twentieth century Americans had become "conspicuous consumers."[66] In this era, many Americans were more interested in the impact science and industry would have on the quality of their lives than on the influence religious doctrine would have on national culture. When popular attention was focused on the realm of ideas, secular philosophies emphasizing psychological and economic explanations for man's alienation often dominated national debate. In response to the agnostic nature and growing popularity of these concepts, some religious scholars began characterizing these ideologies as the causes, rather than explanations of modern strife. A new breed of evangelical Christians began to push for a return to doctrinal Christianity.

The rise of the modern evangelical movement began in 1909 in California when two oil magnates published a volume of books called *The Christian Fundamentals*. The same publishers produced a series of pamphlets that made similar arguments advancing Christian doctrine and rebuking modernist secular education. Many of *The Christian Fundamentals* essays lambasted secular ideologies such as Darwinism, Hegelian Marxism, and Freudian Psychoanalysis. Most were especially critical of evolution. One critique suggested that evolution was responsible for bringing together "the Reds of Russia, the university professors of Germany, England and America . . . and every bum from the down-and-out sections in every city in America."[67] By 1914, millions of *The Christian Fundamentals* pamphlets were in circulation. They were distributed in churches and began to influence school boards and educational professionals.

The influence of religious lobbies on the public school system became a national controversy when a group of concerned parents sued John Scopes, a Tennessee high school teacher who was instructing students on the theories of evolution. In truth, the American Civil Liberties Union asked Scopes to test a statute, called the Butler Act, which prohibited teachers from introducing students to ideas that "contradicted the Bible's instruction regarding the Divine creation of man."[68] The Scopes Trial captured national attention because it featured the riveting performances of the talented Clarence Darrow and the populist William Jennings Bryan. More importantly, the trial pitted evangelical interests against the increasingly secular culture dominating modern American politics. Citing *The Christian Fundamentals* pamphlets, Bryan began a critique of the secularization of educational institutions, attacking false apostles and "false" or radical science. When Clarence

Darrow countered this critique and the press published the Scopes debate, the very public and sobering nature of the trial permanently cooled national ardor for both "fundamentalism" and Creationism.

The evangelicals were defeated in court, but the loss was magnified by the national press, which portrayed the "fundamentalists" as preening hillbillies.[69] Evangelicals withdrew from political life for the next few decades.[70] Their suspicion of the ACLU and the press probably deepened in the years after the Scopes Trial. It is quite likely that the evangelical mood regarding "new" scientific theories, such as those surrounding environmental protection, probably remained rather dim, as well. In a larger sense, the Scopes Trial was a national repudiation of the massive evangelical effort to influence national politics and educational policy in the years preceding the First World War.

Despite lingering unease with the science of Darwinian evolution, by the early decades of the twentieth century, the science of industry was capturing more attention than religion or politics. The Ford Motor Company and its rival car companies, inaugurated a new era in American industry—the age of science. Dubbed the second Industrial Revolution, and spanning the decades of the 1910s to the 1950s, this era was celebrated because it inspired succeeding generations to cultivate their appetites for reflexive consumption. The mobilization of World Wars I and II created the infrastructure for the mass production of various household accessories. Some of the chemicals produced for refrigeration, industrial and domestic, led to the other innovations, including the development of air conditioning and aerosol propellant for a range of pharmaceutical products. Chlorofluorocarbons, or CFCs, were astounding in their capacity to "pollute," including one 10,000 times more potent than carbon dioxide in trapping heat.[71]

Activists would not sound the admonition against chemicals such as CFCs and pesticides like dichloro-diphenyl-trichloro-ethane, or DDT, until the early 1960s. The public's attention only became focused on the harm caused by "toxins" associated with mass production when a lone voice finally considered the legacy of industrialization pollution. In 1962, Rachel Carson published a small book titled *Silent Spring*, which became as important a study for environmentalists as *Uncle Tom's Cabin* had been for Second Great Awakening abolitionists.[72] Scientists confirmed the environmental damage such toxins caused a full decade later when DDT was banned.[73] CFCs would be banned in aerosol cans in 1978, and they were banned in all other forms by international agreement nine years later. The battles over DDT and CFCs were important fights because they were a harbinger of the coming contest over carbon dioxide, and also because these early skirmishes galvanized dilettante greens to become professional environmental advocates. In the meantime, throughout America's growing suburbs, refrigeration and air conditioning flourished, having been transformed from superfluous accessories to domestic necessities.[74]

A scientist by training and employed as a researcher for the U.S. Fish and Wildlife Service, Carson argued her case based on rigorous scientific analysis. *Silent Spring*'s specific campaign was to save endangered animals, in particular the bald eagle and peregrine falcon, from extinction. The culprit, DDT, was a known quantity, a man-made product sold to eliminate "pests." It also just happened to exterminate pets, and in some cases, people.[75] As the Vietnam War raged, Agent Orange, a dioxide, was used to clear Asian forests and to establish better military targets. Those who had not read Carson's book went out and bought a copy. Eventually, Agent Orange was roundly castigated, while DDT, a popular product among large agro-business firms, continued to be an acceptable product in the United States and elsewhere.[76] Despite Rachel Carson's best efforts, the struggle to regulate chemicals and protect the environment lasted beyond her death.

However, and in no small part because of *Silent Spring*, national leaders began paying attention to the devastating effects of pollutants on the environment.[77] Between the years 1967–1970, a variety of environmentalists formed various organizations, including the Environmental Defense Fund, the National Resources Defense Council, and Friends of the Earth. Congress also passed the National Environmental Policy Act. In the midst of the distractions of the Vietnam War, President Lyndon Johnson created the Environmental Protection Agency and the Council on Environmental Quality.[78] Thus, by the late 1960s environmental activism had become a popular social trend, and "legal secularism" dominated popular political culture.

In 1968 the Supreme Court revisited the *Scopes* decision and ruled that Arkansas' Butler Act, which had been devised to prevent discussion of evolution, "violated constitutional requirements regarding state neutrality toward religious doctrine."[79] Excluding the evangelical community, this reaffirmation of the 1925 ruling went all but unnoticed amidst the social and political disruptions of the late 1960s. Evangelical Christians watched mutely as popular culture became more liberal, and became especially taciturn after the 1968 ruling. A few religious intellectuals broached the decline of evangelical authority on popular culture. These included Paul Tillich and Richard Neuhaus, who argued that America needed a spiritual renewal, a "communal covenant" to challenge "the relentless secularism of the public realm."[80] Despite this call to action, the evangelical community remained largely silent, while President Nixon made his commitment to the "silent majority."

Meanwhile, the unpopularity of the military campaign in Vietnam led toward raucous opposition to the draft. This rebellious mood spread through the American public, and the growing success of *Silent Spring* emboldened a greater number of green activists to raise their profile, voicing their support of environmental protection. Between the years 1970–1980, environmental scientists waged a literary campaign, offering scientific analysis comprehendible to the average reader.

After *Silent Spring*, the environmental legislation that succeeded it, and the popular books that followed, the political habitat became more hospitable to pure scientific inquiry regarding the dangers of pollution.[81] The menacing attributes of industrialization were finally a safe topic for national dialogue. In 1974, Sherwood Rowland and Mario Molina wrote a report concerning the impact CFC had on depleting the ozone layer.[82] The report garnered international attention when it was awarded the Nobel Prize for Chemistry.[83]

Green activism blossomed during the 1970s, and environmental activists created a variety of organizations that promoted a range of environmental policies. Some greens, such as Ralph Nader, became consumer or political advocates, running for office as independent or Green Party candidates. However, the vast majority of environmental activists formed advocacy and fund-raising organizations.[84] These organizations had many environmental concerns that they wanted government to address. The primary areas of concern were ozone depletion, global warming, and the impact humans were having on the earth's land, forests, and waters.[85] Throughout the 1970s, the struggle to control DDT and CFCs had exhausted the funds and vitality of "mainstream" environmental activists. In 1987, their efforts were rewarded when the multilateral United Nations Montreal Protocol banned CFC production.[86] Evangelical participation in this era was limited due to the fact that the Evangelical Environmental Network, the foremost alliance of American evangelicals promoting "creation care," was not formed until 1994.

Ironically, two years before parties met in Montreal to discuss CFCs, the International Council of Scientific Unions reported on the intense increase in carbon dioxide and other "greenhouse" gases. Once again, the carbon dioxide problem and the academic study of climate change found its way to the back burner because industry attention was focused elsewhere.[87] A hundred years after the first Industrial Revolution, Edelson's study of the *carbonaria* moth, and Arrhenius's study of carbon dioxide-driven climate change, there seemed to be little popular consensus about curbing the global consumption of fossil fuels. While environmental advocates kept an unflinching focus on banning manmade chemicals such as DDT and CFCs, their gaze was a little blurred when it came to carbon dioxide.[88] At the core of this pedagogical fog was a debate within the "mainstream" environmental movement. On one side of the debate, there were green activists who wanted to find ways to reduce carbon dioxide emissions. On the other side of the debate, some greens still wondered whether "too much" carbon dioxide was really a problem.

While girding themselves for the impending carbon dioxide brawl, many greens seemed to be asking whether human intervention was really necessary. More precisely, many were wondering whether the earth's atmosphere was capable of "correcting" climatic imbalances caused by an excess of "organic" effluvium, or whether attempting to reduce carbon dioxide emissions was an obligatory mission. Arrhenius and Callendar's wistful refrain that global warming may be beneficial seemed to characterize many of these internal debates. As the public would soon learn, wishful thinking was a distraction from the scientific reality. In 1979 the National Academy of Sciences released a major scientific study.[89] The NAS report stated, simply, "If carbon dioxide continues to increase, the study group finds no reason to doubt that climate changes will result, and no reason to believe that these changes will be negligible . . . A wait-and-see policy may mean waiting until it is too late."[90]

Aware, perhaps, that the history of scientific research on carbon dioxide emissions has resulted in little more than a whimper or a yawn by much of the American public, the Carter Administration sought to publish the NAS findings for a broader national audience. In 1980, the Carter Council of Environmental Quality completed a report that circulated widely. The report disclosed the fact that:

Many scientists now believe that, if global fossil fuel use grows rapidly in the decades ahead, the accompanying carbon dioxide increases will lead to profound and long-term alteration of the earth's climate . . . Clearly a deeper appreciation of the risks of carbon dioxide build-up should be spread to leaders of government and business and to the general public. The carbon dioxide problem should be taken seriously in new ways: it should become a factor in making energy policy and not simply be the subject of scientific investigation.[91]

President Carter established the largest wildlife refuge known to man, but he also lost the 1980 election. A promising environmental agenda perished with his frustrated re-election bid.[92] Many of President Reagan's powerful patrons pressed for policies that emboldened industry, especially "big businesses" such as petrochemical firms, car manufacturers, and their advocates, the "Wise Use" conservationists.

Ron Arnold, executive vice president at the Center for the Defense of

Free Enterprise (CDFE) is widely considered the founder or de facto leader of the Wise Use Movement. Along with Arnold, Charles Cushman of the National Inholder's Association and Alan Gottlieb of the National Rifle Association emerged as the co-directors of "Wise Use." The Wise Use Movement grounds its political philosophy in property rights law.[93] It derives its name from a phrase first uttered by naturalist Gifford Pinchot. As President Theodore Roosevelt's "chief forester," Pinchot challenged John Muir's sweeping vision of environmental protection. Though Gifford Pinchot and John Muir were friends and longtime associates of Teddy Roosevelt, they had different conceptions of environmental conservation. Muir believed in preserving nature for its own sake. By contrast, Pinchot advocated "wise" industrial development. Wise Use tended to put human interest on par or ahead of environmental protection. President Roosevelt supported Pinchot's vision in most cases, ultimately constructing a dam in Yellowstone National Park.[94] From then on, Pinchot became the protagonist for Wise Use "hard" green aficionados.

In the early 1980s, a coalition of western logging, hunting, and mining organizations banded together. They decided that environmental regulation was encroaching on their right to earn a living. In the mid 1980s the Wise Use conservationists held various meetings and conferences, bolstering their attendance rolls and refining their ideology until 1988, when they sponsored a "founding conference" with a coalition of over 200 organizations in attendance.[95] Ron Arnold published *The Wise Use Agenda*, an aptly named manifesto, that same year. The agenda advanced more than twenty goals, but the most important Wise Use objectives concerned eliminating restrictions on land development by using legal property rights protections, amending the Endangered Species Act to exclude so-called "non-adaptive species," and promoting oil and mining exploration in all national parks or wildlife preserves. The latter initiative would require the Forest Service to replant ancient forests with young, carbon dioxide-absorbing trees.[96]

Throughout the 1980s, Arnold and his Wise Use staff expanded their legal and political strategies, and by the early 1990s, the Wise Use trend was more than anti-environmental backlash. It was a profound political movement, and Ron Arnold believed its message was ready for broadcast into mainstream publications.[97] Around the same time, Wise Use operatives thought they might expand to ride a wave of conservative Christian revival. It proved to be a successful strategy, because in 1988 the Wise Use Movement had a hardy roster of approximately 200 organizations, yet by the mid-1990s the movement was 1,500 organizations strong. This boost could be best described as a Wise Use leap of faith.

In the late 1980s and early 1990s, American politics was approaching the pinnacle of what could be described as a Third Great Awakening.[98] This revival was a campaign that was both political and religious. It constituted one of the most significant cracks in the proverbial church-state wall since it was first constructed by the founding fathers and subsequently fortified by succeeding generations of American leaders.[99] In many respects, the outcome of the Scopes Trial upheld the Jeffersonian Deist notion that church and state should be kept separate, but this victory came at price. In the decades following the trial, evangelical ideologues would challenge public institutions, especially those that promoted evolutionary science, secular education, and the "liberal" press. In some instances, this suspicion permeated their discussion of environmental protection. Evangelical aversion to scientifically oriented public policy diminished somewhat with the emergence of maverick evangelicals who believed that Americans could promote science and believe in God.

THE THIRD GREAT AWAKENING AND THE WISE USE MOVEMENT

Having recovered from the ignominy of the Scopes Trial by the mid-1940s, evangelical leaders renewed their call for religious Americans to engage in intellectual and civic activism. A Boston preacher, the Reverend Harold Ockenga, led the effort to create the National Association of Evangelicals, or NAE, as an alternative to both the Southern Baptist Convention and the National Council of Churches.[100] A few years later, the bright new mood of evangelicals was described in the *Remaking of the Modern Mind*, a book penned and published by a midwestern Baptist minister named Carl Henry. The evangelical revival spread further west when Charles Fuller, a popular California radio evangelist, invited Rev. Ockenga to become the president of the seminary that bore his name.[101] Eventually, Fuller asked Carl Henry to teach on the school's faculty. These men called their ministry "Cal-tech" evangelism.[102] In another corner of the evangelical revival tent, Reverend Billy Graham began his popular public ministry.

Graham was unequaled in his ability to raise the standing of the itinerant preacher to the status of celebrity. Then, by his own particular talents and his singular station, he ascended to the role of American minister without portfolio. From the 1950s to the 1970s, the evangelicals fortified themselves. Rev. Graham, who appeared to be solidly centrist, became a popular confidant to a succession of presidents when the federal government was engaged in national recovery from World War II, conquering Communism, and venturing into outer space. Meanwhile environmental protection seemed to be a hobby pursued by obscure scientists and eccentric activists.

Silent Spring environmentalists, like the nation writ large, paid little attention to the revival of evangelicals. Few outside the evangelical movement were aware of their views on public policy or their attitudes towards environmental protection. The religious orientation of American presidents was not a major issue in most spheres of public debate. Then, the glamorous Kennedy clan ran for office. Their religious values seemed cool and meditative. John Kennedy spoke of universal themes such as "opposing foes and defending friends," and it appeared for a time that a man of any confession might become president.

Meanwhile, in the Baptist evangelical tent, Rev. Graham projected an elegance that lent the often boisterous evangelical movement gentility and decorum. Rev. Graham's success opened the civic arena to other charismatic evangelicals who considered entering the political arena. This was especially true of a group of preachers who commanded mega-churches in growing and prosperous communities. These new Christian leaders welcomed public spectacle and found an enormous audience in televised church services.

The 1980s became the era of the televangelist. A series of political, economic, and social trends encouraged the spread of evangelism. These developments included the resuscitation of conservative politics after the deluge of Watergate, the steady decline of the Soviet power, and a growing Goldwater backlash against the "radicalism" of the 1960s and 1970s.[103] Evangelicals had come into their own and were feeling somewhat confident. Their wealth derived from their partisan constituents and their televangelist empires. These resources allowed them to build a number of institutions of higher learning dedicated to promoting evangelical religious values. The evangelical community had a young energetic base and rich powerful patrons, so naturally they considered using these political resources to influence public policy.

The Third Great Awakening was characterized by a foremost alliance of televangelical power, educational might, and political authority. These influences coalesced in two important religious organizations.[104] Jerry Falwell founded the first of these groups, the Moral Majority, in 1979. Later, Pat Robertson founded the Christian Coalition after his attempt to secure the Republican presidential nomination in 1988 proved unsuccessful.[105] The Moral Majority and the Christian Coalition, which grew out of the tradition of Rev. Graham, the legacy of "Cal-tech" evangelism, and the popularity of a variety of televangelists, seemed increasingly at odds with the deliberate secularism of mainstream Republican leadership.[106]

President Reagan exemplified the popular face of Republicanism. His screen-guild persona brought a worldly ambience to Republican Party, which countered the drudgery of neoconservative scholarship that focused almost exclusively on promoting "less government." As such, candidate Reagan captivated the National Association of Evangelicals.[107] Similarly, George Herbert Walker Bush projected diplomatic cosmopolitanism that was rare, especially in the far-right corners of the Republican Party.[108] Yet in both instances, conservative evangelicals found a nesting place in the Reagan and Bush Administrations, and they used this roost to promote the Wise Use agenda.

Alan Gottlieb, a founding member of the Wise Use Movement and a leader in the National Rifle Association, raised more than a hundred million dollars for President Reagan's 1980 and 1984 campaigns.[109] As a payment in kind, President Reagan appointed Charles Cushman, a Wise Use Movement co-founder, to the National Parks System Advisory Board. There, Cushman promoted oil and mining exploration, a policy consistent with *The Wise Use Agenda*.[110] Ronald Arnold, the other Wise Use Movement co-founder and executive in the Center for the Defense of Free Enterprise, the CDFE, was a public relations expert and an expert fundraiser. While helping secure money for the Reagan campaign, he wrote a biography about James Watt. After the election, Watt was appointed Reagan's Secretary of the Interior.[111]

As secretary, Watt's environmental policy displayed a zeal for allowing loggers and construction firms to "develop" public land without restriction. Watt's political ideology was energized by what some evangelicals, especially those associated with the Wise Use Movement, call the "dominion theology." Dominion theology argues that man has the right to "subdue the earth."[112] Ultimately Secretary Watt's proposed policy of selling or leasing public lands for coal mining proved unpopular to a broad range of interests, including real estate, environmental, and hunting organizations. Secretary Watt eventually stepped down from office.[113] Around the time of his dismissal, Watt's EPA staff stood accused of trying to misdirect congressional oversight, shredding documents in an attempt to camouflage agency negligence of environmental protections.[114] After Secretary Watt left the White House, the head of the EPA and several other EPA staff had to resign, as well.[115]

Vice President George Herbert Walker Bush was given the task of executive oversight of the EPA. His area of responsibility included working on the Presidential Task Force on Regulatory Relief, which essentially promoted a Wise Use agenda.[116] However, when George H.W. Bush became President, he appointed two men to lead the EPA and the U.S. Fish and Wildlife Service who seemed to be fairly committed to environmental protection. They were, respectively, Bill Reilly and John Turner.[117]

These appointments alarmed the Wise Use-affiliated organizations, including the Wilderness Impact Research Foundation, or WIRF, and Ron Arnold's organization, the CDFE.[118] While Reilly and Turner were moderate, environmentally conscious Republicans, most of their efforts would be countered by Vice President Dan Quayle's Council on Competitiveness. An irony not lost on the Wise Use, the Council on Competitiveness seemed a lot like President Reagan's Task Force on Regulatory Relief.[119] Through the Christian Coalition, the Wise Use advocates continued to make inroads to the Bush White House. During the last years of George H.W. Bush's Presidency, Ralph Reed, Pat Robertson's foremost deputy, became directly associated with White House efforts to temper environmental policy.[120]

After making inroads into the Reagan White House and the Bush Presidency, the Wise Use advocates and the Christian Coalition decided they would have more influence if they also swept Congress. In 1994, the Wise Use Movement helped underwrite many Congressional reelection campaigns, most notably that of Newton Gingrich.[121] The reelection of Gingrich, the future Speaker of the House, was a watershed moment for the Wise Use Movement. When Reagan ran for national office, Gingrich, a junior congressman, began his rise to prominence. Newt Gingrich and other members of the National Republican Congressional Committee planned an event in honor of the candidates called the Capitol Steps Event. The candidates presented their "statement of pledges," which became the Republican presidential campaign platform.[122] Several years later, when Newt Gingrich was elected Speaker of the House, he hosted another gathering on the Capitol steps where he presented the Republican Contract with America.

The Contract was the brainchild of various factions of the Republican party, especially those disenchanted with their minority status in the Congress. However, the core strategists were none other than Newt Gingrich and Ralph Reed of the Christian Coalition.[123] The planks of the 1994 contract bore a striking resemblance to and fleshed out the sentiments of the "statement of pledges" found in the 1980s.[124] The Contract with America made explicit the types of cuts Republicans would make to social programs and the nature of legal and fiscal reforms they would pursue. It also committed the signatories to support Social Security, the military, and family-based initiatives such as adoption and elder care.[125]

Many of the initiatives Gingrich and other Republican leaders would pursue in the years leading to the 1996 and 2000 presidential elections were not, however, covered by the Contract. These included specific efforts to re-conceive environmental protection. Contract Republicans of the 104th Congress led the attack on the Kyoto Protocol and reversed several years of increased funding for the EPA.[126]

In the years leading to the 1996 elections, the Contract Republicans devised a strategy to refute the science of global climate treaties.[127] Vice President Albert Gore, a noted environmental author, was at the forefront of the White House environmental protection during the 1990s, directing the President's Council on Sustainable Development, the PCSD.[128] The influence of the Contract with America, however, was stronger than ever, and certainly much stronger than the PCSD. Its congressional adherents, various conservative civic alliances, and several religious organizations helped promote Contract ideology, which caused Washington public policy to drift right.[129] Despite this fact, in 1996 the Clinton Administration agreed, in principle, to reductions of carbon dioxide.[130] The Wise Use Movement leadership was not amused, and the campaign to capture the Kyoto Protocol commenced. Ultimately, it was the Senate that voted to kill the Kyoto Protocol. Meanwhile, Congress drafted appropriation bills to slow expenditures that might encourage its implementation.[131]

The plain facts of the Kyoto Protocol suggest that it might be a reasonable agreement. The Protocol required the United States to reduce carbon dioxide emissions 7 percent by 2020. To many environmental activists, this seemed like sound policy.[132] The most contentious part of the Kyoto Protocol was that it required large industrialized nations to sign the Protocol first.[133] American politicians across the ideological spectrum were concerned that newly industrializing countries, or NICS, would continue to spew diesel fuel, nitrous oxide, and even chlorofluorocarbons, while the United States would be forced to stretch its resources to build "cleaner cars."[134]

In 2000, President George W. Bush began his campaign for the presidency, criticizing Kyoto and suggesting that it was indifferent to the issue of NIC pollution.[135] However, to the joy and utter bewilderment of Greens, including Green Party political candidates, candidate George W. Bush suggested that the United States should try to control carbon dioxide emissions.[136] In the early months of 2001, President Bush indicated to his staff that his administration should work on implementing a "mandatory cap" on carbon dioxide emissions.[137]

By the end of 2001, however, Contract Republicans and Wise Use lobbyists eager to mute G-8 efforts to coordinate an endorsement of Kyoto brought pressure to bear on the White House.[138] President Bush, to the quiet consternation of EPA administrator Christine Whitman, began to distance himself from the campaign to reduce greenhouse gases.[139] Political strategists in the Bush Administration adopted the tried and true Wise Use strategy of questioning the scientific models used to describe the causal relationship between carbon dioxide and global warming.[140]

THE GLOBAL ECONOMY, AMERICAN POLITICS, AND THE GROWING OPPOSITION TO KYOTO

American opponents of the Kyoto Protocol presented a range of arguments as to why the United States should not adhere to the mandates of the agreement. These critiques can be grouped into three categories. There are those who believe that global warming is either a myth, or, if it is a problem, the dangers are remote. They warn that environmental advocates have exaggerated the hazards for political gain. John McManus, an engineer and member of the John Birch society, suggests that a variety of notable scientists dispute the significance or perils of global warming.[141] McManus cites scientific research regarding Arctic warming during the eighteenth century, which indicates that global warming is a recurring phenomenon. He claims the media and politicians who favor commercial regulation in various sectors of the American economy distort or exaggerate the scientific consensus.[142]

A second group of Kyoto dissenters argue that global warming may be a problem, but that it is not caused by human or anthropogenic activity and therefore cannot be addressed by the prescriptions advanced by the protocol. William Gray, a professor of atmospheric science, suggests that the assumptions animating the majority of scientific models used to show carbon dioxide's role in trapping water vapor may be inaccurate. As a result, Gray and similarly situated scientists argue that the assumption that the humans cause global warming is also incorrect. Citing a history of global warming between 1900–1945 that was followed by a period of cooling, Gray suggests that global warming—and for that matter, global cooling—are cyclical atmospheric phenomenon that are unrelated to anthropogenic activity and not in need of any form of human intervention.[143] Another scientist who defends this position is Ian Clark, a professor of hydrogeology, who argues that "there is no chance that we will effect [control] measurable climate changes with Kyoto or any other accord," because, Clark suggests, carbon dioxide has little effect on the climate. Further, Professor Clark contends that solar wind has a far greater effect on the earth's climate than anthropogenic carbon dioxide emissions.[144]

The third group of Kyoto dissenters maintains that climate change may be a positive development, while the "cures" for reducing carbon dioxide are worse than the global warming malady itself. Sallie Baliunas, an astrophysicist, advises that the findings of the United Nations Intergovernmental Panel on Climate Change (IPCC) and those of other reports supporting a negative impact of global warming are based on climate models that may be "too simplistic."[145] Baliunas recalls earlier speculation by Arrhenius and

Callendar, who argued that increased carbon dioxide and the global warming it generates may beneficially increase crop yields.[146]

Even those who do not necessarily endorse the argument that global warming may be beneficial to crops worry about the new forms of energy that will replace fossil fuels. A coalition of environmental, safety, and energy organizations suggest that switching from petroleum and gas to nuclear power would be dangerous and may produce far more/far worse toxic waste than carbon dioxide.[147] Still others suggest that alternative sources of energy, such as solar or wind power, will neither be cost effective nor reliable.[148] Well before these arguments were publicly expressed, or widely known, Wise Use lobbyists suggested that the "science" of the global warming debate was not settled. Since the ratification of the Montreal Protocol of 1987 concerning CFCs, global warming opponents began an intense campaign to halt a carbon dioxide-reducing protocol.

In March 2001, the Bush Administration abandoned the Kyoto Protocol. The following month, the White House removed the lead chemist, an American they appointed to the United Nations Intergovernmental Panel on Climate Change.[149] In May, President Bush appointed Vice President Dick Cheney as chair of his National Energy Policy Development Group.[150] For several months of 2001, the issue of Kyoto and political intransigence on the issue of global warming remained a subject of Washington debate. Then, on September 11, 2001, global warming, like several other pressing social policies, disappeared into oblivion.[151]

In 2003, the same year 20,000 Europeans died in an unprecedented heat wave and in which Dr. Wangari Maathai, a Kenyan political activist, received the first Nobel Peace Prize for environmental protection, the Bush Administration replaced EPA administrator Christine Todd Whitman with Dr. Gale Norton.[152] Soon after her appointment, Norton stunned the environmental community when she declared that the EPA lacked authority under the Clean Air Act to regulate carbon dioxide. Further, Norton argued that even if the EPA had the authority, it declined to regulate carbon dioxide as a precaution to global warming.[153]

A GREEN REVIVAL: THIRD WAVE ENVIRONMENTALISTS BREACH A WISE-USE FORTRESS

In response to the EPA's new environmental credo, twelve state attorneys general took the Bush Administration to court.[154] The twelve states and the other "petitioners" assert that according to the language of relevant statues, the EPA does indeed have authority over greenhouse gas emissions.[155] The petitioners included a wide range of environmental organizations from

Greenpeace to the Sierra Club, as well as important scientific organizations, including the International Center for Technology Assessment and the Union of Concerned Scientists.

In a break from routine, academic scientists and environmental activists made a concerted effort to work together to provide a unified critique of national environmental policy. This was a unique development in the epic history of the politics of carbon dioxide–driven climate change, which heretofore had been governed by an all-too-human dynamic. Very often, the communities who produced, observed, and encountered pollution were unable or unwilling to work together to resolve this problem. Beginning in the late 1800s and continuing until the first half of the twentieth century, the American government promoted vast industrial expansion while industrial and academic scientists continued to work at cross-purposes. When, in the 1970s, environmental activists began to organize a focused national conservation/protection strategy, they had to convince the majority of the American population that pollution was a serious problem. Meanwhile, the Wise Use Movement capitalized on religious misgivings about environmental science, forming a strong alliance with powerful evangelical communities. In 2006, because of the intransigence of the EPA or despite it, at least one group of evangelicals began to petition the White House to change its stance on global warming.

When various evangelical communities swept a born-again George W. Bush into office, several prominent evangelical community leaders were appointed to positions in the White House.[156] Many of these evangelical appointments were made to President Bush's Office of Faith-Based Initiatives, an evangelical re-assertion over government sponsored social welfare policy.[157] By 2003, an emerging group of "liberal" evangelical leaders worried that the faith-based initiatives would drain resources from better-established governmental programs.[158] In his popular evangelical journal *Sojourners*, founding editor Jim Wallis scolded the White House. Wallis suggested that "the administration is breaking faith with the faith-based initiative by not providing resources."[159]

In 2003, providing the economic and policy resources for climate change was an issue that seemed to elude many political activists, including many evangelicals, with the possible exception of an emerging network of evangelical Greens. In October 2004, these "creation care" evangelicals, under the auspices of the National Association of Evangelicals, published their declaration of evangelical independence.[160] The *Call for Civic Responsibility*, which announced the NAE's formal support of a variety of "left-wing" environmental protection policies, was among the organization's most revolutionary ventures.[161] The document was notable not only because of what it said, but because as of 2001, when the NAE published the document, the NAE was tens of millions strong and was among the fastest growing evangelical organizations in the U.S.[162]

One of the first reactions to the report came from a Wise Use Republican who warned Rev. Richard Cizik, the NAE Vice President for Governmental Affairs, not to allow a flirtation with environmental concerns to distract his organization from promoting policies more traditionally associated with mainline evangelical organizations.[163] These traditional issues included, among other things, the revival of fundamentalist resistance to Darwinian evolution. Drawing on William Paley's natural theology, conservative evangelical scholars have renewed their efforts to induce school boards to teach Creationism, which they dub "Intelligent Design," and which they argue is an alternate or complementary explanation for the existence of life on earth.[164]

Despite the warning from the Wise Use conservatives, Rev. Cizik pressed the "creation care" agenda of his constituents. Many of the NAE's left-leaning "creation care" evangelicals emerged as part of a large counter-revolution within the Southern Baptist Convention during the early years of the 1980s.[165] In the late 1970s, religious neoconservatives led a doctrinal revival that captured much of the SBC leadership, and some "fundamentalist" trends resurfaced. Progressive social justice champions as well as environmentalists and other peaceniks found themselves on the margins of the evangelical tent.[166]

These fragmented "liberal" evangelicals coalesced, establishing various environmental and social welfare organizations. Ultimately, these individuals helped the NAE lead many evangelicals back to centrist positions that were consistent with many moderate Republicans.[167] Increasingly, the Christian Coalition and Moral Majority strained under the weight of controlling a colossal and highly regimented church structure. Meanwhile, the large network of small social action organizations, including a variety of green organizations, strengthened the NAE. When the NAE made the call for environmental civic responsibility, it was led by powerful Greens who promoted "creation care" as a challenge to "fundamentalist" Creationism, Intelligent Design and Wise Use "dominion theory." However, despite the gathering carbon dioxide storm, the majority of "creation care" green evangelical organizations focused on endangered species rather than regulating pollution.[168]

Things changed in mid January 2007 when Reverend Cizik announced that officials from some of the 45,000 churches NAE represents were meeting to address the issue of global warming.[169] These new evangelical "alliances" prompted immediate attention. Political analysts suggested that if green evangelicals were to be successful, they would first have to convince their religious constituents. Then, perhaps, these Evangelical Greens could win Republicans, but only with innovative market-friendly carbon dioxide-capturing technology, and not the type of industry regulations traditionally favored by Democrats.[170] Despite these small matters of strategy, the good news that evangelism might "save" Republican environmentalists from oblivion had been delivered.[171]

Between the years 2003–2006, *The Call for Civic Responsibility* and the growth of NAE's "creation" constituents indicated that environmentalists could make inroads to bastions of creationism. Even further, it appeared that green evangelicals might carve a tunnel into the White House, challenging dominion theory and the Wise Use policies it animates.[172] Meanwhile, during the same year, but in a parallel environmental universe, several scientists brought their considerable knowledge of climate change to a legal challenge of the EPA. The scientific nature of the challenge helped to coordinate divergent civic, economic, and governmental organizations into a massive rejoinder to Wise Use rhetoric. The pressing topic that remains unanswered is whether these developments will make an impression on the Bush White House.

By December 2006, the Bush Administration suggested that it might return to a campaign promise and address environmental concerns when the Department of the Interior added polar bears to the list of threatened species. It would be a stretch to attribute this addition directly to the influence of "creation care" evangelicals, especially since Greenpeace led a 2005 suit against the Department of the Interior asserting that polar bears are a species threatened by global warming.[173] The administration parsed its response to the suit, suggesting that polar bears were threatened and that "green-house gases played a role in climate change," but it also suggested that climate change was beyond the scope of the Endangered Species Act.[174]

A few days later, and continuing throughout the month of January 2007, a flurry of debate on the environment seems to have induced the White House to change its position again. In mid-January, the Ford Motor Company introduced a hybrid electric car that could run on two sources of electric power. Many years ago, Henry Ford, the great-grandfather of the current CEO, tried to introduce an electric car without success.[175] Now one hundred years later, Ford CEO William Clay Ford was building an electric car promoted and sponsored by the U.S. government.[176]

Throughout January 2007, politicians outside the White House announced various policies to address carbon dioxide emissions and global warming. Governor Arnold Schwarzenegger, with the counsel of the environmental advocate Robert Kennedy, Jr., devised a plan for California that was similar to the guidelines of the Kyoto Protocol and that would reduce carbon dioxide emissions by 10 percent by 2020.[177] On January 9, Governor Schwarzenegger issued an executive order to the California Air Resources Board with a recommendation that they use the assistance of scientists from UC Berkeley to implement the directive.[178] The following week, Democratic House and Senate leaders introduced two different bills to cap carbon dioxide emissions.[179] An evangelical organization, the Church of the Brethren, immediately endorsed one of those bills, the McCain/Liberman Energy Bill.[180]

Then, a week after the announcement of the two bills, industry leaders—whose alliance, the U.S. Climate Action Partnership, or USCAP, had been working on the issue of global warming—made their own surprising announcement.[181] They argued that America, as the world leader in renewable energy, must reduce carbon dioxide emissions immediately, and that the USCAP would be at the forefront of developing this technology.[182] A week following the USCAP National Press Club announcement, on January 23, 2007, President Bush gave his State of the Union Address. In his speech before Speaker Nancy Pelosi, the first female speaker of the House or Representatives, President Bush tipped his hat to evangelicals, environmentalists, and scientists when he enumerated the alternative energies and technologies that make Americans "better stewards of the environment." He then made the astonishing concession that global climate change was "a serious challenge."[183] The following day, *The Real Truth*, a magazine associated with the United Brethren in Christ, an NAE-affiliated organization, hailed the historic State of the Union Address as singular for its focus on energy policy.[184] Other more prominent media took a dimmer view of the president's speech, suggesting that the Bush Administration was merely focusing on energy to prime the nation for a new subsidy of large agro-industries that wanted to promote ethanol.[185] A few months later, on April 2, 2007, the Supreme Court finally handed down its decision regarding carbon dioxide emissions. The Court ruled in favor of the twelve states that sued that government in 2003. It specifically stipulated that the EPA could not decline to regulate greenhouse gases emitted from cars.[186]

CONCLUSION: THE FUTURE OF GREEN EVANGELICALISM

Since the foundation of the Environmental Evangelical Network in the mid-1990s, environmental consciousness-raising has intensified in various Christian organizations, especially the National Association of Evangelicals. Many green evangelicals, unable to penetrate Wise Use fortresses located throughout Congress and the White House, have turned to science and industry for leadership on climate change. President Bush, like other politically sensitive leaders, is aware of an emerging alliance between scientists and industry regarding the need to create environmentally friendly technologies. Whether the Evangelical Greens will be able to add their committed constituents to this alliance is unclear, but it is possible. Third Wave environmental advocates are increasingly both Republican and Democratic. They work in industry, regulation, and advocacy. Third Great Awakening evangelicals have a range of views that span the arch of the political spectrum. A variety of outcomes could emerge as a result of these alliances, including a fresh commitment to alternative fuels, a new canon of environmental law, or an expansion of the Green Movement that draws on academic and religious environmentalists.[187]

One question remains: will the Jeffersonian ideal of keeping religion out of politics survive in the midst of these new coalitions? Will the wall between church and state become more porous? More specifically, will the impact of Wise Use leadership and Intelligent Design lead to other breaches, and, if it does, what impact will this have on the nature of party politics, especially in light of the reassertion of the evolutionary party into presidential politics?

In Europe, a hundred years before the Revolution of 1776, after the disruptions of the Protestant Reformation and the Thirty Years War, the Treaty of Westphalia helped restore the peace.[188] Aware of a potential conflict between politics and religion in their own country, America's founding fathers promulgated the Bill of Rights, which created a wall between church and state.[189] Drawing on Jeffersonian logic and recalling the politics of the First and Second Great Awakenings, nineteenth-century proponents of separating church and state continued to defend this political philosophy for a variety of reasons. Defenders of the wall favored protecting the secular republic from religious politics. To the chagrin of religious conservatives, secular ideals began to displace religious values in much of public life.[190] By the early decades of the twentieth century, even social issues, such as the prohibition against alcohol were framed as health issues, rather than moral causes.

Unlike Europe, where Darwinism triumphed, in America Creationism still had powerful advocates, at least until the national debacle of the Scopes Trial. Recently, the controversies of the Scopes Trial have resurfaced with the reemergence of a Creationist ideology called Intelligent Design. Proponents of Intelligent Design have led a less than successful campaign and have been challenged and defeated in the courts. By contrast, politicians promoting evangelical Wise Use conservation have enjoyed great success, expanding and contracting the parameters of White House involvement in environmental protection, and more specifically influencing its position in the global warming debate.

Since its first days of the Bush Administration, Wise Use philosophies have animated the EPA's global warming policy. Amidst the frenzy of the 2007–2008 presidential debates, there seems to be a bubbling up of industry evangelicals and a trickling down of scientific lawmakers. If so, this paradigm shift—one in which Evangelical Greens may focus national attention on climate change—could finally coax the White House toward environmental protection that seeks to reduce carbon emissions. Perhaps some or all of these outcomes can prevail. However, if traditional evangelicals resist or defeat this endeavor, the debate over global warming may stall and environmental protection may continue to demur to wise use. Currently, the most sensitive issue political observers may want to consider is whether evangelicals and Third Wave environmentalists can formulate a permanent agenda for addressing climate change that is based on scientific fact, without offending more traditional evangelicals who promote religious truth and Intelligent Design. Perhaps a coalition comprised of scientists, green evangelicals, and industry leaders can address the contentious issue of reducing carbon dioxide emissions. This coalition will only thrive if its members can lead an awakening that makes its case for social change without demeaning conservative evangelicals. Evangelical environmentalism will succeed if they can lobby the White House while keeping the ghosts of the Scopes Trial at bay.

NOTES

1. The record of rising temperatures, the frequency of regional hurricanes, floods, and of course, most dramatically, the brisk melting of polar ice caps, have pushed the issue of global warming to the peak of popular American consciousness. In 2006, at least two films addressed the global warming phenomenon: *An Inconvenient Truth*, based on the book by Vice President Al Gore and featuring Mr. Gore, and *Happy Feet*, an animated children's movie which followed the "plight" of Arctic Penguins. These films won Best Documentary Feature and Best Animated Feature Film at the 2007 Academy Awards.

2. A significant portion of traditional evangelical Christians subscribe to dispensational theology, which suggests that the world will descend into chaos before the return of Jesus. Various signs will herald this "end of days" scenario. See Tim LaHaye and Jerry Jenkins, *Are We Living in the End Times* (Carol Stream, IL: Tyndale House Publishing, 1999). Regarding the melting of melting ice in the Arctic Ocean see, Andrew Revkin, "After 3,000 years, Arctic Ice Shelf Broke Off Canadian Island, Scientists Find," *New York Times*, December 30, 2006. Evangeli-

cal Greens may face resistance within their own party because some promote left-leaning strategies which put them at odds with more politically dominant evangelicals who promote the right-leaning Wise Use "environmentalism."

3. In the early months of 2007, James Dobson, founder of Focus on the Family, and leaders of other conservative Christian organizations called on the National Association of Evangelicals to silence the Reverend Richard Cizik, an NAE vice president. Cizik, along with leaders in the Evangelical Environmental Network, has led the evangelical effort to address climate change. See Alan Cooperman, "Evangelical Angers Peers with call for Action on Global Warming," *Washington Post*, March 3, 2007.

4. Political historians suggest environmental consciousness, especially concerning the connection between carbon dioxide and climate change, was not part of the public perception during these decades. The scientific community was not very vocal regarding their research concerning energy conservation; finding alternative energy supplies was the focus of national policy debate. See Thomas Friedman, "The First Energy President," *New York Times*, January 5, 2007.

5. Dr. H.A. Des Voeux coined the term "smog." See Gale E. Christianson, *Greenhouse* (New York: Walker and Co., 1999), 149.

6. Among lawmakers who are subscribing to this reading of the science are Senators John McCain and Joseph Lieberman, who have introduced legislation that would limit carbon dioxide emissions. See Steve Lohr, "The Cost of an Overheated Planet," *New York Times*, December 12, 2006.

7. For a review of the global warming debate and an introduction to the arguments of the various scientific camps, see Andrew Rivkin, "A New Middle Stance Emerges In Debate Over Climate," *New York Times*, January 1, 2007.

8. Gail Collins and Andrew Rosenthal, eds., "Global Warming Goes to Court," *New York Times*, November 28, 2006.

9. Second Wave activists such as Greenpeace have shifted strategy from public acts of environmental resistance to more stayed practices, such as suing the Department of the Interior to include polar bears to the list of endangered species. See Felicity Barringer and Andrew Rivkin, "Agency Proposes to List Polar Bears as Threatened," *New York Times*, December 28, 2006.

10. Robert Merton, *Science at the Cross-Roads* (London: Cassell, 1932): 435, and R.K. Merton, "Puritanism, Pietism, and Science," *Sociological Review* 28 (1936), 1. Some scholars suggest that the broader Protestant Reformation, as opposed to Puritanism more specifically, is responsible for increased tolerance of the sciences. See Jean Pelseneer, "Les Influences dans l'Histoire des Sciences," *Archives Internationales d'Historie des Science, Annee 1948,* 349.

11. C.A. Russell, *Science and Religious Belief* (London: University of London Press, 1973), 58, 80.

12. Alexander Koyre, *From the Closed World to the Infinite Universe* (Baltimore: Johns Hopkins Press, 1957), 219.

13. Robert Boyle, *The Works of the Honourable Robert Boyle* (A Millar, 1744), 394.

14. The important Deist texts were written by British authors which were read widely in intellectual circles in the United States. They included John Toland's *Christianity Not Mysterious*, Samuel Clarke's *Discourse Concerning the Being and Attributes of God*, and perhaps most importantly, Mathew Tindal's *Christianity as Old as Creation* (White Fish, MT: Kessinger Publishing LLC, 2004).

15. Allen Brooke, *Moral Minority: Our Skeptical Founding Fathers* (Ivan R. Dee, 2006), 87–90, 96–97, 101.

16. For an analysis of Paine's views on the matter, see Harvey Kaye, *Thomas Paine and the Promise of America* (New York: Hill and Wang, 2005), 81–84. For a discussion of Jefferson's views, see Allen, *Moral Minority*, 89–94.

17. Allen, *Moral Minority*, 87.

18. Europe's "Protestant upheaval" is found in Sydney Ahlstrom, *A Religious History of the American People* (New Haven, CT: Yale University Press, 1972).

19. Herbert Hovenkamp, *Science and Religion in America* (Philadelphia: University of Pennsylvania Press, 1978), 4.

20. The Tennents, a family of five evangelical Presbyterian preachers who were leaders in the Great Awakening movement, helped establish a seminary to train revivalist clergymen. The seminary was later named Princeton University. See Jerry Wayne Brown, *The Rise of Biblical Criticism in America*, (Middletown, CT: Wesleyan University Press, 1969). Thomas Paine often questioned the veracity of Biblical scriptures, and due in party to his notoriety, he bore a large measure of evangelical wrath. See Herbert W. Schneider, *A History of American Philosophy* (New York: Columbia University Press, 1963); Thomas Paine, *The Age of Reason* (New York: Liberal Arts Press, 1948), 3–5.

21. Hovenkamp, *Science and Religion in America*, 59.

22. Various British evangelicals, including George Whitfield, traveled to America and visited various American communities preaching as itinerant ministers and leading raucous revival meetings often held in the outdoors, see Christine L. Heyrman, *Commerce and Culture* (New York: Norton, 1984).

23. Towards the end of the First Great Awakening, John Witherspoon, a Scottish Presbyterian scholar was recruited to America in order to mend a cleavage between "new and old side" Presbyterians at Princeton. Witherspoon introduced Scottish Realism, which promoted scientific investigation with equal enthusiasm to matters of secular and religious thought. See Varnum Collins, *President Witherspoon: A Biography* (Princeton, NJ: Princeton University Press, 1925), 75; see also Douglas Sloan, *The Scottish Enlightenment and the American College Ideal* (New York: Columbia University Press, 1971), 62.

24. A. Williams, *The Common Expositor: An Account of the Commentaries on Genesis, 1527–1633* (Chapel Hill: University of North Carolina Press, 1948), 176–178.

25. C.E. Raven, *Science and Religion* (Cambridge: Cambridge University Press, 1953). In the 1990s, Paley's natural theory resurfaced as part of the Intelligent Design movement, a modern rebuttal of Darwinian evolution.

26. Jared Diamond, *Guns, Germs and Steel* (New York: Norton, 1997), 358–359;

Paul Mantoux, *Industrial Revolution in the Eighteenth Century* (London: Macmillan, 1961).

27. Anita Louise McCormick, *The Industrial Revolution in American History* (Berkeley Heights, NJ: Enslow Publishers, 1998), 50.

28. Gale E. Christianson, *Greenhouse* (New York: Walker Publishing Co., 1999), 152–153.

29. Christianson, *Greenhouse*, 2.

30. Ibid., 149.

31. The earliest record of lung disorders attributed to coal-burning fires dates back to the seventeenth-century observations of London residents John Evelyn and John Grant. See Barbara Frees, *Coal: A Human History* (Cambridge, MA: Perseus Publishing, 2003).

32. These gray- and white-speckled moths made their home alternately in the city and countryside near London. In the day they rested on trees covered with a gray- and white-speckled bark. The moths blended in, thereby avoiding the unwanted attention of predatory birds. At night *B. betularia* flew unnoticed.

33. Here Darwin suggests that adaptations animals make to moderate changes in climate are indicative of "acclimation" rather than adaptation. See Charles Darwin, *Origin of the Species*, ed. Ciliam Beer (Oxford: Oxford University Press, 1996), 114–117.

34. While Charles Darwin suggests that most animals have a "flexible constitution," he identifies changes in rhinos and elephants as a millennial "adaptation," rather than as the rapid "acclimation" seen among some insects. See Darwin, *Origin of the Species*, 70, 116. The connection between climate change and the current endangerment of various breeds of rhinos and lions is discussed in R. Ellis, *No Turning Back: The Life and Death of Animal Species* (New York: Harper Collins, 2004), 131–142.

35. Edward Hitchcock, a professor of natural theology and geology, wrote a number of scientific "proofs" of religious "truths." Hitchcock hoped to reconcile science with religion, and his scholarship included a book in which he spoke of the "catalytic power of Gospel" and "Mineralogical Illustrations of Human Character." See E. Hitchcock, *Religious Truth Illustrated from Science* (Boston: Philips Sampson, 1857), 35–36. Other theologians who promoted scientific analysis of religious truths included Joseph Haven of Harvard Church, Princeton theologian Archibald Alexander, and James Richards of the Auburn Seminary.

36. Cited in Elwyn Smith, *The Presbyterian Ministry in America Culture* (Philadelphia: Westminster Press, 1962), 182.

37. Whewell's treatise was called *Astronomy and General Physics Considered with Reference to Natural Theology*, cited in Charles C. Gillispie, *Genesis and Geology* (Cambridge, MA: Harvard University Press, 1951), 209.

38. Brooke, *Moral Minority*, 991, 221, 242; Hovenkamp, *Science and Religion in America*, 26.

39. Hovenkamp, *Science and Religion in America*, 43.

40. The idea that there were multiple origins and distinct species was called the

polygenist theory. Scholars who suggested there was only a single origin for common species were called monogenists. The polygenist-monogenist debate preceded Darwinian evolutionary theory by several decades. See Brooke, *The Moral Minority*, 279.

41. Beecher was a student at Yale University and classmate of Nathanial Taylor. Both men were credited with a central role in articulating New Light Calvinism. See William McLoughlin, *The American Evangelicals*, 42. Garrison was a leading abolitionist and Robert Owen was an advocate of popular education.

42. Nathan O. Hatch, *The Democratization of American Christianity* (New Haven: Yale University Press, 1989); Charles Foster, *An Errand of Mercy: The Evangelical United Front, 1790–1837* (Chapel Hill: University of North Carolina Press, 1960).

43. One such scholar was John William Draper. British by birth, Draper was raised and schooled in America. He taught Chemistry at New York University, where he was the administrative supervisor of the medical school. Draper traveled to Oxford to deliver a lecture on natural theology akin to the theme of the *Bridgewater Treatises*, but his lecture/publication was overshadowed by the Wilberforce-Huxley debate held at the same venue. See Edward White, *Science and Religion in American Thought* (Palo Alto, CA: Stanford University Press, 1952), 9.

44. Bertrand Russell, *Religion and Science* (Oxford: Oxford University Press, 1997), 75.

45. Hovenkamp, *Science and Religion in America*, 209.

46. In his personal correspondence with scientific theologians such as Asa Gray, Darwin revealed a personal faith in an "omnipotent" God who guided the universe, thereby determining the relative fitness of creatures and promoting natural selection. See David Griffin, *Religion & Scientific Naturalism: Overcoming the Conflicts* (Albany, NY: SUNY Press, 2000), 260.

47. John Hedley Brooke, *Science and Religion: Some Historical Perspectives* (Cambridge, UK: Cambridge University Press, 1991), 36. Huxley and Bishop Wilberforce debated evolution at Oxford University in 1860. Huxley debated a range of individuals, including representatives of the Roman Catholic Church and the defenders of conservative political ideology, including William Gladstone. See Peter W. Bowler, *Reconciling Science and Religion: The Debate in Twentieth Century Britain* (Chicago: University of Chicago Press, 2001): 15. Huxley coined the term agnosticism in the late 1860s. See Bowler, *Reconciling Science and Religion*, 16. Opponents of Huxley's philosophies on nature included Arthur Balfour, of the Balfour declaration, who suggested that scientific naturalism was deterministic materialism.

48. Francis Galton, Charles Darwin's cousin, made a variety of extrapolations from his relative's scientific inquiry. These extrapolations became part of popular political philosophy in late-nineteenth-century England. Some of these ideas came to be known as Social Darwinism, while others were called eugenics. See J.H. Brooke, *Science and Religion*, 1991, 306.

49. Hovenkamp, *Science and Religion in America*, 209–212.

50. Ibid., 48, 109, 186. Gray believed that the Bible supported pure science

and as such argued against the multiple creations promoted by Spencer and Huxley.

51. See William A. Dembski, *Intelligent Design* (Downers, IL: InterVarsity Press, 1999) and W. Dembski, *No Free Lunch* (Lanham, MD: Rowman & Littlefield, 2001).

52. For a discussion of the various proponents of Social Darwinism—notably, the industry leaders of the gilded age—see Frank Ryan, *Darwin's Blind Spot* (Boston: Houghton Mifflin Co., 2002), 34–36.

53. Whereas Britain led other nations in manufacturing in the 1880, by the First World War, America was leading Germany and Britain two-to-one in the share of world manufacturing. See Herman Schwartz, *States versus Markets* (New York: St. Martin's Press, 1994), 184–185.

54. Tyndall's research focused on the hypothetical relationship between drops in the level of the earth's carbon dioxide and the possible onset of another ice age. He did not hypothesize what effect a rise in carbon dioxide, a phenomenon that could come to define the Industrial Revolution, would have on changing the earth's atmosphere. A few years later in 1881, an American astronomer, Samuel Langley, added to the literature concerning the earth's absorption of solar heat. See Christianson, *Greenhouse*, 110. Glen Trewartha, a geography professor at the University of Wisconsin, described the earth's "insulating blanket," which trapped water vapor and carbon dioxide, thereby increasing temperatures and causing what he called "a greenhouse effect." See Glen T. Trewartha, *An Introduction to Weather and Climate* (New York: McGraw-Hill, 1937).

55. Joseph Priestly, "Observation on Different Kinds of Air," *Philosophical Transactions* 62 (1722): 147–264, and Humphry Davy, "On the Application of Liquids Formed by the Condensation of Gases as Mechanical Agents," *Philosophical Transactions* 113 (1823): 119–205. Arvid Gustav Hogbom, colleague and advisor to Svante Arrhenius, steered his student toward the topic of the environment. Hogbom was a geologist fascinated with Louis Agassiz's trendy and popular premise that for several millennia most of Europe had been buried in glacial ice. Like John Tyndall, who measured carbon dioxide in the hopes of solving the riddle of the ice age, Hogbom was not able to secure a definitive answer as to the relationship between carbon dioxide and a climate changing deep freeze. Hogbom did, however, identify a relationship between the annual burning of coal and increasing amounts of carbon dioxide. Once again, like Tyndall, Hogbom was unable to project what affect burning coal or other fossil fuels would have on global climate.

56. Tim Flannery, *The Weather-Makers* (New York: Atlantic Monthly Press, 2006), 40, and Christianson, *Greenhouse*, 111–113.

57. Today, various scientific reports concerning contemporary global warming and future climate change suggest that past ice ages were preceded by a "warming period" and a resulting re-direction of freshwater. Terrence Joyce, Chairman of the Department of Physical Oceanography at the Woods Hole Oceanographic Institute stresses the link between global warming and the possibility of a serious deep freeze similar to the glacial ice age of 12,000 B.C that was responsible for an ice bridge

connecting Siberia to North America. See Terrence Joyce, "The Heat Before the Cold," *New York Times*, April 18, 2002. William Curry, Director of the Climate Change Institute and colleague of Mr. Joyce at WHOI, suggests that current warming could lead to a freeze, but he emphasizes the likelihood that it might produce a "little ice age" similar to the one that characterized George Washington's winter at Valley Forge. See "Testimony to the Senate Committee on Commerce, Science and Transportation," available online at www.whoi.edu. Here Richard Wright's haiku gives this phenomenon a poetic rendering.

58. Alfred Chandler, *Scale and Scope: The Dynamics of Industrial Capitalism* (Cambridge, MA: Harvard Press, 1990), 61.

59. Before petroleum, whale blubber/oil was used extensively to light homes, as well as businesses and city streets. See Alexander Starbuck, *History of the American Whale Fishery* (Victoria, British Columbia: Castle Books, 1989), 85.

60. Edwin Black, *Internal Combustion: How Corporations and Governments Addicted the World to Oil and Derailed the Alternatives* (New York: St. Martin's Press, 2006), 32–33.

61. Lynwood Bryans, "The Origins of the Four-Stroke Cycle," *Technology and Culture* 8, no. 2 (April 1967): 178–198. The internal combustion engine, or ICE, was first developed in 1863 by Nikolaus August Otto, a German salesman who had studied the design of the Newcomen steam engine. In 1876, after years of tinkering, Otto patented the four-cycle engine. The ICE weighed less than steam engines and used fuel more efficiently. A few years later, Karl Benz, Gottlieb Daimler, and Wilhem Maybach invented a carburetor to work with the ICE. The novelty of the carbonator was that it used a previously useless byproduct of kerosene that was later named gasoline. In 1885, Benz and his associates produced an automobile based on the ICE/carburetor technology they perfected. In 1900, the company produced the first series of Mercedes-Benz available for public purchase. In the United States, Otto's ICE garnered the attention of Henry Ford, who worked as an engineer at the Edison Illuminating Company and who began tinkering with the German engine, ultimately adapting it for his famous Model T cars.

62. Black, *Internal Combustion*, 4–5, 154–155, 162–166.

63. Among the industrial giants that were recruited for this super "cartel" were the Ford Motor Company, U.S. Steel, Standard Oil, General Motors, and General Electric. See Leroy Pagano et al., *The Rise and Progress of American Industry* (Richmond, VA: U.S. Historical Society Inc., 1970), 45.

64. In a later publication, Callendar argued that carbon dioxide levels had risen 11 percent between the years 1900 and 1956. See Christianson, *Greenhouse*, 143–145.

65. S. R. Weart, *The Discovery of Global Warming: New Histories of Science and Technology and Medicine* (Cambridge, MA: Harvard University Press, 2003).

66. Philip Dolce, *Suburbia: The American Dream and Dilemma* (Garden City, NY: Anchor Press, 1976); Dolores Hayden, *Building Suburbia: Green Fields and Urban Growth 1820–2000* (New York: Pantheon Books, 2003).

67. The citation is from *The Christian Fundamentals*, cited in Edward White,

Science and Religion in American Thought: The Impact of Naturalism (Palo Alto, CA: Stanford University Press, 1952), 112.

68. The local legislature enacted the Butler Act a few months before the trial in the spring of 1925. See Edward Larson, *Summer for the Gods* (New York: Basic Books, 1997), 40–41.

69. George Marsden, *Fundamentalism and American Culture* (Oxford: Oxford University Press, 2006), 184–185.

70. Jeffery Sheler, *The Believers* (New York: Penguin Group, 2006), 57–59.

71. Dichlorotrifluoroethane is 10,000 times more efficient at capturing heat than is carbon dioxide. See Flannery, *The Weather-Makers*, 31.

72. On the eve of the Civil War, there was an astounding lack of knowledge within communities living in the northern and western regions of the United States regarding the intimate details of slave life in the South. President Abraham Lincoln credited Harriet Beecher Stowe, author of *Uncle Tom's Cabin*, with writing the book that "started the war."

73. DDT was banned in the United States in 1972. See Matthew Black et al, eds., *The Encyclopedia of the Environment* (New York; Franklin Watts, 1999), 30.

74. The same could be said of products that used aerosol propellants, such as bug and hair sprays.

75. In the 1980s, DDT was still used in many third world countries to the detriment of the population. In India, Mexico, and China, DDT was found in high levels in nursing mothers' breast milk. See James Gustav Speth, "Environmental Pollution," in *Earth 88: Changing Geographic Perspectives* (Sierra Club Books: National Geographic Society, 1988), 268–269.

76. According to various estimates, 260 pounds of chemical fertilizers were used per acre on most farms in the late 1960s. See Wendell Berry, *The Unsettling of America: Culture and Agriculture* (Sierra Club Books: National Geographic Society, 1977), 62. For a discussion of a number of large farms or "agro-businesses" that as of the 1970s did not use DDT and promoted organic farming, see Berry, 194–196.

77. Erik Reece, *Lost Mountain: A Year in the Vanishing Wilderness* (San Francisco: Penguin Publishers, 2006), 185–195. Reece discusses Robert Fitzgerald Kennedy's visit of eastern Kentucky in 1968 and the on-going "devastation" to the Appalachian environment from coal mining.

78. J. Brooks Flippen, *Conservative Conservationist: Russell E. Train and the Emergence of American Environmentalism* (Baton Rouge, LA: Louisiana State University Press, 2006), 6, 60.

79. Noah Feldman, *Divided by God* (New York: Farrar, Straus, and Giroux, 2005), 185.

80. Richard Neuhaus established an anti-war organization called the Clergy and Laity Concerned About Vietnam (CALCAV) in response to President Lyndon Johnson's characterization of anti-war debate as treason. See Damon Linker, *The Theocons: Secular America Under Siege* (New York: Double Day, 2006), 17, 30–34.

81. Three of the most important books written on the environment during this

era were published between the years 1970–1973. They included an MIT report called *Man's Impact on the Global Environment*, and two popular volumes, *This Endangered Planet* and *The Limits to Growth*. During the years these books were published, The United Nations established its environmental program (UNEP) and sponsored a conference on the Human Environment in Stockholm, Sweden. In America, Dennis Hays formed an umbrella organization for green activists called the Earth Day Network, and President Nixon ratified the Endangered Species Act. In 1970, this organization fought and won the right to establish a holiday named "Earth Day" to raise environmental awareness. For a discussion on Nixon environmental policy, see J. Flippen, *The Conservative Conservationist*, 114–136.

82. This report, entitled "Stratospheric Sink for Chloro-fluoro-methanes: Chlorine Catalyzed Destruction of Ozone," was published in *Nature* 249 (1974), 810. See Vijay V. Vaitheeswaran, *Power to the People* (Farrar, Straus, and Giroux, 2003), 159, 180, 188.

83. Dr. Wangari Mathaai was awarded a Noble Peace Prize in 2003 for her tree-planting campaign in Kenya.

84. A list of American environmental organizations and the dates they were founded is located on the Wikipedia website. See wikipedia.org/wiki/list_of_environmental_organizations.

85. See James G. Speth, *Protecting Our Environment: Toward a New Agenda* (Lanham, MD: University Press of America, 1985).

86. Wealthy signatories, especially those countries with large chemical manufacturers, wanted a gradual phase-out of production of CFCs over a 14-year period. The coalition of unwilling chemical producers and hesitating signatory countries only adopted the freeze on CFCs when global chemical giant Dupont indicated it could come up with alternative to CFCs. See James G. Speth, *Red Sky at Morning* (New Haven, CT: Yale University Press, 2004), 94. In 2006, Dupont helped form an alliance with other industry leaders, dubbed USCAP, which calls for a reduction in carbon dioxide. See "A Call for Action," available at www.us-cap.org.

87. CFCs and DDTs are manmade, difficult to capture or degrade, and are thousands of times more potent at capturing heat than is carbon dioxide. However, carbon dioxide emitted by manmade machines is the most prevalent ingredient in global warming. See Flannery, *The Weather-Makers*, 31.

88. Though most scientists of this era were not studying the impact of carbon dioxide on the atmosphere, in 1975 Roger Revelle, a graduate student, and Dr. Han Suess, of the Scripps Institution of Oceanography, published a study based on Arrhenius and Callendar's historical analysis. They tested the ocean and found rising carbon dioxide levels in water. Revell and Suess's analysis was ultimately confirmed by a young chemist name Charles Keeling, who had devised a very sensitive gauge to test rising carbon dioxide levels in the atmosphere. Charles Keeling found that no matter where in the world he traveled, wherever he tested the air, the carbon dioxide levels were the exactly the same. He arrived at the conclusion that pollution in one area was not confined to that area and the world's air was a blend of various pollutants. Keeling's subsequent readings of the atmosphere

between 1958 and 2000 indicated a rise in CO2 due to human consumption of fossil fuels. See Flannery, *The Weather-Makers*, 25, 155.

89. In the summer of 1979, four concerned scientists presented their own research to J. Gustav Speth, chair of President Carter's Council on Environmental Quality. The authors of this report predicted a "warming" that would require ambitious policies to regulate the long-term impact of consuming fossil fuels. See George Woodwell et al., "The Carbon Dioxide Problem: Implications in the Management of Energy and Other Resources," July 1979. Speth suggests that this little circulated report helped direct his attention, and the attention of the Carter White House, to the specific issues of reducing carbon dioxide emissions. See Speth, *Red Sky at Morning*, 3.

90. National Research Council, *Carbon Dioxide and Climate: Report of an Ad Hoc Study Group on Carbon Dioxide and Climate* (Washington, D.C.: National Academy of Sciences, 1979).

91. U.S. Council on Environmental Quality, *Global Energy Futures and the Carbon Dioxide Problem* (Washington, D.C.: Government Printing Office, 1981), iii–viii.

92. President Carter wanted to expand alternative sources of energy, including nuclear power.

93. The theory that environmental protection constitutes an "unreasonable" Fifth Amendment "taking" of private property by the federal government was a reinterpreted formulation of a discussion on land use derived from Richard Epstein, *Takings, Private Property and the Power of Eminent Domain* (Cambridge, MA: Harvard University Press, 1985).

94. Theodore Roosevelt, *Autobiography* (New York: Charles Scribner's Sons, 1958). John Muir founded the Sierra Club.

95. Some of the very prominent and important organizations, such as the Western Cattlemen's Association, the American Mining Congress, and the American Farm Bureau Federation are affiliated with the WUM and lobby on its behalf.

96. See Ron Arnold, *Ecology Wars: Environmentalism as if People Mattered* (Washington, D.C.: Free Enterprise Press, 1993); Philip Brick and R. McGreggor Cawley, *A Wolf in the Garden: The Land Rights Movement and the New Environmental Debate* (Lanham, MD: Rowman & Littlefield, 1996); Alan Gottlieb, ed., *The Wise-Use Agenda: The Citizen's Policy Guide to Environmental Issues* (Washington, D.C.: Free Enterprise Press, 1989).

97. Ron Arnold discussed the goals of the WUM in a 1991 interview with *Outside* magazine. He argued that WUM's spin strategy would win many converts because "facts don't matter: in politics everything is perception." See Jon Krakauer, "Brown Fellas," *Outside* (December 1991): 67–69.

98. Noah Feldman, *Divided by God: America's Church-State Problem and What We Should Do about It* (New York: Farrar, Straus, and Giroux, 2005), 217.

99. For another discussion of the Jeffersonian "wall of separation," the effort to protect religion from the state, and the effort to protect political leaders from organized religion, see Feldman, *Divided by God*, 40. See also Philip Hamburger,

Separation of Church and State (Cambridge, MA: Harvard University Press, 2000), 113–117.

100. In the 1940s, the National Council of Churches was called the Federal Council of Churches. See Joel A. Carpenter, *Revive Us Again: The Re-awakening of American Fundamentalism* (Knoxville: University of Tennessee Press, 1997), 144–147.

101. Jeffery Sheler, *Believers: A Journey into Evangelical America* (New York: Viking Adult, 2006), 61.

102. Christian Smith, *American Evangelicalism: Embattled and Thriving* (Chicago: University of Chicago Press, 1998), 11.

103. For a discussion of Barry Goldwater's position on civil rights, see Jonathan M. Schoenwald, *Time for Choosing* (Oxford: Oxford University Press, 2001), 147–151.

104. Several other important evangelical organizations were created during the end of the Carter Presidency and the beginning of the Reagan era. These included Focus on the Family, founded by James Dobson in 1978, and Family Research Council, founded in 1983. See Christine Todd Whitman, *It's My Party Too: The Battle for the Heart of the GOP and the Future of America* (New York: Penguin Press, 2005), 74.

105. The televangelist scandals of the previous year hurt Pat Robertson's presidential campaign. His Christian Coalition would resurface in the 1990s with the 1994 conservative sweep of Congress. See "The Gospel According To Ralph," *Time* (May 15, 1995): 28.

106. Noah Feldman suggests that Jerry Falwell may have specifically coined the term Moral Majority to recall Nixon's "silent majority." See Feldman, *Divided By God*, 192.

107. Johnathan Schoenwald, *A Time for Choosing: The Rise of Modern American Conservatism* (Oxford: Oxford University Press, 2001), 256. In order to get a sense of how—despite fairly unconventional credentials—Ronald Reagan was able to attract conservative evangelical patrons, see Allan J. Mayer, "A Tide of Born-Again Politics," *Newsweek* (September 15, 1980): 28. By the 1980s the NAE was the fastest growing evangelical organization within the larger movement, and by 2005 it accounted for one half of America's evangelical population. See Sheler, *Believers*, 61.

108. George Bush, "The Republican Party & the Conservative Movement," *National Review* (Dec. 1, 1964): 1053.

109. The NRA broke with its tradition of not endorsing candidates and officially endorsed President Reagan. See David Helvarg, *War Against the Greens* (Boulder, CO: Johnson Books, 2004), 36.

110. The *Agenda* was published in the last year of the Reagan presidency. See Helvarg, *War Against The Greens*, 36.

111. Ibid., 35.

112. Genesis 1:28, in *The Holy Bible*. See also Philip Shabecoff, *A Fierce Green Fire* (New York: Farrar, Straus, and Giroux, 1993), 208.

113. Lou Cannon, *President Reagan: The Role of a Lifetime* (New York: Simon and Schuster, 1991), 86, 531.

114. "The Terrible 20 Regulations," *Washington Post*, August 4, 1981.

115. Robert F. Kennedy, Jr., *Crimes Against Nature* (New York: Harper Collins, 2004), 23–25.

116. Ibid.

117. Helvarg, *War Against the Greens*, 42.

118. Ibid., 42.

119. Ibid., 4.

120. John Stauber and Sheldon Rampton, *Toxic Sludge is Good for You!: Lies, Damn Lies and the Public Relations Industry* (Monroe, ME: Common Courage Press, 1995), 75–85.

121. Kennedy, *Crimes Against Nature*, 29.

122. Major Garrett, *The Enduring Revolution: How the Contract with America Continues to Shape the Nation* (New York: Crown Forum, 2005), 33–38. It is worth noting that three of the five 1980 pledges referred to cuts to the national budget, especially various social programs and public salaries. The fourth pledge promoted urban economic development, or what Jack Kept would call "enterprise zones," and the fifth pledged to strengthen the military. See Garrett, *The Enduring Revolution*, 34.

123. Garrett, *The Enduring Revolution*, 30. For Republican strategies to defeat Democrats, see Ibid., 56, 64.

124. *New York Times*, September 16, 1980.

125. Newton Gingrich, Dick Armey et al., *Contract with America* (New York: New York Times Books, 1994).

126. Some attribute the attempt to diminish the role carbon dioxide plays in global warming to Karl Rove, the senior strategist in the George W. Bush White House. See Carl Pope and Paul Rauber, *Strategic Ignorance: Why the Bush Administration is Recklessly Destroying a Century of Environmental Progress* (Washington, D.C.: Sierra Club Books, 2004), 26. Others suggest that the Wise Use lobbyists were responsible for White House ambivalence towards Kyoto. See Kennedy, *Crimes Against Nature*, 50–53. Still others assert that the attack on Kyoto came from the Republican congressional leadership. See Whitman, *It's My Party Too*, 192–196.

127. Garrett, *The Enduring Revolution*, 22–23; Speth, 2004, 6 and Peter Huber, *Hard Greens: Saving the Environment from the Environmentalists: A Conservative Manifesto* (New York: Basic Books, 1999), 19.

128. Mark Dowie, *Losing Ground: American Environmentalism at the Close of the Twentieth Century* (Cambridge, MA: MIT Press, 1995).

129. For a sense of the type of Congressional environmental policy that was in place in the year before the Contract with America, see "Odd Trio Could Kill Nature Pact," *Chicago Tribune*, September 30, 1994. For a discussion of how the WUM tried to gain access to establish policy in President Clinton's White House, see Pope, *Strategic Ignorance*, 40–41.

130. In September 1995, the United Nations Intergovernmental Panel on Climate Change suggested that global warming, due to greenhouse gas emissions,

could lead to dangerous climatic changes, including droughts, (super) hurricanes, and floods.

131. Whitman, *It's My Party Too*, 168–170.

132. Brian O'Neill and M. Oppenheimer, "Dangerous Climate Impacts & the Kyoto Protocol," *Science* 296 (2002): 1971.

133. Speth, 2004, 62–67, 108.

134. For a discussion of the relationship between economic growth and industrial waste, see Speth, *Red Sky at Morning*, 108, 137. Governor Christine Todd Whitman, EPA administrator from 2001–2003, discusses the Kyoto Protocol's silence on the NICs of China and India. Whitman suggests that it is estimated that Asia will produce 70 percent of greenhouse gases in the next 15 years. See Whitman, *It's My Party Too*, 168–170. For a comparative discussion of current and projected emissions in the United States, China, and India, see "Emission Standards," available at http://en.wikipedia.org/wiki/Emission_standards. Regarding India and China's reliance on diesel fuel, see Keith Bradher, "Clean Air or T.V.: Paying in Pollution for Energy Hunger," *New York Times*, January 9, 2007.

135. The Bush Administration's critique of Kyoto regarding lax standards for NICs is discussed in a "special report" *Time* magazine issue that is devoted to global warming. See Bryan Walsh, "The Impact of Asia's Giants: How China and India could save the planet—or destroy it," *Time* (April 2, 2006): 61–62.

136. Regarding some of President Bush's campaign commentary on environmentalism, see Pope, *Strategic Ignorance*, 216. For a range of views regarding Bush Administration policy concerning carbon dioxide emissions, see Howie Hawkins, *Independent Politics: The Green Party Strategy Debate* (Chicago: Haymarket Books, 2006). For a discussion of how the Green Party takes an avowedly secular stand with regard to addressing spiritual aspects of nature conservation, see Michael Lerner, "The Democratic Party Should Appeal to Religious Voters," in *How Does Religion Influence Politics?* ed. James Torr (San Diego: Greenhaven, 2004), 70–72.

137. Whitman, *It's My Party Too*, 170.

138. Christine Todd Whitman traveled to a 2001 G-8 meeting in Italy to discuss carbon dioxide and the Kyoto Protocol with G-8 environment ministers. For a copy of the letter from Whitman to President Bush regarding the issues discussed at the G-8 meeting, see www.washingtonpost.com/wpsrv/onpolitics/transcripts/whitmanmemo032601.htm.

139. EPA administrator Whitman suggests several Republican Senators began a letter writing campaign to stop her from discussing mandatory CO_2 caps with foreign leaders. See Whitman, *It's My Party Too*, 178; Garrett, *The Enduring Revolution*, 23. For an example of WUM and White House views regarding greenhouse gases and global warming, see Senator James Inhofe's website, www.Inhofe.senate.gov and scroll to press releases for a July 28, 2003, speech, entitled "Inhofe Delivers Major Speech on the Science of Climate Change."

140. An international author who suggests that global warming is not as bad as it seems is Bjorn Lomborg, *The Skeptical Environmentalist* (Cambridge, MA: Cambridge University Press, 2001), 4. For a different take on the enforcement of inter-

national treaties and on the dismissal of science warning about global warming, see David Levy and Peter Newell, "Oceans Apart? Business Responses to Global Environmental Issues in Europe and the United States," *Environment* 42, no. 9 (2000): 9; Martha Honey and Tom Barry, *Global Focus: U.S. Foreign Policy at the Turn of the Millennium* (New York: St. Martin's Press, 2000), 120.

141. Friends of Science, a Canadian organization, is one of several groups that disputes the link between carbon dioxide and global warming. The Cato Institute, the Robert Pielke Sr. Research Group, and the Marshall Institute are other organizations that list a variety of scientists who are skeptical of causes and existence of climate change. Website links to these organizations and a range of scientific reports disputing the significance of global warming can be found on the website of Congressman Dana Rohrabacher, available at www.rohbacher.house.gov.

142. John McManus, "The Sky Is Falling! Or is it?" *The New American* 19 (September 8, 2003). For a similar argument also suggesting that the harms caused by global warming are exaggerated, see Patrick J. Michaels, "Global Warming: So What Else is New," *San Francisco Chronicle*, February 2, 2007.

143. William M. Gray, "Get Off the Warming Bandwagon," November 16, 2002, www.bbcnews.com, and Patrick J. Michaels and Robert C. Balling, Jr., *The Satanic Gases* (Washington, D.C.: Cato Institute, 2000). Another research scientist, Jens Bischof, suggests that this cycle of warming is leading to a period of cooling, while polar ice cap melting has been occurring unrelated to carbon dioxide emissions since the 1970s. See Bischof, "Ice in the Greenhouse: Earth May be Cooling, Not Warming," *Quest* 5 (January 2002).

144. Ian Clark, "Blame the Sun/Back to Copernicus: Is it all too Human to Connect Global Warming with Human Activity," *National Post's Financial Report*, July 15, 2004.

145. S. Baliunas, "Studies Lack Hard Evidence That Warming is Human Induced," *American Legion Magazine*, 1/02.

146. Scientists who are leery of the harm caused by global warming suggest that it leads to higher crop yields in the short-run but causes long-term drought. See Thomas Karl and Kevin Trenberth, "Modern Climate Change," *Science* 302 (December, 5, 2003).

147. Groups who resist adopting nuclear power as an alternative source of fuel are listed on the Public Citizen website. See "Environmental Statement on Nuclear Energy and Global Warming," 6/05, available at www.citizen.org.

148. Jerry Taylor and Peter Van Doren, "Evaluating the Case for Renewable Energy: Is Government Support Warranted?" *Cato Institute for Public Analysis* (January 10, 2002).

149. "Battle Over IPCC Chair Renews Debate on U.S. Climate Policy," *Science* (April 12, 2002). The 2001 IPCC Third Assessment Report concluded that even if the United States and other nations aggressively sought to reduce carbon dioxide, there would still be a rise in average global temperatures, and the sea level would also rise. See IPCC 2001 Report at http:/en.wikipedia.org/wiki/IPCC. At the end of March 2001, leaders of various non-evangelical denominations—mainly Presby-

terians, Methodists, and Jewish congregations—sent a letter to President Bush asking him to reconsider his position on global warming. See Bob Edgar, *Middle Church: Reclaiming the Moral Values of the Faithful Majority from the Religious Right* (New York: Simon and Schuster, 2005), 46–55.

150. Much like Vice President Bush's efforts on President Reagan's Task Force on Regulatory Relief and Dan Quayle's services on the Council on Competitiveness, Dick Cheney would be responsible for coordinating executive environmental policy during George W. Bush's presidential administration. David Helvarg suggests that the Wise Use-affiliated Center for the Defense of Free Enterprise recruited Dick Cheney to sit on its board. See the Sierra Club website for "Wise-Use in the White House" (http://www.sierraclub.org/sierra/200409/wiseuse.asp) and Harvey Blatt, *America's Environmental Report Card: Are We Making the Grade?* (Cambridge, MA: The MIT Press, 2005), 130.

151. In August 2002, when the World Summit on Sustainable Development held its meeting in South Africa, American representatives to the conference fought to keep the Summit from endorsing the Kyoto Protocol and won. American environmental organizations were aware of this development, but to a large extent, the American public was either unaware or disinterested. See J.G. Speth, "Perspectives on the Johannesburg Summit," *Environment* 45, no. 1 (2003): 24.

152. In the 1980s, Gale Norton worked under Wise Use aficionado and former Reagan Department of the Interior Secretary James Watt. These alliances are discussed in Pope, *Strategic Ignorance*, 54–55. For a discussion of the weather in 2003, see "How it Affects your Health," by Christine Gorman (Special Report—Global Warming Edition), *Time* (April 3, 2006): 44–45. Dr. Wangari Maathai is a Kenyan activist whose Green Belt Movement is responsible for planting 30 million trees. Since receiving her award, she has argued that carbon dioxide-driven global warming needs to be addressed. See Simon Ross, "Time 100," *Time* (April 2005) and "Nobel Winners Call for Justice," *The Nation*, January 24, 2007.

153. The Norton EPA maintained that there was "substantial scientific uncertainty surrounding global climate change," see Mark Sherman (Associated Press), "Justices Hear Global Warming Case," *The Courier-Journal*, November 30, 2006; Gail Collins et al., eds., "Global Warming Goes to Court," *New York Times*, November 28, 2006.

154. On September 13, 2005, the U.S. Court of Appeals for the District of Columbia Circuit decided to uphold the EPA's decision. See http://www.cadc.uscourts.gov/bin/scripts/isysweb.

155. The plaintiffs are the states of California, Connecticut, Illinois, Maine, Massachusetts, New Jersey, New Mexico, New York, Oregon, Rhode Island, Vermont, and Washington. Other organizations joining these plaintiffs are the Sierra Club, the Union of Concerned Scientists, Greenpeace, and the International Center for Technology Assessment, among several others. Section 202(a)(1) of the Clear Air Act requires the EPA administrator to set emission standards for pollutants from motor vehicles. See *Massachusetts v. Environmental Protection Agency* (case #05–1120). See also http://en.wikipedia.org/ wiki/Massachusetts v. EPA.

156. It is instructive to note that none other than Rev. Billy Graham, a friend and confidant of the extended Bush clan, is attributed with George W. Bush's recommitment to Christianity. See George W. Bush, *A Charge to Keep* (New York: William Morrow and Co., 1996), 136. For an evangelical view of political life in the Bush White House, see David Kuo, "Putting Faith Before Politics," *New York Times*, November 16, 2006.

157. Organizations such as People for the American Way and Americans Untied for Separation of Church and State, as well as a variety of religious scholars, worried that the creation of this new executive "cabinet," would create a crack in Thomas Jefferson's wall that might become a religious floodgate. For a related discussion on faith-based ideology and the Iraq war, see Jim Wallis, *God's Politics* (San Francisco: Harper San Francisco, 2005), 141, 144.

158. David Aikman, *A Man of Faith: The Spiritual Journey of George W. Bush* (Nashville, TN: Thomas Nelson Publishing Group, 2004), 144–145.

159. Gary McMullen, "Increased Need, Smaller Resources," *The Ledger* (Florida), July 12, 2003.

160. For the document entitled "For the Health of the Nation an Evangelical Call to Civic Responsibility," see www.nae.net/images /civic_responsilbility2.pdf.

161. Sheler, *The Believers*, 231. Church of the Brethren, a ministry associated both with evangelical and Methodist organizations, issued a pro-environment statement as early as 1991 entitled "Called to Care," which they feature on their website, available at www.brethren.org/genbd/washof/environment.

162. Harold Ockenga created the NAE in the 1940s. Several enlightened journalist and theologians, such as Billy Graham, joined this association looking for intellectual revival and moral fellowship.

163. Michael Janofsky, "When Clean Air Is a Biblical Obligation," *New York Times*, November 7, 2005.

164. The principal use of the term Intelligent Design occurred in 1987, when the Supreme Court ruled, once again, that teaching Creationism in public school was unconstitutional. Scholars at the Discovery Institute coined the term in the year following the trial, and it was first published in Charles Thaxton ed., *Of Pandas and People* (Richardson, TX: Foundation for Thought and Ethics, 1989). Since then, an avid evangelical proponent of ID, William Dembski, has written numerous books and articles refining natural theory "proofs" in support of ID. Dembski and his Discovery colleagues have lectured on ID, presenting their theories to evangelical congregations and political organizations alike. See www.discovery.org. In 2005, President Bush indicated that students should be allowed to learn alternative theories of evolution, including ID. See "Bush: Schools Should Teach Intelligent Design," at www.msnbc.com. That same year a U.S. Federal Court ruled that a public school district's requirement to teach ID violated the First Amendment of the Constitution. See www.Wikipedia/intelligent-design. For objections to ID, see Jerry Coyne, "The Case Against Intelligent Design, *The New Republic* (August 22, 2005), and William Safire, "On Language: Neo-Creo," *The New York Times Magazine* (August, 21, 2005).

165. Sheler, *The Believers*, 16.

166. Christian Smith, *Christian America? What Evangelicals Really Want* (Los Angeles: UCLA Press, 2000), 120–122.

167. Susan Page, "Christian Right's Alliance Bends Political Spectrum," *USA Today*, June 15, 2005.

168. The Noah Alliance website has a list of approximately 30 environmental organizations. Their evangelical nature and their emphasis on protecting endangered species are available at www.Noahalliance.org.

169. Associated Press, "Evangelicals, Scientists Tackle Warming," *Courier-Journal*, January 16, 2007.

170. John Green as cited in Peter Smith, "Environmentalists Get New Ally," *Courier-Journal*, January 21, 2007.

171. David Kuo, former Deputy Director of the White House Office of Faith-Based Initiatives, suggests that whatever disagreements social welfare evangelicals have with Bush policy, they will not leave the Republican Party to join Democrats. By extension, Evangelical Greens will probably not join green or independent parties, who are left of the Democrats. See "Putting Faith Before Politics," *New York Times*, November 16, 2006.

172. For a first hand account of "counter-culture conservative" challenges of dominion theory and other evangelical concerns regarding climate change, see Rob Dreher, *Crunchy Cons* (New York: Crown Forum, 2006), 150–178.

173. Felicity Barringer and Andrew Rivkin, "Agency Proposes to List Polar Bears as Threatened," *New York Times*, December 28, 2006, A16.

174. Earlier in 2006, perhaps November or December, The National Snow and Ice Data Center in Boulder released a study to the White House suggesting the carbon dioxide-driven global warming was leading to a whole-scale thinning of ice in the Artic. The report's authors suggest that by 2040, most of the ice in the Arctic could be water, which would lead to a series of other environmental problems. See Andrew Rivkin, "By 2040, Greenhouse Gases Could Lead to an Open Arctic Sea in Summers," *New York Times*, December 12, 2006; William J. Broad, "Long-term Global Forecast? Fewer Continents," *New York Times*, January 9, 2007; John Collins Rudolph, "The Warming of Greenland," *New York Times*, January 16, 2007.

175. Edwin Black, *Internal Combustion* (New York: St Martin's Press, 2006), 124–162.

176. See Matthew L. Wald, "Ford Shows a Hybrid Car with 2 Modes: Electric and Electric," *New York Times*, January 23, 2007.

177. Kennedy, *Crimes Against Nature*, 42–43.

178. Jennifer Steinhauer and Felicity Barringer, "Schwarzenegger Orders Cuts in Emissions," *New York Times*, January 10, 2007.

179. Prominent Senators sponsoring carbon dioxide-reducing bills include Diane Feinstein, Barack Obama, John McCain, and Joseph Lieberman. This debate ensures that carbon dioxide-driven global warming will be an issue central to the presidential debate in 2007–2008. See Felicity Barringer and Andrew Rivkin, "Bills on Climate and Global Warming Move to Spotlight in the New Congress," *New*

York Times, January 18, 2007. After California Governor Arnold Schwarzenegger made his pledge to reduce carbon dioxide, the state government of Wyoming quickly offered to sell California wind energy. See Dustin Bleizeffer, "Wyoming has Opportunities in California's 'green' Energy Market," *Star-Tribune*, January 27, 2007.

180. See the Church of the Brethren website, www.brethren.org/genbd/washofc/environment.

181. The USCAP alliance includes: Alcoa, BP American, Caterpillar, Duke Energy, DuPont, and General Electric, among others, along with environmental organizations such as the Pew Center on Global Change, Environmental Defense, National Resources Defense Council, and World Resources Institute. See www.us-cap.org.

182. The USCAP alliance reflects more that $750 Billion of "combined market capitalization." See "FPL Group Joins Major Business and Environmental Leader in Call for Swift Action on Global Climate Change," available at www.dBusiness-News.org.

183. See http:www.whitehouse.gov/stateoftheunion/2007/index.html.

184. "The State of the Union Address: What the Media Missed," *The Real Truth*, January 24, 2007, available at www.realtruth.org.

185. Paul Krugman, "The Sum of All Ears," *New York Times*, January 29, 2007.

186. By the end of April, however, the EPA administrator Stephen Johnson said he would not give the Senate Environment and Public Works Committee a specific timetable for regulating gasoline emissions, "National Briefing," *New York Times*, April 25, 2007.

187. For a range of legal and scientific discussions of alternative energy sources, see Edwin Black, *Internal Combustion* (New York: St. Martin's Press, 2006). Black speaks of a "new Manhattan project of hyper-engineering," and "hydrogen solutions," 293–361. Regarding natural gas and nuclear power, see Michael Klare, *Blood and Oil* (New York: Metropolitan Books, 2004), 180–202 and Vijay Vaitheeswara, *Power to the People* (Farrar, Straus, and Giroux, 2003), 317–327, 276–282. Regarding a range of alternative technologies, see Harvey Blatt, *America's Environmental Report Card: Are We Making the Grade?* (Cambridge, MA: MIT Press, 2004), 115–126.

188. Herald Berman, *Law & Revolution: The Formation of the Western Legal Tradition* (Cambridge, MA: Harvard University Press, 1983).

189. William E. Nelson, *Americanization of the Common Law: The Impact of Legal Change on Massachusetts Society, 1760–1830* (Cambridge, MA: Harvard University Press, 1975), 105–108.

190. In America, Catholics, and a few other religious communities, insisted on establishing their own schools. See Robert F. Drinan, S.J., *Can God and Caesar Coexist: Balancing Religious Freedom and International Law* (New Haven, CT: Yale University Press, 2006), 59. Catholic educational "separatism" became a contentious issue among Second Awakening evangelicals.

FURTHER READING

For a discussion of the impact of the modern environmental movement on American industry, see Ron Arnold, *Ecology Wars: Environmentalism as if People Mattered* (Free Enterprise Press, 1998). Regarding communities that are already suffering from the effects of global warming, see Mark Lynas, *High Tide: The Truth about our Climate Crisis* (St. Martin's Press, 2004). Concerning a future marked by increased global warming and a depleted oil supply, see Paul Roberts, *The End of Oil* (Houghton Mifflin, 2004). For an economic study that considers the costs of cleaning up environmental damage, see Lombor Bjorn, *The Skeptical Environmentalist* (Cambridge University Press, 2001). For a survey of Christian viewpoints on environmental protection, see R.J. Berry (ed.), *Environmental Stewardship: Critical Perspectives* (T&T Clark, 2006). Regarding the damage carbon dioxide is causing to the oceans, see David Helvarg, *Blue Frontier* (Sierra Club Books, 2006).

Religious Liberty and Authority in Biomedical Ethics

Courtney S. Campbell

In February and March 2005, the attention of the nation was riveted by a life-and-death drama unfolding in the courtrooms and hospital corridors in Florida, as well as within the U.S. Congress and the White House. A national controversy erupted during the dying days of Terry Schiavo, nearly seven years after her husband had requested withdrawal of her life-sustaining feeding tubes, and some fifteen years after a cardiac arrest had inflicted permanent, irreversible brain damage on Ms. Schiavo. The Schiavo case was complicated not only because of disagreement between the family of Terry Schiavo and her husband, Michael Schiavo, but also because of political pressure and media engagement by conservative Roman Catholics and evangelical Christian denominations who advocated for continued treatment as consistent with constitutional protections of the right to life. In turn, many arguments for removal of the feeding tubes maintained that this religious-based advocacy and intervention in the case inappropriately entangled religious convictions with matters of medicine and the state and sought to legally enact religious teaching about dying on all citizens.

The Schiavo case presented many salient lessons for understanding the relationship between church, synagogue, and mosque and the interests of the state as mediated in the context of medical care. While many faith traditions have articulated moral teaching on a range of issues in medical ethics, historically these commitments most frequently come into conflict with state interests when the stakes are highest; namely, when a decision quite literally can mean the difference between life and death. In some of these life-or-death contexts, religious traditions may not only develop moral positions, but also request of their adherents, and of public officials, that these religiously based moral values become the foundation for the laws of the secular state.

My intent in this essay is to provide an overview of several church-state issues and conflicts that emerge in the setting of medical care decisions about the generation or preservation of human life or the manner and timing of death. (The scope of my analysis will not address the questions of abortion or embryonic stem cell research, as such issues are covered elsewhere in this volume.) Although there is a vibrant academic discussion regarding the public significance of religious views about medical ethics, my concerns will be those circumstances in which a policy or law of the state is deemed to infringe on the freedom of religious practice, as well as circumstances in which advocates of a moral position on a particular medical intervention on religious grounds appear to infringe the compelling interests of the state in oversight and regulation of medical practice. That is, church-state questions in medical ethics can pose difficult policy and ethical dilemmas that invoke both the Free Exercise and the Establishment Clauses of the First Amendment.

In a liberal, pluralistic, and democratic society, the free exercise of religious liberty is held to be a fundamental right of citizens. This entails that the democratic state, which derives its authority from citizen consent, has a presumptive responsibility and interest in protecting and securing religious freedom. The range of religious freedom, while most commonly manifested in political contexts, also is no less relevant and compelling in health care decision-making. In the context of decisions about health care and biomedical procedures, the prevailing trend has been that the state should seek modes of accommodation of religious liberty to the extent that other basic interests of the state are not threatened or compromised. However, in some circumstances of religious-state conflict, laws have imposed restrictions on the extent of religious liberty to protect other compelling social values.

This essay will draw on and discuss numerous concrete examples in biomedical ethics to illuminate understanding of possible accommodations of conflicts between religious faith convictions and state interests. Whether and how these accommodations are feasible requires observance of three principal distinctions:

1. The constitutional setting—that is, whether the conflict in a democratic society is rooted in the extent of freedom of religion (liberty) or in restrictions on religion as a basis for law (non-establishment);

2. The decision-making capacity of the individual—that is, whether they are a competent adult or a child; and
3. The nature of the medical decision at stake—that is, whether it involves a claim for medical treatment to generate or preserve life, or a claim of treatment refusal or withdrawal that likely will bring about death.

In general terms, the state has been willing to recognize religious grounds for refusals of treatment by adults as having equal moral and legal standing with treatment refusals of adults in general; however, state accommodation of treatment requests or refusals on behalf of children are considerably more controversial, while directives for public law to be informed and shaped by religious influences are customarily held to be at odds with the requirements for binding law in a secular, liberal democratic culture.

RELIGION IN THE LIBERAL DEMOCRATIC STATE: COMMUNITIES OF RESISTANCE AND MEANING

The prevailing models of the church-state relationship include a spectrum of possibilities that range from civic exclusion of religion to a separation and toleration model to a near-theocratic or establishmentarian model in which religious (and particularly, Christian) values are claimed to be the basis for legitimate laws promulgated by the state. While evaluating these models is a subject for more extensive discussion in political philosophy (and in other essays in this collection), it is important at the outset to acknowledge that any account of the church-state relationship, including the one delineated below, will contain assumptions and presuppositions that will impose ethical and legal presumptions in favor of the interests of one domain or the other. It is also important to acknowledge that these normative models seldom fully capture the church-state relationship as it is *experienced* in circumstances of conflict in the context of decisions about medical care.

With these caveats in mind, I want to sketch briefly the parameters of the model that will inform this discussion. This relationship is comprised, though not exhausted by, the following features:

1. The commitment of the liberal state to the principle of liberty and respect for autonomy includes providing social space for the free exercise of religious belief and practice.
2. This commitment means that individuals within society possess the freedom to choose whether to believe and practice religion, and the freedom to choose which (if any) religious denomination—church, synagogue, mosque, or other form—they will enact their freedom of association with.
3. This commitment further entails that the state grants to religious associations

the autonomy of self-governance over ecclesiastical matters internal to the denomination. For example, ecclesiastical discourse and rules regarding controversial topics, such as qualification for ordination to an ecclesiastical office or a position of authority, or matters of sexuality, are properly subjects for the religious community to articulate free of interference from state intervention.
4. The liberal democratic state is agnostic about what constitutes the good life for human beings. The state is committed to ensuring that individuals and intermediate associations (including religious communities) are provided that amount of liberty consistent with individuals and associations articulating and enacting their own view of the good life for themselves to the extent that they do not pose a risk of harm or injury to others exercising their own freedom. Moreover, securing these freedoms means the state can legitimately reject efforts to establish or impose particularistic, or religious, views of the good life (or good death) on civic society. The state thereby seeks to balance an interest in ensuring freedom of religion with an interest in prohibiting the establishment of a religious worldview as socially normative.
5. This means, on one hand, that individuals and communities have the liberty to share their own particular views of the good life with other citizens through persuasive means; on the other hand, the "harm" restriction on the exercise of liberty means the state can intervene to regulate or prohibit the practices of individuals or communities that do present a risk of serious bodily harm or injury to vulnerable individuals. Furthermore, the state can neither promote nor dissuade from religious belief and practice but should instead seek for neutral ground both between religious and secular realms, as well as between specific religions.
6. The state is required to establish procedures that ensure equal opportunity, particularly as the social arrangement of power may situate some persons with substantial authority (political, economic, professional, religious, and so on) and situate other persons in circumstances of substantial vulnerability.
7. While disavowing a view of the good life for human beings, the state does bear a responsibility to ensure that each citizen receives a share of basic needs—food, shelter, clothing, education, security, health care—that allows them to participate meaningfully as citizens in society and to take advantage of guarantees of equal opportunity. In large nation-states, often the meeting of basic needs of a substantial portion of the population can be achieved only through coordinated bureaucracy—including coordination with religiously affiliated health care facilities—and compulsory taxation methods.
8. The claims of religious belief or practice to political power or authority in affairs of the state must not overstep the realm of personal freedom and ecclesiastical autonomy guaranteed by the state. Religious convictions can exert influence in public discourse and practices through reliance on persuasive means, but an effort to ground public laws in religious values, or otherwise to align a religious community with state power and its coercive mechanisms is not only misguided politically, but compromises the integrity and vitality of the religious tradition.

Indeed, as de Tocqueville observed, "Any alliance with any political power whatsoever is bound to be burdensome for religion. It does not need their support to live, in serving them it may die."[1]

Clearly, this is only a sketch of the parameters of one view of the relationship of church and state, and each of the above features is worthy of its own fuller discussion. However, these features should suffice for present purposes to examine the controversies and conflicts that arise between church and state in the context of the provision of medical care. My account is most heavily indebted to the ecclesiology developed by legal scholar Stephen Carter as presented in *The Culture of Disbelief*.[2] Carter offers a middle ground between the "exclusion" of religion from public discourse (a feature he finds increasingly prevalent in the civic culture of the United States) and a dominance of civic culture by one particularistic religious worldview, which fails to ensure a realm of the political-legal immune from religious authority and may neglect to protect the liberty rights of religious (and other) minorities.

By contrast, Carter presents an alternative understanding of the role of religious communities that he maintains avoids both the extremes of exclusion or theocracy. In a democratic society, religions "can serve [first] as the sources of moral understanding without which any majoritarian system can deteriorate into simple tyranny, and second, they can mediate between the citizens and the apparatus of government, providing an independent moral voice."[3] The central characteristic of "moral understanding" that Carter attributes to religions in a democratic society is "the power of resistance," that is, the affirmation of moral values that deny ultimate authority to dominant social institutions, including the state. This characteristic of resistance entails that religious communities function as a social check on the power of government and seek to keep the state "honest" according to its own political values.

In addition, Carter does not frame the primary moral relationship as that between the individual and the state (or put more cynically, between anarchy and tyranny). Rather, the self is embedded in various intermediate or mediating communities, such as family and religious tradition, which issue the set of primary moral responsibilities for the person. These mediating relationships provide access for the religious adherent to personal and collective sources of meaning and purpose, an especially vital role given that the liberal state has declared itself agnostic on such matters.

In this account, then, a religious community must, at times, say "no" or resist the state on vital matters of meaning and purpose, including decisions about life and death in medical care. At the same time, religious communities, as intermediate institutions, renounce pretensions to political authority and power. Whether and how this "no" or power of resistance and this renunciation of power can be accommodated by religious communities and the state when life is at stake is a matter best exemplified by concrete examples in medical ethics. I will begin with conflicts presented by decisions presumptively protected by exercise of the Free Exercise Clause of the First Amendment, and then turn to circumstances in which religious teaching on medical ethics is perceived to present a risk of sanctioning an establishmentarian model.

THE FREE EXERCISE OF RELIGION: REFUSAL OF TREATMENT FOR THE SERIOUSLY ILL CHILD

Some of the most intractable conflicts between state-sanctioned exercise of religious freedom and the state interests in preserving life and ensuring due process for vulnerable persons occur in cases involving children. In some circumstances, a child might be born dying and parents, based on religious commitments to the sanctity of life, may wish for treatment continuation even if it provides negligible medical benefit, or may even be harmful from a medical perspective. The contrary situation holds when parents appeal to religious grounds to refuse treatment for a seriously ill child who could benefit from treatment, but who will likely die without treatment. A variation on this latter circumstance transpires when parents appeal to religion as grounds for conscientious objection to vaccination of their healthy child, thus potentially exposing both the child and the larger community to the risk of infection. I will first consider examples in which the state presumption in favor of protecting and respecting religious liberty is challenged because of parental refusal of treatment for a seriously ill but medically treatable child.

Perhaps the most publicized of such situations are those involving treatment refusals, and when legally allowed, vaccination refusals by Christian Science parents. Christian Science teaching does not deny the biological reality of disease, but it does hold that disease is but a symptom of a deeper spiritual estrangement from God. Christian Scientists maintain that it is not possible to combine medical treatment and the ministry of spiritual healing; at the same time, they differentiate their methods from "faith healing." Thus, when a child is seriously ill, recourse to medical "treatment" is deemed less efficacious than "spiritual healing" through prayer, moral regeneration, and ministry by Christian Science practitioners.[4] According to one bioethical analysis, there are approximate five thousand Christian Scientist spiritual healers, and their fees are reimbursable through some insurance programs and some state and federal programs.[5]

Treatment refusals by parents for their children do arise in other faith communities that affirm beliefs in "faith healing." For example, an evangelical church in Oregon City, Oregon, relies on faith healing when a child in the community becomes seriously ill. Adherents of the Followers of Christ Church cite authorization for faith healing from New Testament passages that promise believers recovery from disease through practices of "a prayer of faith" and "laying on of hands." Yet the Followers have become nationally known because, biblical passages notwithstanding, an estimated 25 children in the community have died from medically treatable illnesses in the past half-century.[6] Nationwide, a study in *Pediatrics* documented 172 deaths of children in faith-healing communities between 1975 and 1995; 140 of the children died from conditions in which there is a success rate from medical treatment of over 90 percent. The authors of the study believe, moreover, that their fatality figures are substantially under-reported.[7]

A final illustration of religious freedom invoked by parents to refuse medical treatment that can endanger their children involves the Jehovah Witness tradition of refusing blood transfusions. Unlike the faith or spiritual healing traditions described above, this tradition accepts many procedures of modern medicine. However, the tradition affirms a prohibition on eating or consumption of "blood" that is derived from biblical passages in both the Hebrew Bible and the Christian New Testament. When applied to modern medicine, such as in surgical procedures, this prohibition means Jehovah Witnesses are forbidden by God from "nourishing of the human body with blood transfusions."[8] This applies to all adherents of the tradition, whether or not they have reached an age of decision-making capacity by which they could affirm their own beliefs in the tradition.

These claims for extensive religious liberty have been facilitated by a federal requirement initiated in 1974 that states provide for religious exemptions to child abuse and neglect charges. While the requirement was rescinded in 1983, laws in some 40 states permit parents to claim a religious exemption from statutes prohibiting child neglect or abuse so long as the parents appeal to religious reasons or faith healing as a basis for opposing medical treatment of ill children.[9] The repeal of such laws has been an ongoing preoccupation of organizations such as the American Academy of Pediatrics (AAP) for the past two decades. The AAP and its Committee on Bioethics has argued that "constitutional guarantees of freedom of religion do not permit children to be harmed through religious practices, nor do they allow religion to be a valid legal defense when an individual harms or neglects a child."[10] Moreover, the Committee has affirmed that as important as family and public education can be, as a last resort, pediatric physicians who encounter parents who make a decision to deny their child necessary medical care should seek court authorization to disqualify the parents. In addition, parents who make such decisions should not be immune from civil or criminal statutes of neglect or abuse.

Religious-based refusals of treatment by parents for seriously ill, medically treatable children (rather than by seriously ill children) are complicated by a collision of important state interests. These include the general presumptions of respect for parental authority and responsibility for the welfare of their children, the protection of religious liberty, the protection of vulnerable persons from harm (often phrased in this context as not permitting parents to make "martyrs" of their children), and the lack of legally acknowledged decision-making capacity by the children themselves. In a 1944 case, *Prince v. Massachusetts,* which concerned the constitutional protections of Jehovah Witness parents in having their minor children sell religious literature contrary to child labor laws, the U.S. Supreme Court addressed many of these conflicting claims: "The right to practice religion freely does not include the liberty to expose the community or child to communicable disease, or the latter to ill health or death . . . Parents may be free to make martyrs of themselves. But it does not follow [that] they are free, in identical circumstances, to make martyrs of their children before they have reached the age of full and legal discretion when they can make that choice for themselves."[11]

The key distinction in this argument is not about the validity of the content of religious claims to spiritual or faith healing, but rather whether the person is of such an age as to avow or disavow the religious beliefs as his or her own. Thus, the presumption in favor of respecting religious liberty can legitimately be overridden when the person is too young to make a meaningful commitment to the religious values of the community.

In some circumstances, it may be possible for the state to accommodate and not infringe on religious freedom while seeking to ensure appropriate medical care for the child. In some cases involving Jehovah Witness children, the child may not be suffering from a life-threatening condition, or it may be possible for non-blood products, which do not violate the Witness prohibition, to be used in treatment. Both Jehovah Witnesses and Christian Scientists also have cultivated hospital liaison staffs to educate professional caregivers about the beliefs of the tradition. If none of these alternatives are accessible or beneficial and a court order authorizing treatment or transfusion is sought, Martin Smith argues that the parents' religious beliefs can still be respected through informing the parents of this decision before the medical procedure is performed.[12]

Both substantive questions about what should be decided and procedural questions about who should decide are implicated in this church-state conflict. States have accommodated parental treatment refusals for their minor children through passage of religious exemption laws. Moreover, society continues to evolve in the direction of tolerating and accepting "alternative" medicine as potentially therapeutic and it is striking, for example, that a prominent bioethics publication has presented Christian Science under the category of "alternative medicine."[13] If such a pattern persists, it will be increasingly difficult to draw a line and justify why religious resistance to treatment for children in favor of an alternative mode of healing is a socially illegitimate and legally intolerable practice.

THE FREE EXERCISE OF RELIGION: PARENTAL REQUESTS FOR FUTILE TREATMENT FOR THE DYING CHILD

The converse of the situations previously described is that in some circumstances, religious belief and an appeal to religious liberty may be invoked by parents to request medical treatment that seems futile in terms of survival of the child. A representative example of this conflict is the situation of Baby K, a child who was born with anencephaly in October 1992. At birth, Baby K had difficulty breathing and mechanical ventilation was provided in order to provide the treating physicians a chance to confirm the diagnosis and to give the mother, Ms. H., time to understand the diagnosis and prognosis. After diagnostic confirmation, medical staff informed Ms. H that they anticipated Baby K to die within a few days, as is customary with infants diagnosed with anencephaly, and recommended the withdrawal of mechanical ventilation and that Baby K be provided with supportive and comfort care only. Given the prognosis, continuation of respiratory support served no therapeutic or palliative purpose.

Ms. H refused both a recommendation of abortion upon prenatal diagnosis of anencephaly as well as the discontinuation of mechanical ventilation on religious grounds: she was reported to have a faith conviction that "all human life has value, including her anencephalic daughter's life." Furthermore, the mother held a "firm Christian faith . . . [and] believes that God will work a miracle if that is his will . . . God, and not other humans, should decide the moment of her daughter's death."[14]

Surprisingly, Baby K continued to live and was subsequently transferred to a nursing home. She was readmitted three times to the hospital to stabilize her respiration; after the second re-admission, the treating hospital brought a court case contending that health care personnel and institutions should not be required to render what they considered "medically and ethically inappropriate treatment" or treatment "outside the prevailing standard of medical care." The Fourth Circuit Court found that the Emergency Medical Treatment and Active Labor Act mandated providing stabilizing treatment to a person with an emergency medical condition, and thus a duty to provide respiratory support when Baby K was admitted with breathing difficulties.[15]

Baby K continued to receive occasional respiratory stabilization until her death in 1995, living a life span of exceptional duration for an infant with a diagnosis of anencephaly. In the Baby K case, the issue before the courts was not the legitimacy of the religious beliefs of her mother, but rather the obligations of caregivers. The case itself does not reflect a full church-state conflict, although the legal process does reveal how significant the presumption in favor of religious liberty can be when invoked to *prolong* life. However, is this presumption so compelling that it can require health care professionals to practice medicine in what they believe to be an unprofessional manner, at the risk of compromising their professional and personal integrity and values? Coupling the Baby K case with that of a seriously ill adult with impaired decision-making capacity can illuminate the scope of religious liberty when it conflicts with the integrity of medicine.

THE FREE EXERCISE OF RELIGION: RELIGIOUS REQUESTS AND PROFESSIONAL INTEGRITY

Helga Wanglie was a married elderly woman of eighty-six years when she was admitted to a hospital in Minnesota subsequent to respiratory failure. She was placed on a respirator for over five months before she experienced a cardiopulmonary arrest; her physicians believed she had suffered severe and irreversible brain damage. Repeated medical evaluations confirmed a diagnosis of persistent vegetative state or permanent unconsciousness and permanent respirator dependency because of chronic lung disease.

Although hospital staff believed Ms. Wanglie's prognosis for any recovery in these circumstances to be negligible and recommended to her family limiting or withdrawing life-sustaining treatment, the family refused and instead requested continuation of all forms of treatment, including life support. The family's refusal was attributed to religious values: "Mr. Wanglie has said that only God can take life and that doctors should not play God."[16] Or, as stated by the hospital's ethics consultant, familial objections to discontinuation of treatment reflected a view that "Physicians should not play God, that the patient would not be better off dead, that removing her life support showed moral decay in our civilization, and that a miracle could occur."[17]

After several months of continued treatment and mediated consultation between treating staff and the family, the attending physicians reached the conclusion that continued respirator support would not be in Ms. Wanglie's benefit; that is, to provide such treatment would violate the medical commitment to the principle of beneficence. As articulated by the medical director of the hospital in a letter to the family, life support is "no longer serving the patient's medical interest. We do not believe that the hospital is obliged to provide inappropriate medical treatment that cannot advance a patient's personal interest."[18] The hospital subsequently filed a petition in district court to disqualify Mr. Wanglie as the proxy decision-maker and have a court appointed guardian make a determination about continuation of treatment. The court rejected this petition.[19]

The central church-state concern in the Wanglie case, much as it was in the case of Baby K, is the extent to which the state presumption in protecting freedom of religion can sanction requests of physicians to provide treatment that, in the assessment of the physician and other health care professionals, provides no medical benefit to the patient. In such conflicts, the state clearly has additional concerns besides those of preserving religious liberty. This includes a (rebuttable) presumption in favor of the family as qualified proxies for the patient, and an interest in ensuring that patients are not abandoned by a health care institution or its physicians. Of no less importance, however, the state must ensure that medical professionals are not requested to act in an unprofessional manner. Physicians, as agents and stewards for an important social institution, should be protected from requests that they violate the principle of beneficence by providing treatment that does not provide medical benefits to the patient (although it may not cause any harms, either). The societal commitment to religious liberty should not be allowed to override respect for the autonomy, professional judgment, and integrity of professional caregivers.

It is also important to examine the reported arguments of the Wanglie family for continued treatment, because even though they were presented as appeals protected by religious liberty, closer scrutiny reveals that they actually offer an evaluation of various social roles that can be assessed on non-religious grounds. The claim that "physicians should not play God" does not provide a religious mandate for continued treatment; it rather is a claim about the social status of the medical profession, one that inevitably includes misjudgments attributable to finiteness and fallibility. The claim that Ms. Wangle "would not be better off dead" could be interpreted as a religious claim about the sanctity of life, but it also is plausibly an appeal to patient welfare—an appeal disputed by the physicians, but not necessarily one protected by religious liberty. The argument that non-treatment of Ms. Wanglie is symptomatic of moral decline in society is an observation, one that is presumably subject to empirical testing, rather than a statement of religious revelation (even though it would be compatible with the social assessments of many conservative religious traditions). Finally, the language of "miracle" does invoke a hope for divine intervention; in contrast to the other appeals reflecting familial concerns about physician integrity, patient welfare, and social decline, this appeal does require a specific religious commitment. It is, however, no less a claim about the relation of history and scientific medicine; that is, that scientific diagnosis and prognosis presumes a form of closing of history to the unexpected, in contrast to an "open" account of history that may be more compatible with certain religious beliefs. My intent is not to dispute a genuine claim to freedom of religion that may ground requests for, as well as denials of, medical treatment, but rather to ensure that moral analysis distinguishes between religious and non-religious argumentation.

Society does have a method for accommodating conflicts between what appear to be irreconcilable claims of patient (or proxy) requests and professional integrity: when a patient makes a request for a treatment or procedure that would violate the moral values of the professional (or the mission of the institution), the professional can object on grounds of conscience and refuse participation. This recognized form of accommodation is typically accompanied with a requirement to transfer the care of the patient to another provider for whom the request does not present such conflicts. This process respects patient autonomy without subjecting the objecting physician to a charge of abandonment. However, in neither the Baby K or the Wanglie case did the participating physicians invoke a right to conscientious refusal; the familial request for continued treatment was viewed not as an infringement on personal conscience, but rather as a violation of a defining principle of the profession as a whole, that of beneficence. There were, nonetheless, unsuccessful efforts in both cases to transfer the patients to other care settings for the required respirator support.

Physicians should not in any event be compelled to participate in unprofessional medical procedures out of regard for the religious liberty of patients. Conversely, religious liberty can give to patients in their religious communities a similar right of conscientious objection to medical policies deemed morally oppressive, as the following example illustrates.

THE FREE EXERCISE OF RELIGION: EXEMPTION FROM BRAIN DEATH

Since the late 1960s, which witnessed technological developments in life prolongation and life-extension such as organ transplants, the United States has undergone a transformation in the standards for defining death. A brain-oriented standard has emerged to supplement, or in cases of organ transplantation, supplant a more traditional standard that relied on vital fluids such as blood circulation and respiration. In 1981, the President's Commission recommended the adoption of the Uniform Determination of Death Act by all jurisdictions in the nation: "An individual who has sustained either (1) irreversible cessation of circulatory and respiratory functions, or (2) irreversible cessation of all functions of the entire brain, including the brain stem, is dead. A determination of death must be made in accordance with accepted medical standards."[20]

In making this recommendation, the Commission was explicit in attributing diminished significance to ongoing respiration and circulation, especially as such functions can be maintained mechanically even with the irreversible loss of brain function. The brain is identified as the organ that provides for a complex and integrated wholeness of the human biological organism; hence, "breathing and circulation are not in themselves tantamount to life," but rather are "surrogate signs" for the presence or irreversible cessation of brain functioning."[21]

While social and legal movement to a brain-oriented definition of death has facilitated medical decision-making about termination of treatment or of organ transplantation, the fact that an individual could be declared dead either by vital signs or by brain criteria has been objectionable to certain religious traditions who do not equate life and death with integrative brain functioning in the way the President's Commission and the UDDA do. For members of such traditions, a person could be declared legally dead by whole brain criteria even though, by the values of their tradition, they were still a living person.

In writing about pluralism in the standards for death, medical ethicist Robert M. Veatch maintains: "the constitutional issue of separation of church and state presses us in the direction of accepting definitions [of death] with religious groundings."[22] The most salient state accommodation to religious resistance to a brain death standard is illustrated in the New Jersey Declaration of Death Act enacted in 1991. In the language of the act, a declaration of death should not "violate the personal religious beliefs of the individual."[23]

As articulated by Robert Olick, "the Act recognizes a religious exemption (a conscience clause) designed to respect the personal religious beliefs of those who do not accept neurological criteria for the determination of death . . ."[24] The "personal" religious beliefs acknowledged by the New Jersey Act pertain primarily to those held within Orthodox Judaism, and among some Asian Americans and Native American cultures. In the following, I will focus on the religious exemption as it pertains to Orthodox Jewish concerns with a brain death standard.

As articulated by Orthodox Jewish scholars J. David Bleich and Fred Rosner, death in Jewish tradition occurs upon the separation of the soul from the body. Both scholars recognize, however, that dis-ensoulment is not a phenomenon subject to empirical testing and confirmation. It is nonetheless significant in that it suggests a more complex metaphysical reality to death than envisioned by the President's Commission.

Bleich contends that the definition of death is not a medical or scientific problem but one pertaining to theological and moral values, and that Jewish law (Halakhah) must be governing for the Jewish physician and patient "whether or not these determinations coincide with the mores of contemporary society."[25] Thus, the states commitment to respect and secure free exercise of religion permits Orthodox Jews to say "no" to the statutory criteria for death. For Bleich, "Brain death and irreversible coma are not acceptable definitions of death insofar as Halakhah is concerned. The sole criterion of death accepted by Halakhah is total cessation of both cardiac and respiratory activity."[26]

Rosner's analysis of biblical and Talmudic passages indicates why circulation and respiration are of such significance within Orthodox Jewish teaching. A passage from the Talmud indicates that "life manifests itself primarily through the nose as it is written: *In whose nostrils was the breath of the spirit of life* (Genesis 7:22)."[27] This interpretation suggests respiration and breath is the essence of life. Rosner affirms that the irreversible cessation of respiration is "the classic definition of death in Judaism," for "the soul departs through the nostrils at death, just as it is in the nostrils into which the Lord blows the soul of life at birth (Genesis 2:6)."[28] Nonetheless, rabbinic commentary on the same passage in some cases reveals that cessation of respiration was itself a "sign" of "prior cessation of circulation of blood from cardiac activity." Moreover, Rosner contends that other Talmudic sources can render a conclusion compatible with a whole brain standard of death. This itself is a compelling illustration of how diversity and pluralism can be discerned within a religious tradition, but at bottom, there is a traditional religious ground within Orthodox Judaism for resisting social redefinitions of death to encompass a brain-oriented standard.

The state-synagogue question in this regard then turns on whether the state—which has an interest in uniformity in legal statute, particularly because so much turns on a declaration of death (insurance, inheritance, disposition of the body, transplantation, communal rituals, etc.)—can compel (that is, infringe on religious liberty) an individual or community to accept a standard for their own death that is contrary to their religious and moral values. The New Jersey Declaration of Death Act, which is the only one of its kind in the country, holds that "the societal need for uniformity should yield to and accommodate the personal interests of a distinct minority of the population in the exercise of their religious beliefs."[29] This is interpreted as a claim of "conscience," because the individual who utilizes the exemption is not making a generalizable claim about the standard of death that everyone ought to subscribe to, but rather advances a dissent from the majority based on their personal religious convictions.

Unlike religious exercise of what Carter refers to as the "power of resistance" against medical treatment for ill children who may be endangered by treatment refusal against or without knowledge of their will, the accommodation of the state to religious liberty in the case of dissent from a brain death standard does not pose a risk of involuntary premature death to anyone. The New Jersey religious exemption then seems less difficult to justify than religious exemptions for faith healing as a defense against child neglect or abuse. It is, of course, not without its own internal problems. For example, as has been the case with conscientious objection to conscription into the military historically, it may prove hard for the state to hold firmly to "religious" grounds for the exemption; at some point, debate may ensue about the legitimacy of an exemption for beliefs that are the moral or philosophical equivalent of a religious conviction. Moreover, if that deeply-held moral or philosophical position is one that adheres to not simply whole brain death, but a higher brain or neocortical standard of death, what began as a narrow legal exemption will have culminated in undermining the regulatory act.

THE FREE EXERCISE OF RELIGION: CONSTRAINTS ON TREATMENT REFUSALS BY ADULTS

The status of patient rights by competent adults to refuse treatment has evolved significantly in the past quarter century. In contemporary medical ethics, competent adult patients are recognized to possess a right to refuse any medical treatment, even if in some circumstances such a refusal will eventuate in death. The rationale for such a refusal, be it religious or non-religious, is itself not grounds for denial of the right or paternalistic coercion by the state.

Prior to this contemporary consensus, refusals of blood transfusions by adult Jehovah Witnesses in the 1960s–1980s became paradigmatic cases of the conflicts between church and state and between liberty and paternalism. Most frequently, a refusal of a transfusion on religious grounds was sufficient to raise questions about the believer's rational decision-making capacities. A classic illustration was a case litigated by Georgetown University Hospital in 1964, in which the health care providers sought a court order to authorize a transfusion of a seriously ill female Witness in order to save her life following a ruptured ulcer. The husband refused to authorize the transfusion, but indicated that he would not be responsible should the court order a transfusion. The wife was in such a dire physical condition that her competency was questionable, but the intervening judge interpreted her words to mean that she also would not experience responsibility should a transfusion be ordered by the court. It appears that state infringement on religious liberty in this case not only saved the life of the woman, but also allowed both the husband and wife, even though they refused to authorize a transfusion, to live with a clear conscience, as well as preserving the integrity of medicine.[30]

While this infringement was accomplished because of the disavowal of responsibility for the transfusion by the patient and her husband, other objections have been raised regarding treatment refusals by competent adults on religious grounds. One such objection, alluded to above, is that an appeal to religious directives when it appears the consequence of professional acquiescence in the appeal will be patient death concerns constraints internal to the decision-making process of patients. The state has an interest in ensuring the voluntary, informed consent of patients to treatment and in refusals of treatment. Yet ethicist Margaret Battin argues in an analysis of "high-risk religion," including refusals of treatment by Jehovah Witnesses, as well as Christian Scientists and some faith healing denominations, that such refusals are permeated by coercion and manipulation, which undermines the conditions for voluntary choice, and by incomplete, partial, or misleading information, which undermines the basis for informed choices.

However, Battin does not find grounds in the case of refusals by Jehovah Witnesses for attributing "coercion, deception, or impairment of the individual's reasoning processes."[31] Instead, Battin finds the Witness tradition to engage in "risk encouragement by a reevaluation of outcomes,"[32] that is, the choice presented to the Witness in the context of a transfusion refusal is not the choice seen by the professional or society of life or death, but rather that of something much more momentous, between personal salvation and damnation. This provides stronger grounds for the state to accommodate such refusals under the auspices of the protection of religious liberty. Nonetheless, Battin's analysis means the presumption of respecting religious liberty is rebuttable even in circumstances of treatment decisions by apparently competent adults. At a minimum, patient refusals of treatment on religious grounds in circumstances when treatment provision will likely restore health and prolong life should not be accepted without inquiry into the background conditions of the choice.

A second ground for caution and further inquiry on treatment refusals by adults concerns not the constraints internal to a person's decision-making processes, but rather the risks of harm to an identified person with whom the patient has a significant relationship. It is a morally and legally significant feature of the Georgetown case that the woman was the mother of a seven-month-old child. The state's interest in protecting vulnerable persons from harm, neglect, or abuse becomes very complicated in such situations because there are at least two vulnerable persons—in the Georgetown case, the reversibly dying mother and her child, who can be raised by others, of course, including the husband, but will live without the nurturance of her biological mother. In the intervening years, numerous cases have been adjudicated in which a refusal of a transfusion has implications for an already vulnerable person, with some courts intervening to preserve life while others have supported the patient's refusal. Smith observes currently that there is "neither a consistent ethical nor legal consensus" for transfusion refusals that bear on the interests of vulnerable third parties.[33]

Persons with religious convictions should not be held to a higher standard of scrutiny when they refuse treatment than persons who refuse treatment on secular grounds. However, it may be that part of what it means for a religious community to function as an intermediary between the liberal state and the believer is to assume responsibilities for the provision of medical care in situations similar to those described above. It is noteworthy in this regard that the Jehovah Witness tradition has established hospital liaison committees to provide information and consultation for both providers and religious practitioners in circumstances of conflict between medical and religious best interests; the committees can also identify physicians, including surgeons and anesthesiologists, and health care institutions that will provide medical care in accord with Witness convictions. The state's attempt to accommodate both religious liberty and third-party considerations can, nonetheless, lead to polarizing cultural politics, as reflected most recently in the Terry Schiavo case.

LIBERTY OR PRIVACY?: RELIGIONS AND THE PROBLEM OF FEEDING TUBES

The national controversy engendered by the 2005 case of Terry Schiavo came as a surprise to many in academic medical ethics. The large questions about the legal and ethical permissibility of refusing or withdrawing feeding tubes were considered generally resolved by the 1990 decision of the U.S. Supreme Court in its *Cruzan* ruling.[34] That decision categorized the provision of nutrition and hydration through tube feedings as "medical treatment," and this allowed patients (or their proxies) to legitimately refuse or withdraw them as part of a patient's right to refuse medical care and to freedom from unwanted bodily invasion. The Court did allow for states to establish a "clear and convincing" evidentiary standard to ensure that such a decision was consistent with patient autonomy and values.

However much the *Cruzan* decision may have resolved the legal, ethical, and academic controversies about the extent of patient rights to refuse medical treatment, the verdict was the subject of protests by religious conservatives. The feeding tube issue has remained a vexing question for many religious communities and their adherents over the past two decades. While for some religions a decision to remove feeding tubes is compatible with and protected by religious liberty, for others, it is a symbol of moral decline in medicine and society and possibly grounds for activism in the political and legal sphere. Three general kinds of arguments have been offered in religious reflection and ecclesiastical teaching in opposition to feeding tube removal.

A first argument disputes the classification of nutrients delivered by feeding tubes as "medical treatment." Instead, the provision of food and fluids to a seriously ill or impaired patient is held to be part of the essential comfort care that is obligatory to provide to any member of the human community. Legal permission to remove or refuse feeding tubes thereby symbolizes callousness rather than caring and undermines commitment to a foundational value, that of the sanctity of human life.

A second argument contends that the central mistake in the feeding tube issue is not conceptual but moral. Withdrawal or refusal of feeding tubes will with certainty bring on death. Thus, the moral intent behind such a treatment decision cannot be portrayed as one of "allowing the patient to die" from an underlying natural pathology, but rather as "intentionally hastening death," and perhaps even "aiming to kill."[35] That intent makes a decision to refuse feeding tubes morally indistinguishable from euthanasia and crosses a moral and legal line that should not be disturbed.

A third argument is that social acceptance of feeding tube removal displays and perpetuates continued diminishment of respect for the value of life. Society is deemed to be at a tipping point between what the late Pope John Paul II referred to as "the struggle between the 'culture of life' and the 'culture of death.'"[36] Removal of feeding tubes, in some accounts, opens the door more widely to social acceptance of hastening death immorally through physician assistance in suicide and physician-administered euthanasia. This anticipated outcome is stated succinctly by conservative Christian ethicist Gary E. Crum, "Withholding food and water leaves no hope. A genuine 'slippery slope' ethical argument develops that says that this practice will lead to the next step of legally sanctioned, active euthanasia... Since death is assured anyway, the impetus for just giving the patient an overdose of drugs becomes almost overpowering."[37]

The Roman Catholic tradition in which Terry Schiavo was raised, and to which her parents continue their adherence, has for decades used the categories of "extraordinary" and "ordinary" in addressing medical treatment decisions. Based on criteria of burden and proportionate benefit, extraordinary treatments refer to those that are optional morally, while ordinary treatments refer to those that are morally obligatory. Applying these categories, many, although not all, Roman Catholic moralists have argued that feeding tubes could be considered extraordinary treatments in certain circumstances and therefore refused or withdrawn by Catholic patients.[38]

This seemed to be the "consensus" within Roman Catholic bioethical teaching until an "allocution" or address by John Paul II in March 2004 on "Care for Persons in a Permanent Vegetative State." A person in a vegetative state, the Pope claimed, retains the "right to basic health care," or "minimal care," which includes nutrition and hydration, in addition to comfort for hygiene and warmth. Moreover, the papal allocution concluded that "the administration of water and food, even when provided by artificial means, always represents a natural means of preserving life, not a medical act." The use of feeding tubes was therefore morally assessed as "in principle, ordinary and proportionate, and as such morally obligatory;" cessation of such care, when done knowingly and willingly, constitutes "euthanasia by omission."[39]

Given the prior "consensus," moral theologians Shannon and Walters anticipated "monumental implications for the relationship between church and state" were the papal allocution to be strictly interpreted and applied by Roman Catholics in their health care decision-making and in Catholic health care facilities. Despite prior court holdings,[40] that prediction was quickly realized when the parents of Terry Schiavo argued that the papal allocution created "new circumstances" that required the Florida courts to reconsider their previous authorizations of feeding tube removal from their daughter. Indeed, they maintained that, contrary to prior holdings of the courts, in view of the papal interpretation of the religious values to guide Catholics in end-of-life decision-making, their daughter would not have wanted the feeding tubes removed.

This argument, put forward in good conscience as a statement of personal belief by the Schindler family, was then employed publicly by a variety of conservative Catholic and Protestant advocates for life, as well as leading political figures in the federal government, to claim that the fundamental rights of Terry Schiavo, including the right to life, as well as the religious liberty of her parents, were being denied by the judiciary of the state. To others, however, the political involvement of religious-based advocates (not to mention the unprecedented intervention of the Congress and White House in the case) reflected an attempt to enshrine religious values into law. As physician Eric Cassell observed, "Fundamentalist religions expect personal relationships and professional activities to accord with their religious principles and values. As these religions in the United States have extended their political influence, their principles have come into conflict with the values of privacy and individual liberty, as in the case of Terry Schiavo."[41]

In this regard, the question of the ethics of providing or withdrawing feeding tubes may become the cultural equivalent at the end of life what the question of abortion is at the beginnings of life. Arguments for the state interest in protecting and respecting religious liberty seem to elide readily into occasions for questioning or dismantling the separation of church and state. It is not a surprise that the central values that Cassell invokes as moral and legal protections for Terry Schiavo from religious fundamentalism—privacy and liberty—are precisely the same values invoked to protect a woman's right to abortion; ironically, they are no less invoked to protect religious practices from state intervention. It is striking, moreover, that Cassell's critique echoes the observation of de Tocqueville that the moral influence religions can have is vital to a democratic society, but what Cassell refers to as the "political influence" of religions may compromise values the religious traditions embody and endorse. The extent of political accommodation for religious claims with respect to law can be illuminated through some further examples in medical ethics.

PROCESS AND JUSTIFICATION: RELIGIOUS APPEALS IN PHYSICIAN-ASSISTED SUICIDE

The free exercise of religion guaranteed by the state permits substantial personal autonomy in belief and practice (including the right not to believe or practice), as well as the freedom of religions to develop and enact ecclesiastical standards without intervention by the state. Religious communities function as intermediate associations interposed between the self and the liberal state that embody moral understanding and wisdom to serve as personal, communal, and even societal resources for resistance and for meaning. Yet because the matters at the core of religious practice, ritual, and liturgy—including the meanings of birth, life, sexuality, and death—involve the most profound and intimate of human experiences, there may arise occasions in which the influence of religious values assume a mantle of authority such that, for some adherents, the values should be enshrined in law. While demanding state protection of religious liberty, religious communities or traditions are not immune from voicing arguments or appeals to audiences broader than their ecclesiastical walls, whether to adherents of other faith traditions, or to citizens and/or civic authorities of the state to change or revise laws in conformity with the moral teaching of the religious tradition. These arguments demand careful scrutiny, as some appeals can be accommodated while others should not be.

In 1994, citizens in Oregon were confronted with a unique opportunity for social reform. Through the state's initiative process, Ballot Measure 16, known as "The Death with Dignity Act," was placed before voters for approval or rejection. The unique feature of the Act was that it permitted physicians to prescribe a lethal medication for terminally ill patients that could be self-administered in order that the patient could experience what was described as a "humane and dignified death." In more commonly used language, citizens were participating in a binding referendum on "physician assistance in suicide."

The public campaign to persuade citizens of the necessity of the act relied on medical, political, and occasionally, ethical argumentation, but one of the more memorable features of the campaign was the treatment of religious values and discourse. Oregon is demographically the "least-churched" state in the country, with approximately 30 percent of the state's residents claiming affiliation with a religious denomination. Thus, religious life is rather peripheral to the civic ethos of the state, in contrast to other states. Nonetheless, proponents of the act commonly argued that the only ground for opposition to its passage would be based on religious values, such as a commitment to the sanctity of life, or opposition to freedom of choice about options in dying. However, religiously based opposition was portrayed as coercive and as authoritarian in civic life, as "imposing" values on the citizenry without or against their consent. State legislators who considered proposing revisions to the act were targeted by electoral ads reminding voters of the repercussions of "imposing religious beliefs on citizens." In general, those opposed to passage of the act were described as "held hostage" by the "raw political power" of religious organizations.[42]

The implication of this perspective on religion was that religious discourse might be all well and good for adherents within the confines of ecclesiastical settings, but that it should be excluded from having a voice in the public square. And by and large, the civic exclusion of religion was the prevailing parameter for discussion in public education forums, community meetings, and even public debates. The culmination of this view was displayed in litigation subsequent to the passage of the act, when the Ninth Circuit Court, in overturning a Washington state statute prohibiting physician assistance in suicide, came to the following conclusion in its majority opinion: "Those who believe strongly that death must come without physician assistance are free to follow that creed . . . They are not free, however, to force their views, their religious convictions, or their philosophies, on all the other members of a democratic society, and to compel those whose values differ from theirs to die painful, protracted, and agonizing deaths."[43]

The language of the majority comes rhetorically close to suggesting that all opposition to physician assistance in suicide has a religious character, or must be ground in religious values; that is, such opposition is part of a "creed." Empirically, this is clearly fallacious. Constitutionally, however, the majority endorses the civic exclusion of religion in its finding that to express a religious objection on the matter constitutes "force" or "compulsion." The concluding clause raises the specter of religious tyranny, even inquisitorial methods, for the majority portrays those persons who affirm a different set of values as experiencing a brutal and undignified death.

This seems to get the balance a democratic society should want between protecting religious liberty and avoiding establishing religion as a basis for law entirely wrong. No argument was made in public discourse over either the Oregon Death with Dignity Act or the disputed Washington statute that the justification for law in end-of-life decisions should assume religious grounding or be determined by a "creed." However, if the question is not about the basis or justification for law, then it seems respect for religious liberty should allow for more than just individuals "following" their own personal life plans or enacting their own concepts of a good death. Religious values, no less than professional positions, or ethical principles, should have a voice in democratic discourse in the public square and in the process that leads to the formulation of policy or citizen referendums. Religious positions should be tested in the forums of democratic deliberations for persuasiveness, reasonability, tolerance, and coherence. Some positions may not meet those tests, but to contend as the Circuit Court did that such positions are not expressible in public discourse without subjecting an audience of citizens to "force" and "compulsion" is a draconian violation of the state's responsibility to protect freedom of religion. It seems therefore necessary to distinguish reasoning in public processes from reasoning for public justification.

THE LIMITS OF ACCOMMODATING RELIGION: MORAL AND CIVIL LAW

In circumstances when public justification is at issue, and where religious argumentation is directly addressed to civil or political authorities with the intent to revise or propose a law based on particularistic religious beliefs, religious appeals have overreached the limits of the state's interests in accommodating religious liberty. This happened to some extent in the *Schiavo* situation. Here, I wish to examine illustrations that reflect much more careful thought than was demonstrated by right-to-life activists in Florida.

Roman Catholicism, the largest of U.S. denominations, has articulated prohibitions on numerous practices—contraception, abortion, infertility procedures such as in vitro fertilization and surrogacy, and research on embryos and embryonic stem cells—that are categorized in secular bioethics as matters of "reproductive rights" and "scientific freedom." Moreover, the Catholic tradition has sought to cultivate a "seamless" culture of life in opposition to the "culture of death." It has thus rejected physician assistance in dying and euthanasia (as well as other non-medical social practices like capital punishment and warfare).

In advancing and defending these bioethical prohibitions, the Catholic tradition is exercising its power of refusal to endorse or participate in medical practices it deems contrary to central values of the tradition. In many cases, Catholic teaching is addressed to an audience broader than its congregants, namely, "persons of good will" that include citizens, policymakers, and civic authorities in secular society. I will focus on two important Catholic documents on bioethical issues, the 1987 Vatican teachings in *Donum Vitae*, The Gift of Life: Instruction on Respect for Human Life in Its Origin and the Dignity of Procreation[44] and the 1994 papal encyclical *Evangelium Vitae* (The Gospel of Life),[45] to illustrate some church-state tensions when the scope for the tradition's teaching is extended broadly to civic society.

Donum Vitae presents theological analyses and moral assessments of an array of beginning of life medical technologies within the context of Catholic moral theology about the respect and dignity of human life and of procreation. The principles used in moral assessment of the technologies are derived from "divine law" and the "natural moral law." These complementary sources mean the basic norms are knowable through both revelation and reason, by both believer and non-believer. *Donum Vitae* refers to the natural moral law, for example, as "the rational moral order whereby man is called by the Creator to direct and regulate his life and actions and in particular make use of his own body."[46] The appeal to reason in this context means the moral teachings are not limited to those who affirm the particular theological beliefs of the Catholic tradition but encompass all persons capable of rationality. Through appeal to the norms of the moral law, and a rational method of moral reasoning, *Donum Vitae* argues, for example, that the creation of extra embryos through IVF or judgments of embryo worth through prenatal diagnosis offends the dignity of the human person; such biomedical procedures are assessed as "not in conformity with the moral law."[47] The unitive and procreative features of procreation lead to similar judgments about such procedures as AIH, AID, IVF, surrogacy, and embryo transfer.

The question of particular interest here is not the validity of these moral judgments but rather the relationship articulated in *Donum Vitae* between the moral law and civil laws. *Donum Vitae* contends that interventions of public authorities in regulating procedures and technologies concerned with the beginnings of life are inevitable, but that such oversight "must be inspired by the rational principles which regulate the relationships between civil law and moral law." Indeed, legislators have a "duty . . . to ensure that the civil law is regulated according to the fundamental norms of the moral law."[48]

The regulation of civil law by the moral law entails legal respect for the "inalienable rights of the person," which include the "right to life and physical integrity from the moment of conception until death," and the inherent rights of the family, marriage, and the child to be raised within a family of biological origins. These "regulatory" rights mean that specific laws must prohibit non-therapeutic research on embryos, IVF that creates embryos that will be discarded, donor gametes, and surrogacy. *Donum Vitae* affirms that it is a responsibility of legislators, and indeed, "all men of good will," to advocate for reform of unacceptable civil laws, and to engage in conscientious objection to laws contrary to human life and dignity.

Evangelium Vitae, an encyclical of John Paul II, is rhetorically memorable for situating these beginnings of life procedures along with professional practices at the end-of-life that embrace physician assisted suicide and euthanasia as a manifestation of "the struggle between the 'culture of life' and the 'culture of death.'" This coupling of beginning and end of life procedures that are permitted and tolerated by society in fact reflect "the systematic violation of the moral law."[49] Interestingly, the pope draws attention to the "widespread development of bioethics" in promoting reflection and dialogue on such matters, which should contribute to a generalized awareness that "we are facing an enormous and dramatic clash between good and evil, death and life, the 'culture of death' and the 'culture of life.'"[50] The "gospel of life" developed and defended by John Paul II includes a responsibility to love, serve, defend, and promote human life; while displayed fully in Christ and in revelation, the gospel of life "can also be known in its essential traits by human reason."[51]

The papal encyclical devotes substantial attention to the relation of moral and civil law, in part because of recognition that many laws permitting the practices opposed by Catholic moral teaching and the encyclical have been approved by the citizenry through democratic processes. Similar to *Donum Vitae*, cultural practice or custom is rejected as morally or politically determinative; rather, "the 'natural law' written in the human heart is the obligatory point of reference for the civil law itself."[52] Further, "the doctrine on the necessary conformity of civil law with the moral law is in continuity with the whole tradition of the church."[53]

Citing the teachings of Thomas Aquinas on just and unjust laws, the pope contends that laws that do not protect the inviolable right to life of innocent human beings (especially laws that regulate but do not prohibit abortion, euthanasia, and assisted suicide) completely lack juridical authority; it follows that moral conscience presents "a grave and clear obligation to oppose them by conscientious objection."[54] The encyclical calls civil leaders to assume a "particular responsibility" to refrain from passing or supporting laws that "disregard the dignity of the person," but instead requires them to construct, especially through legislative measures, a social order in which "the dignity of each person is recognized and the lives of all are defended and enhanced."[55]

The theology of the moral law in both *Donum Vitae* and *Evangelium Vitae* is quite consistent. Its central elements seem to be these:

1. Catholic moral teaching has an invariable commitment to the protection of innocent human life.
2. This value is presented both in revelation and through reason, or the natural moral law.
3. Certain contemporary biomedical procedures pertaining to both the beginnings and endings of human life are directly contrary to the culture of life.
4. Civil laws permit these practices in the name of freedom, democratic consensus, and social coexistence.
5. Catholics as well as conscientious citizens of good will have a responsibility to re-affirm socially the fundamental rights of human persons, including the protection of human life.

6. Civil laws should conform to or be regulated by the principles of the moral law.
7. Civil laws that are not regulated by moral law have no binding authority (in short, society is just a small step away from moral anarchy, or the "culture of death") and Catholics have a duty to engage in conscientious objection regarding these laws.
8. It is a moral and political responsibility of both legislators and citizens to enact civil laws that reflect the moral law and its commitment to protection of innocent human life.

There are elements of this perspective that can and should be accommodated by a liberal democratic state. For example, the values articulated in these documents can be expressed in the discourse of the public square out of respect for freedom of religious expression and in seeking to ensure a substantive and informed discourse rather than one that is primarily procedural in nature or one that has adopted an attitude of civic exclusion of religious values. The state can also accommodate the ecclesiastical requirements for conscientious objection to morally compromising biomedical procedures. At the least, accommodations for personal conscientious objection should be accommodated in the same way that Orthodox Jewish objections to brain death criteria can be accommodated.

It is more complicated and controversial for institutional conscientious objection to be accommodated. This would require coordination of patterns of health care delivery, due to managed care options and/or health care insurance coverage and reimbursement. Should patients, be they Catholics or non-believers, seek treatment for fertility or for end of life care at a Catholic health care facility because of their health plan or insurance requirements, depending on the kind of care or treatment requested, some institutional accommodation to patient requests may be necessary. The principle of non-abandonment of patients may impose some restrictions on the freedom of institutional care providers, a concern expressed by Shannon and Walter with respect to the papal allocution on the moral status of feeding tubes.[56]

The claim that civil law should conform to the natural moral law, as interpreted within the Catholic faith tradition, is a relationship that should not be accommodated by the state. In a liberal democratic society in which moral pluralism predominates, it is far from clear that the religious-based moral values instantiated in the natural law are accessible through reason for all persons. At the very least, the Catholic bioethical teaching would need to supply an account of moral epistemology that would inform a democratic audience how they are supposed to become cognizant of the values of the moral law. Moreover, although Catholic teaching has commonly indicated that the clarity by which norms of the moral law can be recognized will seldom be reflected in their concrete application in practice and civil law, an argument must be presented as to why it is that persons can with a clear conscience espouse values, practices, and laws that directly conflict with teachings of the moral law.

Even though the religious character of the values civil law is supposed to conform to recedes to the background by the language of "moral" or "natural" law, it is evident that the totality of the tradition's teaching on ethical issues at the beginnings and endings of human life are illuminated and ultimately grounded in religious teaching. The ecclesiastical context and source for such teachings may be found in revelation from Scripture, or in the reflection of the tradition over time. In either case, such an effort to regulate civil law by the natural moral law is not compatible with the commitments of the liberal democratic society of neutrality between religion and non-religion or amongst religions. The limits of state accommodation of religion have been breached when religious values are aligned with the coercive power of the state and political authority.

CONCLUSION

This essay has examined features of the relationship between church and state as illuminated by the context of conflicts in biomedical ethics. Such conflicts arise most frequently in circumstances where a decision about medical treatment has life and death consequences. My analysis has approached such wrenching situations from a societal and constitutional presumption in favor of respect for and protection of religious liberty. Within the framework of this presumption, the state has a responsibility to accommodate the claims of religious liberty by respecting many (but not all) treatment decisions rooted in appeals to religious values, through the sanctioning of religious exemptions from certain statutes (such as brain death legislation), or by permitting conscientious objection to offensive laws on religious grounds.

However, as with any presumption in moral analysis, this presumption to respect religious liberty is rebuttable and can be overridden when weightier moral and legal claims conflict with the free exercise of religion. State infringement of religious liberty can occur in several kinds of circumstances, including (a) a treatment refusal that endangers the health or life of a child who is not of an age of moral accountability to avow or disavow the religious values invoked on his or her behalf; (b) a treatment request that denies professional or personal integrity of a health care provider; (c) constraints of coercion, manipulation, or incomplete information with respect to decision-making; (d) a treatment decision that can pose risks of harm to vulnerable third parties or dependents; (e) treatment decisions that may violate other fundamental rights of persons, such as privacy or freedom from unwanted bodily invasion; and (f) the instantiation in civil law of religious justifications for values under the guise of an appeal to religious liberty.

I have argued, following the political ecclesiology developed by Stephen Carter, that religious communities function as intermediate associations between the state and the individual and that the protection of religious liberty enables such communities and their adherents to say "no" to political authority when fundamental values of the tradition would be compromised. At the same time, recognizing that the state commitment to religious liberty is a moral presumption, not an absolute, means that it is appropriate in the circumstances delineated above for the state to say "no" to the claims of religious liberty.

This infringement of religious liberty in the context of bioethical decisions does not mean the value of religious liberty is cancelled or diminished in general, or even in the specific case. Rather, the state has the burden of proof to justify its infringement of religious liberty, and such infringements should meet most, if not all, of the following conditions: (a) state infringement must be an effective means to securing the social good (a child's life, professional integrity, autonomous choice, and so on) jeopardized by the exercise of religious freedom; (b) state infringement must be a necessary means to secure the social good, that is, there are no other alternatives to secure the good but by restrictions on religious liberty; (c) the social mechanism (education, ethics committee, court order, and so on) adopted to secure the social good should be the least restrictive alternative of religious freedom; (d) public justification of the infringement is required to signify ongoing respect for the value of religious liberty.

NOTES

1. Alexis de Tocqueville, *Democracy in America*, ed. J.P. Meyer (Garden City, NY: Anchor Books, 1969), 298.

2. Stephen L. Carter, *The Culture of Disbelief: How American Law and Politics Trivialize Religious Devotion* (New York: Basic Books, 1993).

3. Ibid., 36–37.

4. *Freedom and Responsibility: Christian Science Healing for Children* (Boston: First Church of Christ Scientist, 1989).

5. Margaret P. Battin, *Ethics in the* Sanctuary (New Haven: Yale University Press, 1990), 78–80, 94–100.

6. Mark Larrabee, "The Battle Over Faith Healing," *The Oregonian,* November 28, 1998.

7. Seth M. Asser and Rita Swan, "Child Fatalities From Religion-Motivated Medical Neglect," *Pediatrics* 101 (April 1998): 625.

8. Martin L. Smith, "Jehovah's Witness Refusal of Blood Products," in *Encyclopedia of Bioethics, 3rd ed.*, ed. Stephen G. Post (New York: Macmillan Reference USA, 2004), 1341–1346, at 1342.

9. Ontario Consultants on Religious Tolerance, "Faith Healing: Legal Aspects," available at www.religioustolerance.org.

10. American Academy of Pediatrics, Committee on Bioethics, "Religious Exemptions from Child Abuse Statutes," *Pediatrics* 81 (January 1988): 169–171; "Religious Objections to Medical Care," *Pediatrics* 99 (February 1997): 279–281.

11. *Prince v. Massachusetts,* 321 US 158 (1944).

12. Smith, "Jehovah's Witness Refusal of Blood Products," 1345.

13. James F. Drane, "Alternative Therapies," in *Encyclopedia of Bioethics, 3rd ed.*, ed. Stephen G. Post (New York: Macmillan Reference USA, 2004), 159–161.

14. George J. Annas, "Asking the Courts to Set the Standard of Emergency Care: The Case of Baby K," *New England Journal of Medicine* 330 (May 26, 1994): 1542–1545.

15. *In the Matter of Baby K,* 16 F.3d 590 (4th Cir. 1994).

16. Ronald E. Cranford, "Helga Wanglie's Ventilator," *Hastings Center Report* 21 (July–August 1991): 23–24.

17. Steven H. Miles, "Informed Demand for Non-Beneficial Treatment," *New England Journal of Medicine* 325 (1991): 512–515.

18. Cranford, "Helga Wanglie's Ventilator," 24.

19. *In re the Conservatorship of Helga M. Wanglie*, No. PX-91–283, District Probate Division, 4th Judicial District of the County of Hennepin, State of Minnesota.

20. President's Commission for the Study of Ethical Problems in Medicine and Biomedical and Behavioral Research, *Defining Death: Medical, Legal, and Ethical Issues in the Definition of Death* (Washington, D.C., U.S. Government Printing Office, 1981), 2.

21. Ibid., 32–38.

22. Robert M. Veatch, "The Conscience Clause," in *The Definition of Death: Contemporary Controversies*, ed. Stuart J. Younger, Robert M. Arnold, and Renie Schapiro (Baltimore, MD: Johns Hopkins University Press, 1999), 138–160.

23. Legal Resources, "New Jersey Statute," available at www.braindeath.org.

24. Robert S. Olick, "Brain Death, Freedom, and Public Policy," *Kennedy Institute of Ethics Journal* 1, no. 4 (1991): 275–288.

25. J. David Bleich, "Establishing Criteria of Death," in *Ethical Issues in Death and Dying, 2nd ed.*, ed. Tom L. Beauchamp and Robert M. Veatch (Upper Saddle River, NJ: Prentice Hall Press, 1996): 31.

26. Ibid.

27. Fred Rosner, "The Definition of Death in Jewish Law," in *The Definition of Death: Contemporary Controversies*, ed. Stuart J. Younger, Robert M. Arnold, and Renie Schapiro (Baltimore, MD: Johns Hopkins University Press, 1999), 215–220.

28. Ibid.

29. Olick, "Brain Death, Freedom, and Public Policy."

30. *Application of President and Directors of Georgetown College*, 331 F 2d. (D.C. Cir.).

31. Battin, *Ethics in the Sanctuary*, 105.

32. Ibid., 101–107.

33. Smith, "Jehovah's Witness Refusal of Blood Products," 1344.

34. *Cruzan v. Director, Missouri Dept. of Health*, 497 U.S. 261, 1990.

35. Gilbert Meilaender, "On Removing Food and Water: Against the Stream," *Hastings Center Report* 14 (December 1984): 11–13.

36. John Paul II, "Evangelium Vitae," *Origins* 24 (April 6, 1995): 697.

37. Gary E. Crum, "Dying Well: Death and Life in the 90's," in *Life at Risk: The Crises in Medical Ethics*, ed. Richard D. Land and Louis A. Moore (Nashville, TN: Broadman & Holman Publishers, 1995), 163.

38. Thomas J. Shannon and James J. Walter, "Implications of the Papal Allocution on Feeding Tubes," *Hastings Center Report* 34, no. 4 (2004): 18–20.

39. John Paul II, "Care for Patients in a Permanent Vegetative State," available at www.catholicculture.org.

40. *In re: Guardianship of Theresa Marie Schiavo, Incapacitated. Robert Schindler and Mary Schindler, Appellants, v. Michael Schiavo, as Guardian of the person of Theresa Marie Schiavo, Appellee*, Case Number: 2D02–5394, *Florida Second District Court of Appeal,* June 6, 2003.

41. Eric J. Cassell, "The *Schiavo* Case: A Medical Perspective," *Hastings Center Report* 35, no. 3 (2005): 22–23.

42. Courtney S. Campbell, "Give Me Liberty and Death," *The Christian Century* 116 (May 5, 1999): 498–500.

43. *Washington v. Glucksberg*, 1996; reversed on appeal to the U.S. Supreme Court 117 S. Ct. 2258, 1997.

44. Congregation for the Doctrine of the Faith, *Instruction on Respect for Human Life in its Origin and on the Dignity of Procreation: Replies to Certain Questions of the Day*, February 22, 1987, available at www.vatican.va/roman_curia/congregations/cfaith/documents/.

45. John Paul II, "Evangelium Vitae," 689–730.

46. Congregation for the Doctrine of the Faith, *Instruction on Respect for Human Life in its Origin and on the Dignity of Procreation*, 3.

47. Ibid., 8.

48. Ibid., 17–18.

49. John Paul II, "Evangelium Vitae," 697.

50. Ibid., 700.

51. Ibid.

52. Ibid., 714.

53. Ibid., 715.

54. Ibid.

55. Ibid., 720.

56. Shannon and Walter, "Implications of the Papal Allocution on Feeding Tubes," 20.

FURTHER READING

For a thoughtful and unique philosophical discussion of the ethics of religious practices on confidentiality, conversion, and refusals of treatment, including "faith healing," see Margaret P. Battin, *Ethics in the Sanctuary: Examining the Practices of Organized Religion*. The issues of religious liberty in the context of both ecclesiastical culture and secular society are carefully examined in Stephen L. Carter, *The Culture of Disbelief: How American Law and Politics Trivialize Religious Devotion*. For a compelling argument from the view of liberal political philosophy on the status of religious conscience in matters of life and death, especially abortion and euthanasia, see Ronald Dworkin, *Life's Dominion: An Argument about Abortion, Euthanasia, and Individual Freedom*. A compelling narrative of how different world views—Hmong and medical science—create anguishing moral and legal dilemmas in the treatment of an ill child is presented in Anne Fadiman, *The Spirit Catches You and You Fall Down: A Hmong Child, Her American Doctors, and the Collision of Two Cultures*. For a careful examination of the extent to which citizens and elected officials in a liberal democratic society can rely on religious convictions in making political decisions and legislation, see Kent Greenawalt, *Religious Convictions and Political Choice*. For an overview of the religious values and positions in bioethics of major American denominations as well as of classic world religions, see the anthology by John F. Peppin, Mark J. Cherry, Ana Iltis, eds., *Religious Perspectives in Bioethics*. An indispensable resource about ethical and legal issues in biomedicine, with many articles specifically devoted to moral teachings of religious traditions on bioethics, is found in Stephen G. Post, ed., *Encyclopedia of Bioethics*, 3rd ed.

Appendix: Selected Cases

The following cases are discussed or referenced by the chapters in this volume. Only precedent-setting decisions or important clarifications are included in this appendix. Though not all the cases here are, strictly speaking, matters of church and state jurisprudence, all have important ramifications for the issues covered in the volume.

Badoni v. Higginson (1981): The Dine and Hopi Nations in southern Utah faced loss of their lands due to the planned flooding of Lake Powell for downstream water storage and recreational boating. Federal courts found the latter interests to be more compelling than the concerns of the Native American groups and dismissed their challenge to the National Park Service.

Baehr v. Lewin (1993): The Hawaii Supreme Court ruled in 1993 that the legal prohibition against gay marriage might be unconstitutional and sent the case back to the lower courts for the state to prove that there was a compelling reason to forbid same-sex marriage. In 1996, the lower court found no such reason and sent the case back to the Hawaii Supreme Court. By then, the legislature, following an amendment to the state constitution, had banned same-sex marriage.

Bear Lodge Multiple Use Association v. Babbitt (1983): In this case, the Wyoming federal district court ruled against a group of climbers who argued that the National Park Service's management plan for protecting sites sacred to Native Americans, including in this case the Devil's Tower, amounted to an establishment of religion. Following the *Lemon* Test (*Lemon v. Kurtzman),* the court ruled a voluntary ban on climbing to be a reasonable accommodation to Native American religious interests.

Crow v. Gullet (1982): A South Dakota district court ruled that construction projects on sites sacred to Native Americans did not violate their religious freedom. The Constitution, the court ruled, does not mandate that the government provide the means for carrying out religious obligation.

Cruzan v. Director, Missouri Dept. of Health (1990): After a severe automobile accident, Nancy Beth Cruzan entered a "persistent vegetative state." Though her parents wanted to end her life support, the hospital refused to do so without court approval, citing a state policy against ending life in this way. The Supreme Court determined that individuals in a state such as Cruzan did not enjoy the same rights to refuse medical intervention given to competent individuals and that since Cruzan's own wishes were not clear, the State of Missouri's decision to continue life support must stand.

Doe v. Bolton (1973): The state of Georgia's abortion legislation limited the procedure to extreme cases involving rape, severe fetal deformity, or concerns regarding the mother's health. Moreover, the law required approval by three doctors and a committee before an abortion could be performed and prohibited non-state residents from receiving abortions within Georgia. The Supreme Court overturned this law, thus supporting *Roe v. Wade* and maintaining the constitutional right to abortion in Georgia and all states in the country.

Employment Division, Department of Human Resources of Oregon v. Smith (1990): After ingesting peyote as part of religious practice in the Native American Church, two counselors in a private drug rehabilitation organization were fired and denied unemployment compensation. The Supreme Court concluded that religious beliefs do not excuse an individual from just laws of the state. To allow such excuses, the Court argued, would be to open a Pandora's box of religious exceptions to laws necessary to maintain an ordered society.

Everson v. Board of Education (1947): New Jersey instituted a law allowing for the reimbursement of funds to parents who sent their children to both religious and public schools on public transportation buses. Everson charged that this violated the Establishment Clause by enacting state support of religious schools. The Supreme Court upheld the constitutionality of the law by claiming the reimbursement was available to religious and non-religious individuals alike and did not constitute direct support of religious organizations.

Gillette v. United States (1971): Gillette sought conscientious objector status due to his opposition to the Vietnam War and despite his support of other wars. His claim was denied due to his lack of an absolute moral stance against all wars. The Supreme Court found that Congress was within the law when it required opposition to all war as a limiting criterion for conscientious objector status.

Goodridge v. Massachusetts Department of Public Health (2003): In this case, the Massachusetts State Supreme Court ruled that legislative prohibitions against same-sex marriage were unconstitutional and that a civil union bill was also unacceptable. The state legislature opted for a marriage bill giving legal recognition to same-sex marriage, and thus Massachusetts became the first state to legally recognize marriage rights for homosexuals.

Griswold v. Connecticut (1965): The Executive Director and Medical Director of the Planned Parenthood League of Connecticut were charged under a Connecticut law prohibiting any counseling or medical treatment of married individuals aimed at preventing pregnancy. The Supreme Court overturned the Connecticut law as a violation of the privacy in marital relations suggested by the First, Third, Fourth, and Ninth Amendments.

Jacobson v. Massachusetts (1905): After Cambridge, Massachusetts followed a state law allowing cities to require vaccinations of its citizens against smallpox, Jacobson refused and was fined five dollars. Citing the state's power to enforce the public health and safety of its citizens in extreme circumstances, the Supreme Court denied that this vaccination requirement violated Jacobson's Fourteenth Amendment right to liberty.

Lawrence and Garner v. Texas (2003): After entering John Lawrence's house due to a report of a weapons disturbance, Houston police discovered Lawrence and another adult man, Tyron Garner, engaged in a sexual act. The two men were arrested and charged with deviate sexual intercourse in violation of a Texas law. The Supreme Court concluded that the law violated the Due Process Clause and constituted an inappropriate involvement of government in private affairs, thus overturning *Bowers v. Hardwick*.

Lyng v. Northwest Indian CPA (1988): The U.S. Forest Service planned to build a paved road through the Chimney Rock area of the Six Rivers National Forest, land used by Native Americans to conduct religious rituals. Citing the Forest Service's research showing the damage such a road would cause, the Northwest Indian Cemetery Protective Association charged Secretary of Agriculture Richard Lyng with violating the Free Exercise Clause. The Supreme Court upheld the Forest Service's right to build the road because its primary interests were economic and the effects on the Native Americans' land were incidental.

Planned Parenthood v. Casey (1992): One of the most divisive cases in recent memory, this decision upheld a number of provisions regulating access to abortion in Pennsylvania, including parental notification and a waiting period. In its decision, the Supreme Court adopted Justice O'Connor's "undue burden" standard for regulating abortions, meaning that only restrictions that did not place "a substantial obstacle" in the path of a woman seeking abortion were permissible. Only spousal notification was found to place such a burden on women.

Prince v. Massachusetts (1944): This case concerned child labor laws and the conviction of a Jehovah's Witness woman whose children routinely distributed and sold religious magazines. The Supreme Court upheld her conviction, finding that her religious rights had not been violated since the activity in question occurred on public property.

Reynolds v. United States (1879): George Reynolds, a member of the Church of Jesus Christ of Latter-Day Saints, was charged with bigamy in Utah. Along with certain procedural arguments, Reynolds held that religious duty obligated him to marry more than one woman at a time. The Supreme Court upheld Reynolds' conviction and drew a distinction between what religious people might believe and what they can practice in the public sphere.

Roe v. Wade (1973): This case established reproductive freedom for women in the United States. Based on the right to privacy established in *Griswold*, the Supreme Court struck down a Texas law that prohibited abortions except to save the mother's life. The Court gave women control over the first trimester of their pregnancy and established different rules for subsequent trimesters.

Sequoyah v. Tennessee Valley Authority (1980): This case was brought by the Cherokee against a plan by the Tennessee Valley Authority to build the Tellico Dam. The Sixth Circuit Court held that while the damage to Cherokee culture was unavoidable, there was no expressly religious interest in the land. The court held that since it was culture and tradition that were at issue, and not religion, the First Amendment did not apply.

Sherbert v. Verner (1963): A member of the Seventh Day Adventist Church was fired from her job for refusing to work on Saturday, which was for her the Sabbath. She was denied unemployment compensation by the South Carolina Employment Security Commission. The Supreme Court held that the state's attempt to restrict her unemployment compensation violated her rights to the free exercise of her faith.

Stenberg v. Carhart (2000): This case struck down a Nebraska law that prohibited partial birth abortions unless the life of the mother was at stake. The Court found that the Nebraska law violated the constitutional right to reproductive freedom as determined by *Planned Parenthood v. Casey* and *Roe v. Wade*.

Tennessee v. John Scopes (1925): This is the famous case dramatized in the movie *Inherit the Wind*. John Scopes was a high school teacher convicted of violating Tennessee's Butler Act—a new law banning the teaching of evolution in the classroom. The prosecution won the trial and the Butler Act was affirmed.

United States v. Seeger (1965): This case concerns the definition of religion as it related to claims for religiously based conscientious objector status. Federal law required that applicants for conscientious objector status be able to affirm a theistic, rather than a political, sociological, or philosophical understanding of reality. The Court held that the opinions of the individuals themselves must be taken into account and thus that Congress could not define what was or was not religious in this setting by mandating certain beliefs—for instance, the existence of a Supreme Being—as part of a religiously justified claim for conscientious objection.

Webster v. Reproductive Health Services (1989): The State of Missouri enacted several restrictions on access to abortion, including the requirement that no public employees or resources could be used to perform abortions outside of a procedure necessary to save the mother's life, the requirement that there could be no counseling for abortion, and the requirement that viability tests had to be performed on women seeking abortions after the twentieth week of pregnancy. While the Court specified that they were not revisiting *Roe*, it held that these restrictions were constitutionally permissible.

Wisconsin v. Yoder (1972): This case revolved around whether or not Amish families could absent their children from school facilities after a certain age on the basis of religious conviction. The Supreme Court held that public schooling was in direct conflict with the Amish way of life and that the State of Wisconsin could not therefore compel students to attend after the eighth grade.

About the Editors and Contributors

THE EDITORS

ANN W. DUNCAN is a Ph.D. Candidate in American Religious History at the University of Virginia. She received her M.A. in Religious Studies from the University of Virginia in 2005 and her B.A. from Duke University in 2000. Her research, publications, and conference presentations have focused on intersections of religion and politics, American Christianity in wartime, and, more recently, motherhood and American Christianity.

STEVEN L. JONES is Associate Professor of Sociology at Grove City College and is the former associate director of the Center on Religion and Democracy at the University of Virginia. He received his M.T.S. degree from Duke University and holds a Ph.D. from the University of Virginia. A former fellow of the Center for Children, Families, and the Law and the Institute for Advanced Studies in Culture, his main areas of academic interest are political sociology and family, state, and church conflicts. He is currently finishing a book on patriotism and church schooling in America.

THE CONTRIBUTORS

FRANCIS J. BECKWITH is Associate Professor of Philosophy and Church-State Studies, Baylor University, where he teaches in the departments of philosophy and political science as well as the J.M. Dawson Institute of Church-State Studies. A graduate of Fordham University (Ph.D.) and the Washington University School of Law, St. Louis (MJS), he is the author of over a dozen books, including *Defending Life: A Moral and Legal Case Against Abortion Choice* (Cambridge University Press, 2007) and *Law, Darwinism, and Public Education: The Establishment Clause and the Challenge of Intelligent Design* (Rowman & Littlefield, 2003). A former James Madison Research Fellow at Princeton University, he was the 2006–2007 president of the Evangelical Theological Society.

COURTNEY S. CAMPBELL is Professor and the Chair of the Department of Philosophy at Oregon State University. Prior to joining the OSU faculty in 1990, he was the Associate for Religious Studies at The Hastings Center and the editor of the *Hastings Center Report*. He received his M.A. and Ph.D. degrees in religious studies from the University of Virginia and his B.A. degree in religious studies from Yale University. Campbell's teaching and research interests at Oregon State include biomedical ethics, death and dying, philosophies of the body, and religious traditions and public policy.

JAMES F. CHILDRESS is the John Allen Hollingsworth Professor of Ethics at the University of Virginia, where he teaches in the Department of Religious Studies and directs the Institute for Practical Ethics and Public Life. He has written several books and numerous articles on a range of topics in ethics, including just war theory and pacifism, biomedical ethics, and methods in ethics.

NADRA HASHIM has a bachelor's degree in psychology from Georgetown University where she also received an Arab Studies Certificate. She completed her Ph.D. work in International Relations at the University of Virginia. She has taught as an Adjunct Professor at the University of Louisville in the Pan-African Studies Department and has been a visiting Ford Fellow in the Women's Studies Department at Amherst College. She currently works as a freelance researcher and writer and is finishing a book which concerns contemporary partisan/linguistic conflict in Zanzibar.

ERIC MATTHEWS serves as Director of the Center for Public Service and Assistant Professor of Political Science at Mount Union College. His research interests include evangelicalism, dimensions of religiosity, political culture, civic engagement, and welfare reform. A graduate of Kent State University, Dr. Matthews's dissertation involved interviewing 30 evangelical ministers in central Appalachia on topics ranging from Charitable Choice to the mega-church movement. He is also a graduate of the Pollsters and Parishioners Methods Workshop held at Calvin College on a bi-yearly basis.

ERIN O'BRIEN is Assistant Professor of Political Science at the University of Massachusetts-Boston. Her work examines issues of intersectionality and social welfare policy. Dr. O'Brien's research appears in journals, including *The American Journal of Political Science* and *Women and Politics*.

S. ALAN RAY is Senior Vice Provost for the University of New Hampshire, where he holds appointments as Affiliate Associate Professor of Political Science, Philosophy, and Justice Studies. A citizen of the Cherokee Nation, his research and teaching focus on federal Indian law and policy, race and law, religion and public policy, and political theory. He holds a Ph.D. in religion from Harvard University and a J.D. from the University of California, Hastings College of the Law.

SAMUEL S. STANTON, JR., is Assistant Professor of Humanities and Political Science at Grove City College. He earned his Ph.D. in Political Science in 2004 from Texas Tech University. Dr. Stanton specializes in the study of conflict processes and has been involved in research covering the effect of migration and immigration on civil conflict. His current research concerns the effects of divergent forms of globalization on civil conflict.

KATHERINE STENGER is Assistant Professor in the Department of Political Science at Gustavus Adolphus College in Minnesota. Her research centers on the role of religious interest groups in the policy process, with a particular focus on the contrast between the Religious Right and Left in terms of political strategy and policy success.

CHAD MICHAEL WAYNER is an instructor in the Department of Religious Studies at the University of Virginia and a research fellow at the Institute for Practical Ethics and Public Life. He is also currently studying for a doctorate in religious studies at the University of Virginia, with a concentration in religious ethics in general and Christian ethics in particular. Other research interests include the relationship between sanctification and the moral life in Christian theology, the theological virtues, the moral theology of St. Thomas Aquinas, and the Christian ethic of John Calvin. He studied philosophy and political science at Calvin College in Grand Rapids, Michigan, and received his bachelor's degree there.

Index

abolitionist movement, 144–45
abortion: Constitution and, 1–2; current law and, 3–12; First Amendment and, 23–24; history of, 7–8; proposed definition of, 1; stem cell research and, 123; undue burden standard and, 10. *See also Roe v. Wade*
accidental properties, 13, 17
accommodation of religion: biomedical ethics and, 248–49, 258, 259, 261; cases about, 192 n.90; limits of, 269–73; Native American, 181–83, 185–86, 279
Adalberto United Methodist Church, 141, 157
adaptation, biological, 203
affiliative dimension of religiosity, 127–28
AIRFA (American Indian Religious Freedom Act), 170, 171, 173, 174, 177
AIRFA (American Indian Religious Freedom Act) Amendments, 182
air pollution, 198, 199
Akron v. Akron Center for Reproductive Health, Inc., 28 n.28, 29 n.41
Alaska, 55
Allard, Wayne, 52, 53
Alliance Defense Fund, 56
Alliance for Marriage, 52
Alliance for Traditional Marriage, 46, 47
alternative service, 104

American Center for Law and Justice, 40, 46
American Civil Liberties Union, 82
American Family Association, 49, 53; Law Center, 40
American Friends Service Committee, 46, 48
American Indian Religious Freedom Act (AIRFA), 170, 171, 173, 174, 177
American Indian Religious Freedom Act (AIRFA) Amendments, 182
American Peace Society, 78–79
Arellano, Elvira, 141, 155–56, 157
Arizona, Proposition 107, 37–38, 56
armed forces, morale and effectiveness of, and conscientious objection, 98–99
Arnold, Ron, 213–14, 217
Arrhenius, Svante August, 207

B. betularia, 203
Baby K, 255–56
Bacon, Francis, 200
Badoni v. Higginson, 172, 173, 176–77, 279
Baehr v. Lewin, 45, 279
Baker v. Nelson, 69 n. 25
balancing test, 178, 179–80
Baldwin, Roger, 82
Baliunas, Sallie, 220–21

Barclay, Scott, 49
Barr, Bob, 48
Basso, Keith, 165
Battin, Margaret, 262–63
Bear Butte, 172–73
Bear Lodge Multiple Use Association v. Babbitt, 184–85, 279
Beck, Alison, 65
Beer, David, 42, 55
Bible, interpretation of, 201
Bill of Rights, 201, 226; conscientious objection and, 77–78
biological adaptation, 203
biomedical ethics. *See* medical ethics
Black, Joseph, 207
Blackmun, Harry, 4–5, 7–8, 177–78
blastocyst, 124
Bleich, J. David, 260
blood transfusions, refusal of, 253, 262–63
bodily rights, extent of, 17–22
book, religions of, 163–64, 165–66
Boonin, David, 13, 17–18, 19, 21, 22
Bowers v. Hardwick, 281
Boyle, Robert, 200, 203
brain death, exemption from, 259–61
Brennan, William J., Jr., 3–4, 177–78
Bridgewater Treatises, 203
Bryan, William Jennings, 209–10
Burton, Lloyd, 164
Bush, George H. W., 8, 217
Bush, George W.: carbon dioxide emissions and, 219; environment and, 225; evangelicals and, 222; faith in campaign of, 198; Marriage Protection Amendment and, 53; partial birth abortion ban, 12; on stem cell research, 118
Butler Act, 209, 211

Cadge, Wendy, 39
Callendar, 208–9
"can't help" and conscientious objection, 91–92
carbon dioxide emissions, 199, 207, 212–13, 219, 224–25
Carens, Joseph, 150
Carpenter, Kristen, 187
Carson, Rachel, *Silent Spring*, 198, 210–11
Carter, Jimmy, 213

Carter, Stephen, *The Culture of Disbelief*, 251
Cassell, Eric, 266
Catholic Church: bioethical prohibitions of, 269; *Donum Vitae*, 269–70; *Evangelium Vitae*, 270–71; feeding tube issue and, 265–66; liberation theology and, 153; same-sex marriage and, 40; sanctuary and, 144; stem cell research and, 128
Central America, 152, 156–57
Chauncey, George, 42
Chidester, David, 165
Childress, James, 92, 96
child support laws, 19–21
chlorofluorocarbons (CFCs), 210, 212
Christian Coalition: Robertson and, 216; same-sex marriage and, 40, 48, 49; stem cell research and, 123, 134–35; Wise Use Movement and, 218
Christian (Evangelical) Right, 42, 43, 55–56, 197
The Christian Fundamentals, 209
Christianity: Deloria on, 165–66; Free Exercise Clause and, 168; as religion of book, 166; right belief and, 163–64. *See also specific denominations*
Christian Legal Society, 46
Christians, born-again, 128
Christian Science, 252–53, 254, 262
Churchland, Paul, 16–17
Church of Jesus Christ of Latter-day Saints, 40, 47
civil initiative, 153
civil law and moral law, 270–71, 272–73
Cizik, Richard, 223, 228 n.3
Clark, Ian, 220
Clergy for Fairness, 54
Clinton, Bill, 182
cloning, 2
Clovis I, 144
Cohen, Carl, 100
Colautti vs. Franklin, 28 n.28
Coleman, Walter, 156
Cole-Turner, Ronald, 117
communities: Native, and culture, 162, 164; religious, and power of resistance, 251–52
conception, 13

Concerned Women for America, 135
conscientious objection: all-volunteer military and, 107; Bill of Rights debates and, 77–78; church, state, and, 106–7; Civil War and, 79–80; definition of, 75; history and development of, 76–87; by institutions, 272; judicial recognition for, 82–83; legal and ethical analysis of, 87–88; penalties and fines for, 78–79; Quakers and, 76–77; Shakers and, 77, 105; Vietnam War and, 85–86; World War I and, 80–82; World War II and, 83–85. *See also* selective conscientious objectors
conscious formation, 105
consequentialist reasoning, 90–91, 93–95
consistency and conscientious objection, 104
conspicuous consumption, 209
Constitution: abortion and, 1–2; Bill of Rights, 77–78, 201, 226; First Amendment, 23–24; Fourteenth Amendment, 33 n.110. *See also* Establishment Clause; Free Exercise Clause
constitutional jurisprudence, assumptions of, 167–69
contraceptive use, 3–4
Contract with America (Republican Party), 218–19
Convention Relating to the Status of Refugees, 146–47, 152
Cooper, Stephen, 154
Corbert, James A., 153
Cousineau, Phil, 164
Crow v. Gullet, 172–73, 176, 280
Crum, Gary E., 265
Cruzan v. Director, Missouri Dept. of Health, 264, 280
culture: Free Exercise Clause and, 167–68, 169; Native communities and, 162, 164
The Culture of Disbelief (Carter), 251
"culture wars" thesis and same-sex marriage, 38
Cushman, Charles, 214, 217

Darrow, Clarence, 209–10
Darwin, Charles, 202–3, 204–5
Davy, Humphry, 207
DDT (dichloro-diphenyl-trichloro-ethane), 210, 211, 212

D & E abortions, 12
Defense of Marriage Act, 40, 48–49
Deism, 200–201
Dellapenna, Joseph W., 7, 24
Deloria, Vine, Jr., 165–66
democracy frame and same-sex marriage debate, 61–62
deontological reasoning, 90–91, 122–23
Department of Defense Directive 1300.6, 86–87
developmental view of embryo, 123
Devil's Tower National Monument, 183–85
devotional dimension of religiosity, 130–31
Dignity USA, 65
dispensational theology, 227 n.2
distributive justice, 150–51, 155
DNA, 124
Dobson, James, 54
Doe v. Bolton, 5–6, 280
dominion theology, 217
Douglas, William O., 3
drug use, sacramental, 179–80, 182, 186–87
Dupuis, Martin, 49
Dworkin, Ronald, 23
D & X abortions, 11–12

easements, 187
Eastmay, Crystal, 82
economics frame: immigration and, 147–50; same-sex marriage debate and, 61–62
Edelson, R. S., 203
Edison, Thomas, 208
Eisenstadt v. Baird, 3–4
Eller, Cynthia, 83–84
embryo: Catholic Church and, 270; moral status of, 123
embryonic stem cell research. *See* stem cell research
Employment Division, Department of Human Resources of Oregon v. Smith, 179–80, 280
English Common Law, 144
Enlightenment, 201
environmental activism, 211–12
environmental organizations, 211

Environmental Protection Agency (EPA): creation of, 211; scientific legal challenge to, 224; state suits against, 199, 221–22, 225; Watt and, 217; Wise Use Movement and, 227
Episcopal Church, 135–36
equal respect and conscientious objection, 92–93
equal rights frame and same-sex marriage debate, 63–64
"erroneous conscience," 102–3
essential properties, 13, 17
Establishment Clause: abortion and, 24, 34 n.113; conscientious objection and, 85, 94; *Everson v. Board of Education* and, 280; land management plans and, 183–85, 186, 187–88; overview of, 181; states and, 33 n.110
Ethelbert, 144
eugenics, 205, 231 n.48
Evangelical (Christian) Right, 42, 43, 55–56, 197
Evangelical Environmental Network, 212
Evangelical Greens: Bush and, 198; emergence of, 222–23; future of, 225–27; global warming and, 199, 223–24; Republican Party and, 197
Everson v. Board of Education, 280
evolution, 204–5, 209–10, 211
exemption from military service. *See* conscientious objection

fairness principle and conscientious objection, 92–93
faith healing, 253, 262
Falwell, Jerry, 52, 54, 216
family, "traditional" model of, 42
family values frame and same-sex marriage debate, 62–63, 65–66
Faraday, Michael, 207
federalism, 151–52
feeding tubes, 264–66
fee simple estate, 187
fertilization, 13
fetal viability, 5, 9, 10
Fife, John, 153
First Amendment, 23–24. *See also* Establishment Clause; Free Exercise Clause

First Great Awakening, 201
Fisher, Shauna, 49
Fletcher, Joseph, 14
Focus on the Family: same-sex marriage and, 37, 40, 47, 48, 49, 53–54, 65–66; stem cell research and, 123, 134
Ford, Henry, 208, 224
Ford, William Clay, 224
Fourteenth Amendment, 33 n.110
Fox, George, 76
framing of same-sex marriage debate, 58–62
Frazee v. Ill. Department of Employment Security, 190 n.31
Free Exercise Clause: abortion and, 24; cases about, 190 n.31; conscientious objection and, 94; constitutional jurisprudence and, 167–69; exemption from brain death and, 259–61; Native American religious liberty claims and, 169–71, 172–74, 176–80, 182, 186, 281; refusal of treatment by adult and, 261–63; refusal of treatment for child and, 252–55; religious liberty and, 167; religious requests, professional integrity, and, 256–58; request for futile treatment for child and, 255–56; sacred sites and, 171–75; *Wisconsin v. Yoder* and, 190 n.27
Frist, Bill, 52
Fuller, Charles, 215
Full Faith and Credit Clause, 45
futility, medical, 255–56

Gabbard, Mike, 46
Galton, Francis, 231 n.48
Garrison, William Lloyd, 78–79
Gearhart, John, 125
genes, 124
Gillette v. United States, 86, 93–94, 280–81
Gingrich, Newton, 218
Girouard v. United States, 109 n.44
global warming: carbon dioxide emissions and, 199, 207, 212–13, 219, 224–25; climate change and, 198, 219; Evangelical Greens and, 199, 223–24; ice ages and, 232 n.57; polar bears and, 224

Goldberg, Arthur J., 3
Gonzales v. Carhart, 2, 12
Gonzales v. O Centro Espirita Beneficente Uniao Do Vegetal, 186, 192 n.84
Goodridge v. Massachusetts Department of Public Health, 53, 281
Gordon, Doris, 24
Gore, Albert, 219, 227 n.1
Gottlieb, Alan, 214, 217
Graham, Billy, 215, 216, 242 n.156
Gray, Asa, 206
Gray, William, 220
Greek Orthodox Archdiocese of America, 135
Green Movement: first wave of, 200–205; future of, 225–27; history of, 198; Kyoto Protocol and, 220–21; second wave of, 206–15; third wave of, 215–19, 221–25
Griswold v. Connecticut, 3, 281
Gulliford, Andrew, 166

Haider-Markel, Donald, 49
Hand, Augustus, 84
Harrison, Beverley, 14
Harrison, James, 39
Hawaii, 45–48
Hawaii Christian Coalition, 47
Hawaii Council of Churches, 47
Hawaii Family Forum, 47
Henry, Carl, 215
Henry VIII, 144
Hentoff, Nat, 24
Herman, Didi, 40
High Country, 175–76, 181
Hobbie v. Unemployment Appeals Commission, 190 n.31, 192 n.90
Hodge-Gray debate, 206
Hogbom, Arvid Gustav, 232 n.55
homosexuality, debate over within churches, 41–42. *See also* same-sex marriage
Hull, Kathleen, 47, 59
human beings: extent of bodily rights of, 17–22; fairness and respect for, 92–93; nature of, 1–2, 13–17
humanitarian approach to sanctuary, 156
Huxley, Thomas, 205

immigration, 147–52
Indian Reorganization Act, 171
indirect burdens on religion, 169–70, 173–74, 176, 186
"industrial melanism," 203
Industrial Revolution, 202, 206–7
In Pursuit of Equity (National Advisory Commission on Selective Service), 95
Intelligent Design, 206, 223, 226
in vitro fertilized embryos, 125

Jacobson v. Massachusetts, 281
James I, 144
Jefferson, Thomas, 201
Jehovah's Witnesses, 81, 84, 253, 254, 262–63
Jews, 128, 260
John Paul II, 153, 265, 270–71
Johnson, Lyndon, 211
Jump Dance, 165
just-war tradition, 89, 91, 102

Keller, Helen, 82
Kellogg, Walter, 81
Kennedy, Anthony, 8, 10, 11, 12
Kennedy, John, 216
Kyoto Protocol, 197, 198, 219, 220–21

Lam, Pui-Yan, 116, 117, 126, 127
land, religions of, 163–64, 165–66, 178–79, 186. *See also* sacred places
land management plans, 183–85, 187–88
law, selective disobedience to, 95–96
Lawrence and Garner v. Texas, 52, 281
Lee, Patrick, 16, 21, 22
legal frame and same-sex marriage debate, 59, 60–61
Lemon test, 184, 279
Levin, Michael, 21
liberal democratic state, religion in, 249–52
liberation theology, 153
Linenthal, Edward, 165
Lippert, Randy, 151
Lynch v. Donnelly, 192 n.90
Lyng v. Northwest Indian Cemetery Protective Association, 175–80, 281

Macintosh, Douglas, 82–83
Mack, Julian, 81
Madison, James, 77–78
Madison Society of Hawaii, 46
Marriage Protection Amendment, 53–54, 57
Marshall, Thurgood, 177–78
Massachusetts and same-sex marriage, 52–53, 56, 57
mass production, 207–8, 210
materialism, 16–17
McCorvey, Norma, 4
McDonagh, Eileen, 17–18
McGivern, Daniel, 46
McManus, John, 220
media and same-sex marriage debate: dueling frames in, 58–62; group representation in coverage of, 62–66
medical ethics: Catholic Church and, 269–73; distinctions among cases related to, 248–49; exemption from brain death, 259–61; feeding tube issue, 264–66; model of church-state relationship and, 249–52; overview of, 247–48; physician assisted suicide, 266–69; refusal of treatment by adult, 261–63; refusal of treatment for child, 252–55; request for futile treatment for child, 255–56; state infringement of religious liberty and, 273–74
Medicine Wheel National Historic Landmark, 185
mereological essentialism, 15
Merolla, Linda, 42, 55
Merton, Robert, 200
Michigan, 56
migration, 147–52
military service. *See* conscientious objection
mini-DOMAs, 49–50
Mississippi, 56
Molina, Mario, 212
Moore, Thomas, 204
moral discourse about war, 100
moral frames: conscientious objection and, 88–93; same-sex marriage debate and, 59–60, 61, 62–64, 65–66
moral law: civil law and, 270–71, 272–73; theology of, 271–72

Moral Majority, 216
Moreland, J. P., 13, 14, 15
Mormons, 128, 167
Muir, John, 214
Musgrave, Marilyn, 52, 53

Nader, Ralph, 212
Nagel, Thomas, 133
National Academy of Sciences report, 213
National Advisory Commission on Selective Service, *In Pursuit of Equity*, 95
National Association of Evangelicals, 215, 222–23
National Campaign to Protect Marriage, 48
National Historic Preservation Act amendments, 182
National Interreligious Service Board for Conscientious Objectors, 86
National Park Service, 183–85, 187
Native American Graves Protection and Repatriation Act, 181, 182
Native Americans, 162–66. *See also* spiritual practices of Native Americans
natural theology, 203–4
Natural Theology (Paley), 202
Navajo Nation v. U.S. Forest Service, 180
Neuhaus, Richard, 211
New Jersey Declaration of Death Act, 259–61
Newsom, Gavin, 55
Newton, Isaac, 200, 203
Norton, Gale, 221
no-subject view, 16–17

Ockenga, Harold, 215
O'Connor, Sandra Day, 8, 10, 176, 177, 281–82
Office of Faith-Based Initiatives, 198, 222
Ohio, 56
Olick, Robert, 260
Olson, Laura, 39
Oregon, 56
Oregon Death with Dignity Act, 267–68
Origin of the Species (Darwin), 204–5
out-marriage, 162

pacifism, 91, 102, 104, 106
Paine, Thomas, 201, 229 n.20
Paley, William, 202, 206, 223
"parallel belief" test, 102, 105
parental obligation objection, 19–21
"partial-birth abortion," 2, 11–12
participatory dimension of religiosity, 129–30
personal identity, 16
personal morality, 42
petroleum, 208
peyote, use of, 179–80, 182
physician assisted suicide, 266–69
Pinchot, Gifford, 214
place-making, 165
Planned Parenthood of Missouri v. Danforth, 28 n.28
Planned Parenthood v. Casey, 8, 9–10, 23, 281–82
pluripotent, 124
political action and religious conviction, vii–viii
political asylum and sanctuary, 145–47
politics frame: same-sex marriage debate and, 59, 60; sanctuary and, 156–57; selective conscientious objection and, 88–92
praying and support for stem cell research, 130–31
Prince v. Massachusetts, 254, 282
privacy, right of, 3, 266, 274
Pro-Family Hawaii, 46
property rights, 187, 214
Protect Marriage Arizona, 37–38
public opinion on stem cell research, 118–22, 126–32
public policy: religious values and, 39–40; stem cell research and, 133–34
Puritans, 164, 200

Quakers, 76–77, 145
quickening, 7

Rainbow Bridge National Monument, 172, 185
Rainbow of Aloha Metropolitan Community Church, 47–48
rape and abortion, 22

Rawls, John, 150
Reagan, Ronald, 8, 152, 156–57, 213, 216–17
Reed, Ralph, 218
Refugee Act, 147, 154
refugees and sanctuary, 145–46
refusal of treatment: by adult, 261–63; for child, 252–55
Reilly, Bill, 217–18
reliance interest, 10
religion: definition of, 168; indirect burdens on, 169–70, 173–74, 176, 186. *See also* accommodation of religion
Religion and Public Life survey (Pew), 127
Religion Clauses and *Roe v. Wade*, 23
religiosity, dimensions of, 126–32
Religious Action Center, 65
Religious Coalition for Reproductive Choice, 14
religious conviction and political action, vii–viii
religious freedom and medical decision-making, 248
Religious Freedom Restoration Act, 179–80, 186
Religious Land Use and Institutionalized Persons Act, 180
religious liberty, 169–71, 273–74
"religious motive" test, 24
religious tradition and abortion, 22–23
religious values, definition of, 126
Republican Party, 197, 216–17, 218–19
resistance, power of, and religious communities, 251–52
responsibility objection, 19–21
Reynolds v. United States, 167, 170, 282
right conduct, 164–65
Robertson, Pat, 54, 216
Roe v. Wade: overview of, 4–6, 282; reasoning of, 6–8; Religion Clauses and, 23; Supreme Court actions after, 8–12
Rogers, Alexander, 78
Rogers, Jack, 42
Rohr, John, 91
Roman Catholic Church. *See* Catholic Church
Roosevelt, Theodore, 214
Rosner, Fred, 260

Rowland, Sherwood, 212
Russell, Bertrand, 204–5
Rutherford Institute, 40, 46

sacred places: accommodation of, 185–86; Clinton, Executive Order of, and, 182; future of, under federal law, 186–88; human agency and, 165; judicial struggles with, 171–75; land management plans and, 183–85, 187–88
same-sex marriage: Arizona and, 37–38; debate over, 38; Defense of Marriage Act and, 48–49; federal marriage amendment and, 52–53; future of, 56–57; Hawaii and, 45–48; Marriage Protection Amendment, 53–54, 57; Massachusetts and, 52–53; media coverage of debate over, 58–66; religion, policymaking, and, 39–40; religious voices in debate on, 40–42, 43–44; states and, 49–50, 55–56, 57; venues for policymaking regarding, 45; Vermont and, 51–52
sanctuary: Biblical inception of, 142–43; dilemmas of, 156–57; as form of punishment, 143; in historical context, 144; political asylum and, 145–47; in U.S. history, 144–45
Sanctuary Movement, 141, 142, 145, 152–56
Scalia, Antonin, 8
Schiavo, Terry, 247, 265–66
Schlissel, Lillian, 81–82, 106–7
Schwarzenegger, Arnold, 224–25
science, age of, 210
scientific naturalists, 205
Scopes, John, 209–10
SCOs. *See* selective conscientious objectors
Scottish Realism, 229 n.23
Second Great Awakening, 204
security and immigration, 147–50
Seeger, Daniel, 85
selective conscientious objectors (SCOs): consequentialist arguments and, 93–95; description of, 87–88; fairness and respect for persons and, 92–93; morale and effectiveness of armed forces and, 98–99; nature of claims of, 88–92; numbers of, 96–98; positive consequences of, 99–101; selective disobedience to law and, 95–96; sincerity of, 101–5
Selective Training and Service Act, 83, 85
Sequoyah v. Tennessee Valley Authority, 171–72, 174, 176, 177, 282
Shacknove, Andrew, 150
Shakers, 77, 105
Shannon, Thomas J., 265, 272
Sheldon, Lou, 48, 52, 54
Sherbert balancing test, 178, 179–80
Sherbert v. Verner, 169–70, 172, 173–75, 282
Shows, Ronnie, 52
Silent Spring (Carson), 198, 210–11
Simmons, Paul, 16, 23–24
sincerity and selective conscientious objectors, 101–5
Singer, Peter, 13
Six Rivers National Forest, 175–76
Smith, Martin, 254, 263
smog, 202
Social Darwinism, 205, 206, 231 n.48
Soule, Sarah, 49
Souter, David, 8, 10
Southern Baptist Convention, 135
sovereignty, 151–52
space: Native American notion of, 165; religions and, 166; Western notion of, 164
Spencer, Herbert, 205
spiritual practices of Native Americans: accommodation of, 181–83, 185–86, 279; assumptions of constitutional jurisprudence and, 168–69; *Badoni v. Higginson,* 172; *Bear Lodge Multiple Use Association v. Babbitt,* 184–85; *Crow v. Gullet,* 172–73; *Employment Division v. Smith,* 179–80; as land-based, 165–66; *Lyng v. Northwest Indian CPA,* 175–79; overview of, 161–62; right conduct, 164–65; *Sequoyah v. TVA,* 171–72; *Wilson v. Block,* 173–74
states: conscientious objection and, 78; constitutional amendments in, 55–56, 57; Defense of Marriage Acts in, 49–50; policies in, favorable to same-sex couples, 58; religious liberty and, 273–74; stem cell research policy in, 117–18; suits against EPA by, 199, 221–22, 225

states (sovereign), and Convention Relating to the Status of Refugees, 146–47
stem cell, definition of, 124
stem cell research: debate over, 132–34; dimensions of religiosity and views on, 126–32; dominant discourses regarding, 122–23, 125–26; influences on views of, 121–22; overview of, 115–16; procedures of, 124–26; public opinion on, 118–22; questions about, 2; religion and, 116; status of, 117–18; terminology of, 124
Stenberg v. Carhart, 2, 8, 11, 282
Stevens, John Paul, 24
Stone, Harlan, 81
Sumner, L. W., 13
Supreme Court, 167–69, 225. *See also specific cases; specific justices*
Swomley, John, 14

televangelists, 216
Tellico Dam, 171–72
Tennessee v. John Scopes, 209–10, 282–83
Theodosius the Great, 144
theological dimension of religiosity, 128–29
Thiloreir, Charles, 207
Third Great Awakening, 215–19
Thomas, Clarence, 8, 12
Thomas v. Review Board, 190 n.31
Thomson, James, 125
Thomson, Judith Jarvis, 17, 18–21, 22, 23
Thoreau, Henry David, 79
Thornburgh v. American College of Obstetricians and Gynecologists, 28 n.28, 29 n.41
Tillich, Paul, 211
Tomsho, Robert, 153
Tooley, Michael, 13
totipotent, 124
Traditional Values Coalition, 48, 49, 52, 53–54
transfusions of blood, refusal of, 253, 262–63
trimester framework, 5, 9, 10
Turner, John, 217–18
Tyler, Samuel, 201

Udall, Morris, 177
unborn, as person, 7
undue burden standard, 10, 281–82
Uniform Determination of Death Act, 259
Union of American Hebrew Congregations, 135
United Nations Montreal Protocol, 212
United States v. Aguilar, 154, 155
United States v. Berman, 84–85
United States v. Downer, 84
United States v. Kauten, 84
United States v. Macintosh, 82–83
United States v. Seeger, 85, 102, 105, 283
universal conscientious objectors, 87–88
U.S. Climate Action Partnership, 225
U.S. Conference of Catholic Bishops, 134
U.S. Immigration and Nationality Act, 147

Veatch, Robert M., 259
Vermont, civil unions in, 51–52
Vietnam War and conscientious objection, 85–86
vigilante justice, 155

wall between church and state, 226
Wallis, Jim, 222
Walter, James J., 265, 272
Wanglie, Helga, 256–58
War Industrial Board, 208
Warren, Mary Anne, 13
Watt, James, 217
Webster v. Reproductive Health Services, 8–9, 283
Weiner, Myron, 147
Welsh v. United States, 85–86
Whewell, William, 203
Whitman, Christine Todd, 219, 221, 239 nn.134, 138, 139
Wilcox, Clyde, 42, 55
Wilson v. Block, 173–74, 176
Wisconsin v. Yoder, 190 n.27, 190 n.31, 283
Wise Use Movement, 213–14, 217–18, 222, 226–27
Witherspoon, John, 229 n.23
World War I and conscription act, 80–82
World War II and conscientious objection, 83–85